A CONCISE HISTORY OF SUNNIS AND SHI'IS

ALSO BY JOHN MCHUGO

A Concise History of the Arabs

Syria: A Recent History

John McHugo

A CONCISE HISTORY OF SUNNIS & SHI'IS

SAQI

Published by Saqi Books 2017

Copyright © John McHugo 2017

ISBN 978-0-86356-163-4
eISBN 978-0-86356-158-0

John McHugo has asserted his right under the Copyright, Designs
and Patents Act, 1988, to be identified as the author of this work.

First published in Great Britain in 2017 by

Saqi Books
26 Westbourne Grove
London W2 5RH

www.saqibooks.com

A full CIP record for this book is available from the British Library.

Printed and bound by CPI Group (UK) Ltd, Croydon CR0 4YY

To the memory of my parents, with love and gratitude

Christopher Lawrence McHugo, 1909–1987

Jan McHugo, 1913–2001

May they rest in peace

Contents

List of Maps

Glossary

Abbasid: the dynasty of Caliphs who were descended from the Prophet's uncle Abbas and who ruled during the period 750–1258.

Akhbari: a school of Twelver Shi'i theology which rejects the rationalist methods of the rival Usuli school.

Alawi: a member of a secretive Shi'i sect; the Alawis predominate in the mountains above Lattakia in Syria and in parts of the Orontes valley further east. There are also Alawis in Turkey.

Alevi: a Shi'i grouping in Turkey who are the present-day spiritual descendants of the Kizilbash.

Ansar: the Muslims during the time of the Prophet who were natives of Medina.

Ashura: the Shi'i commemorations of the martyrdom of Hussein, the Prophet's grandson, on the 10th day of the month of Muharram.

Ayatollah: literally 'sign of God'. A pre-eminent religious scholar in Twelver Shi'ism.

Al-Azhar: a university mosque originally founded in Cairo by the Fatimids during the 970s. Today it is the most influential teaching institution of Sunni Islam.

Batini: literally, 'esotericists'. A derogatory name for the Fatimid Ismailis.

Caliph: the word can mean either 'deputy' or 'successor': a title adopted by the successive leaders of the Muslim community after the death of the Prophet Muhammad; hence 'caliphate' for the caliph's office, or the area under the caliph's stewardship.

Da'i: an Ismaili missionary

Da'wa: the 'call' or the 'preaching'

Druze: a member of a secretive sect that is an offshoot of Shi'i Islam. They are numerous in parts of Lebanon and the Hawran plateau, southeast of Damascus. There is also a Druze community in Israel.

Faqih: a Muslim religious scholar who is versed in the detail of the Sharia.

Fitna: civil disturbance or discord.

Gnostic Shi'is: Shi'i movements preserving heterodox beliefs that predate Islam.

Hadith: the sayings or traditions ascribed to the Prophet Muhammad.

Hijra: emigration, specifically the Prophet's emigration from Mecca to Medina.

Ijtihad: independent judgement, especially in a legal or theological context.

Imam: a religious leader. The word may mean no more than a prayer leader or preacher, but for Shi'is the word is used for the divinely inspired and infallible teacher whom all Muslims are bound to follow. See the discussion of the term in Chapter Four.

Ismailis: the second largest Shi'i sect. They believe that the line of the Imams descended through Ismail, who died before his father, the sixth Imam, Ja'far al-Sadiq. His line has continued until today and is now represented by his descendant, the Aga Khan.

Jahiliyah: literally, 'the age of ignorance', the age before the preaching of Islam.

Jazeera: 'island' or 'peninsula' in Arabic. Also the name of the large area of steppe between modern Iraq and Syria.

Jihad: literally, 'expenditure of effort' or 'endeavour'. Jihad is the struggle a Muslim should wage against his ego and for his religion. This includes religious warfare in the name of the Muslim community, which is the most common use of the term today.

Ka'ba: the shrine in Mecca.

Kharijis: a Muslim sect that rejected both Ali and Mu'awiya as the leader of the Muslim community and is neither Sunni nor Shi'i.

Kizilbash: literally 'redheads'. The Kizilbash were a confederation of Turkic tribes who supported Shah Ismail and subsequent rulers of Iran.

Madhhab: a doctrinal law school in Sunni Islam that is considered valid by all Sunnis.

Madrasa: a religious school or seminary.

Mamluk: a slave soldier usually brought as a boy from a distant country and brought up to be a member of a military elite.

Maronite: a member of a Christian sect predominant in parts of Lebanon but also with followers scattered throughout Greater Syria. This sect has retained its own traditions and autonomous structure while being in communion with the Roman Catholic Church since the time of the Crusades.

Mufti: a religious scholar of sufficient eminence to give opinions on questions of Islamic law that it is reasonable for other Muslims to follow.

Muhajirun: literally 'the emigrants', those Muslims who followed Muhammad to Medina.

Muharram: the month in the Muslim calendar in which Hussein was killed.

Mujtahid: an expert jurist whose degree of learning and piety is such that he is able to use his independent reasoning to interpret and develop questions on the Sharia.

Munafiqun: 'the hypocrites', those Muslims who converted to Islam in Medina for reasons of expediency and were judged to be insincere.

Mu'tazili: a movement in the Abbasid era that applied the logical techniques of Greek rationalism to developing Muslim theology.

Notables: the elite, aristocratic families of the Ottoman Empire and its successor states.

Rashidun: the first four caliphs, Abu Bakr, Umar, Uthman and Ali, who are accepted by Sunni Muslims.

Safavids: the dynasty that ruled Iran from 1501 to 1722 and converted most of the country to Twelver Shi'ism.

Salaf: ancestors, predecessors, specifically *al-salaf al-salih*, 'the righteous ancestors' or 'forefathers', namely the first three generations of Muslims.

Salafi: literally 'a follower of the forefathers'. The term is generally used for a Sunni Muslim who follows a rigid and literalist form of Islam and tries to base his life as closely as possible on that of the Prophet and his Companions in the seventh century. Hence, 'Salafism'.

Sharia: the religious, or canonical, law of Islam.

Sheikh: literally, 'old man'. The term denotes respect and is used of a tribal or religious elder or leader. A man who learns the entire Qur'an by heart is automatically a sheikh whatever his age.

Shi'i: a follower of Shi'i Islam, the second largest Muslim sect.

Shirk: polytheism, idolatry.

Shura: the Arabic word for consultation.

Source of emulation: a Twelver religious scholar whose learning is so deep and his piety so great that ordinary members of the faithful adopt his teachings as the model they will follow in their spiritual lives.

Sultan: literally 'authority' in Arabic. The word came to mean a Muslim ruler who is the supreme political authority within his dominions and whose authority stems from the fact that he implements the Sharia.

Sunna: habitual practice or custom; specifically that of the Prophet Muhammad, which came to be regarded as legally binding precedent.

Sunni: a follower of Sunni Islam, the largest Muslim sect.

Takfir: declaring another Muslim to have betrayed the faith by apostasy and to be worthy of death. Hence *takfiri*, a person who makes such declarations.

Taliq (plural Tulaqa'): a Meccan who converted to Islam only after

Muhammad had entered the city.

Taqiyya: a doctrine followed by Shi'is under which it is permitted, when need arises, to dissemble about one's true religious beliefs in order to avoid persecution by the Sunni Muslim majority.

Tawhid: the affirmation of the unity of God.

Twelver: the largest sect of Shi'i Islam. They believe that the Prophet was followed by twelve divinely-guided imams who were his direct descendants. The last went into hiding as a boy in the ninth century and is still alive although in hiding (or 'occultation') until he reappears in the End Times. The Twelver methodology for discerning the Sharia is substantially different from that of Sunni Muslims.

Umayyad: founded by Mu'awiya, the dynasty of caliphs that ruled the Islamic world until supplanted by the Abbasids in 750.

Umma: 'community', especially (but not necessarily) the community of Muslims.

Usuli: a school of Twelver Shi'i theology in which rational argument deployed by learned and pious religious scholars (mujtahids) is used to develop theology and religious law.

Velayat-e faqih: government by the mujtahid, who is expert in the Sharia: the principle developed by Ayatollah Khomeini and now enshrined in the constitution of the Islamic Republic of Iran.

Wahhabi: a strict, puritanical Muslim sect founded by Muhammad ibn 'Abdal-Wahhab in Central Arabia in the mid-eighteenth century. It is the prevailing ideology of Saudi Arabia. Today, it overlaps with Salafism, which Saudi Arabian Wahhabis seek to export to Muslim communities across the world.

Zaydi: a small Shi'i sect that believes any descendant of the Prophet may become the imam by unsheathing his sword and establishing righteous rule. Today, there is a large Zaydi community in Yemen which includes slightly over a third of the population.

Preface

We live in a time of appalling violence across large swathes of the Arab world and many other Muslim countries. When people ask how this has come about, they often find themselves presented with an answer citing the Sunni-Shi'i divide.

Muslims often disagree among themselves about the meaning of particular Qur'anic verses and the way of life God wishes them to follow. Nevertheless, these disagreements are minor in the scale of things when set alongside the essentials of the faith that are shared by Sunnis and Shi'is, and put a certain cultural stamp on Muslim societies everywhere.

Sectarianism is frequently given as the ultimate cause of the bloodshed in Syria, Iraq, and even Yemen. Behind these conflicts lurks the regional rivalry of Sunni Saudi Arabia and Shi'i Iran. The appearance of the so-called Islamic State (which we will call by its Arabic acronym, Daesh) led to some tens of thousands of young Sunni men travelling to Syria and Iraq to establish a new caliphate in which an extreme version of the Sharia was to be the law of the land. The world – including, it is important to stress, the overwhelming majority of Muslims – has watched in horror at the atrocities Daesh has committed in the name of Islam. Many are carried out against non-Muslims such as Christians and Yazidis. These are the ones that generally hit the headlines. Most, however, have been perpetrated against Shi'is, whom Daesh see as heretics who have deserted the faith: in other words, as traitors.

Islam is the world's fastest-growing religion. It is predominant from the Atlantic Coast of Morocco and Mauritania across a vast belt of land all the way to the islands of the Indonesian archipelago, the major exception being largely-Hindu India. Its predominance also extends north into Central Asia and parts of southern Russia, and southwards into large chunks of Sub-Saharan Africa. There are also Muslim minorities in many other countries, some of which have come into existence as a result of immigration that began only in the second half of the twentieth century. Most Muslims are Sunnis. Although reliable figures are hard to come by, it is generally assumed that they make up 85–90 per cent of the world's Muslim population of some 1.6 billion people or more. Most of the rest are Shi'is.

There are only four countries in which Shi'is are the majority: Iran, Iraq, Azerbaijan and Bahrain. Lebanon is the only country in which the Shi'i minority outnumber their Sunni co-religionists. Although Shi'i minorities also exist outside the central Islamic lands, they tend to be very small proportions of the total Muslim population. They have either arrived as traders or other migrants, or have converted to Shi'ism since the Iranian Revolution of 1979.

The Shi'is, being the minority among Muslims, have often been the underdogs and marginalised. As long ago as the eighth century, they even developed a doctrine called *taqiyya*, which allowed them to conceal their true beliefs from other Muslims so as to avoid persecution. Throughout the history of the caliphate from the death of the Prophet in 632 to the sack of Baghdad in 1258, the Muslims we now call Sunnis were the rulers of the Muslim empire that the Arab conquests built in the seventh and eighth centuries. The only ruling caliph during this period whom the Shi'is recognise is Ali. In 661, after less than five years of a reign characterised by civil war, he was murdered (his murderer was not a Sunni, incidentally). After Ali's son Hussein was martyred at Karbala in 680, many Shi'is came to despair of the establishment of a just Islamic society ruled by a descendant of the Prophet. This frequently led to an attitude of quietism, of withdrawal from politics and worldly power, and putting faith in the ultimate triumph of God's justice. Many aspects of Shi'ism, especially the ritual commemoration of the martyrdom of Hussein, provide strength to sustain the oppressed.

It thus becomes easy to see the Shi'is as the victims in the long history of Sunnis and Shi'is. There is much truth in this. The Iraqi dictator Saddam Hussein's pitiless repression of Shi'is is still very recent memory. But the overall picture is more nuanced. In the early centuries of Islam, there were many Shi'i rebellions against Sunni rule. One of these led to the great Shi'i empire of the North African/Egyptian Fatimids, who disdainfully ruled over many more Sunnis than Shi'is. Later on, there was another sparkling Shi'i empire, that of the Iranian Safavids, who forcibly converted their Sunni subjects to Shi'ism in the sixteenth century. The commemorations of Ashura (the date on which Shi'is mourn the killing of Hussein) were not purely for the oppressed and downtrodden. In India in 1784, during the time of the Shi'i kingdom of the nawabs of Awadh (also called Oudh), the ruler Asaf-ud-Daula built a magnificent structure in Lucknow called the Imambarah, to provide a fitting location for the commemoration of Ashura. It would also house his own tomb. The Ashura procession in Lucknow was led by royal elephants and was joined by large numbers from both the Sunni community and the Hindu majority population, who reinvented Hussein as a Hindu god of death.[1]

It is often forgotten that many of the giants of medieval Persian literature such as (Jalal ad-Din Muhammad) Rumi (1207–73) and Hafez (Khwaja Shams-ud-Din Muhammad Hafez-e Shirazi: 1315–90) were Sunnis rather than Shi'is, although sectarian issues tended to be of little importance to them. This brings us to an important point. These literary giants, whose works are so full of Islamic allusions that some understanding of Islam is needed in order to appreciate translations of their work, are still at the heart of the culture of Shi'i Iran today. Their Sunni background does not prevent this. Sunnism and Shi'ism have always been interlinked and able to cross-fertilise. A leading scholar has recently pointed out that Sunnism can be understood only by differentiating it from Shi'ism, and vice versa.[2] Even when Sunnis and Shi'is are clearly distinguished from each other, they have often lived harmoniously together and combined forces against invaders.

The aim of this book is to explain the great divide in Islam throughout the entirety of its history. There is no other route to understanding the divide, or to seeing why in recent years it has suddenly led to so much conflict. When we describe Sunnism and Shi'ism as 'sects' (a term I use because I cannot find a better alternative) we have to be careful not to import subconscious assumptions taken from Christian theology, where the word 'sect' originated. We tend to think of a sect as a religious grouping that split off from the mainstream at some identifiable historical point, possibly under the leadership of a charismatic spiritual figure. It did so in order to preach and practise the ancestral faith in a way that was sufficiently different as to be incompatible with the faith of those who decided not to join the new movement. Yet in Islam, the split between Sunnis and Shi'is did not arise in this way. Instead, there were two different conceptions of who should exercise religious authority among Muslims, more or less from the moment of the Prophet's death. This led to a civil war breaking out between Muslims while many of those who had been closest to the Prophet were still alive. These questions of authority were the central issue in that conflict.

Only four decades ago, the words Sunni and Shi'i were virtually unknown in Western countries outside specialist academic circles. If an ancient feud between Sunnis and Shi'is is truly the faultline that has divided the Muslim world ever since the death of the Prophet Muhammad in 632, why did it receive so little attention before the late 1970s? To take just one example, but a hugely important one: in 1947, British India was partitioned on independence into predominantly Hindu India and predominantly Muslim Pakistan. At the time, the Sunni-Shi'i divide received almost no attention and was clearly of little significance, even though India and Pakistan each contained both Sunni and Shi'i Muslims.

Nevertheless, an ancient religious dispute, a focus for primordial hatreds, can appear to fit the bill for today's many disasters in the Middle East. Important figures in the West have fuelled this kind of simplistic perception. The idea that Sunnis and Shi'is are now going through a period of bloodstained hatred similar to that experienced by Europe during the Reformation has become almost commonplace. Thomas Friedman, a columnist with a good background in Middle Eastern matters, wrote in a flippant piece in the *New York Times* on 1 April 2015 that 'the main issue [in Yemen today] is the 7th century struggle over who is the rightful heir to the Prophet Muhammad – Shiites or Sunnis.'[3] Such a perception needs to be challenged, as will become clear in the final chapter of this book. Another figure who has encouraged the spread of such contagious oversimplifications is Barack Obama. In his January 2016 State of the Union address, he stated that 'the Middle East is going through a transformation that is going on for a generation, rooted in conflicts that date back millennia'. When seen in the context of his speech, this could only be a reference to the Sunni-Shi'i divide. He has also implied on other occasions that 'ancient sectarian differences' are the drivers of today's instability in the Arab world.[4]

A simplistic narrative is in danger of taking firm hold in the West: that Sunnis and Shi'is have engaged in a perpetual state of religious war and mutual demonisation that has lasted across the centuries; and that this is the root cause of all that is wrong in the Middle East today. This is a very convenient narrative. It deflects attention from the immediate causes of the increase in sectarian violence between Sunnis and Shi'is over the past few years. Where bloodshed between Sunnis and Shi'is occurs it is usually entwined with political issues. The way to stop today's bloodshed is to sort out those political problems. Unfortunately, that runs up against the vested interests of many players.

It is quite wrong to see sectarian strife as endemic to Islam or the Middle East. Nevertheless, it is unquestionably growing at the moment. It has done so since 1979, and at a turbo-charged rate since 2003. Many mischievous hands have played a role in this, but there are also important forces that work against it. So there is no reason to despair – at least, not yet.

Note on Terminology

The names of cities, countries and even people can change over time, especially when a book covers history spanning more than 1,400 years. I have tried to use the best-known names that require least explanation. For consistency, I refer to Istanbul rather than to Constantinople, even though Constantinople was the form used throughout most of the centuries covered by this book. I do, however, refer to the city as Constantinople in the paragraphs dealing with its fall to the Ottomans in 1453. I also refer to the founder of the Turkish republic as Kemal Ataturk, although at the time he is mentioned he was still Mustapha Kemal. Iran and Persia provide a particular difficulty, since each name can carry very different overtones in English. It was not until 1935 that Persia officially changed its name to Iran, but it would have been confusing to start referring to Iran only at that point. This is especially so as the name Iran is also ancient, and has been used by the Iranian people to describe their land throughout the period covered by this book. Yet they call the language they speak Persian (Farsi, the language of the province of Fars). I have therefore tended to say Iran and Iranians when referring to the land and its people, but to use Persian when referring to the language and its culture. In any case, culture written in the Persian language has extended well beyond the borders of Iran, and sometimes may have little that is specifically Iranian about it. I have also referred to the Sasanian Empire – which the Arabs conquered in the seventh century – as Persian, because that felt right.

I use the term 'Greater Syria' for the land extending south from the Taurus mountains (which are now inside Turkey) all the way along the coast of the Mediterranean to the Sinai peninsula. In doing this I am not trying to make a political statement. Greater Syria is primarily a geographical, rather than a political, expression; the term is useful because in the twentieth century this area was split up by modern boundaries that are irrelevant and misleading if mentioned in the context of earlier periods. Similarly, 'Greater Bahrain' refers not just to the islands of Bahrain but a large area of adjacent Arabian mainland.

When discussing the concept of the Islamic Sharia, which is described in the glossary as 'the religious, or canonical, law of Islam', I have avoided the debate in modern scholarship over questions such as the extent to which the Sharia genuinely reflects the practice of the Prophet. Some modern scholars have argued that much of the Sharia, as we know it today, consists of existing customary laws which were recast as Prophetic and Islamic law. This question lies outside the scope of this book, as does the related one of the extent to which pre-Islamic Persian and other practices influenced Islam, and particularly Shi'ism.

John McHugo
June 2017

PART ONE

CHAPTER ONE

In the Beginning:
Before There Were Sunnis and Shi'is

The split in Islam between Sunnis and Shi'is is often traced back to the question of who should have led the Muslim community after the death of the Prophet Muhammad in 632 AD. Failure to resolve that question to the satisfaction of all resulted in a great scandal: a civil war among Muslims over the leadership of the community. This began less than twenty-five years after the Prophet had been placed in his grave, and while there were still many people alive who had known him well and loved him.

One side to that civil war is often presented today as consisting of those who said that Muslims should choose the best available leader for their community. There were only two provisos. The first was that he should be a leading figure who was known for his devotion to the faith. This meant that he should be chosen from among the Prophet's eminent Companions while they still lived. The other was that he must be from the tribe of the Quraysh to which Muhammad had belonged. This requirement may seem rather unnecessary to a modern reader who is unfamiliar with the history of Islam, but there were sound reasons for it at the time, as we shall see. The opposing party, it is frequently said, was made up of those who argued that leadership could be provided only by someone who was in the bloodline of the Prophet: initially, his cousin Ali, who was his closest living male relative at the time of his death and was married to his daughter Fatima. According to this view, the community should thenceforth always be led by a male descendant of that union.

Looked at this way, the dispute appears as much political as religious. It can even be interpreted as the pitting of those who favoured a somewhat more democratic form of religious authority (the Sunnis) against those who supported a strictly monarchical one (the Shi'is). As time passed, the split would appear to take the form, at least on the surface, of struggles between rival dynasties. Yet there has not been a caliph with a strong claim to universal acceptance among Sunni Muslims since 1258, the year in which Hulegu the Mongol sacked Baghdad. According to the most widely known account, he ordered the last of the Abbasid caliphs to be wrapped in a carpet and trampled to death by a soldier on horseback. This form of execution was chosen because Mongol protocol dictated that royal blood should not be seen to be spilled. As for the Shi'is, apart from a few groups such as the Ismaili followers of the Aga Khan who are a small minority even among them, none today pledge their allegiance to a worldwide religious community in which the supreme authority is a living descendant of Ali and Fatima.

Yet today the division between Sunnis and Shi'is seems very much alive. It is frequently seen as an important aspect of the conflicts that have been ravaging Syria and Iraq over the past few years, and of the power politics playing out between Saudi Arabia and Iran. There must therefore be something more behind it than ancient civil wars and half-forgotten dynasties. We have to follow the history from the beginning right through to the present if we wish to understand the division and its impact on us now. Over time, incompatible narratives to explain the history of the early Muslim community emerged. These would split Islam. In Islam, as perhaps in other religions, history and theology became permanently intertwined.

I

Islam's central tenet is faith in the one true God. It shares this with Christianity and Judaism, alongside belief in the Last Judgement, the Resurrection of the Body, Heaven and Hell. Even though the three religions have important differences which divide them, each enjoins its followers to live their lives in accordance with core virtues that are shared by them all, such as compassion, honesty, generosity and justice.

Islam's sacred scripture, the Qur'an (literally 'the recitation'), consists of passages which Muhammad believed were revealed to him by the angel Gabriel. From the earliest days of the faith, the revelations that make up the Qur'an were known to be distinct from everything else the Prophet said. The Qur'an is not the sole source of Muslim teaching, however, since all Muslims agree it is to be amplified by following the example of the Prophet and emulating the way he lived his life.

The hallmarks of Islam are to be found in Muslim devotional practices – such as the formal prayers that are to be said at prescribed times over the course of the day, the fasting during the holy month of Ramadan, and the pilgrimage to Mecca known as the Hajj. But the religious laws that govern the way Muslims should lead their lives are also key to living the religion. These, too, are based primarily on the teachings contained in the Qur'an and the customs established by the Prophet. After his death, the community was faced with many important questions. Among the most important was how to formulate and interpret these rules that govern the way Muslims perform their devotions and lead their lives. They make up what came to be known as the Sharia (literally, the path to the watering hole in the desert).

The Prophet had died fairly suddenly, and had not made any clear arrangements accepted by the whole community as to who was to lead it after his death. He had not instituted any kind of priesthood or left behind an uncontested teaching authority on spiritual matters. Moreover, ever since the Prophet's *Hijrah*, or emigration, from Mecca to the oasis of Medina some ten years before he died, the Muslim community had been a political entity. It had since grown into what today we would call a sovereign state, and required political leadership. This had been ably supplied by the Prophet himself while he was alive. Who was best qualified to supply it now? There were pressing problems of statecraft that had to be addressed at once. These were likely to involve murky compromises and messy decisions by a leader who would also be required to have the purity of heart needed to give guidance on spiritual matters. Sooner rather than later, this was likely to lead to a hard choice for the community: the person best able to exercise authority over it as an effective political leader might not be the most suitable candidate to be its spiritual guide.

By the time Muhammad died, the community he had founded had

come to dominate the desert subcontinent of Arabia. He had made Medina his capital, but Mecca, not Medina, was his native city and the place where he had begun his mission. Apart from the relatively small band that had responded to his initial preaching, the Meccans had been indifferent to his message or had actively opposed it. After a while, the city's fathers had made the situation of the first Muslims very uncomfortable. The result had been that Muhammad had gone to Medina, a large oasis with considerable settled agriculture that lay more than 250 miles to the north, where he already had some followers. This was in response to an invitation to act as a kind of resident arbitrator in disputes between the tribes living there – a position that would imply a degree of leadership. He had charisma and wisdom, and was known for his trustworthiness. He would have appeared an ideal outsider to fulfil such a role.

To the Muslim Muhajirun or 'emigrants', who set out for Medina from Mecca in unobtrusively small groups, there were now added Medinan converts who became known as the Ansar or 'helpers'. They were able to consider the Prophet one of their own, since his paternal grandmother had originally come from Medina. Yet not all the inhabitants of Medina converted. The Jewish tribes in the oasis retained their own religion, and substantial numbers of the other inhabitants remained polytheists. Despite this, over time Muhammad became the most powerful man in the oasis and its de facto leader. That leadership eventually consolidated into rule. Initially, however, his authority was on sufferance, except as far as his Muslim followers were concerned. His position of pre-eminence stemmed from agreement, especially treaties of alliance with the major tribes. While he was still in Mecca, conversion to Islam had involved the risks of ostracism, discrimination and active persecution. We can therefore assume that all conversions while he had been in Mecca had been sincere. But now, in Medina, it became expedient for many to accept Islam for reasons of self-interest. This large group was referred to as the Munafiqun, generally called 'the hypocrites' in English, who are frequently attacked in the Qur'an.

War with Mecca broke out almost immediately after Muhammad went to Medina, and seems to have been initiated by him and his followers. In contrast to the agricultural lands of Medina, Mecca was situated in a dry, rocky valley and had little or no agriculture of its own.

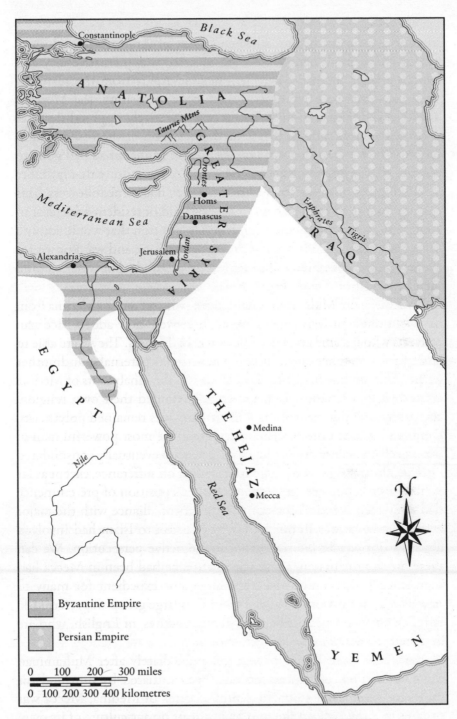

Black Sea

Constantinople

ANATOLIA

Taurus Mtns

GREATER SYRIA

Orontes

Homs

Damascus

Mediterranean Sea

Jerusalem

Jordan

Alexandria

EGYPT

Nile

Euphrates

Tigris

IRAQ

THE HEJAZ

Medina

Red Sea

Mecca

N

YEMEN

Byzantine Empire

Persian Empire

0   100   200   300 miles

0   100 200 300 400 kilometres

ARABIA IN THE TIME OF THE PROPHET

Its prosperity depended on trade and, to a lesser extent, on its status as a pilgrimage destination, since it possessed the shrine of the Ka'ba, which tradition stated had originally been built by Abraham and his son Ishmael (Ibrahim and Ismail in Arabic), although it was now a crowded house of idols. Meccan caravans had to pass Medina on their way to and from Syria, and it was this trade that Muhammad and his followers began to raid as a source of booty. By attacking its trade with Syria, he was threatening Mecca's lifeblood.

Raiding of this sort was permitted by long-established Arabian custom. The tribe was the basic social and political unit of pre-Islamic Arab society, and rights and obligations were limited to those towards other members of the tribe, and the upholding of whatever agreements the tribe may have entered into with others. Third-party arrangements included relations with other tribes, as well as engagements with individuals or groups who might seek the tribe's protection. The deterrent of vengeance, the old cry of an eye for an eye and a tooth for a tooth, was the cornerstone of justice and the only way in which law and order were maintained. It could be exacted not merely against the perpetrator of a wrong, but against any member of the wrongdoer's tribe. Not for nothing was 'persistence in the pursuit of vengeance' a cornerstone of the central Arab virtue of *hilm*, the quality which also combined steadfastness, courtesy, generosity, tact and self-control, and was the characteristic most sought after in the leader of a tribe.

This illustrates just how hard and lawless life was in seventh-century Arabia. It was not just the barrenness of the desert that was harsh. It had produced a brutal society that practised, among other extreme acts, the infanticide of unwanted baby girls. Not only was the physical environment hostile, but the lack of any settled government meant that there was no social unit above the tribe. Islam was something entirely new. When somebody became a Muslim, this meant that he or she had a new allegiance and a new code of conduct that overrode that of the old tribal customs. Tribal relationships were modified among those who had accepted the new religion, and the brutality of those relations softened by the teachings of Islam. If one tribe had a claim against another for the murder of one of its members, the Qur'an taught that the life of the murderer was forfeit – but it would be better and more praiseworthy to renounce the right to the murderer's death and accept blood money instead. Islam forbade the killing of another member of the murderer's tribe on the old basis of an eye for an eye, so vengeance could now be exacted only against the murderer himself. The death penalty for the murderer or acceptance of compensation was the choice for the victim's family, and the victim's family alone, to decide.

Islam provided a kind of 'super-tribe', of which all Muslims were members. Yet Islam did not replace tribalism as such. That would have been impossible in seventh-century Arabia, and there is no sign that the idea even occurred to the Prophet. The converts to the new faith formed a community that closed ranks against outsiders, such as the polytheists of Mecca, but the community's relations with the tribes of Mecca (and elsewhere) were still based on the old tribal customs. The Muslim attacks on Meccan caravans would have been understood in these terms by everybody in Arabia. Tribes which had converted to Islam would now focus their energies on spreading Islam, rather than dissipating it on raids against each other and blood feuds.[1]

II

During the ten years between Muhammad's *Hijrah* from Mecca to Medina and his death, he gradually rose to be the undisputed leader of much of Arabia. This was an extraordinary feat of political skill. First he had to make himself the leader of the whole oasis, then overcome the opposition of the Quraysh tribe which ruled Mecca, and finally spread his message far and wide across a desert subcontinent.

The first major military encounter between the Muslims and the Quraysh was at the wells of Badr, when a smaller force of Muslims defeated a Meccan army sent to escort a trading caravan returning from Syria. Muhammad received a revelation that divine help, in the form of legions of angels, had aided the Muslims. The victory simultaneously boosted Muslim morale, lifted their prestige among the non-Muslim inhabitants of Medina, and turned the struggle with Mecca into open warfare. For the sake of the tribe's own standing, the Quraysh needed to take revenge.

This is what they sought a year later. A large Meccan force approached Medina. Muhammad met them at Uhud, a mountain outside the oasis.

Initially, it looked as though the Muslims were gaining the upper hand. Excited rumours spread through the Muslim ranks that the Meccan camp was about to fall, and soldiers rushed forward in the hope of booty. The result was that archers guarding a flank abandoned their posts, and the Meccan cavalry were able to wheel round and attack the Muslims from the rear. Most of the Muslims were able to escape to high ground and lava-flows where they were safe from the enemy cavalry, but the Meccans were left in possession of the main battlefield. Muslim casualties were heavy. The Prophet himself was wounded. One of the men closest to him, his uncle Hamza, was killed. Hamza's body was mutilated and Hind, the wife of the Meccan leader Abu Sufyan, ritually chewed part of his liver in revenge for the death of her father, son, brother and uncle who had all been killed at Badr.

The defeat also demonstrated that Muhammad's leadership was still fragile. A large party of Munafiqun under Abdullah bin Ubayy, a tribal leader in Medina who aspired to rule the oasis and resented the prominent position Muhammad had acquired, deserted him before the battle. At the same time, the Jewish tribes and some others had remained neutral. Muhammad had clearly not consolidated his control of Medina at this point, yet he was able to ensure that Uhud was no more than a setback. The defeat made it necessary for him to redouble his efforts to extend his authority.

The Jewish tribes in the oasis presented him with a problem. They rejected his status as a messenger of God and argued that the truth lay in their own scriptures, not the Qur'an. On the ideological level, this made them his most dangerous opponents. One of the Jewish tribes, the silversmiths of Banu Qaynuqa', had already been exiled after the Battle of Badr. Now, Muhammad moved against the wealthiest Jewish tribe in the oasis, the Banu Nadir. Following allegations of their treachery, he laid siege to their village. It was eventually agreed that they would surrender their arms and leave the oasis with their moveable property. The siege of the Banu Nadir had demonstrated the weakness of Abdullah bin Ubayy's position, since he was bound to extend his protection to them. However, it had now been shown that he was not strong enough to challenge Muhammad. The departure of the Jewish tribe was therefore a humiliation for him and another major step towards Muhammad consolidating his authority in Medina.

The Quraysh now sought to destroy Muhammad once and for all. A much larger army than the force that had fought at Uhud was assembled and joined by major confederations of tribes. This time, rather than march out of the oasis to meet them and risk defeat by superior numbers, the Medinans fortified their oasis and surrounded it with a trench wherever there were no walls or lava-flows impenetrable to cavalry. The siege that resulted was known as the Battle of the Trench. The Meccans soon began to run out of supplies. Their Bedouin confederates drifted away, and they had no alternative but to return to Mecca.

Muhammad now took the final steps to assert his authority in Medina. The Banu Qurayza, the third of the Jewish tribes in the oasis, had plotted with the Meccans to rise up during the siege and attack the Muslims from the rear. Muhammad delegated the decision as to what should happen to them to Sa'd bin Mu'adh, a leader of the Ansar who had been mortally wounded in the Battle of the Trench. Sa'd decreed that the adult males of the tribe should be executed and the women and children enslaved. Medina, now indisputably under Muhammad's leadership, had become at least as powerful as Mecca. The Quraysh's commercial route to Syria was at his mercy, and Medina rivalled Mecca in the trade with Syria. Muhammad's envoys made agreements with tribes in the area between Medina and Greater Syria, as well as seeking alliances with tribes in the area between Medina and Mecca.

In achieving the final submission of Mecca, Muhammad practised magnanimity and subtle diplomatic skill. He announced that he wanted to lead his followers to perform a pilgrimage to the sanctuary at Mecca. This dismayed the Quraysh, because it would have involved, for all practical purposes, allowing him to lead a Muslim army into the city. A compromise was reached at Hudaybiyya, a place about nine miles from Mecca where Muhammad and his followers halted. A truce was agreed for the next ten years. The Muslims would turn back from making a pilgrimage that year but they would be permitted to perform it the following year. While the Muslims made their pilgrimage, the Meccans would evacuate the city for three days so as to make sure there was no disorder. When the pilgrimage took place, it happened without incident. The Muslims then returned to Medina and the Meccans re-entered their city.

In January 630, very probably after secret negotiations, Muhammad

led a large army to Mecca, which arrived unexpectedly. There was almost
no resistance to his arrival. He guaranteed the lives of the Meccans and
the safety of their property, although a few men who had abandoned
Islam and poets who had satirised the Prophet were executed. Once
assured that he would not seek revenge for their earlier opposition to him,
the merchants of the Quraysh flocked to accept Islam. As the idols were
taken from the Ka'ba and their shrines in neighbouring towns pulled
down, Arabian polytheism lost its force and its appeal. The advantages
of the new order were plain to see. Only three weeks after the submission
of Mecca, the tribe of Thaqif from nearby Ta'if were defeated after
marching on the city. The Thaqif had been a long-standing rival to the
Quraysh, but had been too powerful for the Quraysh to defeat on their
own. Now, however, as a result of the union with Medina, they were able
to do so. A new, successful, political order had been born. Muhammad's
emissaries travelled across Arabia in all directions spreading his message
and receiving the allegiance of the tribes, something that usually entailed
acceptance of the new religion. Muhammad's community of Muslims
had evolved into a state, and were now beginning to acquire what can
only be called an empire.

Alongside the categories of Muhajirun and Ansar, a third category of
Muslim now appeared. These were the Tulaqa' (singular, Taliq), those
Meccans who accepted Islam only after the fall of Mecca. They included
the leadership of the Quraysh, who had opposed Muhammad so
stubbornly, and are best exemplified by the Meccan leader Abu Sufyan
and his wife Hind. Muhammad forgave them for their opposition.
He even pardoned Hind for mutilating the body of his uncle Hamza.
Abu Sufyan was given a position that reflected his status and became
Muhammad's governor of Yemen, which at that time was probably the
richest province of the nascent Muslim empire. Hind travelled with the
Muslim armies on some of their conquests (it was a tradition for women
to accompany their men-folk to war so as to encourage them to fight
bravely), and cheered them on as she had once cheered the Quraysh as
they fought against the Muslims at Uhud.

III

Muhammad died in 632 AD, only two years after the submission of Mecca. His death was peaceful, and happened only a few days after he had first been taken ill. Before his final few hours, he may not have realised that the illness was likely to be fatal.

Losing him was deeply shocking for the Muslim community, and left it facing an unprecedented crisis. At the time of his death, an observer might easily have concluded that the odds were stacked against the survival of Muhammad's new religion and the polity that he had established. Although he had been acknowledged as the Prophet of God over most of Arabia, many of the tribes – especially those in the regions some distance from Medina and Mecca – had seen their relationship with him as entirely personal. Some had agreed to send payments of alms known as *sadaqa* to the Prophet. This money was used to help finance the Muslim state, to help the poor and to be used for other purposes that we would now call charitable. Yet the reality was that paying it would often have appeared more like sending tribute to a suzerain than performing a religious duty. One faction of a tribe might have agreed to make the payment so as to acquire a powerful ally in a struggle for supremacy with a rival faction. There were also tribes that had agreed to pay tribute but had not acknowledged Muhammad as a prophet, and Christian tribes that had retained their own faith but made individual arrangements with him. Now, many of these groups would not feel bound to enter into similar relations with whoever took the Prophet's place – assuming anyone succeeded in stepping into it. The new leader of the Muslim community, whoever he might be, was likely to face considerable resistance collecting taxes and tribute. Rebellions and attempts at secession were to be expected, and they began as soon as the news of the Prophet's death spread.

But what of the Muslims in the areas where Muhammad had preached – Mecca, Medina and nearby – where the new faith was much more firmly established? Here there was potential for friction between different groups within the community. As we have already seen, the most distinguished Muslims were those who had been early converts in Mecca and had loyally followed Muhammad throughout his mission. They were to be found among the Muhajirun and were predominantly

Meccans from one branch or another of the Quraysh, although people who travelled to Medina from other parts of Arabia to join Muhammad up to the time of the submission of Mecca were also listed as Muhajirun. Quraysh, however, was not only the tribe of the Prophet but also that of the Meccan merchant oligarchy who had opposed him so vehemently.

Now, however, things had changed. Opposition from the Quraysh's Meccan oligarchy had ended. All of the Quraysh were puffed up with pride at the fact that the Prophet had been one of their number, while at the same time the tribe's traditional prestige still counted for a great deal, and this was now ready to be deployed in the service of the new faith and Muhammad's polity. Its leaders and eminent men were rich merchants with more political experience and a greater awareness of the wider world than most other Arabs, a knowledge gained in the hard school of commerce. Many of them had travelled to Greater Syria (where some of them owned property) as well as to other far-flung areas. As the Prophet's early Companions were from the Quraysh, there would be little difficulty finding Qurayshi candidates for leadership who were devout Muslims and would also satisfy this tribal pride.

But there was also an important group of Muslims who were not members of the Quraysh. These were the Ansar of Medina who, like the Muhajirun, were distinguished by their devotion to the new religion. Three quarters of the Muslim fighters at Badr had been Ansar, and only one quarter Muhajirun,[2] while the Ansar suffered disproportionately at Uhud: seventy of them were killed, while only four of the Muhajirun lost their lives.[3] Muhammad tried to bind the Ansar and Muhajirun together, but few of the Ansar seem to have been granted leadership roles by him. Interestingly, too, the Prophet never took a daughter of one of the Ansar as a bride, although scholars have found it easy to discern political motives behind most if not all the marriages he made after the loss of Khadija, his first (and, at that time, only) wife. Khadija had died two or three years before the *Hijrah*. Indeed, the removal of her moral support and encouragement may have been an important factor behind his decision to leave Mecca. The divide between the Muhajirun and the Ansar was a threat to the harmony and stability of the community. The Qur'an presents the two groups as equal in rank,[4] but they seem to have stayed apart and it may be significant that there appears to have been little intermarriage.[5]

As soon as they heard of the Prophet's death, the Ansar met together and debated the choice of a leader from among themselves: someone who would either lead the whole community, or at least head the Ansar and thus rule Medina, where Muhammad had died and which he had retained as his capital after the submission of Mecca. The fact that these alternatives were both possible showed that there was a real risk that the community might split. Yet these deliberations were cut short. Two key figures from the early days of Muhammad's preaching in Mecca entered the roofed area or hall where they were congregating. These were Abu Bakr and Umar. They were accompanied by Abu Ubaidah bin al-Jarrah, another important early convert, and several others. Abu Bakr and Umar had both been very close indeed to the Prophet. Some historians have noted parallels between them in this closeness, as well as the remarkable fact that it does not seem to have led to jealousy between them.[6] Yet they were very different people.

Abu Bakr had been a friend of Muhammad from the earliest days in Mecca, and became known by the epithet al-Siddiq, 'the truthful', or 'he who affirms the truth'. He is said to have been three years younger than Muhammad and is often listed as the first adult male convert to the Prophet's message. He had an unshakeable faith in his friend's mission and was good at dispelling the doubts of others, especially when Muhammad took controversial or unpopular decisions. He was a skilful politician and was good at giving his friend sound and careful advice, which he expressed in a gentle and diplomatic way. At the same time, there was a steely side to his character. He has been described as 'a stern and ambitious father',[7] and at least two of his children, his daughter Aisha and his son Muhammad, would play important but controversial roles in the years after the Prophet's death. He was known to be utterly uncompromising in his faith, and would follow the Prophet's instructions to the letter. He had the honour of being Muhammad's sole companion on the *Hijrah*. This was a journey that had involved taking dangerous risks, and the two men had needed to hide in a cave to be safe from the Qurayshis who were searching for them, and would almost certainly have killed them if they had found them.

For Abu Bakr to leave Mecca at that point had meant jeopardising his considerable commercial interests, since he had been a successful, although not particularly wealthy, merchant there. Apart from one son who had not yet converted to Islam, his family joined him soon after he reached Medina, where he betrothed his nine-year-old daughter Aisha – Muhammad's only virgin bride – to the Prophet, for the marriage to be consummated soon after she reached puberty (as was normal practice at the time). Abu Bakr was the nearest Muhammad had to a constant companion. In his final illness, when the Prophet was too sick to lead the prayers, he asked Abu Bakr to take his place. According to many sources, Muhammad died in the arms of Aisha, who was always his favourite and most influential wife. His relationship with Aisha added additional cement to his bond with Abu Bakr.

Umar could not have been more different in temperament from Abu Bakr. He began by being fiercely opposed to Islam, but is said to have been swayed by the beauty of some Qur'anic verses he heard chanted in the house of his sister who, together with her husband, had already converted. This happened in Mecca about four years before the *Hijrah*. Yet, once he became a Muslim, he took up the cause with a pugnacious zeal that had characterised his earlier opposition. He was a natural leader in a way that Abu Bakr may not have been. He was tall, and was said to tower over other people as though he were on a horse. He was also noted for obstinacy, impulsiveness and a certain roughness (the latter not least by his wives), and had an overbearing temperament that could inspire fear. He was instrumental in helping Muhammad organise the polity in Medina, often acting as his right hand. Like Abu Bakr, he gave a daughter in marriage to the Prophet: Hafsa, whose husband had been killed at the Battle of Badr.

When they strode into the hall, Abu Bakr and Umar presented the assembled Ansar with a fait accompli. Abu Bakr stated that, as a purely practical matter, the leader of the community after the Prophet's death had to come from the Quraysh, or he would not be accepted by the Arabs across the length and breadth of Arabia. He then said that he was prepared to swear allegiance to either of the other two distinguished Companions of the Prophet who had accompanied him to the meeting, Umar or Ubaidah bin al-Jarrah, and commended the Ansar to do the same. At this point Umar intervened, and stated that for him it was inconceivable that he should swear loyalty to anyone other than Abu Bakr (Abu Bakr was roughly twenty years older than Umar). Abu Bakr accepted Umar's allegiance. With the two men united in their view as to the succession, it would now be very difficult for anyone to oppose their decision.

Yet when the two men and their followers had arrived at the hall, they had found Sa'd bin Ubadah, himself a distinguished Companion of the Prophet, lying on the ground wrapped in a cloak, and clearly ill. He was one of the most eminent among the Ansar and the paramount chief of the important Medinan tribe of Khazraj. He was a man whose views would certainly have held great weight with those present, and the Ansar were probably preparing to acknowledge him as the leader to represent their community. There seems to have been an element of intimidation in the meeting. Umar and some others are reported to have assaulted Sa'd for daring to challenge the right of the Quraysh to rule.[8] Sa'd never swore allegiance to either Abu Bakr or to Umar, who would himself take over leadership of the community after Abu Bakr's death two years later. Some other Ansar present at the meeting probably also never gave their allegiance to either of them, and maintained a sullen silence. Yet they would have felt that, if it had to be one out of Abu Bakr or Umar, they definitely preferred Abu Bakr.

A consideration in the backs of the minds of all present would have been the position of the Tulaqa', those converts from the Quraysh who had joined Islam only late in the day, for reasons that smacked of expediency. The group included powerful people such as Abu Sufyan, the aristocratic leader of the leading Umayya branch of the Quraysh, who had led the Meccan opposition to Islam almost to the bitter end. Men such as he would inevitably tend to see Islam through the lens of their tribal allegiance. If they remained within the fold of Islam, they could help the religion and its polity expand yet further. The Tulaqa' knew they were taking part in a hugely successful political project, and wanted to join the side that had won. There would be opportunities for glory and prestige, for booty and amassing wealth, as well as for spreading the message of the new religion. The Muslim community needed them. It was even an open question whether the Muslims could remain united as a community if they lost the support and skills of the Tulaqa'. It would have been crucial for the Tulaqa' that the leader should come from the Quraysh. If he did not, here was a strong risk that the Tulaqa' would revert to the ways that had served them so well until the days of Muhammad. For this reason, Abu Bakr was a ruler whom they, too, were able to accept.

But there was another possible candidate, apart from Abu Bakr and Umar, who seemed to fulfil the requirements for leadership. Unlike both of them, he had a following among the Ansar. This was Ali. His links with Muhammad were even closer than those of Abu Bakr or Umar. He was the son of Abu Talib, the Prophet's uncle, who had played a major role in Muhammad's own upbringing. When Muhammad had begun preaching and received hostile reactions, Abu Talib had given him protection under the tribal code (even though Abu Talib was not a Muslim, and never converted). Ali became a Muslim while still a boy or teenager, even before the adult Abu Bakr.

On the night of the *Hijrah*, Ali stayed behind to deceive the Meccans about Muhammad's departure. He courted danger by sleeping in Muhammad's own bed so that any potential assassins who peered through the window would not realise Muhammad was gone. He also tidied up Muhammad's affairs in Mecca before leaving for Medina. In Medina, he married the Prophet's daughter Fatima, and gave Muhammad two grandsons, Hassan and Hussein, whom the Prophet knew as small children and adored. Later, Ali also married a granddaughter of the Prophet, Umamah bint Abu al-'As.[9] Ali proved himself to be a mighty warrior and is reported to have received sixteen wounds at the Battle of Uhud. This is a characteristic that the sources do not attribute to Abu Bakr or Umar in quite the same way – although Abu Bakr did carry the battle standard on at least one occasion, and it is safe to assume that Umar was no mean warrior.

One practical and legitimate reason to exclude Ali from consideration would have been his youth. He seems to have been at least thirty years younger than Muhammad and Abu Bakr, and over a decade younger than Umar. It might have been difficult for him to assert his authority over the quietly voiced charisma of Abu Bakr or the forceful Umar, with their greater age and experience. Both had been playing important roles in the Prophet's mission while Ali was still a boy. There are also suggestions that Ali's judgement was sometimes poor – something that his subsequent career would arguably demonstrate – in a way that the judgement of the two older men was not.

There were, then, understandable reasons why Ali may have been passed over. It is possible that Abu Bakr and Umar both dismissed him as a serious candidate and considered that he would make a disastrous leader.

But they may also have had personal reasons to reject him. The hasty meeting at which Abu Bakr was proclaimed leader of the community took place in Ali's absence, since Ali was engaged in preparing the Prophet's funeral rites. There has always been suspicion that Abu Bakr, Umar and the other Companions who elected Abu Bakr were acting swiftly so as to pre-empt Ali's candidature. It is possible – some would say likely – that if a formal assembly of the Prophet's Companions had been convened Ali might have been chosen.

Aisha was intensely hostile to Ali, which may well have influenced Abu Bakr against him. This ill-feeling arose from an incident during the Prophet's life that could have had dire consequences for her. Within a year or two of her marriage to Muhammad, she had mislaid a necklace at an encampment. She slipped out of her covered litter and found it but, when she returned, the caravan had set off, the camel drivers assuming that she was still inside the litter. Expecting them to come back to look for her, she waited. A young man riding a camel, who had fallen behind the army, came upon her and rescued her. However, that evening when she arrived riding his camel, which he was leading by the halter, malicious gossip began.

If Muhammad had been cuckolded, it would have caused immense damage to his prestige. It would also have tested relations between him and Abu Bakr to destruction. The gossip was blamed on the Munafiqun, whose malicious intention was to weaken Islam. Even though the gossip was not widely believed, there seems at first to have been a nagging doubt in Muhammad's mind – or possibly he was just disconcerted by the gossip. Eventually, that doubt was dispelled when he received a Qur'anic revelation that Aisha was innocent. By then, however, he had already questioned many about what they thought. When he asked Ali, he received the following response: 'God hath not restricted thee, and there are many women besides her. But question her maidservant, and she will tell thee the truth.'[10]

The maidservant told Muhammad she was confident of Aisha's innocence. By suggesting that Muhammad ask her, Ali might almost be said to have appeared supportive of Aisha. But his other words cannot be ignored. When he said 'there are many women beside her', this would have been devastating for Aisha. It could only be encouragement for Muhammad to divorce her. His words were also interpreted as attempting to pressurise the maid into making a confession of her mistress's guilt. What Ali said infuriated Aisha, leaving her with a long-lasting enmity towards him.

After Muhammad's death, it took Ali six months to offer his allegiance to Abu Bakr, and even thereafter the relationship between the two men remained cool. Towards the end of those six months, Ali's wife, Fatima, died. Her burial took place at night, so that Abu Bakr could not attend – a very pointed snub indeed to the leader of the Muslim community, especially as she was the Prophet's daughter. Could it be that she always considered Ali the rightful successor to Muhammad? It is also possible that while she was still alive she prevented Ali from accepting Abu Bakr as the leader. Ali does not seem ever to have renounced completely the hope of leading the community at some stage in the future.[11] He would subsequently say that he considered himself to be the rightful successor to Muhammad, and only gave way to Abu Bakr for the sake of the unity of the community. This can be seen as part of a pattern of behaviour that reflects well on Ali since, as we shall see, there would be other occasions when he put the harmony of the community before his own interests and ambitions.

Accounts have survived from two of those involved in what happened during those crucial hours that followed the Prophet's death.[12] One is that of Aisha. The other is that of Ali's (and the Prophet's) cousin Abdullah bin Abbas. Not surprisingly, they provide very different narratives that support the position of the person each is closest to: Abu Bakr, in the case of Aisha, and Ali in the case of Abdullah (although relations between Ali and Abdullah would not always prove to be cordial).[13]

Aisha presents her father as the Prophet's choice. She also portrays Abu Bakr as concerned with ensuring that the Prophet's own blood relatives received their full inheritance rights; at the same time she goes out of her way to paint those relatives in a negative light, even mentioning an attempt by the Prophet's uncle Abbas to force medicine on the dying Muhammad, which he did not want. For his part, Abdullah bin Abbas maintains that the Prophet did not make a will in favour of Ali as his successor, but this was probably because Aisha and Hafsa prevented Ali being on his own with Muhammad during his final hours. They always made sure that the father of one or other of them, that is to say Abu Bakr or Umar, was present. When Muhammad suggested that he should write a letter of guidance to the Companions – the Muslim faithful who knew him personally – Abdullah asserts that Umar prevented it. 'The Messenger of God is overcome with pain,' he said. 'You have the Qur'an. The Book of God is sufficient for us.'[14] Abdullah also states that his father, Abbas, suggested to Ali that he should raise the question of the succession directly with the Prophet. Abbas was confident that Muhammad would either tell Ali he should be the successor or at least insist that the Quraysh take good care of Ali and the Prophet's other relatives. But Ali declined. For her part, Aisha has a story to counter that of Abdullah: the dying Muhammad asked her to call her father because he wanted to write him a letter. The Prophet feared there was 'someone else' – and this could only be Ali – who would have vain hopes of leadership once the Prophet was dead.

Aisha and Abdullah, then, give opposing views as to who the successor should be. They were adamant in those views, but both their accounts are self-serving. Aisha claimed that the Prophet died in her arms. Abdullah maintained that he died in the arms of Ali.[15] It is also unsurprising that an atmosphere of distrust between supporters of Abu Bakr and Ali can be clearly detected at this time. It mirrored the pre-existing loyalties of competing families, as well as the splits in the Muslim community that we have already discussed. The Prophet's clan, the Banu Hashim, excluded Abu Bakr from any part in the funeral rites, while Ali took a leading role in them. In what may have been an act of retaliation, Abu Bakr deprived them of their share of inheritance of state lands acquired from unbelievers, even though this was provided for in the Qur'an.

Abu Bakr was already quite elderly at the time of his election and died only two years later. By then he had proved a decisive leader who had certainly repaid the trust placed in him by those who chose him. Not only did he quash the rebellions that broke out after the death of the Prophet and secure Arabia for Islam, but he directed the Muslim armies – largely led by members of the old Qurayshi aristocracy[16] – towards Greater Syria, which at that time was part of the Byzantine, or Eastern Roman, Empire, which had its capital in Istanbul. Abu Bakr was noted for following the instructions of Muhammad to the letter, but used his authority to make sure that the Quraysh received their reward for supporting him.

One of Abu Bakr's first tasks as the successor to the Prophet had been to send armies out to make sure that the tribes across Arabia remained within Islam and continued to make the payments they had agreed to send to Muhammad. From a strictly Muslim standpoint, this was problematic. As Umar is reported to have put it: 'I was ordered to fight all people until they say "there is no god but God". If they say this, they safeguard themselves and their property from me.'[17] While Abu Bakr took away the inheritance of the Prophet's family, including the shares of the prophet's daughter Fatima and his grandchildren Hassan and Hussein, he did not deprive the Prophet's widows of their legacies. Aisha, of course, was the most prominent widow. He transferred the large land holdings belonging to the Prophet to the treasury. This decision increased the funds available for the armies. As Abu Bakr's health failed, he nominated Umar as his successor and persuaded the community to accept him. There was no suggestion of any elective process. Umar was far from popular, even among some of the other early Companions. Abu Bakr's success in choosing his successor, and persuading the community to accept that choice, must therefore be seen as another sign of his strong charisma.

IV

After Umar succeeded Abu Bakr he tried to arrange a compromise over the issue of the inheritance that should be due to members of the Prophet's family, and even admitted that the appointment of Abu Bakr had been over-hasty. But he was unswerving on the point that leadership could not, under any circumstances, go to the Prophet's family. Others were already jealous of the fact that the Banu Hashim could claim the honour of being the family of the Prophet; the rest of the Quraysh would not tolerate them also acquiring leadership of the community.

The success of Umar's ten-year reign vindicated Abu Bakr's decision to nominate him as his successor. Those ten years were a period of truly dramatic conquest. Umar's headstrong and outspoken nature made him another formidable champion of Islam. During the Prophet's life he had taken a hard line towards the pagan aristocracy of Mecca. He had wanted the Meccan captives at Badr killed rather than ransomed, had objected to the compromise over pilgrimages to Mecca reached at

Hudaybiyya, and had suggested that Abu Sufyan should be executed rather than pardoned after the final surrender of Mecca.[18]

Muslim armies had occupied the whole of Greater Syria and Iraq, Egypt and part of modern Iran by 644, when Umar was assassinated by a Persian slave in an incident that seems to have had no political motivation. Umar had also begun to organise the Muslim state on a more formal basis than hitherto, most notably by using lands expropriated in the conquered territories to pay pensions to the conquerors. Now that he was ruling over the Muslim community he did not question the fundamental role of the Quraysh, but stressed the precedence of those who were early converts at the expense of the old aristocracy. The conquests of Greater Syria and Iraq were now proceeding apace, swelling the coffers of the state with booty. The riches at his disposal for distribution were thus of an altogether different order than those which Muhammad or Abu Bakr had commanded.

The leading positions during his reign were largely occupied by early Muhajirun Companions. For Umar, precedence in acceptance of Islam was the most important qualification for leadership, but he also gave important roles to some of the Tulaqa' (the late-converts from the Quraysh). After the death from plague of the distinguished Companion Abu Ubaidabin al-Jarrah, who had been Umar's first choice as governor of recently conquered Greater Syria, he seems to have had little option but to appoint members of Abu Sufyan's family to replace him.[19] He nominated Abu Sufyan's son Yazid, who had been one of the generals leading the invasion of Greater Syria, to become the governor of Damascus. When Yazid, too, died from the plague, Umar replaced him with his brother Mu'awiya, whose role expanded to that of governor of the whole of Greater Syria.

By contrast, few Ansar were promoted to significant positions during Umar's reign. They seem to have been notably absent, for instance, from the lists of those who fought at the Battle of Yarmouk, the Muslim victory that led the Byzantines finally to abandon Greater Syria. There were others, too, who were overlooked in the new order of precedence. These were proud members of old, non-Qurayshi tribal aristocracies whose positions had been diminished with the coming of Islam and the consequent ascendancy of the Quraysh. Some of the Ansar and tribal leaders from these aristocracies played significant roles in conquering and occupying Iraq, in a way that seems to have been denied to them elsewhere. It may have been significant that Iraq had always been less important to the Quraysh than Greater Syria.

V

In the space of a couple of decades –including the twelve-odd years since the death of the Prophet – events had taken place that would transform the history of the world. Islam was not yet securely established as a new religion, and internal tensions that threatened its unity and survival can already be detected, despite the impressive expansion of the Arab conquerors riding under the banner of the new faith. There was now a vigorous new empire that was Arab and Muslim, but there were cracks beneath its surface – rivalries, jealousies and conflicts of interest between those leading it and among the warriors who provided its armed might.

The geography of the Middle East was also changing to accommodate this new empire. The empire's capital was still Medina, but its main source of wealth was now the rich, conquered territories of Greater Syria, Iraq and Egypt. In all of these it now exacted tribute on a scale that would have been unimaginable to the people of Mecca and Medina just ten years before. In the new provinces, the Arab warriors were settled in cantonments near the edge of the desert. Sometimes, as in the case of Damascus, this would be in centres that were conveniently placed for their connection to Medina, and Arabia generally. In other cases, new cities had to be built. Most of the Arab warriors in Iraq were settled in the new towns of Kufa and in Basra, both equally handy for a quick return to Arabia if this should prove necessary, as well as for the arrival of reinforcements from Medina. Cities like Damascus, Kufa and Basra were now beginning to take on an importance that, in a fairly brief period of time, would mean they would become the main political centres of the new world the Muslims were creating.

CHAPTER TWO

How Civil War Came to Islam

I

Umar died on 3 November 644. He was not killed outright. He lived long enough to summon six of the most eminent survivors among the Prophet's Companions to decide on his successor. Their task of finding a successor who could keep the community united would not be easy. The focus was on two candidates, Ali and Uthman bin Affan.

As we have seen, Ali would have been the Ansar's choice. He was a member of this six-man college convened to choose a successor, but there was no member of the Ansar among the other electors. He was decisively rejected, partly at least because he was perceived as the Ansar's candidate. Uthman, the other leading contender, also had strong religious credentials. He was an early convert and was known to be devout. As with Abu Bakr, Umar and Ali, his closeness to the Prophet was underlined by marriage alliances. He had married two of the Prophet's daughters. First, he took the hand of Ruqaiya. When she died, he married Umm Kulthum.

Despite these marriage ties, Uthman seems to have been a less prominent figure during the Prophet's mission than Abu Bakr, Umar or Ali. However, as has been pointed out by Wilferd Madelung, a renowned scholar of early Islamic history, the fact that Muhammad successively gave Uthman two of his daughters in marriage was an even greater honour than that he accorded Abu Bakr and Umar by taking the hands of a daughter of each of them.[1] Uthman had played no military role whatsoever during or after the Prophet's life; it was something for which it would seem he was unsuited. Yet he was important for the Prophet because he was a rare early convert from the Banu Umayya, the dominant section of the Quraysh, which had been implacably hostile to Muhammad and his mission until the submission of Mecca. Uthman was a wealthy merchant – something that was rare among the early converts. Coming from the Banu Umayya, he was a close kinsman of Muhammad's former arch-enemy, Abu Sufyan. For the main body of the Quraysh, he was now an acceptable choice in a way that Ali was not. The fear was that Ali would have opened the leadership of the community to the Ansar and more recent converts from all over Arabia, in a way that would have ended the privileged position of the Quraysh.

The six therefore chose Uthman, and it is easy to see hard-nosed, practical realities behind that decision. It was the first – and last – occasion on which there was a genuine election by a group of the leading Companions. Uthman was chosen because he was the candidate around whom opposition to Ali could unite. The fact that he had married not one daughter of the Prophet, as had Ali, but two, would have strengthened his candidature. He had not sought the office. Others had chosen him for it, and almost thrust it upon him. This may have given him a misplaced confidence as to the strength of his position as ruler. He adopted the new title of *Khalifatu'llah*: 'God's deputy [on earth]', a more imposing title than Abu Bakr's 'successor to the Prophet of God'. The difference between the two titles tends to get lost in English translation, since the holder of each title is usually just referred to as 'the Caliph'. Yet, as we shall see in Chapter Four, the word *khalifah* or caliph can mean two different things: 'successor' (the way Abu Bakr used the title as the successor to the Prophet) or 'deputy' (as Uthman used it to describe himself as 'God's deputy [on earth]'). His choice of title must have indicated his own belief in the strength of his authority. Unfortunately, this showed itself in a highhandedness and tactlessness which in time would drain almost all mainstream support away from him.[2]

Like it or not, and despite Umar's policy of promoting those who had been early converts, the Qurayshis were providing the main body of leadership for the new empire – for that is what the polity established by Muhammad had now become. The Muslim, Arab warriors had lost their freedom to raid each other, but instead had become the empire's military caste, which lived on the labours of the indigenous, non-

Muslim and non-Arab populations of the conquered lands. Now the warriors were subject to military discipline which could be brutal, and involved floggings for various offensives – a development that was the very antithesis of the old tribal ethos in which a tribal leader's authority was based on the consent of his followers. Their stipends and pensions, as well as the hope of once unimaginable quantities of booty, were the price they were paid in return.

Umar had been able to send the Muslim armies out of Arabia to carry out undreamed-of conquests. This must have appeared as a mark of divine favour, but could not alter the fact that this Arab and Muslim empire, which had existed for only a decade or so, was fragile. Byzantium had been defeated in Greater Syria and Egypt, but counterattacks were still possible and the core of the Byzantine Empire was intact. The other great empire the Muslims had attacked was Persia, which at that time covered Iraq as well as the whole of Iran and considerable territories further east. The King of Persia had been repeatedly defeated in battle, but he was still at large as a focal point for resistance, and the Iranian heartland was unsubdued. The grip of the conquerors on the vast territories they had occupied was tenuous. Although internal frictions and disputes over the spoils of victory had not yet erupted into bloodshed, they could easily do so at any time. Umar may have taken the very first steps towards putting the government of the empire onto some sort of formal basis, but that work had scarcely begun. The prestige of being Muhammad's successor was the source of his authority. Now that Umar's immense force of personality was absent, the Muslim community was entering a new and very difficult period.

The empire was constantly expanding as the Arab warriors surged on, and Uthman's reign was concerned with maintaining its unity. Internal pressures that could tear it apart had begun to build up. On the one hand, further expansion was needed in order to avoid the risk of the Arab conquerors turning against each other. On the other, provincial governors were now becoming very powerful figures in their own right, and it was frequently they – rather than Uthman himself – who initiated further campaigns of conquest. Thus, the governors of Greater Syria and Egypt built fleets manned by local (and therefore Christian) sailors who defeated the Byzantine navy off the Lycian coast in 655 and forced Cyprus to pay tribute. In Iran, organised resistance was finally ended as the Arabs pushed their way across the Iranian plateau. This, too, was to a considerable extent an initiative of local governors in Kufa and Basra, the Arab garrison towns that had been established in southern Iraq during Umar's reign.

Uthman's greatest achievement in religious terms was to produce an approved text for the Qur'an. This removed one serious source of potential discord, especially as the Companions of the Prophet who could recall him receiving the revelations were now ageing. As more of them died, there was the risk that crucial recollections of parts of the sacred text would be lost. Uthman also tried to exert a greater degree of control over the provinces and their governors. This was an implicit admission that he lacked some of the authority that had radiated from Abu Bakr and Umar. The establishment of greater control meant challenging vested interests, especially when he reduced the financial position of the garrisons and tried to ensure that more of the revenues of the provinces went to the central government. Many early converts and individuals who had fought bravely for Islam during the campaigns of conquest found they were losing out.

Uthman's response was to appoint new governors on whom he knew he could rely. These were invariably from the Banu Umayya, the dominant section of the Quraysh to which he belonged. Their task was to enforce his authority. Right from the start of his reign he gave preference to relatives, who soon occupied all the major governorships. Some of his closest relatives, especially his cousin Marwan bin al-Hakam, became key figures behind his rule. Despite criticism, which he brushed aside, he continually made grants to his extended family from state funds. He even argued in his own defence that he was implementing the Qur'anic injunction to provide for one's kin.[3] He also transformed rich estates in the conquered territories that had been considered communal lands of the Muslim community into crown lands of which he could dispose at will.

As a result of these policies, Uthman gradually lost the support of the surviving Companions of the Prophet. Some of those who had elected him were openly critical, while others remained silent. The same applied to the mass of the Quraysh, who were jealous at the way in which he was favouring his closer relatives.[4] Beyond the Quraysh, there were those who felt excluded by the prominence of that tribe. Discontent grew in the Iraqi garrison city of Kufa, among the army in Egypt, and in Medina itself – the original home of the Ansar. Eventually there was even talk among the Companions of jihad against Uthman.[5]

All this put Ali in a delicate position. He became a focus for those who were discontented with the way things were going. He disagreed with the Caliph on some questions of devout Muslim practice, and the interpretation and enforcement of religious law. Uthman had a half-brother, Walid bin Uqba, whom he appointed as governor of the garrison town of Kufa in Iraq, even though he was a habitual drunkard. Ali had him punished by flogging – and may even have carried out the sentence himself.[6] At the same time, he stood up for individuals whom he considered to be devout and worthy Muslims but who might have incurred the Caliph's displeasure. He publicly called on Uthman to acknowledge past mistakes and apologise for them. For a while, Ali tried to help Uthman by mediating and urging him to repent. At one point, Uthman did acknowledge his mistakes, but his cousin Marwan believed this had been a fatal sign of weakness, and he angrily dismissed aggrieved soldiers with threats of violence. In frustration, Ali washed his hands of the situation.[7]

The atmosphere grew steadily worse. By 655, the same year in which an Arab fleet defeated the Byzantine navy off the coast of Lycia while victorious Arab soldiers were pushing further across the Iranian plateau, Uthman faced serious discontent at home. In the early summer of 656, an angry and potentially violent crowd of mutineers surrounded his house in Medina, telling anyone who cared to listen about their demands. In the final sermon Uthman preached, he was interrupted by volleys of pebbles. These knocked him unconscious and he had to be carried out of the mosque. Several days later, a group of mutineers from Egypt, whom he had persuaded to return home in the belief that he had listened to their grievances and would look into them, reappeared. They were carrying a letter, ostensibly written by Uthman himself, to the governor of Egypt, telling him to have the mutineers flogged on their return. They had taken it from a messenger who had tried to pass them on the road. Whether or not the letter was a forgery – as Uthman insisted it was – it seems clear that his cousin Marwan was behind it.[8] Ali, for one, was convinced the Caliph had not written it. Uthman, however, did not help himself. He seems to have swung between moods in which he publicly acknowledged that he had made mistakes and others in which he imperiously clung to the prestige and dignity of his office. It has even been suggested that these vacillations could have been signs of a breakdown that impaired his judgement.[9]

As Egyptian army rebels besieged his house, demanding his replacement by another ruler, Uthman justified himself by writing letters in which he maintained that he had kept his promises. He claimed that he had ordered appropriate redress for grievances, and stated that the punishments in the Qur'an would be applied to all wrongdoers without fear or favour. At the same time, he stressed the dignity of his office. He pointed out that Abu Bakr and Umar had not been held to account in the way that he had been. Nor had they been threatened with retaliation for their actions, or asked to resign. He repented of whatever sins he might have committed, but refused to step down as demanded. It is also clear that he did not envisage using force to defend his position. Instead, he looked to the Companions and the widows of Muhammad, 'the Mothers of the Faithful', for powerful moral support. Despite this, a number of men went to his house to guard it. These included Ali's son Hassan.

Up to this point violence had been unheard of between Muslims, save for punishments for crimes. Now it began to look ominously possible. The mutineers would not back down from their demand that the Caliph resign, while Uthman stubbornly refused to do so. Niyar bin Iyad, an elderly Companion of the Prophet, called for Uthman to appear before the crowd outside the gate. When the Caliph came out onto the balcony, Niyar insisted that he step down. A former slave of Marwan dropped a rock on Niyar, killing him instantly. When the crowd demanded that the murderer be handed over, Uthman asserted that he did not know the identity of the killer. The following day, 17 June 656, after crowds had gathered during a noisy night, the palace was stormed. Uthman told the defenders to go to their own houses and protect themselves, saying that the assailants wanted only him. Despite the Caliph's wishes, there was fighting and a number of the participants were killed. One of those who are alleged by tradition to have slain the Caliph was Muhammad, a son of Abu Bakr, who was one of the leaders of the mutineers from Egypt. He is said to have grabbed Uthman by the beard while he was sitting reading the Qur'an, and to have shoved his sword into the Caliph's forehead.

The murder of Uthman brought violence to the heart of the community's political life. As his position weakened in the period leading up to his death, his kin reproached Ali for failing to act more decisively to protect him. Ali seems to have been pulled in two directions. On the one hand, he owed Uthman loyalty as the head of the community and as a kinsman. On the other, he believed Uthman was misgoverning the community and not acting in accordance with Islam's true principles.[10] Both the community itself and its new empire were unstable. The old rivalries between Mecca and Medina, Muhajirun and Ansar, early converts to Islam and latecomers, Qurayshis and non-Qurayshis, the devout and the cynical, had become more intense as a result of the vast wealth that came from the revenues of the conquered territories, the spoils of war and payments of tribute.

II

There is no doubt that Ali believed he was now entitled to the succession. He had once told Abu Bakr that he had a better title than the latter to succeed the Prophet. The only reason he had finally offered his allegiance to Abu Bakr, then subsequently to Umar and Uthman, was concern for the unity of Islam and the good of the community. Mu'awiya bin 'Abi Sufyan, the powerful governor of Greater Syria who would in due course emerge as Ali's rival, satirised the manner in which Ali had acquiesced in the authority of the first three caliphs. He wrote Ali a deliberately insulting letter in the run-up to the civil war that was to break out between them:

> Yet each one [Abu Bakr, Umar and Uthman] you envied, and against each one you revolted. We knew that from your looking askance, your heavy speech, your heavy sighing, and your holding back from the caliphs. To each one of them you had to be led as the male camel is led by the wood stick through its nose in order to give your pledge of allegiance while you were loath.[11]

After the murder of Uthman, the situation was very different to that which had prevailed on those earlier occasions. Now Ali believed that the community was turning to him to lead it. As news of Uthman's murder spread, Companions of the Prophet approached Ali and offered their allegiance. It is reported that initially he refused to accept, but then asked that the pledges should be made publicly in the mosque. When he went to the mosque the day after the murder, he seems to have been acclaimed as the leader by an excited congregation. This included pledges by Zubair and Talha, two of the leading Companions who had been members of the electoral college of six that had selected Uthman as caliph. They would have been potential candidates for the leadership themselves. Subsequently, they had become openly hostile to Uthman's policies. Although they now offered Ali their allegiance, they would later claim that they were coerced into doing so, as would a few others.

The fact is that there does seem to have been an atmosphere of intimidation created by some of Ali's supporters, such as Malik al-Ashtar, but this was probably without the approval of Ali himself. Malik al-Ashtar was a physically imposing man who was known to be a brave and very able warrior. He had led a party of 200 men from Kufa to Medina to protest against Uthman, and had been one of the murdered caliph's most vociferous critics. He and his men had taken part in the siege of the caliph's house. It is easy to believe that he could be very intimidating. Yet this was not Ali's approach. He excused some leading figures who did not wish to swear him allegiance, and let them depart.[12] Others simply absented themselves, and he did not try to prevent them from so doing.

Opponents to his rule gathered in Mecca. These consisted of two main groups. First, there were those who believed the caliphate should remain in the hands of the Quraysh, because they were uneasy about the main sources for Ali's support: the Ansar and soldiers from non-Qurayshi tribes. Although Ali himself was from the Quraysh, this support made him unsuitable in their eyes. Another group went further. They might be described as loyalists to Uthman, who believed that a kind of dynastic principle had now been established and that the successor should come from his family.

For Ali, it did not matter that he had not been formally elected by a college of the most eminent surviving Companions, nor that he lacked the backing of the grandees of the Quraysh. He was convinced of the rightness and justice of his position, and for him that was the end of the matter. His sermons and speeches were uncompromising. In one report of his first homily as caliph, he is said to have warned the congregation that God had prescribed two remedies for the community: the sword and the whip. Now he was the imam, or leader, he might forgive past misdeeds. This was a hint that he might show clemency to those who had not supported him in the past, but a warning that he would not to those who transgressed in the future. He compared Uthman to a raven that had thought only of his stomach. It would have been better for that raven if his wings had been clipped or his head cut off, since he had left a Muslim community that was now lukewarm. Hard work was now needed to restore it to what it should be. Ali is also said to have reminded the congregation that the virtuous among the close relatives of the Prophet had a high spiritual status. This family had divine knowledge that enabled them to sit in judgement in the way that God would do. The faithful should follow them, and would then receive right guidance. If they failed to do so, God would lead them to perdition.[13]

Ali was a courageous man who was determined to act in accordance with his religious conscience. He forthrightly reproached the community for its backsliding and tepidness, as well as its disloyalty and failure to give him the support he needed. Such pronouncements were occasionally offset by warm praise for acts of loyalty. Ali did not attack the memory of the rule of Abu Bakr and Umar – in fact, he seems to have admired the austerity and sternness that were characteristics of Umar's rule, and often followed the precedents he had set. He is also on record as describing them both as righteous emirs who had followed the Qur'an and the Prophet's custom. By contrast, he believed that the community had gone astray under Uthman, or at least it had become apparent during his reign that it had done so. Uthman had himself provoked the rebellion that led to his death. However, on the question of whether Uthman's death had been justified or it had been murder, he generally tried to remain silent or at least to avoid committing himself to a position.[14]

One of Ali's first policies was to set about removing the provincial governors appointed by Uthman. This may have been politically unwise – but a lack of political judgement was a character flaw in Ali.[15] The existing governors of the major provinces had all been appointed by Uthman (save for Mu'awiya in Syria who had already been appointed by Umar but was closely related to Uthman). He was warned that the governors would stir up opposition to him if he deposed them, and that they could easily rally behind the cause of justice for Uthman. This might tempt Talha and Zubair to go back on their pledge of allegiance to him. Nevertheless, he pressed ahead and decided to remove them all except for the governor of Kufa, Abu Musa al-Ash'ari, who had been the choice of the Kufan rebels against Uthman.

If these changes at the top in the major provinces of the empire had led to a successful consolidation of Ali's authority, it would have been a revolution against the dominance of the Quraysh. His success, however, was limited. He established control of Basra and appointed Qays bin Sa'd as governor of Egypt. He was the son of Sa'd bin Ubadah, the leader of the Ansar who had been roughly treated by Umar at the meeting of the Ansar on the night after the death of the Prophet.

But Ali had a weakness that prevented him strengthening his grip on power across the empire in its entirety. This was the fact that Uthman had been murdered, and that his relatives were entitled to justice. This meant that Ali's own position had been made uncomfortable by his attempt to stay neutral on the question of whether Uthman's death had been justified.

Mecca refused to acknowledge him. As an act of disrespect, a young member of the Quraysh even chewed up the letter he wrote calling for the city to pledge allegiance.[16] The allegation that Ali was responsible for the murder of Uthman was made publicly by Aisha, who was now living in the city. It was frequently repeated, often in poetry written to lampoon him. The city soon became resolutely hostile to his cause, although there is no doubt that, for many of the worldly-wise Quraysh, the call for justice for the murder of Uthman was primarily a convenient excuse.

Aisha flung her weight behind Talha and Zubair, the two Companions who had the most credible claims to lead the community as an alternative to Ali. As we have seen, Aisha had a deep-seated hostility to Ali. It has been suggested that her real motivation was the removal of Ali rather than justice for Uthman,[17] since she had also incited a rebellion against Uthman herself.[18] Alongside Talha and Zubair, she was opposed to Uthman's policy of relying on Tulaqa' (Meccans accepting Islam only after the fall of Mecca) and other relatives from his immediate clan, but the three of them were all Quraysh loyalists in a wider sense. They argued that there should be another electoral college, a Shura or 'consultation', as instituted by Umar. They went to Basra where they hoped to raise support, but found that loyalties there were divided, and they had to fight a battle before they could even enter the city. While Aisha used her natural charisma and status as the Prophet's pre-eminent widow to encourage men to enlist in the rebellion against Ali, there were disputes between Zubair and Talha as to who should have seniority over the other. These were demonstrated when one of them led the congregational prayers, thus taking precedence. Ali's response was to go to Kufa, the other big garrison town in Iraq. He had very substantial support there, and it would become his de facto capital.

The rebellion of Aisha, Talha and Zubair was defeated fairly easily when the armies met on the occasion that has gone down in history as the Battle of the Camel. It took place on 8 December 656, just over six months after the murder of Uthman and the acclamation of Ali as his successor. Zubair seems to have fled from the battle scene at an early stage and to have been murdered nearby, while Talha was killed in the fighting. The last stand was a melee around the camel that carried Aisha in an armoured litter. This was ended when Ali ordered the camel to be hamstrung, so that it threw off its load. Fleeing Basrans pleaded that they belonged to 'the religion of Ali' in order to save their lives – but this probably meant no more than a statement that they had now, in their defeat, belatedly accepted that Ali was the leader of the community.[19] A chastened Aisha, who had been wounded by an arrow through her arm, threw herself on Ali's mercy. His cousin, Abdullah bin Abbas (the same who had given an account of the Prophet's last hours that was inconsistent with Aisha's) was given the task of sending her back to Medina. Entering the house where she was staying without asking her permission, he rudely told her that she was nothing but one of the nine 'stuffed beds' (i.e. widows) the Prophet had left behind, and that she owed everything to the Prophet's blood relatives.[20] She was sent back to Mecca and prevented from having any further political involvement. She lived out her final years in remorse for her role in leading Muslims to fight each other, and also regretted her incitement against Uthman.[21]

III

The immediate challenge to Ali's supremacy had been dealt with. But the underlying problem of deciding how to respond to the call from Uthman's kin for justice remained. Ali's position was that he needed to establish his authority before he could do so. He therefore required Mu'awiya in Syria to pledge allegiance before he could take action. Mu'awiya had originally been appointed by Umar and had deep roots in the province. His family had had strong trading connections there for generations, and had already owned property in what is now Jordan before the coming of Islam. He had built up the Syrian army and made sure that it was loyal to him personally. It faced the Byzantine frontier, and was the largest and most professional army in the Arab empire.

Mu'awiya consistently refused to swear allegiance, and stated that he held Ali responsible for the murder.[22] His position was that, once the murderers had been dealt with, there should be a Shura ('consultation') – but it should be dominated by the Syrians, who now had the right 'to be judges over the people' – code for the almost certain selection of Mu'awiya himself.[23] Uthman's widow sent him the bloodstained shirt her husband had been wearing when he was killed. It was taken round the Syrian garrisons to whip up war fever. Mu'awiya called on Ali to punish the murderers. Yet in Syria, as in Iraq, there were many who did not want the matter resolved by war.

Some of the leaders of the mutineers against Uthman were among Ali's principal supporters, especially Malik al-Ashtar, who was Ali's enforcer in Kufa. Another was Abu Bakr's son Muhammad – who it will be remembered was one of the leading mutineers, and allegedly the murderer of Uthman. Muhammad was now part of Ali's family. He had been only two when his father died. Ali had then married Abu Bakr's widow, Asma, who was Muhammad's mother. This was an attempted gesture of reconciliation, which may have been intended to heal the rift with Aisha but was also designed to bring the whole Muslim community together. Muhammad had therefore grown up in Ali's household and was his stepson. It would have been inconceivable for Ali to repudiate him now.

A kind of catch-22 had arisen: it was not realistic for Ali to withdraw his support for these men, even if he wished to do so, before he had

Mu'awiya's pledge of allegiance. Ali's consistent position was one of neutrality: he did not say that Uthman was wrongfully killed, nor that he was killed as a wrongdoer.[24] Yet there was no possibility of obtaining Mu'awiya's allegiance unless he came off the fence. The impasse probably suited Mu'awiya well. History shows him to have been a coldly calculating individual. The cynicism of his quest for justice for Uthman was apparent to many. It was also demonstrated by a secret offer he made to pledge allegiance to Ali on condition that he continued to control Syria and Egypt, and would not be bound to accept any successor designated by Ali on his death.[25] If Ali had accepted this offer, it might well have led to the permanent fragmentation of the Muslim empire.

On Mu'awiya's side of the divide, there were the Qurayshi loyalists and the forces that made up the army of Greater Syria, which Mu'awiya was able to swing behind him. Although the forces Ali might be able to bring against him were potentially more numerous, they were less united. Kufa was notorious for infighting among its garrison, which was composed partly of devout early converts to Islam who had been among the original conquerors, and tribesmen who were late-comers to the religion. The two groups also had very different financial interests when it came to the revenues of the conquered land. Ali's response was an appeal to the brotherhood of all believers and to emphasise the spiritual nature of his leadership. In rousing speeches he was able to describe Mu'awiya and his followers as 'the enemies of God' and 'the murderers of the Muhajirun and Ansar'.[26] Some remained neutral, and refused to take sides, but Ali won many of the early converts over to his cause. Support for him snowballed as tribal leaders returning from campaigns in Iran joined him. In the early summer of 657 he led an immense army up the Euphrates towards Syria. It encountered Mu'awiya's forces at Siffin, north of Raqqa. There was a clear reluctance to settle the issue on the battlefield, and the armies remained in encampments near each other for three months, skirmishing intermittently.

Eventually, Ali declared that Mu'awiya's Syrians had failed to answer his call to the Qur'an and to repudiate their falsehood.[27] As was customary in the run-up to battles among the Arabs, individual combats took place as well as skirmishes between prominent figures and tribal leaders with small retinues. When full-scale fighting eventually started, about a week after these first exchanges, the Syrians seem to have had the better of the first day. But thereafter the battle ebbed and flowed, and there was even a suggestion that Ali and Mu'awiya should decide it by single combat. Mu'awiya refused, but Ali is reported to have 'cleft in two' a champion foolhardy enough to decide to stand in Mu'awiya's place.[28] Eventually, towards noon on the third day of fighting, it looked as though Ali's forces were gaining the upper hand. Some soldiers in the centre of the Syrian army tied copies of the Qur'an to their lances (or probably just verses of the Qur'an) and cried out 'Let the Book of God decide between us and you. Who will protect the border towns of the people of Syria after they are all gone, and who will protect the border towns of the people of Iraq after they are all gone?'[29]

This could be seen as an offer by the Syrians to surrender. Mu'awiya had claimed to be leading his army in a moral cause: justice for the slain caliph. Hitherto, his position had been that the sword should be the judge between his forces and those of Ali. Now, however, he had in effect appealed to arbitration on the basis of the Qur'an. He can only have done so because he sensed he was losing the battle. For his part, Ali called on his men to continue the fight. He knew that Mu'awiya and those around him were not religious people, and that their sudden appeal to the Qur'an was nothing more than a stratagem to stop the battle before they lost. Yet many of the devout men in his own army had been fighting to call the Syrians to the Qur'an and to repentance. They therefore demanded that he stop the battle. One of their leaders even said to him, ominously: 'Ali, respond to the Book of God since you have been summoned to it. If not, we shall hand you over to these people or we shall do with you as we did with [Uthman].'[30] Threatened with mutiny, Ali had no alternative but to order his great captain Malik al-Ashtar to stop his advance towards the Syrian camp – something that Malik al-Ashtar at first refused to do, as he was reluctant to see victory slip from Ali's grasp.

When the fighting was over, Mu'awiya proposed that each side appoint a representative. The two men appointed would discuss the issues that had led to the fighting, and find a way to restore peace. They would use the Qur'an as the basis for their arguments. This made the proposal very hard to reject. Needless to say, Mu'awiya appointed a representative who could be relied upon to further his interests. This was Amr ibn al-'As, the original conqueror of Egypt. Ali, on the other hand, was forced by pressure from devout soldiers to appoint an individual who would be even-handed between him and Mu'awiya. The pause in the fighting had left his camp in disarray. He and many of his followers had wished to continue the fight until victory, but he had to accommodate the wishes of the devout majority whose interests were not necessarily identical to his own.

Not only had Mu'awiya saved his army from defeat, but he had cleverly manoeuvred Ali into a position where they appeared as equals, even as rival claimants to the leadership of the community. This implicitly denied Ali any right to consider himself the caliph. Mu'awiya objected to Ali's styling himself with the caliphal title 'Commander of the Faithful' in the agreement. Reluctantly, Ali omitted it. He saved face before his followers by reminding them of a precedent: Muhammad's consent to the omission of the title of 'Prophet of God' in the agreement with the pagan Meccans at Hudaybiyya.

Ali was also compelled to nominate Abu Musa al-Ash'ari as his representative in the forthcoming peace talks. But Abu Musa was a less-than-ideal person to nominate to protect Ali's interests. Although Ali had confirmed him as governor of Kufa at the start of his reign, Abu Musa had stayed neutral in Ali's struggle with Talha, Zubair and Aisha. Ali had had to dismiss him when he approached Kufa on the way to confront the rebels. Although Abu Musa was clearly loved in Kufa, he had had a controversial record on the distribution of booty to his men when campaigning during the conquests. But there were reasons why he might appeal to the devout. He was known for his beautiful recitations of the Qur'an and the care with which he said his prayers.

The arrangement reached is often described as an arbitration agreement, but in reality it was an agreement to find a way as to how the Muslim community should now proceed. It did not state the question the two representatives were to decide. Their task was to take a just decision that would restore peace, and end division and war in the community. It is hard not to see acceptance of the agreement, which was on terms suggested by Mu'awiya, as a failure of leadership by Ali. The majority of his army may have wished to stop fighting, but he also had robust supporters who were charismatic leaders of their own men and who had protested when it stopped. As soon as it became apparent that Mu'awiya's conduct was cynical, they wished to resume fighting. If

Ali had shown resolution, he could probably have persuaded many if not most of the 'peace party' to resume fighting. It has been suggested that Ali may have been haunted by the way in which his supporters had turned away from him at the time when each of Abu Bakr, Umar and Uthman had become caliph, and that this memory of these experiences may have paralysed his resolve. He may also have been influenced unconsciously by the role of a tribal sheikh, the usual figure of authority in Arabia before Islam. A sheikh has to obtain and keep the consent of his followers in order to lead them. This was a much lesser degree of authority than the firm leadership that was now Ali's right as the successor of the Prophet. From the reputation he had already earned as a warrior, we can safely assume that a lack of physical courage was not his reason for compromise and allowing procrastination.[31] He probably knew that the process was doomed, but hoped it would vindicate him by making Mu'awiya's dishonesty plain.[32]

IV

There was another adverse consequence for Ali. Large numbers had been killed in the three days of fighting at Siffin. The civil war in the community – for that was what the struggle between him and Mu'awiya had become – was a scandal, and as such raised a question mark over his claims. It threatened to split the community into two, and left the rather fluid and uncertain frontiers of the expanding empire undefended while the Arabs fought among themselves. Many of the devout men who had followed Ali had turned their swords and spears against fellow Muslims only with the greatest reluctance, and after much soul-searching. Others in the army might have been fighting because of personal loyalty to Ali, or for tribal honour, prestige, or the hope of booty, but these men had been fighting for Islam. Now some of them were devastated and confused. What had it all been for? How could Ali arbitrate with a man who was ultimately nothing more than an unscrupulous war lord, a Taliq who was the son of Abu Sufyan and Hind, the greatest and most cynical Tulaqa' of them all? Furthermore, as one of the two men appointed to reach an agreement was a partisan of Mu'awiya and effectively held a veto, it was not realistic to expect anything positive to result from the discussions. Once the large army Ali had put together began to disperse, everybody knew it would be very difficult to reassemble. Some of those pondering these questions came to a conclusion: sovereignty and judgement belonged to God alone. The question of authority over God's community could not be decided by a kind of arbitration process. By approving this, Ali had shown that he was not the true leader of the community.

The agreement was read out to the two armies by al-Ash'ath, a partisan of Ali who had fought in the battle and had played an important role in the discussions that had followed. He is said to have played a leading part in persuading, or cajoling, Ali into accepting the agreement and consenting to the appointment of Abu Musa al-Ash'ari as the representative for Ali and the Iraqi side. When they heard what al-Ash'ath had read out, two men in Ali's army shouted 'no judgement except God's', and charged the Syrian battle line to meet their deaths. Another cried out, 'Will you appoint men as arbitrators in the affairs of God? No judgement but God's. Where are our dead, Ash'ath?' Then he charged at al-Ash'ath, slightly wounding his horse, before he was called back by his fellow tribesmen.[33]

These were portents of what was to come. While Ali's forces were riding back to Kufa, there were scuffles as groups of men called out, 'No judgement but God's,' while other groups shouted back and angrily accused them of betraying their leader and their community. Men struck each other with their riding whips. As the army reached Kufa, 12,000 men are said to have withdrawn from it, including some who had originally backed the arbitration but had come to view it as a mistake. They swore allegiance to God and to the Qur'anic precept of commanding what is right and forbidding what is wrong.[34] In their view, Mu'awiya and his representative Amr ibn al-'As were no better than polytheists and should have been fought. Ali persuaded some of them to return, but others set out from Kufa and Basra to join them.

These disillusioned men who withdrew from Ali's army are known to history as the Kharijis, literally 'those who left', or 'those who walked out' or possibly, 'those who went forth for jihad'. They preached a faith that was pure and excluded all others who claimed to be Muslims. They rejected the leadership of both the Quraysh and their own tribal leaders. Their departure was over a matter of principle, while those who stayed with Ali had reasons for doing so that were equally principled. His remaining followers offered him a new oath of allegiance, in which they swore they would be friends of those he befriended and enemies of his enemies.

On one occasion, Ali called out in the square in front of the mosque in Kufa for the Companions of the Prophet to come forward and tell the crowd what the Prophet had said at the pool of Ghadir Khumm. This was a place where the Prophet's caravan had paused for the night on its way back to Medina after the farewell pilgrimage to Mecca. Twelve or thirteen elderly men came to the front and gave their testimony as to what had happened on that day. Muhammad had asked whether he was dearer to the assembled throng than they were to themselves. The crowd had enthusiastically shouted that he was. The Prophet had then taken Ali's hand in his own, and said that Ali was the patron of everybody who saw Muhammad as his own patron.

The truth of this testimony given by those ageing Companions of the Prophet in response to Ali's request has generally been accepted, although the meaning and significance of it have been disputed by Muslims ever since. But the context in which Ali called for this testimony to be given is important. By telling the mass of the people about what happened on 'the day of Ghadir Khumm', he was making a very definite public claim: he had been entrusted with a spiritual and political authority by the Prophet that was greater than that which either Abu Bakr or Umar had held. The strong implication was that a true Muslim now had to follow Ali, just in order to be a Muslim. If he did not do so, he had left the community of believers. Ali asked for allegiance on the basis of the Book and the practice (Sunna) of the Prophet. When a warrior who had fought for him in the Battle of the Camel and at Siffin had suggested that this meant the practice of Abu Bakr and Umar, Ali had objected. If Abu Bakr or Umar had followed a practice that was not that of the Prophet on a specific issue, he warned, they would have been 'remote from the truth'.[35] This was another indication of Ali claiming a leadership status that was higher than that of the first two caliphs.

The warrior in question subsequently deserted Ali's cause and joined the Kharijis, dying while fighting against Ali's forces at the Battle of Nahrawan. The Kharijis saw Ali as merely asking his followers to do exactly the same as Mu'awiya expected from his Syrians: to follow him wherever he might choose to lead. For the Kharijis, the leader of the community could lose his status by contravening the law of Islam – as had happened in the case of Uthman. Leadership was not tied up with proximity to the Prophet, whether through blood or companionship. For them, the only two true successors of Muhammad had been Abu Bakr and Umar.

When the arbitrators met, Abu Musa, whom Ali had appointed against his better judgement, was outsmarted once again – as Ali's advisers had feared he would be. The first – and only – point on which they reached agreement was that Uthman had been wrongfully killed. The arbitrators tried to keep their agreement on this point secret until they had reached a full agreement, but the news leaked out. Mu'awiya's followers were ecstatic. Mu'awiya was Uthman's cousin, and was therefore now officially entitled to seek justice. This meant that those involved in his death, including Malik al-Ashtar and Ali's step-son Muhammad bin Abu Bakr, should in theory be handed over to Mu'awiya, who might extract revenge if he chose. Abu Musa probably saw agreeing to this point as a quid pro quo for subsequent acknowledgement by his counterpart Amr that Ali was the leader of the community, but Amr would not budge on that issue. Instead, Amr insisted that Mu'awiya should remain governor of Syria while the question of leadership was resolved.[36] No progress could be made on that question, and the two representatives went their separate ways. Amr returned to Damascus, where he greeted Mu'awiya as 'Commander of the Faithful', a title which Mu'awiya accepted and which implied he was the caliph. This amounted to a declaration of war on Ali. Abu Musa retired to Mecca in disgrace, while there was uproar in Kufa when the news arrived. Ali denounced him and Amr as well as the agreement they had reached from the pulpit, and pronounced a formal curse on Mu'awiya which was to be said every day with the morning prayers. The latter retaliated, cursing not just Ali but including Ali's two sons, Hassan and Hussein, in the curse for good measure.

Ali prepared to invade Syria once again. He tried to enlist the Kharijis in his cause, but their response was that he was not fighting Mu'awiya for the sake of God but for his own purposes. They called on him to admit that he had committed an act of unbelief and to repent, after which they would consider the position. He tried to ignore them and to set his army in motion. He preached a rousing sermon in which he compared Mu'awiya and the people around him to Heraclius and Chosroes, implying that, like that Byzantine emperor and Sasanian king, Mu'awiya was a leader who had no credentials in Islam. However, news reached his army that the Kharijis had killed an envoy and his pregnant wife. This made his men afraid to go so far from home while leaving the Kharijis in their rear as a menace to their families and property. He therefore had no choice but to deal with the Kharijis first.

When he requested the surrender of the murderers of the envoy and his wife, the Khariji response was that they all shared the responsibility jointly. To them, the blood of Ali and his supporters was licit since, in their view, Ali had left the faith. Ali met them at Nahrawan on 17 July 658. He pleaded with them to return. Some did so, but a hard core said to be over 1,500 remained. Ali did not attack them, but waited. They furiously charged at his army, which vastly outnumbered them. The result was a massacre. Only a handful of Ali's men were killed as the Kharijis impaled themselves on his battle line.

The victory, though total, left a bitter taste. The battle showed that sectarianism had now unquestionably arrived in Islam. Both Ali and his Khariji opponents were fighting over points of principle which, somewhat ironically, prevented them from combining against Mu'awiya whom both parties viewed with equal distaste. Ali now wished to push on to Syria so as to finish off the battle that had begun at Siffin. But his soldiers pleaded the need to return to their bases and to re-equip. This may have been a diplomatic excuse. Many of them faded away, and the army dissolved. Ali had no choice but to return despondently to Kufa.

In the period after Nahrawan his position declined. Mu'awiya began to subvert some of his support and to launch raids into the territories loyal to him. These were often raids of a pre-Islamic kind in which booty was the main objective, although they also served to soften up the areas Ali controlled. Ali's principled stance refusing to make concessions over the financial entitlements of tribal leaders and what was now the empire's Qurayshi nobility left important individuals and tribes vulnerable to seduction by Mu'awiya. Mu'awiya is even reported as saying that after the Battle of Siffin he did not need to take any military action against Ali.[37] He made approaches to some of the tribes that had accompanied Ali to Siffin, and wrote them a letter in which he described the murdered

Uthman in glowing terms; he was a pious Muslim who had been fasting and in the ritual state of a pilgrim at the time of his death, and who loved the weak and oppressed. Mu'awiya then called on them to exact revenge.[38] He also won back control of Egypt by sending Amr ibn al-'As, the orginal Arab conqueror of the country, to retake it. One of Amr's subordinates captured Ali's governor, Muhammad bin Abu Bakr, nearly dead from thirst. Despite orders from Amr that he was to be brought to him alive, Muhammad bin Abu Bakr was killed, placed inside the skin of a donkey, and burned. As tribes drifted away from Ali, Mu'awiya was increasingly becoming the stronger party. This enabled him to encourage or intimidate people into recognising his claim to the caliphate. The discord led others to take the view – especially when tax collectors arrived from one or other of the claimants to the caliphate – that the matter of leadership was still undecided and that they were waiting until the successor to the Prophet was confirmed.

A raid ordered by Mu'awiya into the Hejaz and Yemen succeeded in its objective of terrifying the local population and weakening Ali's support. It also led to a new low, since the raiders enslaved some women who were Muslims – apparently the first time this had happened since the beginning of Islam.[39] The implication was that these women, and the community to which they belonged, had left the faith.

The raid forced Ali's supporters to rally round him, and Ali began preparations for another push to invade Syria and dethrone Mu'awiya. It looked as though at last he might be about to finish the war that had been interrupted after Siffin, although major factors motivating his men were fear of Syrian rule and the desire to retain their independence, as well as personal loyalty to him. But there was never to be a final trial of strength between Mu'awiya and Ali. On 28 January 661, less than three years after the Battle of Nahrawan and a mere four-and-a-half years after the murder of Uthman, a Khariji assassin approached Ali as he was entering the mosque to perform his morning prayers. 'The judgement belongs to God, Ali, not to you,' he said, then struck him on the head with a poisoned sword.[40] Ali died two days later.

Hassan, Ali's eldest son by Fatima, believed that leadership was his right, and that it flowed to him as the grandson of the Prophet. As he addressed the congregation in the mosque of Kufa, choking back his grief at his father's murder, he stated, 'I am the shining lamp. I am of the

Family of the Prophet from whom God has removed filth and whom He has purified, whose love He has made obligatory in his Book.'[41] Though he was acclaimed as his father's successor, he stood down some seven months later and acknowledged Mu'awiya's authority as the Commander of the Faithful. Not only does it seem that he lacked ambition to rule, but he also realised that standing up to Mu'awiya would involve yet another bloody war within the Muslim community. Initially, he had summoned Mu'awiya to do him homage, but the latter had replied demanding the same from him, and asserting that he was the true Commander of the Faithful. Just as Abu Bakr had been more suited to leading the Muslims after the Prophet's death, Mu'awiya argued, so was he now better placed to do so than the much younger and inexperienced Hassan. He also made an important concession. In return for Hassan's allegiance during Mu'awiya's lifetime, Hassan would rule after the latter's death.

Although there was some fighting, many of Hassan's followers sensed that he was not prepared to push his rights to the full, and they deserted, some even joining the Kharijis. One fighter accused Hassan of 'associating partners with God as your father did before you.'[42] When Hassan publicly acknowledged Mu'awiya, he told his followers, 'You have pledged allegiance to me on the basis that you make peace with whomever I make peace. I have deemed it right to make peace with him and have pledged allegiance to him, since I considered whatever spares blood as better than whatever causes it to be shed.'[43]

When Hassan submitted to Mu'awiya in 661, the supremacy of the Banu Umayya clan seemed assured. Yet rioting and discontent in the garrison cities of Basra and Kufa were portents of what was to come.

CHAPTER THREE

Of Umayyads and Abbasids

The Political Background to the Split Between Sunnis and Shi'is

I

Something that would once have seemed unbelievable had happened. A son of Abu Sufyan and Hind had become the ruler of the empire of the Muslims. This was not just the triumph of Mu'awiya personally, but of the tribe of Quraysh and of his own branch of that tribe, Banu Umayya, the clan of the murdered Uthman. This clan, which is now known as the Umayyads, would rule the empire for almost ninety years. As we shall see, later rulers from this dynasty would be forced to centralise the empire, but Mu'awiya preferred methods that reflected the subtle and pragmatic ways in which a leading Qurayshi merchant would have done business before the coming of Islam. He preferred negotiation and compromise to using the army to enforce his rule outside Syria, or to ruling through his closest relatives. He would reach agreements with local governors and power brokers and exercise patronage (offering inducements such as prestigious positions), very often buying loyalty with money. Violence and assassination were also weapons in his armoury. Although he was entirely ruthless when he needed to be, these methods were a last resort. Once he had consolidated his power, Mu'awiya was largely successful in ensuring peace within the empire during his lifetime, as well as its continued expansion.

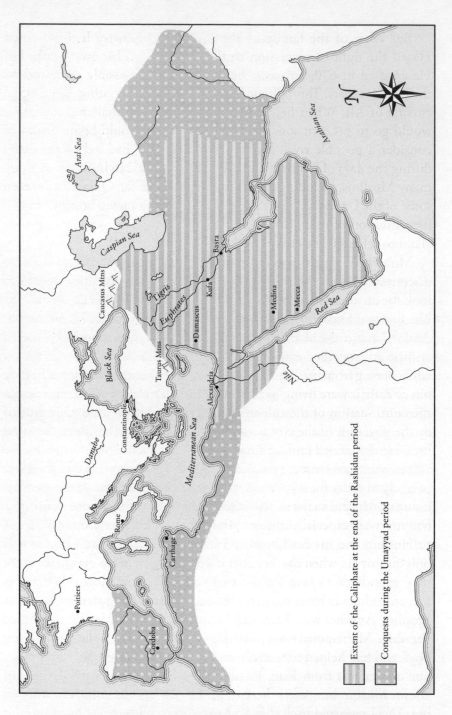

Legend:

Extent of the Caliphate at the end of the Rashidun period

Conquests during the Umayyad period

**THE ARAB CONQUESTS UNDER THE RASHIDUN
AND THE UMAYYADS**

Map labels: Aral Sea, Arabian Sea, Caspian Sea, Basra, Caucasus Mtns, Tigris, Euphrates, Damascus, Kufa, Medina, Mecca, Red Sea, Black Sea, Taurus Mtns, Alexandria, Nile, Constantinople, Danube, Mediterranean Sea, Rome, Poitiers, Carthage, Cordoba

But what of the family of the Prophet? Mu'awiya had promised Hasan the right to succession to the caliphate on his own death, but Hasan died in 670, ten years before Mu'awiya, possibly poisoned on the latter's orders. Throughout his reign, Mu'awiya continued the ritual cursing of Ali. When he died in 680, he ensured that the succession would go to his own son Yazid, and that there would be no Shura to consider a possible rival. But the pressures that had led to the strife during the days of Uthman and Ali had continued to build up. Among many Muslims, including disaffected sections of the Quraysh and even some of the Umayyad family itself, there was widespread hostility to this formalisation of rule of the community by a dynasty with no obvious claim to religious pre-eminence.

Mu'awiya's death was a moment that gave those who were discontented with the rule of the Umayyad family the opportunity to look for an alternative focus. They found two potential rallying points. The first was Hussein, the younger son of Ali and Fatima. The other was Abd Allah bin al-Zubair, the son of that same Zubair who had revolted against Ali together with Talha and Aisha, and who had been killed while fleeing from the Battle of the Camel. Both Hussein and Abd Allah bin al-Zubair were living in Medina. Each was sufficiently dangerous to the continuation of the rule of the house of Umayya to be summoned by the governor of the city as soon as news of Mu'awiya's death reached him. He demanded immediate pledges of loyalty to Yazid.

Hussein temporised, saying that he would need to make the pledge publicly in order for it to be valid, and escaped to Mecca. Loyalty to the house of Ali, and to the idea of rule by a member of the Prophet's family, had survived, especially in Kufa. The closeness that the Prophet had felt to Hussein and his dead brother Hasan was well-known. Hussein was only five or six when the Prophet died, but there were many stories of their grandfather's love for the two boys. 'Whoever loves them loves me, and whoever hates me hates them,' was one saying attributed to the Prophet. Another was, 'Hasan and Hussein are the lords of the youth of Paradise.' Muhammad had crawled around on the floor playing with the boys, and had helped to teach them how to pray. Now, Hasan was dead, but messengers from Kufa invited Hussein to their city. He sent his cousin Muslim bin Aqeel there to find out what was going on. Muslim bin Aqeel reported back that he had gathered thousands of pledges of support. Unfortunately for him and Hussein, however, news of this reached Yazid, who sent the governor of Basra, Ubaydullah bin Ziyad, to Kufa, where he terrorised anyone who might conceivably back a bid by Hussein for the caliphate.

There is a tragic inevitability about the events that followed. Hussein was warned of the dangers, but set out on the long journey across Arabia accompanied only by a small party of perhaps fifty men together with women and children. Soon after leaving Mecca, he encountered a caravan coming from Yemen carrying merchandise consisting of cloth and plants for use in dying. It belonged to the caliph, so he impounded the cargo as rightfully his. Some of those he encountered on the way across the desert joined him, but others were wary and warned him of what might lie ahead. One such was the poet al-Farazdaq, who told him bluntly that the hearts of the Iraqis were for him, but their swords were for the Umayyads. Hussein's reply to those who tried to dissuade him was fatalistic: 'God does as He wishes... I leave it to Him to choose what is best... He is not hostile to him who purposes the just cause.'[1]

Ubaydullah bin Ziyad posted men on the roads to Kufa to control those going in and out of the surrounding territory. News reached Hussein that the governor had captured Muslim bin Aqeel and executed him. He would have turned back at this point, but Muslim bin Aqeel's sons insisted on continuing, determined either to extract revenge or to die as their father had done. Hussein decided to persevere, even though he learned shortly afterwards that other messengers he had sent ahead to announce his impending arrival had also been killed. He asked his companions to let him travel onwards by himself, but the original party that had set out with him refused to abandon him.

Ubaydallah sent a message to Hussein. It was entrusted to a man called al-Hurr, who caught up with Hussein and told him that he had been sent to bring him to the governor without a fight. Hussein refused, but he led al-Hurr in prayers. As Hussein's party set off to continue the journey, al-Hurr followed at a short distance. From time to time, he would call out, 'I remind you of God for your own sake. If there is a battle, you will be killed.'

Shortly before they reached the Euphrates, Hussein's party encamped at a place called Karbala. Four thousand men confronted them under the orders of Umar bin Sa'd bin Abi Waqqas, who had been sent by

Ubaydullah. Umar agreed to grant Hussein one night's respite. Hussein addressed his followers: 'I ask you all to go away. I do not hold you back. The night will cover you. Use it as your steed [to flee].' But only a few left.

The following fateful day, the 10th of the Muslim month of Muharram in the Muslim year 61, calculated from the date of the *Hijrah* and corresponding to 10 October 680, was to be Hussein's last. He reminded his followers and the army opposing them of the words Muhammad had said about him and his brother, and the great virtue of the family of the Prophet. Then he reproached the men of Kufa for summoning him, and asked Umar to be allowed to make his way to a land that would offer him sanctuary. When the response came that he must submit to Yazid, he replied that he would never humiliate himself like a slave. He and his men hamstrung their horses to indicate that they would not be trying to escape.

At first, the attackers shot arrows at Hussein's men and individual combats took place. One co-ordinated attack was repulsed; but in the afternoon the little party was encircled and the end could only be a matter of time. One by one, Hussein's close relatives and supporters were killed. Eventually, Hussein tried to break through to the Euphrates to drink, but was wounded in the mouth and chin. Then he was hit in the head, and began to bleed copiously. He wrapped his head up with a cloth as a turban and continued to fight, suffering other wounds to his hand and his shoulder. Finally, he collapsed on the ground and a soldier decapitated him. His head was taken first to Kufa to show that he was dead, and then to Yazid in Damascus. His body was buried where he had fallen.

The death of Hussein was as traumatic for Muslims as the murder of Uthman or the assassination of Ali. But there was a key difference. Unlike Uthman and Ali, Hussein was killed by agents of a body claiming to be the lawful government of the Muslim community. Nor was it just the Umayyads who were involved. The army that surrounded him was led by the grandson of a distinguished Companion of the Prophet, S'ad ibn Abi Waqqas, the general who had done more than anyone else to conquer the Persian Empire and who had been a member of the Shura that had elected Uthman. In fact, it was not inconceivable that Sa'd ibn Abi Waqqas might have been chosen as caliph himself at some point.

Now his son had commanded the men who had unsheathed their swords to fight and kill the Prophet's own grandson. Ubaydullah, the governor who had despatched Umar to bar Hussein from the Euphrates, was the son of Mu'awiya's right-hand man in Iraq, Ziyad bin Abihi. He was the son of a prostitute whose father had been unknown, and whom Mu'awiya had proclaimed to be his half-brother, thereby making Ziyad a member of his own family and ensuring his loyalty.

Hussein's cause had been to support those excluded from the elite, an elite that now governed the empire. The support of that elite for Yazid, and the length to which they had shown they were prepared to go when their interests were threatened, were now apparent for all to see. The killing of Hussein had removed a grave threat to the Umayyad dynasty, but it would gnaw away at their legitimacy.

II

The other figure of concern to the Umayyads after Mu'awiya's death was Abd Allah bin al-Zubair. His father had been one of the Shura that had elected Uthman and Ali, and thus had also been a potential candidate for the caliphate himself, while his mother was a daughter of Abu Bakr and sister of Aisha. Ibn al-Zubair himself had been a hero of the wars of conquest in Ifriqiya (roughly equivalent to modern Tunisia and the eastern part of Algeria) where he was said to have killed the Byzantine governor in combat. He had also taken part in the campaigns in northern Persia. In addition, he had been appointed by Uthman to the commission he had set up to produce the definitive text of the Qur'an. He thus had impeccable claims to be a candidate to lead the community at the time of Mu'awiya's death. If Hussein was the figure behind whom it was natural for supporters of rule by a member of the Prophet's family to rally, Ibn al-Zubair was a potential candidate for those who did not necessarily believe the caliph need be a member of the Prophet's family, but rejected Umayyad dynastic rule.

After the death of Hussein, a secret following began to grow around Ibn al-Zubair. He began a revolt by declaring that Yazid was deposed. He soon found himself besieged in Mecca by an Umayyad army, but this army withdrew when news reached it of Yazid's death from natural causes. Ibn al-Zubair proclaimed himself the Commander of the Faithful and received support from those opposed to the Umayyads in Syria, Iraq, Egypt and Yemen. These rebellions were all put down, and Ibn al-Zubair was finally killed in 692 on the battlefield outside Mecca, which had been besieged for a second time. The Umayyad dynasty had survived its second major challenge. Ibn al Zubair's revolt had proved far harder to crush than Hussein's, but Ibn al-Zubair is now remembered only by historians of the period. By contrast, the story of Hussein's doomed attempt to reach Kufa had a poignancy and moral impact that would always resonate among Muslims. He lit a lamp that would burn brightly throughout the period of the Umayyad dynasty and beyond. It is still burning very brightly today.

III

After Yazid's death, the caliph chosen by the Umayyad family was Marwan bin al-Hakam, the very same Marwan who had once advised his cousin Uthman to take a hard line in defence of his rights as caliph. He carried as much responsibility for the strife that had torn apart the Muslim community as any other individual –if not more. It will be remembered that he had been behind the letter that Uthman denied sending to the governor of Egypt, asking the governor to have the discontented soldiers who had come to Medina imprisoned and flogged. His freedman, it will also be recalled, had precipitated the first violence between Muslims by dropping a stone from the balcony of Uthman's house, which killed a Companion of the Prophet. This had been the spark that started the riot in which Uthman was murdered. The now elderly Marwan was the strongman of the Umayyad family, but was scarcely a figure likely to appeal to the devout.

Marwan's able son Abdul Malik succeeded him in 685, and it was he who finally triumphed over Ibn al-Zubair and other rebels, and reunited the empire. He also instituted some very important reforms. The old Arab ways of doing business in the Hejaz (the Islamic Holy Land, corresponding to the western region of present-day Saudi Arabia) had become inadequate for such a vast empire. Government needed to become much more formal than hitherto. From now on records were kept in Arabic rather than in Greek and Persian, the old languages of administration of the Byzantine and Persian Empires, which had still been used for that purpose during the first half-century after the conquests. Coins were minted containing inscriptions attesting that Muhammad was the Prophet of God. The first great edifice of Muslim architecture was built. Abdul Malik commissioned the Dome of the Rock in Jerusalem, which was fringed with Qur'anic verses deliberately chosen because they pointedly denied the Christian doctrine of the Incarnation. Imperial Islam was starting to accentuate the differences between the teaching of the Qur'an and Christianity, rather than the similarities.

Abdul Malik died in 705, and the Umayyad Caliphate remained in place until 750. The empire continued to expand – all the way to the Atlantic Ocean and north into Spain and what is now France, as well as eastwards to Bukhara, Samarkand, Kabul and Sind. But its internal problems had not gone away. There were disputes over the revenues of the conquered territories, as well as tribal rivalries almost everywhere, and intermittently simmering disquiet in the rich garrison cities of Iraq. A discontented but important group were the Arab tribes who did not belong to the Quraysh and whose aristocracies from pre-Islamic times inevitably felt excluded from the kind of leading roles they would instinctively have expected for themselves. This group would provide leaders for insurrections.

The Umayyads faced other problems, too. They had to play a skilful game balancing the competing Qaysi and Yamani tribal groupings, the representative names for the northern and southern Arabs, whose rivalry always risked erupting into civil war and had many local variants. The Umayyad power base was largely confined to Greater Syria and the Jazeera – the large steppe area between the Tigris and Euphrates to the north east of Damascus. This left other areas, especially the wealthy province of Iraq, ripe for subversion.

There were also complications caused by the empire's success. The number of converts to Islam grew. Initially, they continued to be taxed as though they were non-Muslims. A compromise was reached under which they were given the same more favourable tax treatment as other Muslims, but land continued to be taxed at the rate applying to non-Muslims, even if the owners had converted to Islam. A sense of exclusion and discontent remained. The converts aspired to treatment equal to that given to other Muslims because they had adopted the faith of their overlords; but it was not granted to them, or only very grudgingly. Because they tended to adopt Muslim names which were also Arab (and because they often needed to attach themselves as clients to an Arab tribe), it can be hard to tell them apart from native Arab Muslims in the source material that has come down to us. For instance, large numbers of Arab tribesmen were sent to settle in the Khorasan area of eastern Iran. Many of them intermarried with the local, Persian-speaking population, some of whom also converted to Islam. By the 740s, there may well have been many tribal fighters in that region whose paternal grandfather was their only source of Arab blood, and who spoke Persian at home. They would have been hard to distinguish – by, say, Arabs in the Hejaz or Syria – from a Khorasani convert to Islam.

The Umayyad caliphs claimed religious authority, but many of them had a reputation for religious laxity and luxurious living, and there were frequently bitter quarrels within the family over the succession. We have already seen how they had difficulty appealing to the devout. Mu'awiya's moral claim of justice for the murder of Uthman might have been a good rallying cry in Syria in the late 650s, but it lost its force with Ali's death. Ali's son Hasan, after all, had stood guard at Uthman's house, and Hasan's reason for not having pressed his claim to the caliphate against that of Mu'awiya was commendable: he had wished to preserve the peace and stability of the community. From that time onwards, it was hard to find any justification, other than the stability of the empire, behind the dynastic rule of the Umayyads. Nevertheless, the desire – or the need – for stability was a very powerful impulse that led many to support or acquiesce in Umayyad rule. Stability was needed for the sake of Islam, but there were plenty of people who might be tempted to back a rival to the Umayyads if only such a rival could gain sufficient traction to stand a chance of replacing the dynasty.

IV

The remorse felt among the men of Kufa for the failure to go to Hussein's aid on that fateful day, the 10th of Muharram, led to the appearance there of a movement known as 'the Penitents' very soon after his death. Seeking revenge, its members first spent a day and a night weeping at the grave where Hussein's decapitated corpse was buried; then they set out for Greater Syria to dethrone the Umayyads. They were intercepted by Syrian troops and easily wiped out in January 685. After this, the call for the replacement of the Umayyad dynasty by a caliph from the Prophet's family increasingly became the rallying cry for rebels, although there were also rebellions that took their inspiration from Kharijism (founded by those who had come to reject Ali's authority). Two of the rebellions in favour of a descendant of Ali need to be mentioned here in passing, although their full historical significance will only become apparent at a later point.

The first took place later in 685. Mukhtar al-Thaqafi, a member of the old, non-Qurayshi tribal aristocracy, took control of Kufa and held it against all-comers for some eighteen months. His revolt was in the name of Muhammad ibn al-Hanafiyyah, Hussein's half-brother born to Ali by his wife from the Hanafi tribe, not the Prophet's daughter Fatima. Mukhtar al-Thaqafi proclaimed Muhammad, who was now Ali's only surviving son, as the Mahdi, or 'rightly-guided one'. Muhammad ibn al-Hanafiyyah was living in Medina at the time and wisely had nothing to do with the revolt. After it had been suppressed, he even travelled to Damascus and paid homage to the Caliph Abdul Malik.

The second revolt occurred only four years later, in 739. Zayd bin Ali, a grandson of Hussein whose father had survived the massacre at Karbala, arrived in Kufa. He unsuccessfully tried to instigate another rebellion but was killed fighting against government troops in the city's streets. His son Yahya fled to Khorasan and thence to Herat, where he raised the standard of revolt but died in battle in 743.

These two revolts were in the name of a specific descendant of Ali. Yet from the 730s onwards, a new idea took shape. The previous concept involved rallying behind a descendant of Ali who claimed the caliphate for himself or whose name was used as the banner behind which opposition to the Umayyads could rally. Now, opponents of the dynasty suggested that the identity of the true caliph was still secret – or might not even have been decided. The leader of the community should be 'the Accepted One from the House of Muhammad' (*al-rida min al-Muhammad*). The only certain thing about him was that he came from the Prophet's family. This preaching became increasingly systematic and effective. Like the three earlier revolts by the Penitents, Mukhtar al-Thaqafi and Zayd bin Ali, it started in Kufa. It soon extended to the garrisons of eastern Iran and beyond, especially to the important city of Marv in what is now Turkmenistan.

Its public face was a mysterious figure known as Abu Muslim. His full name (or at least the name he used – he was evasive about his origins and early life) was Abu Muslim Abdurrahman bin Muslim al-Khurasani. 'Al-Khurasani' means 'from Khorasan', so we know where he claimed his family came from. Abu Muslim means 'father of a Muslim' and therefore tells us very little. It might just mean he had a son whom he called Muslim. Yet when put together with 'ibn Muslim', the patronymic meaning 'son of a Muslim', one suspects the possibility of a coded reference that he was the son or grandson of a convert. Abdurrahman, literally 'worshipper of the merciful' is a common Arab name – but it would not have been an unusual one for a convert to adopt or to give his own son. What does seem certain is that Abu Muslim recognised that the non-Arab converts to Islam and the Arab tribal fighters excluded from the Umayyad establishment were powerful constituencies that he could rally behind his own choice of the Accepted One. And the identity of his Accepted One was a closely guarded secret.

But who was eligible to be chosen as an 'Accepted One'? Questions of succession to the headship of a clan in Arab society were generally decided by consultation among its senior male members, rather than by any automatic right of the first-born. Such was the case with the Umayyad dynasty itself, as happened with the passing of the caliphate from the line of Mu'awiya, after the death of his son Yazid, to that of Marwan. The Arab conception of a family was more of a clan descended from a common male ancestor than what we now call a nuclear family. In a similar way, Muhammad ibn al-Hanafiyyah, the figure who had been put forward by a group of rebels at a slightly earlier stage, was a descendant of Ali but not of the Prophet. Thus, somebody in the line of Ali who did not carry the genes of Fatima was still a member of the *al-Muhammad*, the family of Muhammad, through their common descent from Muhammad's grandfather, and could be seen as a potential candidate to lead the community.

V

In 747 Abu Muslim took control of Marv. He sent armies westwards. They were victorious against the Umayyad forces sent to quell the uprising, and within eighteen months had taken most of Iraq. Although Ibrahim, the first person whom he declared to be the designated Accepted One, was caught and executed by the Umayyads, Ibrahim's brother Abu al-'Abbas was proclaimed as the first caliph of the new Abbasid dynasty. He took the regnal name Saffah in Kufa after it opened its gates to the armies from Khorasan in October 749. The last Umayyad caliph's army was decisively defeated at the Battle of the Zab River after it entered Iraq to evict him, and soon the new movement had swept all before it.

Saffah claimed descent from the Prophet's uncle Abbas, whose name now became that taken by the new dynasty. He was not a descendant of the Prophet through Fatima. The important point was that he was a descendant of Hashim, the male ancestor he shared with the Prophet and who was the founder of the clan to which the three cousins, the Prophet Muhammad, al-Abbas and Abu Talib, the father of Ali, belonged. To many Muslims, descendants of Abbas were equally eligible for consideration as members of the Prophet's family from whom the Accepted One might be chosen, alongside the Prophet's direct descendants through Ali and Fatima. Indeed, according to the norms of pre-Islamic Arab tribal custom, it could be (and was) argued that the uncle and his male offspring should take priority over direct descendants through the daughter of a man who had left no male heir. This explains how an insurgency could be raised in the name of a figure like Muhammad ibn al-Hanafiyyah.

An even more shadowy figure in the overthrow of the Umayyads than Abu Muslim was Abu Salama, the man who originally persuaded Abu Muslim to leave Kufa and travel to Khorasan in order to spark the rebellion. It appears (although we cannot be certain about this) that, before Abu Salama made the initial approaches to the descendants of the Prophet's uncle Abbas, he had also tried to find a descendant of Ali to be the new caliph.

The head of the house of Ali at that time was Ja'far, a great-grandson of Hussein who is known as Ja'far al-Sadiq, 'the faithful' or 'the truthful'. His own grandfather, Ali Zayn al-Abidin, saw Hussein, his own father, killed at Karbala, but he himself had survived the battle because he had been ill and unable to take part. A man known for his intense religious devotion, Ali Zayn al-Abidin had kept well out of politics and was not associated with the revolts connected with his cousin Zayd or Mukhtar al-Thaqafi's revolt in the name of his uncle, Muhammad ibn al-Hanafiyyah. His own son, Muhammad al-Baqir, followed the same pious and careful path. His mother had been a daughter of Hussein's elder brother Hasan. The parentage of Muhammad al-Baqir had thus united the bloodline of the two sons of Ali and, of course, of the Prophet.

Muhammad al-Baqir's son Ja'far al-Sadiq would thus have had an impeccable lineage as the Accepted One if he had become caliph. Like his father and grandfather, he had kept well away from political activity and had spent his life in study and prayer. He also carried immense respect as an authority on the traditions of the Prophet. His pupils included many of the key figures in the early Abbasid period who would go on to formulate the precepts and rules which constitute the religious law of Islam, and which we know as the Sharia. But, if it is indeed true that Ja'far al-Sadiq was invited to become the Accepted One, he declined. He is reported to have read the letter containing the invitation and then burned it without writing a reply.[2] During the preaching in the name of the 'Accepted One', many expected the new caliph to be a descendant of Ali. Despite the definition of the family of the Prophet to include the descendants of his cousins, prestige was attached by all Muslims to the line of the Prophet itself. Many felt disappointment that the new dynasty was not descended from Ali and Fatima. This was a factor behind rebellions during the Abbasid period in which a descendant of Ali provided a focal point, just as had been the case during the Umayyad period. As Tayeb El-Hibri (a specialist in Arabic historiography) has put it, the descendants of Ali were 'in full command of the rhetoric of opposition and sentimental memory'.[3] Yet well before the end of the Abbasid Caliphate, those who preached that the leader of the Muslim community should be a lineal descendant of Ali and Fatima had themselves split into sects.

VI

Right from the start, there was a self-conscious grandeur to the new dynasty. After Abu al-'Abbas had taken the regnal name Saffah, all subsequent Abbasid caliphs adopted this practice of a regnal name. At first the dynasty was in a precarious position, but it wisely preached reconciliation and accepted homage from those who had fought against it. The one exception to this rule was the Umayyad family itself. Its leading members were ruthlessly hunted down and killed. Only one prince escaped. Abdurrahman bin Mu'awiya, a grandson of the Caliph Hisham, managed to reach Spain where he set up a principality which would one day declare itself a separate caliphate.

Saffah died in 754, only four years after his installation as caliph. During that brief period, Abbasid power was consolidated – at least on the surface – but there were portents of things to come in the discord that broke out on his death. He chose his brother Mansour to succeed him, but Mansour faced competition from his uncle Abdallah bin Ali, a strong military leader who had played an important role in the overthrow of the Umayyads. Mansour wisely turned to Abu Muslim to lead his armies against his uncle. Then, when Abu Muslim had been victorious, Mansour showed his ruthless side by inviting him to his tent, where he had him murdered. He also faced a challenge a few years later in 762, when a descendant of Ali through Hasan, known to history as Muhammad the Pure Soul, was proclaimed as caliph by members of the House of Hashim in Medina. The rebellion was crushed without too much difficulty, not least because influential members of the family of Ali, including its head, Ja'far al-Sadiq, refused to support it.

Mansour is one of the most famous of the Abbasid caliphs. His thirty-year reign began what we think of as the golden age of Abbasid civilisation. The centre of gravity of the empire shifted from Syria to Iraq. He built his new capital at Baghdad on the river Tigris, near the point where it and the Euphrates begin to run close together in the rich and fertile agricultural plain called the Sawad. It was also very close to Ctesiphon, which had been the capital of the Persian Empire until the Islamic conquest. Although the caliphs and the elite would always remain very proud of their Arab lineage and genealogy – to display one's Arab ancestry would be an important branch of learning under the Abbasids – this was the period when the empire ceased to be an ethnically 'Arab' enterprise. Instead, it became a genuinely Muslim one.[4]

Arabic was the language of the court, religion, the administration and high culture, but many important figures in the bureaucracy and among the religious scholars came from the Iranian plateau or areas further east. Much of the army came from the now important province of Khorasan, where the rebellion that had brought the Abbasids to power had first gathered steam. Many of those who wrote in Arabic spoke Persian, Syriac or another language as their mother tongue. A strong Persian cultural element infused itself into Abbasid life, as did ancient scientific and philosophical ideas originally developed by the Greeks. Although non-Muslims continued to flourish, much of the empire's elite consisted of converts or those whose fathers or grandfathers had converted. For instance, the famous Barmakid family had originally been Buddhist priests in Balkh, while the descendants of Hunayn bin Ishaq, the leading Christian translator of philosophical and scientific texts into Arabic from Greek and Syriac in the ninth century, also became Muslims.

The empire had internal tensions that one day would bring it to its knees. The old squabbling continued over whether provincial revenues should remain in the province where they were collected or be forwarded to the caliph, and this was a repeated source of friction. The empire was now moving from the model of a state permanently expanding its borders by conquest, in which booty from campaigning was the main source of financing the army, to one in which the army was paid for by taxation from agricultural estates. Tax collection and the use of the revenues became increasingly complex, leading to the growth of a powerful bureaucratic class on which the empire depended because the revenues were needed to pay the military. Unsurprisingly, the bureaucrats and the military had competing interests and were all too likely to clash.

Mansour died leaving a full treasury and an empire that appeared stable. He was succeeded by his son Muhammad Mahdi, who ruled for ten years to 785. He tried to crush the idea that the caliph should be a descendant of Ali and Fatima by asserting that the Prophet had designated his uncle Abbas, not Ali, as his successor.[5] Needless to say, this attempt did not succeed. During his reign there was an uprising in favour of al-Husayn bin Ali, a descendant of Hasan. Although it got nowhere, and al-Husayn bin Ali was killed, two brothers of Muhammad the Pure Soul escaped from custody. One of these, Idris bin Abdullah, succeeded in reaching the Maghreb and establishing an independent dynasty among the Walila Berber confederation in what is now Morocco.

After Mahdi's death, his son al-Hadi died only a year after ascending the throne. He was followed by the famous Harun al-Rashid, who lived until 809. By the end of his reign, many of the features of the new caliphate had been firmly established. Later, in less happy times, these years would be remembered through rose-tinted spectacles as an age of stability and relative prosperity. This was exemplified in the gilded memories of the era of Harun al-Rashid, which the *Arabian Nights* have made part of a worldwide folklore.

The traditions of the Abbasid Caliphate at its highpoint included the resumption of the annual campaign against the Byzantines. These expeditions were more raids carried out by a large army than anything else, because the Byzantines had successfully reorganised themselves after the loss of Greater Syria, Egypt and their other possessions along the north African coast. The days when Muslim armies could conquer large and significant Byzantine territories were long since past. Nevertheless, the caliph mounting his horse to lead his army in person against the infidel Christians, or solemnly appointing a brother or son to do so on his behalf at the start of the campaigning season every year, was highly symbolic. It provided a useful way of demonstrating his leadership of the Muslim community. Another such demonstration was the caliph's active involvement in the annual pilgrimage of the Hajj. This too he would sometimes lead in person – although Harun al-Rashid was the last caliph ever to make the Hajj – or would at least nominate a close family member to lead in his place. At the same time, the spiritual role of Jerusalem was acknowledged, and caliphs made visits to the city whenever they had the opportunity.

In Baghdad, the caliphs tried to surround themselves with religious scholars and to coax them into becoming judges and accepting official positions. At first this had proved difficult, but was becoming common by the time of Harun al-Rashid. A much greater emphasis was placed on court ceremonial than under the Umayyads, a change that reflected the influence of Sasanian ideas of monarchy that had deep roots in Persian culture. These blended seamlessly with the caliph's role as the leader of the Muslims and of the Prophet's own family, as well as his position as guardian of the rituals of the faith and the application of the Sharia. These were roles that the Umayyads had, in general, emphasised to a lesser extent. These changes enhanced the way in which the caliph saw himself, and in the way that he was now viewed. He was firmly placed on a pedestal that separated him from those he ruled. Access to him came to be carefully controlled by the chamberlain or *hajib* (literally, 'the veiler', or 'screener'). The simple *majlis* of the Arabs, in which a leader would sit and give access to all his followers so that they could talk directly to him – or, indeed, challenge him in front of all present– was now a distant memory.

During Harun al-Rashid's reign there were rebellions in outlying regions of the empire, especially in the Iranian east. Sometimes, these took on a religious dimension and were led by Kharijis or advocates of the rule of a member of the house of Ali. These were generally local affairs, and were all crushed, but when he died in 809 the empire descended into civil war between his sons Amin and Ma'moun. He had written a will that imposed a kind of compromise on them both. He had designated Amin as his successor, but decreed that Ma'moun would be Amin's heir apparent and the governor or even semi-independent ruler of the key province of Khorasan. But this strategy did not succeed, and the agreement broke down. Forces loyal to Amin attempted to invade Khorasan. In response, Ma'moun also proclaimed himself caliph and Amin's authority soon disintegrated. After a siege of Baghdad that lasted over a year, Amin was captured and killed.

Now that he was in control, Ma'moun tried to implement two radical policies. The first was to try to rule the entire empire from Marv in Khorasan, where his powerbase was situated, rather than setting himself up in Baghdad in the manner of the earlier Abbasids. The other was a novel plan for what was to happen when he died. He nominated Ali bin Musa al-Rida, the head of the House of Ali, to become the next caliph. Such a step had no precedent, and would have meant the fusion of the rival branches of the Prophet's family. Ali al-Rida was considerably older than Ma'moun, and some writers speculate whether the motives behind this appointment of a successor likely to die before him were cynical. But it does seem to have been part of Ma'moun's plan – albeit a short-lived one – to join the two rival branches of the family of the Prophet. He gave a daughter to Ali al-Rida in marriage, and betrothed another to Ali al-Rida's seven-year-old son, Muhammad al-Jawad. The official flags were changed from the traditional Abbasid black to the green of Ali.

Neither policy succeeded. From Marv, he found he was just too far away from the central provinces of the empire. He was faced with widespread *fitna*, or civil disorder, in many regions. There was even a strong and persistent anti-Muslim and anti-Arab revolt under a leader called Babak in Armenia and Azerbaijan, while many of the western provinces slipped away from central control. He therefore came to realise that he would have to move to Baghdad if he was to survive.

His other policy also failed. Ali al-Rida died. As this was may have been rather convenient for Ma'moun, there has always been speculation that he was poisoned. The colours of the empire's official banners reverted to black, and Ma'moun entered Baghdad in 819. It took him the first decade of his rule to re-establish control over the western provinces. One new and very effective element in his military machine, and one that helped him to achieve this, was an army of Turkish soldiers. Many of them were slaves commanded by his brother Mu'tasim, who would succeed him as caliph. These troops became one of the three mainstays of the Abbasid army. The second was the Arab element, which was now largely confined to the steppe lands to the north of the Arabian peninsula and the all important Byzantine frontier. The final element consisted of the army from Khorasan who had originally overthrown the Umayyads, and many of whose soldiers were now stationed in Iraq.

When Mu'tasim became caliph in 833, he could rely on his slave army of Turks, which had made him the most powerful man in the caliphate while Ma'moun still lived. These troops now became the dominant military force in the empire. But their presence in Baghdad led to friction and sometimes violence. It probably also occurred to Mu'tasim that they might be seduced from their loyalty to him by the powerful families and factions of the capital. His solution was to build a new capital at Samarra, north of Baghdad, to which he and the elite of the caliphate moved. This set a distance between them and Baghdad's troublesome populace, and the relationship between the two cities has been compared to that between Paris and Versailles during the days from Louis XIV to the French revolution. As with the Bourbons at Versailles, parades and court spectacles at Samarra reflected the caliph's exalted status. Mu'tasim, and his successors Wathiq and Mutawakkil, continued this splendour, and were renowned for building new palaces.

Yet, ultimately, the move to Samarra only replaced one problem with another. Its location was unfavourable for the development of the new city as a major centre for agriculture, industry and trade. This may have been a reason behind the original decision to move there – since it meant escaping Baghdad's troublesome populace and urban mob – but it had its downside: the caliph risked becoming a prisoner of the army, while the upkeep of the complex of palaces, mosques and barracks at Samarra was expensive. In 861, the Caliph Mutawakkil was assassinated by Turkish officers who were nervous that they were about to lose their privileges. They were in league with his son Muntasir, who feared that his father was going to remove him as his designated successor. The cold-blooded murder of an Abbasid caliph in this way broke a taboo, but it would soon become almost commonplace. Its immediate effect was an anarchic period that lasted for nine years, in which infighting between rival groups of soldiers probably reflected the decline in the revenues available to pay the army. After four brief caliphal reigns, order was restored; but by now it was clear that real power lay with the mainly Turkish soldiers.

There was a revival under Mu'tamid, who came to the throne in 870, during which the seat of the caliphate reverted to Baghdad from 892 onwards. The revival continued until the death of Muktafi in 908. During this period control had been re-established over the army, and central authority had been regained over the whole of Iraq, Syria, Egypt and the western and central parts of Iran. Thereafter, however, decline reasserted itself, and became unstoppable.

The Caliph Muqtadir, who succeeded Muktafi in 908, seems to have been chosen because he was perceived as likely to be easy for his ministers to manipulate – a disastrous reason for his election. The most pressing problem was shortage of money with which to pay the army. The old system of taxation had decayed. Tax farming and what was for all practical purposes the sale of whole provinces became the only way to raise the revenues needed. Muqtadir was killed by an army leader in 932, which precipitated another period of anarchy. One by one, the outlying provinces slipped out of caliphal control and into the hands of powerful local families who were often essentially warlords. This time, the loss would be for good. Simultaneously, a combination of neglect and fighting between army factions devastated the key agricultural estates of the Sawad around Baghdad. This led to the end of the caliph's political power.

Some kind of change now became inevitable. The caliphate was bankrupt and could only continue on the sufferance of local warlords. This did not, however, bring it to an end. In 945, Ahmad ibn Buwayh, a warrior from the mountainous areas south of the Caspian Sea, entered Baghdad. Finding Mustakfi, the current caliph, not to his liking, he contemptuously replaced Mustakfi with his brother, Muti'. The new caliph, and the institution of the caliphate itself, had effectively become a client of a military strongman. But Ahmad ibn Buwayh preserved the institution, because it was a useful source of legitimacy for his own rule. Although the Abbasid Caliphate would survive for more than two hundred years, it would never regain political control over the empire that the first caliphs had gained for Islam and which the Umayyads had expanded. Ahmad ibn Buwayh's dynasty, known as the Buyids, were ethnically Persian and proud of it. They came from the Alborz mountains, south-west of the Caspian Sea. Ahmad ruled as part of a confederation, since his brothers had already established themselves as rulers on the Iranian plateau in the cities of Shiraz and Rayy (close to modern Tehran). The family even began trying to set up their empire according to ancient, pre-Islamic Persian models of kingship. If this seemed like an insult to the Abbasid Caliphate, we will see in the next chapter how the Buyids would also insult the caliphs in a far greater way.

VII

Turning aside from the political history, two divergent approaches were emerging during these first two Abbasid centuries as to how Muslims should discern the teachings of Islam. For many, the obvious way to do this was to listen to what Muhammad's Companions could tell them about the way the Prophet had wished Muslims to live their lives. As the Companions aged and died, attention became focused on the recollections of the next generation – the 'followers' of the Companions: those who had known the men and women who had walked with the Prophet and could recall things they had passed on about his teaching. The same applied as that generation aged in its turn, and people listened to the memories of 'the followers of the followers'. These first three generations of Muslims became known collectively as the 'righteous ancestors', *al-salaf al-salih*, and the generations after them would treasure and spread the recollections of the Prophet's life that they transmitted. After the text of the Qur'an, the recollections attributed to *al-salaf al-salih* would be used to constitute the core of the material that made up the Sharia as it was lived by those Muslims who would come to be called Sunnis.

But other Muslims followed an alternative way to discern how to live their Islam. This was to look on the Prophet's family as the source of guidance for his teachings. His descendants were seen not only as the great exemplars of how Muslims should perform their devotions and behave in their daily lives, but were believed to be endowed with a special form of knowledge of the true meaning of the religion and the way it should be lived. These were the ancestors of those we now think of as Shi'is.

Although in due course there would be powerful states established on the basis of a Shi'i doctrine, we have seen how political support for rule by a member of the House of Ali and Fatima was invariably crushed during the first centuries of Islam. This began with the passing over of Ali in favour of Uthman, was followed by Mu'awiya's triumph after Ali's assassination, the poignant story of Hussein, and the numerous rebellions in favour of a descendant of Ali during the Umayyad period and the first two Abbasid centuries (only some of these rebellions have been mentioned above). This meant that the Shi'is – or perhaps we should say proto-Shi'is – had a very different view of most of the Prophet's Companions, since they had opposed Ali or at least colluded with those who opposed him. This also meant that, for them, these Companions were not suitable people to transmit the practice of the Prophet, no matter how close they may have been to him while he was alive. For Shi'is, the sad truth was that most of *al-salaf al-salih*, the so-called 'righteous ancestors' of the Sunnis, had betrayed his memory. At the same time, it will have been noted that not all members of the House of Ali necessarily believed in political action or the use of violence to wrest the caliphate from the Abbasids or their predecessors, the Umayyads. The example of the quietism (acceptance of the status quo) shown by Ja'far al-Sadiq when he turned down the offer to proclaim him caliph is instructive on this point.

These, then, were the two approaches to the way in which Muslims should learn the truths of Islam, which led respectively to Sunnism and Shi'ism; yet they overlapped. They were basically trends or tendencies that took a long while to develop into what we might call 'sects', and cannot be completely disentangled even today.[6] You did not have to be a follower of the House of Ali to be moved by the martyrdom of Hussein. He was a figure loved and revered by Sunnis as well as Shi'is. As late as the twelfth century, some Sunni communities took part in the commemorations of his death at Ashura on the 10th of Muharram.[7] Yet for Shi'is there is an extra dimension to Hussein's story. It marked the loss of the best – perhaps the only – chance to usher in the era of justice and righteousness that required leadership of the Muslim community by a descendant of the Prophet. And this happened because Hussein was betrayed by that community. Yazid, his Umayyad opponent, would be remembered for ever as an archetype of the godless ruler, like Pharaoh in the Qur'an (and the Bible).

In time, Shi'is would write down the history of the descendants of Ali whom they considered to be the true leaders of the Muslim community. They came to see the twelve imams – Ali, Hasan, Hussein and the leaders of the House of Ali over the following nine generations – as infallible, sinless and divinely inspired. For their part, Sunnis would often tend to see all the Companions of the Prophet, even controversial figures such as Mu'awiya, as saints. It was historical memory that drove Shi'is inexorably apart from those we have come to call Sunnis. Ali and Hussein had died violent deaths. Some – or all – of the other imams (except, as will be explained later, the Twelfth) may also have been poisoned. Significantly, however, some of the earlier Shi'i biographers, such as the great scholar known as al-Sheikh al-Mufid (d. 1022), tend to be sceptical about some of the stories of murder, while those who held contrasting views as to whether they had been murdered cannot be neatly separated into representatives of opposing Sunni and Shi'i camps. Yet as time passed possibility would harden into sectarian certainty, and the 'fact' that the first eleven imams were murdered by their Sunni opponents would become an article of faith: the only acceptable narrative that a Shi'i biographer could repeat. This was the case by the time of the Iranian Safavids in the sixteenth century.[8] Two rival historical narratives had thus taken hold. For Shi'is, wicked men had hijacked Islam and killed the descendants of the Prophet who had always been intended to lead the community. For Sunnis, the community had been divided and hamstrung by discord spread by the Shi'is.

We have now reached the point at which we must look at how these two rival trends crystallised into sects.

CHAPTER FOUR

The Split Between Sunnis and Shi'is

I

It is during a crucial period of two centuries that we can finally see the crystallisation of Sunnism and Shi'ism as rival sects. This era begins with the Abbasid 'revolution' in 749–50 and ends with the caliphs becoming the prisoners, and at times the puppets, of the Buyid dynasty in 945. It is impossible to examine how most Muslims came to see themselves as either Sunnis or Shi'is without first understanding the political history of this period, as well as the legacy of the first four caliphs and the Umayyads. That is why the first three chapters of this book have set out in some detail the story of the struggles for leadership of the Muslim community from the death of the Prophet onwards. We must now turn to the world of ideas. We will begin by looking at two Arabic words that were frequently used to denote the person who was leading the Muslim community: 'imam' and 'khalifah', or 'caliph'. These have entered the English language, but in English the full range of meanings that they each convey has been lost. We will look at 'imam' first.

The scholars of the Abbasid age preserved pre-Islamic poetry because it shone light on the language of the Qur'an. This can be aptly demonstrated in a line from the pre-Islamic poet Labid: 'Belonging to a people whose forefathers laid down for them a Sunna; every tribe has its Sunna and imam.'

Sunna is a word we have already encountered. It means 'custom' or 'practice'. The imam was the source of that custom or practice. As the historian of Islamic law, Norman Calder, put it, 'an *imam* was a person whose actions became models of right conduct for later generations: his practice, *Sunna*, was to be the practice also of the people who followed him'. In Islam, 'imam' was used especially in religious contexts. In the Qur'an, the word is used in particular to refer to prophets. It was used subsequently to refer to Abu Bakr, Umar, Uthman and Ali as individuals. It could also be used to refer to some of the Companions of the Prophet who never became caliph but whose piety made them exemplars for others to follow.

A revealed book could also be described as an imam, and the term was on occasion applied to the Qur'an. The great scholar Ibn Hanbal, who died in 855, referred to his own, vast collection of hadith (sayings attributed to the Prophet) as an imam. Echoing Labid's line, he said that he had made it 'an imam to settle any dispute concerning the Sunna of the Prophet'. In the legal matters of the Sharia, 'imam' came to carry the sense of 'an authority', meaning a jurist whose teachings were followed. At the same time, it continued to be used in purely secular contexts to denote, for instance, a military leader or governor. It thus carried a generic sense of 'leader' as well as 'authority'. There were times when the caliph was referred to as the imam, but the word could also mean no more than the person who led a congregation in prayer.[1]

While the general sense carried by the word 'imam' is therefore clear, it could carry many different meanings depending on the context in which it was used. It was also perfectly possible for a group to endow it with a special meaning that others would not necessarily use.

By contrast, the other word, 'khalifah' or 'caliph', has an inherent ambiguity. It can mean either 'successor' or 'deputy'. Sometimes the expression *khalifat rasul allah*, 'the caliph (or successor) of the prophet of God' was used. On other occasions, the caliph described himself as *Khalifatu'llah*, 'God's deputy' (the expression 'God's successor' would be blasphemous and meaningless). 'Deputy' and 'successor' are two very different concepts, but they both indicate that, whatever authority the office of caliph held, that authority derived from another: from the Prophet, in the case of 'the caliph of the prophet of God'; and from God Himself in the case of 'God's caliph'. Linguistically, this is not the case with 'imam', since that word does not of itself denote that the imam's authority stems from a higher source of authority. While 'imam' might denote just a humble prayer leader, the word nevertheless carries the potential – linguistically, that is – to be used for a supreme source of authority to a greater extent than the word caliph.

After he became the leader of the Muslims, Abu Bakr used the title *Khalifat Rasul Allah*, or 'the caliph (i.e. successor) of the Prophet of God'. Umar came to be called *Amir al-Mu'minin*, generally translated into English as 'the Commander of the Faithful', although the word amir/emir, 'commander' also carries the ideas of 'prince' and 'governor'. This title was generally used to address the caliph throughout the history of the caliphate and later. To this day, it is a title claimed by the king of Morocco. Umar was also referred to as *Khalifat Khalifat Rasul Allah*, 'the successor of the successor of the Prophet of God'.[2] With Uthman, the first attestations of the use of the title *Khalifatullah*, 'God's deputy', appear. It was the official title used by all the Umayyad and Abbasid caliphs.[3] Under the Abbasids, the expression 'Caliph of the Prophet of God' reappeared, and both designations were used, sometimes side-by-side. Of course, 'the Caliph of the Prophet of God' fitted in nicely with the status the Abbasids promoted for themselves as kinsmen of the Prophet. Its adoption (or re-adoption) did not imply a diminution of the caliph's status as God's deputy on earth.

II

We have focused on these two words because the question of the leadership of the Muslim community, and the source of the leader's authority, was vitally important for Muslims. It was necessary to be a follower of the caliph (or imam) in order to belong to the community. In other words, it was necessary to accept the caliph as the spiritual – and political – leader in order to gain salvation. He was a stronghold in which the faithful should seek refuge, and a rope to which they should hold fast. He could, for instance, be identified with the cord that is mentioned in Qur'an 3:98:

> And hold ye fast by the cord of God, all of you, and break not loose from it; and remember God's goodness towards you, how that when ye were enemies, He united your hearts, and by his favour ye became brethren.[4]

Panegyric poets could play with words, sometimes using imagery fresh from the Arabs' life as nomadic tent dwellers in the desert. The caliphs held religion and community together. They were the 'tent pegs'[5] of Islam that prevented religion and community collapsing to the ground. Without the caliph, neither would survive. The consequence was that anyone who failed to follow the true caliph was courting eternal damnation. Ali and Mu'awiya may have held the same religious beliefs, but that was not the point. There was one Muslim community, and it had one, true leader. To reject the leader meant putting yourself outside the community and courting eternal damnation.[6]

The same applied, of course, to the followers of the other distinct sect that appeared in early Islam. These were the Kharijis who, it will be recalled, rejected both Mu'awiya and Ali as caliph because they saw each as acting for his own selfish ends and not in the path of God. They had their own theology of leadership but, unlike the Sunnis and Shi'is, they never managed to set up a successful imperial project that spread over a wide area of the Muslim world. Today, the only state where the majority of Muslims are Kharijis is Oman, and the reason for that is that Kharijism took root among the tribes of the inaccessible mountains in the north of that country and has retained their loyalty ever since. The one other place where they survive is in part of Algeria. The history and development of Kharijism lie outside the scope of this book, but it will have been noticed how it provided an option for those who disputed the authority of the caliph – an alternative to seeking a leader from the line of Ali.

It was the caliph's duty to uphold the Sharia, the precepts and rules that developed into the detailed, God-given law of the community; but the extent to which the early caliphs could interpret, and even decree, the contents of that law by reason of their office is debated by scholars. As the political and religious leader of the Muslim community, the caliph was its defender and guardian. Abu Bakr, Umar, Uthman and Ali had all been key Companions of the Prophet. Both their office as caliph and their status as Companions gave them the right to be listened to on questions about what the actual practice of the Prophet and the Companions had been. Their own practice was also seen as praiseworthy, and fit for emulation by other Muslims. Right through the Umayyad period, disputes would be brought before the caliph who would give a decision without necessarily referring to a Qur'anic dictum or Prophetic practice. Judges would also write to the caliph asking for his advice on how to decide novel or difficult cases.

The *ra'y* or 'considered opinion' of trustworthy and devout men was originally a source of law, alongside the Qur'an and the practice – the Sunna – of the Prophet. Decisions were inevitably made on the basis of precedents. The caliph himself would seek precedents before giving judgement, although this did not necessarily imply seeking a precedent from the practice of the Prophet himself. A precedent set by an earlier caliph or another revered Companion of the Prophet might be sufficient. Inevitably, the 'considered opinion' of a scholar on a particular matter might well be identical to the practice of the Prophet and the practice of other eminent Muslims.[7]

By the 680s, scholars were beginning to gather material that set out the practice or Sunna of the Prophet. Within a generation or two, this would develop into the specialist and systematic science of 'hadith': amassing the sayings attributed to the Prophet and testing their authenticity by examining the trustworthiness of those who had transmitted them. In effect, the scholars codified the memory of the Prophet's practice in their collections of hadith. As this science of religious learning grew and became more formal, the 'considered opinion' that was used to resolve judicial disputes increasingly had to be based on the Prophet's Sunna, if it was to be accepted as valid.

As the judicial supremacy of the Qur'an and, beneath it, the hadith, became ever more firmly established, the element of personal discretion contained in 'considered opinion' steadily retreated. The jurist Abu Abdullah Muhammad ibn Idris al-Shafi'i, who died in 820, established a rigid hierarchy of sources of law in which it had no place. His aim, which he successfully achieved, was to provide a methodology for unifying Islamic law and ending the risk that it would disintegrate into regional variants. At the top of al-Shafi'i's hierarchy were the texts: first the Qur'an, and then the hadith. Below them, there were the consensus of the Muslim community (*ijma'*) and the use of analogy to reach a decision (*qiyas*). The consequence was that 'considered opinion' gradually disappeared as a source of law in itself. But it would survive in specific judicial tools such as the use of analogy and *istihsan*, interpretation in the way most conducive to achieving justice and the common good.

Another judicial tool that is also ultimately derived from considered opinion would prove to be of major importance in the history of both Sunnism and Shi'ism. This was *ijtihad*, the ability of a devout and trusted scholar to answer a judicial question through his knowledge of the sources of the Sharia. Al-Shafi'i often uses the words *qiyas* and *ijtihad* interchangeably. For him, *qiyas/ijtihad* is merely the bringing out of the meaning or interpretation of revelation in order to deal with a specific case. It is not a source of law in itself; it is a means to 'discover' the contents of that law.[8]

The scholars might disagree about aspects of the religious law, but a caliph gradually came to find that he needed authority from somewhere in the teachings of these scholars to justify the positions he adopted on questions of the Sharia. Revolts against caliphal authority, whatever the grievance behind them might be, were invariably justified on the grounds that in some way or other the caliph was disregarding the teaching contained in the Qur'an and the practice of the Prophet. This was already the case with the mutineers against the Caliph Uthman.

By the time of the Abbasid revolution, if not before, the religious scholars had become the repository of the community's memory of what the Prophet had said and done. There was an interesting case in which Caliph Mansour did not dare to use his authority to judge between three scholars who all produced different rulings on the same legal question. This was despite an appeal from the intellectual Ibn al-Muqaffa', who suggested he should declare which was correct and forbid jurists to follow the rulings he had rejected. The eminent jurist Malik bin Anas told Mansour that to try to establish a legal ruling by the caliph that overrode the judgement of a local judge would actually be seen as *kufr*, unbelief.[9]

The experts on the application of the Sharia, the *fuqaha* (singular *faqih*), soon became an important class of officials at the court of any ruler or provincial governor. Their presence at the caliphal court had become well established by the reign of Harun al-Rashid, if not before.[10] It was around this time that the different 'doctrinal legal schools'[11] of the Sharia began to appear, which the Muslims whom we must now begin to describe as Sunnis recognise as equally valid. Four of these doctrinal law schools or *madhhahib* (sing. *madhhab*) survive to this day. Each is named after its founder: Malik bin Anas (d. 795) for the

Malikis; Abu Hanifa (d. 767) for the Hanifis; al-Shafi'i (d. 820) for the Shafi'is; and Ahmad ibn Hanbal (d. 855) for the Hanbalis.

Each *madhhab* was more, however, than merely a school that was centred on an individual scholar – however eminent and brilliant he might be. There had already been plenty of figures who were outstanding in their learning, from whom other, typically younger, scholars could learn. But there had been nothing exclusive about the opinions expounded by these learned men. Students would come to learn what they could from them, and would then often go off to seek what knowledge they could find from other authorities. This explains, for instance, how Malik bin Anas and Abu Hanifa could both sit at the feet of Ja'far al-Sadiq as well as other scholars. Eventually, they would go on to found their own distinct, doctrinal legal schools.

Wael Hallaq, a scholar of Islamic law, has distinguished four characteristics of the doctrinal legal schools that mark them apart from the purely 'personal' schools. First, although they were named after an individual as their founder, that founder was actually only one among a number of scholars (including, probably, some of his own teachers and pupils) whose legal thinking had cohered as a 'composite school'. Second, the school was concerned as much with legal methodology as with the contents of the substantive law. Third, the schools each had their own boundaries when it came to both substantive law and the methodology of their legal reasoning. Finally, loyalty to the school became a defining feature of membership. It became rare for a scholar (or often for an ordinary Muslim who followed that school) to transfer his loyalty to another school.

This was a new and defining development. In Hallaq's words, an 'axis of authority had been constructed in the name of the school's eponymous founder around which the entire methodology of law'[12] revolved. The founder was now referred to as the school's imam, and was the mujtahid – that is, the practitioner of *ijtihad*– by whose teachings it was defined. He was seen as the teacher who had grappled with the content of revelation, and gained an absolute knowledge of it. This was what had enabled him to articulate the law that he gleaned from the holy texts. He was 'the absolute and independent *mujtahid*'.[13]

Al-Shafi'i, who is often described as the most systematic of these scholars, closed the debate over the caliph's role in debating the Sharia:

in legal matters, the caliph's task was to enforce the law, nothing more.[14] Like all other Muslim jurists, al-Shafi'i gave precedence to the Qur'an as the supreme source of law. Beyond this, priority was given to the Sunna, or practice, of the Prophet as preserved – and therefore as interpreted – by the hadith scholars. The ultimate arbiter for discerning the Sharia was *ijma,* the consensus of the community. In practice, this meant the consensus of the hadith scholars.[15] Any question of the caliph's ability to define the Sharia was ended, while the paramountcy of the class of religious scholars to decide on such questions was confirmed. They would define what we have come to know as Sunni Islam. This meant that they would also set its boundaries. They would decree who was and who was not a Muslim, would lay down rules to set out the relationship between Muslims and members of other religions such as Christians and Jews, and would decide which forms of Islam should be considered deviant and had to be opposed.

Most significant, perhaps, was the fact that the whole process of the development of the class of scholars and of the doctrinal law schools took place without any involvement from the caliphs. If they tried to steer or even influence the direction in which the Sharia developed, they failed. But although the scholars and the rulers now had different functions, the relationship between them inevitably meant that they were intertwined. By approving a particular doctrinal law school, or appointing scholars to positions at court or to positions as judges, rulers gained themselves legitimacy with the broad mass of Muslims who were their subjects, who followed particular doctrinal law schools, and from whose ranks the scholars emerged. The scholars thus provided the ruler with a shade under which to shield himself. Simultaneously, they became dependent on the ruler because of the offices, privileges and salaries they were granted. The relationship was symbiotic.

III

At more or less the same time as the class of religious scholars was emerging into full prominence and codifying the hadith, the tools of Greek logic were becoming available in Arabic and being used in theological debate. This was encouraged by the Caliph Ma'moun, who enjoyed such discussions. In 827, he used his authority to proclaim that the Qur'an had been created by God, and that this should be an article of faith for all Muslims. He even went to the extent of setting up a procedure known as the Mihna (a word which means 'test' but is usually translated in this context as 'inquisition') to examine religious scholars, and check that they subscribed to this belief.

On a theological level, this was a debate similar to that which took place in Christianity over Christ's nature (was Christ human or divine, or both at the same time?). After much discernment, this led Christians to the doctrine of the Trinity. For both religions, God is the fount of all existence. He is beyond existence itself, since nothing that exists can be said to have any reality save to the extent that it is ultimately granted by God. For Muslims, it was only to be expected that this conundrum would lead, sooner or later, to discussion of the nature of the Qur'an. Was the sacred text created by God, or had it existed from all eternity as an eternal manifestation of God's attribute of speech? If the latter was the case, it posed another theological problem. Speech is a human attribute. In what way can God be said to 'speak'? In fact, one of the reasons that Ma'moun himself gave for promulgating the doctrine was that he had been troubled by the fact that those who argued that the Qur'an was uncreated were bringing into Islam a doctrine that was analogous to that which the Christians taught about 'Jesus, son of Mary'.[16]

It was with the new intellectual tools of Greek logic and dialectics that Ma'moun enunciated and promulgated his belief in the created-ness of the Qur'an. Yet this belief was rejected on principle by many religious scholars, who repeatedly endured torture and imprisonment for sticking to their beliefs. They took the view that, as Ahmad ibn Hanbal put it, a Muslim should believe 'without asking how' (*bi-la kayfah*). This meant that reliance on the text of the Qur'an and the hadith should be the prime tools – ultimately the only tools – used for discerning the beliefs Muslims should hold. As we have seen with the emergence of the doctrinal law schools, this was already accepted to be the case with regard to questions of the practice of the Sharia. It followed that analogy and other logical tools should be used as sparingly as possible, and always subject to the greatest possible caution.

Behind the controversy, there lurked a struggle for power. Some modern scholars see Ma'moun's action as a deliberate attempt to assert the power of the caliph over that of the religious scholars to decree what were the contents of the faith. It is interesting that he began to refer to himself as the imam as well as the caliph. By imam, he meant the source of authority in the teaching of religion. The title 'the Imam' was also applied to him by at least some of those who agreed with the position he had taken and, inevitably, by court sycophants.[17] But the hadith scholars emerged victorious from the tussle, and the use of the title by the caliph was discontinued for the time being. Although Ma'moun's successors, Mu'tasim and Wathiq, continued the Mihna, they did so in a half-hearted manner. It was finally discontinued in the 840s by Mutawakkil,who reversed the official position. The caliph now upheld the doctrine of the uncreated-ness of the Qur'an, and enjoined all Muslims to do the same.

Mutawakkil was subsequently assassinated by Turkish soldiers worried about their privileges and pay. It is unnecessary to look further than the decline in the caliphate's revenues as the cause for this, but it is possible that this also marks a decline in the caliph's status. The hallmark of Islam was living according to the Sharia. As this was now seen to be defined and interpreted by scholars, and not by the caliph, it meant that a warrior who was full of zeal to serve Islam no longer needed to enlist in the caliph's army. He could equally well serve in the army of one of the provincial courts. Many of these were now independent of Baghdad for all practical purposes. Yet by doing this, he could still be confident that he was serving Islam. In the words of Tayeb El-Hibri, a specialist in classical Arabic historiography and literature, the caliph himself was no longer 'the anchor of religious and political authority'. In fact, 'the roads of Islamic legitimacy had diversified'.[18]

True Islam was to be found wherever a Muslim ruler kept a court with a staff of religious scholars who could inform him of the contents of the Sharia as contained in the Qur'an and hadith, and interpret it for him. The caliph in Baghdad might still be the source of legitimacy. Prayers would be offered for him all over the Muslim world in congregational mosques every Friday, and his name would appear on coins. He was a potent symbol of the truth and might of Islam. Offering a form of ceremonial allegiance to him was a good way for a Muslim ruler to cement his own legitimacy. But the caliph's political power – and his spiritual authority to define the faith – had drained away.

By the mid-ninth century, if not well before, the Islam of the Abbasids was a religion in which a class of religious scholars defined the faith and how it should be lived. They already enunciated the contents of the Sharia, which might be said to be the embodiment and practice of that faith. This was what became known as Sunnism. In time, the caliph would adopt the title of Imam alongside that of Caliph, and would be referred to as the Imam by Sunnis. This seems to have occurred over the course of the tenth and first half of the eleventh centuries. The timing suggests that it was very probably a defensive measure against the Shi'i movements that came close to swamping the Abbasid Caliphate as the tenth century wore on.[19]

As an idea, Sunnism evolved gradually, but it would outlive the Abbasid Caliphate. The Sunnis were the people of the *sunnah* [the practice of the Prophet] and the *jama'ah* [the community]. Their starting point was that all Muslims should live together in peace and unity. This meant accepting whatever had happened in the past, rather than letting old disputes flare up and create discord. In particular, it meant accepting that each of Abu Bakr, Umar, Uthman and Ali had, in turn, been the legitimate caliph. These caliphs became known collectively as the four *rashidun*, those who had been rightly guided, or those who followed the right way. Later caliphs, too, should be accepted – as should other Muslim rulers, provided that they did not go against the fundamental rules of Islam. There was (and is) no central teaching authority in Sunni Islam. Sunnis discern the precepts and practice of Islam from the religious scholars. Needless to say, these scholars often disagree among themselves. That was already the case at the time the doctrinal law schools emerged in the late eighth and early ninth centuries, and is still so today.

IV

We must now turn to the Shi'is. For them the word 'imam' was used to describe the divinely inspired descendant of the Prophet who was the rightful leader of the Muslim community and the embodiment of religious learning. A consequence of this was that, in theory but not in practice, in Shi'ism the class of religious scholars could never have the same status that they acquired in Sunni Islam. In time, however, practice and theory would become hard to disentangle.

The word *shi'ah*, from which 'Shi'i' comes, just means 'party' or 'faction'.[20] As early as the run-up to the Battle of Siffin there were references to Ali's *shi'ah*, but it is difficult to tell whether at that time this meant anything more than 'Ali's faction', referring to those who supported him. It was only gradually that the expression crystallised to become the term used for a sect whose members held beliefs and had practices that were distinct from those of other Muslims. After all, in the period after the murder of Uthman there are also references to the *shi'ah* of Uthman. These indicate no more than the faction that sought justice for the murdered caliph.[21]

The story of what happened at Ghadir Khumm, which was told in Chapter Two, can be interpreted to suggest that the Prophet had intended Ali to follow him as leader of the community after his death. There are other incidents from Muhammad's life that might suggest that he saw Ali as pre-eminent among his followers, and imply that he chose him as his successor. It was Ali (and Ali alone) who helped the Prophet cleanse the Ka'ba of pagan idols, and it was to Ali that he gave his famous sword Dhu'l-Fiqar at the Battle of Uhud. As we have seen, there is also plentiful evidence that Ali always thought he should have become the leader of the community when Muhammad died, and that he held back from asserting this right only for the best of all possible motives: the peace and wellbeing of the community.

Ali's son Hasan claimed the right to succeed his father. He stood down in favour of Mu'awiya for the same reason that had led Ali to wait so patiently during the reigns of Abu Bakr, Umar and Uthman: peace and harmony in the community. Hasan's younger brother Hussein asserted his claim to leadership of the community only after Mu'awiya's death. The tragic and poignant killing of Hussein left many Muslims with a deep yearning for the just rule of a truly righteous imam from the Prophet's family, the *ahl al-bait* or 'People of the House'. Even if such an imam was not the political ruler of the community, they still saw him as the sole authoritative source of spiritual guidance whom Muslims should follow. The First Imam had been Ali. On his death the role was taken over by Hasan, and then by Hussein. But on whom did this role devolve after Hussein's death?

Some believed it fell on the shoulders of Muhammad ibn al-Hanafiyyah, the half brother of Hasan and Hussein who was Ali's only surviving son after Hussein was killed. Muhammad ibn al-Hanafiyyah himself made no attempt to raise a revolt against the Umayyads, and lived a blameless and virtuous life in Medina, which was now a political backwater. In his life we can thus see a continuation of the quietism, or calm acceptance of things as they are, that had characterised the conduct of Ali during the period of rule by Abu Bakr, Umar and Uthman, and which had then been continued by Hasan and, indeed, by Hussein up to the death of Mu'awiya. But, as we have seen, after the death of Hussein some of those who had followed the cause of Ali and then his sons turned to violence and calls for vengeance. This was the case not just during the Umayyad period, but also during the era of the Abbasids. Even if the Abbasids were genuinely from the family of the Prophet, that does not mean that all Muslims accepted their legitimacy. As we have seen, movements arose that would turn to a direct descendant of Fatima and Ali (or, to be more precise, to somebody who claimed to be one) and answer the call to take up arms against the caliph.

Such movements were both spiritual and political at the same time, and could broadly be characterised as aiming to overthrow a godless order and usher in an era of justice and righteousness. They took inspiration from the martyrdom of Hussein, whose ambition had been to do just that. The first insurrection occurred almost immediately after his death. This was the revolt of 'the Penitents' from Kufa, who were consumed by guilt for their failure to go to Hussein's aid on that fateful day of Karbala. This was swiftly followed by the revolt launched by Mukhtar al-Thaqafi, who proclaimed Muhammad ibn al-Hanafiyyah as the imam and also as the Mahdi – a new title that meant 'the one who is divinely guided'. The word 'mahdi' carried messianic overtones, and implied that the Mahdi would restore Islam to what it was meant to be, establish justice on earth, and free the oppressed from tyranny. Mukhtar's revolt is significant because it seems to have been the first that managed to rally to its cause many of the new, non-Arab converts who felt excluded by Umayyad rule. When Mukhtar took Kufa, he executed anyone he captured who had taken part in the massacre of Hussein's party at Karbala.

Although his revolt was crushed within a couple of years, the movement that it had created survived. It became known as the Kaysaniyya, after Abu Amr Kaysan, who had commanded Mukhtar's guard. The Kaysaniyya condemned Abu Bakr, Umar and Uthman as usurpers of the position that was always intended for Ali. When Muhammad ibn al-Hanafiyyah died in 700, many members of the movement believed that he was still alive but had withdrawn from the world into a state of *ghayba*, a word that means absence, concealment or invisibility.[22] The rather quaint word 'occultation' has become the standard English translation for *ghayba* in the sense that it is used in Shi'i theology, and we will therefore adopt it in this book.

The continuing presence of Muhammad ibn al-Hanafiyyah in this world, even though in a state of occultation, meant that he could have no successors, and that he would reappear at some point as the Mahdi in the last days, in order to usher in an era of justice before the Day of Resurrection. On the other hand, some members of the movement denied that Muhammad ibn al-Hanafiyyah was in occultation, and accepted his son, Abu Hashim, as his successor. When Abu Hashim himself died in 716, the majority of this group believed that he had specified Muhammad bin al-Abbas as the next imam. This was the same Muhammad bin al-Abbas who would become the first Abbasid caliph. Abu Hashim's followers became one of the major religious groups – perhaps *the* major religious group – that rallied to the cause of 'the Accepted One from the Family of Muhammad' against the Umayyads. Nothing shows more clearly how the trends that became Sunnism and Shi'ism had not congealed irrevocably at this time.

Then there were others who did not see Muhammad ibn al-Hanafiyyah as the imam, but believed that the imamate followed the direct bloodline of Ali and Fatima. This passed through Hussein to his son Ali, who was known as Ali Zayn al-Abidin, 'Ali the adornment of the believers', because of his deep piety. According to this group, the imamate then passed to his grandson Muhammad al-Baqir, who died in 732. After Muhammad al-Baqir's own death, it passed to his son Ja'far al-Sadiq, who lived through the Abbasid revolution until 765. These three imams maintained the now well-established tradition of quietism, something that set them apart from the Penitents and Mukhtar al-Thaqafi. But there was also one significant member of the family of Ali who did not follow this tradition. Zayd, a younger half-brother of Muhammad al-Baqir, attempted to start a revolt against the Umayyads in Kufa in 740. The city did not rise to support him, and he and his followers were soon killed by government troops. This rebellion may have been futile and short-lived, but it led to a new, distinct Shi'i movement known as Zaydism, which survives to this day. Together with other smaller Shi'i sects, it is discussed in Chapter Five.

Ja'far al-Sadiq became the rallying point for all those who believed in rule by a descendant of Ali and Fatima but who did not support Zayd's revolt. When Abu Muslim's victorious army took Kufa, Abu Salama, who had originally sent Abu Muslim to raise the flag of rebellion in Khorasan, invited Ja'far al-Sadiq to become the new caliph, 'the Accepted One from the House of Muhammad'. Yet, as we have seen, Ja'far declined. He continued to live quietly in Medina and took no part in the Abbasid revolution or the revolt of Muhammad the Pure Soul. He kept aloof from politics, and is acknowledged as a great religious scholar who was a towering figure in the intellectual development of Islam. There is much about his career that suggests that the currents which we now think of as Sunnism and Shi'ism had not yet entirely formed. He was a major scholar of hadith, and much of his work would be accepted by both Sunnis and Shi'is. He is sometimes seen as having set up his own doctrinal law school of Sharia, or *madhhab*, like his younger contemporaries the scholars Abu Hanifa and Malik bin Anas, who founded the Maliki and Hanafi doctrinal law schools of Sunni Islam. They each revered Ja'far al-Sadiq, who taught them both.

On the other hand, with Ja'far al-Sadiq we can see some of the hallmarks of Shi'ism becoming clear. He saw himself as the sole authoritative figure on the Sharia in his generation. He believed that, in this, he was following the position his father had held before him. But his claims for himself as the imam went much further. Starting with the Prophet's designation of Ali as the First Imam, the imamate had been transmitted to Hasan and then Hussein. Each imam from Hussein onwards had specified a son who was to be his successor. The imam guides humankind. He is even essential for the continuation of the existence of the world, and knows the literal and hidden meanings of the Qur'an – the exoteric (*zahir*) and the esoteric (*batin*). He is therefore possessed of religious knowledge in a special and unique way, and is both infallible and the receiver of divine guidance. He is not necessarily a temporal ruler, and is content to confine himself to teaching until the right time comes for him to ascend to earthly power. Nevertheless, obedience to him in matters of religion is an absolute duty for all Muslims. He is the proof of God on earth.

Ja'far al-Sadiq jealously guarded his position as the imam against any other members of the Prophet's family who might believe they could claim it, and saw himself as the supreme authority on religious matters. However, he did not take the step which some might think would have followed on logically from this. He never attempted to become the political leader of the community, and never supported rebellion against either the Umayyads or the Abbasids. He also taught his followers that, when necessary, they could resort to *taqiyya*, that is to say that they could legitimately hide their true beliefs so as to avoid persecution. *Taqiyya* became an integral feature of Shi'ism, and has made it very hard ever since to be certain whether a Muslim who denies Shi'i claims is doing so sincerely. This has often caused much anger among Sunni Muslims.

V

One of the greatest crises in the history of Shi'ism occurred in 765 when Ja'far al-Sadiq died. He had designated his son Ismail to be his successor, but Ismail had died shortly before Ja'far himself. This was a challenge to the faith of all those who believed in the idea of the Shi'i imam. If God had designated Ismail to succeed his father, why had he predeceased him?

A period of confusion followed. Each of Ja'far's three surviving sons, Abdullah al-Aftah, Musa al-Kazim and Muhammad, now claimed to be the imam, and each had his own supporters, while a fourth group believed the succession should pass through the sons of Ismail. The idea that Ja'far al-Sadiq had not actually died but had disappeared from view and entered into occultation also gained some traction for a while.

The position became even more complex when Abdullah al-Aftah died a few months after his father, leaving no sons of his own. The group supporting him had been the largest, and most of them then transferred their allegiance to Musa al-Kazim.

Of these various groups, the two that would be by far the most significant in the long term were the followers of Musa al-Kazim and the followers of the descendants of Ismail. This became the great split within Shi'ism. The followers of the line of Ismail would come to be known as the Ismailis. The followers of Musa al-Kazim would recognise him as imam and accept a further five imams in his direct line. For this reason, they are generally referred to in English as the Twelvers, since they accepted a line of twelve imams beginning with Ali and of which Ja'far al-Sadiq was the sixth. For convenience, from now on we will refer to those who followed Musa al-Kazim and the following five imams as Twelvers from the time of Musal al-Kazim onwards, although, of course, he was only the Seventh Imam.

Musa al-Kazim received the support of the majority of Ja'far al-Sadiq's followers, including most of the leading Shi'i scholars who had been in his entourage. Ja'far al-Sadiq would be the last of the imams to be buried at the al-Baqi' cemetery in Medina. The Abbasid caliphs feared the imams, both as direct descendants of Ali and because of the status they merited as acknowledged religious scholars. When Harun al-Rashid came to the Hejaz on pilgrimage to Mecca, he ordered Musa al-Kazim to accompany him back to Baghdad where Musa al-Kazim was kept under surveillance and even imprisoned. He died in prison in 799, and Twelver writers would come to take it for granted that he was poisoned. In a pattern that by now will be familiar, some of his followers believed he was not dead but had gone into occultation.

Ali al-Rida, the Eighth Imam, was Musa al-Kazim's son. As we saw in Chapter Three, he was designated by the Caliph Ma'moun to be his successor, and Ma'moun gave him a daughter in marriage. But Ali al-Rida died in 818, only two years later. If this was an attempt by Ma'moun to reconcile the rival branches of the Prophet's family, it had failed. Undeterred, Ma'moun seems to have made another attempt at reconciliation. Ali al-Rida's seven-year-old son Muhammad al-Jawad, the Ninth Imam, was betrothed to one of Ma'moun's daughters. He was kept in Baghdad. Although he was subsequently allowed to go back to

Medina, he was summoned back to Baghdad by Ma'moun's successor, Mu'tasim, when he was twenty-four, and died shortly thereafter.

The Tenth Imam was Muhammad al-Jawad's son, Ali al-Hadi, who, while still a boy, was brought from Medina by the Caliph Mutawakkil and taken to Samarra where he was kept in custody until his death over forty years later in 868. Mutawakkil feared the descendants of Ali. In 850, he destroyed the tomb of Hussein at Karbala and thereby earned himself the lasting enmity of Shi'is. His intention was to stop pilgrimages there, but the custom of visiting the tombs of the imams had become deeply engrained among the Shi'is. Samarra would now also become a place of pilgrimage for visitors to the tomb of Ali al-Hadi and his son, al-Hasan al-Askari, who was the Eleventh Imam and was also held there until his death in 874.

As far as was known at the time of his death, al-Hasan al-Askari had left no son. He was only twenty-eight, and the Twelver movement was thrown into the same sort of disarray as Shi'ism itself had been after the death of Ja'far al-Sadiq. This was called the period of *hayra*, or confusion. It will be recalled that Twelver Shi'is believe that the presence of the imam in the world is necessary for it to continue to exist. Some thought the imamate had transferred to al-Hasan al-Askari's brother Ja'far, while other candidates were also suggested. The idea that eventually won out, however, was that al-Hasan al-Askari had in fact been the father of a son who was only five at the time of his death. The birth of the boy in 869 had been kept secret, and his identity was known to only a few trusted people, because of the risk to him from the Abbasids. His name was Muhammad al-Mahdi, and he was recognised by Twelvers to be the Mahdi as well as the Twelfth Imam. Because he was in hiding (known as the period of 'the Lesser Occultation') he was known as the Hidden Imam.

In 892, the Caliph Mu'tadid finally abandoned Samarra and returned to Baghdad, leaving Samarra to be turned into an additional Shi'i shrine city, because it contained the tombs of the Tenth and Eleventh Imams. Baghdad was also becoming increasingly important at this time as a centre for Twelver Shi'ism, something that occurred at the expense of Kufa. There were members of the sect in high places at the caliphal court, including powerful viziers from the Nawbakhti family. The version of the history of this period that later came to be accepted by the Twelvers asserts that there were four 'ambassadors' who were able to communicate with the Hidden Imam. They would give written answers, like legal opinions, on questions believers wished to put to the imam. The third of them, Ibn Rawh al-Nawbakhti, died in 938. After the fall from favour and execution of his patron, the great vizier Ali al-Furat, in 924, he often had to operate in secret, and died in prison. He nominated Ali bin Muhammad al-Simmari to be his successor, but Ali died only three years later in 941. The channel of communication with the Hidden Imam had been broken.

Tradition would say that it was the imam himself who had broken off contact with his community. He had done this because of his disgust at the sin, tyranny and oppression in the world. He had therefore told the final *safir* or 'ambassador', only a few days before his death, not to designate a successor.

The death of the final 'ambassador' in 941 began what is called the period of the 'Greater Occultation', which Twelvers believe continues to this day. The eventual coming of the imam will be part of the End Times, of eschatology. A saying of the Prophet is said to have predicted: 'Day and night will not end before God has sent forth a man from my house who bears the same name as I. He will fill the world with justice and equity just as it was filled with tyranny and oppression before.'[23] His coming will be preceded by portents and omens, plagues, eclipses and earthquakes. The sun will rise in the west, and the Tigris and Euphrates will flood Iraq, while Baghdad and Kufa will be consumed by fire descending from the sky. False prophets and unbelievers will fight apocalyptic battles before the world is cleansed. Then, the Mahdi (that is, the Hidden Imam) will appear at the shrine of the Ka'ba in Mecca on the 10th of Muharram, the anniversary of the martyrdom of Hussein. He will fight those Muslims who have parted from the true faith and destroy their mosques before ushering in a paradise-like era by the side of a canal stretching from Ali's shrine at Najaf to that of Hussein at Karbala. His righteous rule will see the end of poverty (and therefore of taxes, including the religious *zakat*, defined below) and last until the Day of Resurrection.

VI

The tradition of quietism among Twelver Shi'is did not prevent them from becoming soldiers, and rising to political power as a result. The Buyid dynasty was a case in point. They were a family of mercenary leaders from Daylam to the south of the Caspian Sea. In the 930s, Ali, al-Hasan and Ahmed, the three sons of Buya after whom the dynasty is named, began to carve out principalities for themselves and rule them in a kind of confederation. Ali set himself up in Shiraz and al-Hasan did the same in Isfahan, while Ahmed crossed over the mountains into Iraq. In 945 he marched into Baghdad. As we saw in the last chapter, he replaced the Caliph Mustakfi with his brother, Muti', and thereby showed where real power lay. The mighty Abbasid caliph was now the helpless prisoner and client of a Shi'i ruler.

Propriety, however, was observed. Ahmed was appointed commander of the Caliph's armies (*amir al-umara'*), while the Caliph decreed that his brothers would be the governors of the provinces they held. We do not know the precise nature of their Shi'i sympathies. Were they Twelvers or Zaydis? Although it seems that the family became Twelvers, Daylam had been a stronghold of Zaydism, that is to say of those who considered Zayd bn Ali, the son of Ali Zayn al-Abidin and brother of Muhammad al-Baqir, to have been a true imam.

Whatever the case concerning the form of Shi'ism followed by the early Buyids, they were all prepared to accept the lavish titles they were awarded by the Sunni caliph. The reality was that the majority of the population were Sunni and it would have been politically difficult for the Buyids to end the Abbasid Caliphate – assuming that they wished to do so, which is far from certain. What is quite clear, however, is that the Shi'i-inclined Buyids looked to the institution of the caliphate to legitimise them, just as Sunni rulers did.

They also had another source of legitimisation: the traditions of kingship of ancient Persia. These had never died, especially in remote areas like Daylam from which the dynasty came, and where Arab penetration had been small. The history of the old kings had been preserved, and some Buyid rulers even adopted the ancient Persian title of Shahanshah, 'king of kings', an honorific that would now be used by the Shi'i prince who effectively controlled the Abbasid caliph.

The Buyid era was not a prosperous or a happy one. There were struggles within the Buyid family, revolts by unpaid soldiers, friction between Daylami and Turkish units in the army, brigandage, a steady decline in agriculture, trade and tax receipts, and the emigration of leading families to Egypt in the hope of a better life: all these were features of those times. Another was communal strife, of an increasingly sectarian nature, in Baghdad.

It was in the decades immediately before the Buyids entered Baghdad that sectarian communal violence gradually began in the Abbasid capital. In 925, the Caliph Muqtadir ordered the demolition of a mosque in the Shi'i quarter of Karkh. Ali himself had prayed at this mosque, and it was a meeting place for Shi'is. Nevertheless, the event does not seem to have sparked sectarian rioting. By contrast, ten years later, the Caliph Qahir signed a decree ordering Hanbalis – that is to say, Muslims who followed the doctrinal law school established by Ahmad ibn Hanbal – to stop rioting against Shi'is, a sure sign that sectarian tensions had appeared at street level and had become a real danger to communal life in the capital.

These tensions were initially stoked by fear of the Qarmatis (a militant Shi'i grouping which will be discussed in the next chapter) when they seized and pillaged the pilgrimage caravan to Mecca in 924, and left those pilgrims who were not worth a ransom to die of thirst in the desert. Anger at the government's powerlessness was combined with dread that the Qarmatis might actually take Baghdad and massacre its inhabitants. This led to distrust of Shi'is and the downfall of the vizier, Ibn al-Furat, whose family was known for Shi'i sympathies. The Qarmati threat would ease in the 930s, but by then communal strife was appearing in Baghdad as mobs of Hanbalis began rioting against Shi'is in 933.

The immediate cause was a report (accounts differ as to whether it was true) that Ali bin Yalbaq, a key member of the entourage of the Caliph al-Qahir, had tried to institute the cursing of Mu'awiya from the pulpit. This led to further Hanbali agitation against Shi'is and attempts at the repression of Hanbalis. The next Caliph, Radi, would castigate the Hanbalis as hypocrites who physically assaulted other Muslims who disagreed with them while posing as defenders of Islam, and 'ascribing to the party of the blessed Prophet's house unbelief and error'.[24] But the Caliph did not succeed in calming the situation. While he persecuted the Hanbalis, the response by their mobs was only to intensify their attacks on Shi'is.[25]

We can see in these riots how Muslims were dividing themselves into Sunnis (as represented here by the Hanbalis) and Shi'is over their contestation of the history of Islam. For Shi'is, Mu'awiya was inevitably one of the villains of that history. It was he who had prevented Ali being accepted as caliph by the entirety of the Muslim community. He was also believed by Shi'is to have poisoned Ali's son, Hasan, whom he deceitfully promised would be his successor. On the Sunni/Hanbali side, the view was very different. Mu'awiya had been a Companion of the Prophet and therefore his memory should not be attacked. Mu'awiya's rule, however controversial it may have been, was nevertheless legitimate and had led to stability in the Muslim polity and the further expansion of Islam. The caliphs were trying to hold the ring between the two factions, and finding increasingly that they could not do so as rioters roamed the streets.

Sectarian tension can thus be seen to have been well and truly present in Baghdad before 945 and the coming of the Buyids and their proudly pro-Shi'i Daylami soldiers. In 962, the Buyid Mu'izz al-Dawla had curses on Abu Bakr and Umar painted onto walls in the city. The following year, he gave permission to the Shi'i community for the public commemoration of the mourning rituals of Ashura and the celebration of Ghadir Khumm.[26] Around this time, important figures began asking for their bodies to be buried at Karbala, rather than be interred where they died (as had previously been the tradition). Lawlessness on the roads may also have been a factor in growth of pilgrimage traffic to the Shi'i shrines rather than undertaking the perilous journey across Arabia necessary for the Hajj.

The division between Daylami soldiers who were Twelvers and Turkish soldiers who were Sunnis became a source of violence from 972 onwards. A military expedition against the Christians of Byzantium turned round and went back to Baghdad, where its Turkish soldiers attacked the Buyids, their Daylami troops, and Shi'is in general. The Shi'i suburb of Karkh was sacked and burned down on two separate occasions. Sunnis instituted their own feasts to rival those of the Shi'is. Their counterpart to Ghadir Khumm was the feast to commemorate the night during the *Hijrah* when the Prophet and Abu Bakr took refuge in the cave to hide from the Quraysh after they left Mecca on their way to

Medina. But the damage to the Muslim community was now permanent. Baghdad was divided into quarters that were specifically Sunni or Shi'i. These were often patrolled by thuggish, sectarian gangs, which clashed in the streets. The pattern of sectarian riots and specifically sectarian quarters also began to spread to other cities and regions of the Islamic world.

There were figures such as the gifted Buyid Adud al-Dawla who managed to calm things down to a certain extent, and forbade provocative, sectarian commemorations. Another Buyid, Baha al-Dawla, had rival Shi'i and Sunni gang leaders tied together with rope and thrown into the Tigris to drown. Nevertheless, from now on it was all too frequently a process of containing sectarian violence, as well as sectarian excuses for brigandage and other crimes, rather than stamping them out.

Yet, at the same time, there was much positive and courteous interaction, particularly at the highest levels of society. There was an official representative, the *naqib*, of the descendants of Ali living in Baghdad who attended the caliph's court. Although the descendants of Ali were by no means necessarily all Shi'is, some naqibs such as al-Sharif al-Radi (d. 1015) won the trust and intimacy of the caliph despite being well known to be Twelvers. Al-Sharif al-Radi was a friend of the caliph, wore the official black robe of the Abbasids, and was entrusted with two important positions by him. He was the commander of the pilgrimage caravan to Mecca and was put in charge of the tribunal that dealt with *mazalim* – complaints by members of the public against wrongdoing by government officers. He was also politically useful to the Abbasid caliph. The rival Fatimid caliph in Cairo (see Chapter Five) claimed descent from Ali. Al-Sharif al-Radi was among a number of eminent Twelvers who joined the Abbasid Caliph Qadir and the Buyid prince Baha al-Dawla in signing a document that publicly disputed the authenticity of the Fatimid caliph's ancestry.

VII

It was in the decades leading up to the Buyid period and, above all, during that period itself, that the theory of the Hidden Imam and his occultation was developed by Twelver scholars. The Buyid period has thus been called the era of the Twelver 'church fathers',[27] in which the sect distinguished itself from other Shi'i groups and defended its positions against polemical attack. Although much of this thought was begun in other Buyid cities such as Rayy and Qumm, Baghdad became the epicentre for Twelver learning.

A crucial development in Twelver thinking was the adoption of the rationalist ideas of the Mu'tazili school. This school had become prominent in Baghdad in the early 800s, and had used the techniques of Greek logic and dialectic. It had supported the view that the Qur'an was created. After the end of the Mihna in 847, the opposing view that the Qur'an was an eternal manifestation of God's attribute of speech prevailed and the school fell out of favour among Sunnis. However, its ideas had never disappeared and they resurfaced in the writings of Sheikh al-Mufid (d. 1022), who shaped the form that Twelver thought would take. He gave reasoned argument ('aql – literally 'intellect') a fundamental role in Twelver jurisprudence. This would be the beginning of an intellectual thread that stretches all the way to the ideas of Ayatollah Khomeini, and which would be influential in the establishment of the Islamic Republic of Iran in 1979. Nevertheless, Sheikh al-Mufid taught that reason should be used only within narrowly defined limits, and could never override scripture. Like the Mu'tazilis, he held that man's actions were the product of free will, rather than being predetermined by God, since this was a necessary consequence of God's justice. He also followed the Mu'tazilis in teaching that the Qur'an had been created. His pupil Ali al-Murtada (d. 1044), who was the brother of al-Sharif al-Radi and followed him as the naqib (leader) of the descendants of Ali at the Abbasid court, took the use of reason further, arguing that reasoned argument had to be applied to matters of faith. Merely relying on the authority of others in matters of the transmission of tradition (taqlid) would lead to unbelief, since a saying attributed to the Prophet or one of the Imams would always comply with reason if it was genuine. This rational test therefore had to be applied in order to establish the authenticity of a saying.[28]

The Twelvers now believed that their imam, the ultimate religious authority in Islam, was permanently in hiding and that this would remain the case until the End Times. This position inevitably required some explanation and justification from their scholars. This can be gleaned from the polemical works they wrote during the Buyid period to defend their positions. These were predicated on rational, Mu'tazili arguments. God is just. Man is weak, and in need of God's grace. Man requires guidance, which can be supplied only by the imam. Without leadership from an imam who is divinely inspired, infallible and sinless, human society would descend into perpetual strife, injustice, anarchy and chaos. Indeed, unjust men dominate the world, and it is their tyranny that has forced the imam into hiding. The Abbasid caliphs themselves acted in ways that are tyrannical.

Heinz Halm, a scholar whose speciality is Shi'i history and doctrine, has pointed out how remarkable it is that a figure such as Ali al-Murtada (known as Sharif al-Murtada, d. 1044) who 'went in and out of the Abbasid court' could write in such terms.[29] Yet al-Murtada provided precedents. He pointed out how, according to the Qur'an, Joseph asked Pharaoh, the archetypal oppressor, to put him in charge of his granaries. He also drew attention to the fact that Ali had acquiesced in the Shura that had elected Uthman as caliph, and had actually taken part in the election of Uthman himself. These were precedents that Twelvers could follow when dealing with or serving rulers such as the Abbasid caliph, whom they considered to be intrinsically unjust. Ja'far al-Sadiq was also reported to have said, 'Fulfilment of the needs of fellow believers atones for collaboration with government.'[30] Important Twelver writers repeatedly taught that, when the imam reappeared, he would fight oppression and overthrow all earthly governments, since they were ineluctably unjust. Even the governments of rulers who were themselves Twelvers were frequently considered as tainted in this way. However, Muhammad bin Hassan al-Tusi (d. 1067) taught that a ruler who accepts the Hidden Imam and therefore rules provisionally in his name while applying the Sharia (as taught by the Twelvers) is entitled to obedience.

A second reason for the necessary existence of the imam flowed from the Sharia. Although believers were aware of the existence of the Sharia, they needed the imam in order to enable them to ascertain the detail of its contents. The believers were frail and fallible. Their judgement was questionable both as individuals and when assembled together as a group. The Qur'an required an interpreter and elucidator. It was the imam who could instruct the faithful in the way the Prophet interpreted the holy book. Furthermore, the methodology adopted by the Sunni schools was wrong. *Ijtihad* and *qiyas* (the terms for judgment by use of analogy that, as in some Sunni texts, sometimes tended to be elided together) were only forms of speculative opinion or conjecture (*zann*). They could be no substitute for the imam. In the same way, problems in the transmission of some hadith demonstrated that the imam was necessary in order to provide clarity.

But the absence of the Hidden Imam must at times have seemed an insurmountable problem. His functions included not just the definition of religious truth, but all the tasks that were the prerogative of the imam alone: the exercise of those punishments prescribed in the Qur'an which involve capital and corporal punishment (the *hudud*), leading the congregational prayers on Fridays, raising the religious taxes known as *khums* and *zakat*, proclaiming jihad and administering justice. From the time of the scholars in the Buyid period until the present, debate among Twelvers has continued. Despite disagreement, the trend has been towards the view that more and more of these powers and prerogatives have been delegated to the religious scholars who are experts on the detail of the Sharia, the *fuqaha*. Nevertheless, this was a gradual – and often contested – process. In the sixteenth century, the questions of whether taxes could be collected during the Imam's absence and whether congregational prayers on a Friday could validly be held were still disputed. Only at the end of the eighteenth century was it agreed that religious scholars could enforce the *hudud*, while it was not until the nineteenth century that it was accepted that scholars could proclaim jihad.[31] This trend might be said to have reached its logical conclusion in the twentieth century, when Ayatollah Khomeini would assert that religious scholars should take on the political authority of the imam. This, however, remains extremely controversial among Shi'i scholars today.

The Twelver scholars believed that, if they erred in their elucidation and interpretation of the Sharia, the imam would still find a way to guide and correct them. This meant that, for all practical purposes, the imam's function as the supreme teacher of the Sharia had devolved on them as a class. They therefore accepted the principle of *ijma*, consensus, in order to expound the Sharia. However, this was the *ijma* of the Twelver scholars alone. The opinions of Sunnis, as well as of ordinary people, did not count.

The Twelver scholars therefore acted as judges in their own community, deciding cases on the basis of the Qur'an and hadith. It was *kufr*, unbelief, to seek it from the courts of Sunni rulers, even if the judgement given happened to be based on a correct understanding of the Sharia.[32] When it came to the sources of law, there were obvious similarities to those used by Sunni judges, save that the traditions the Twelvers followed included those ascribed to the twelve imams. They also believed that, by rejecting Ali, most of the Companions had betrayed the Prophet's legacy. Aisha, who was an important transmitter of traditions recognised by Sunnis, is an obvious example. For Shi'is, she was quite simply not a reliable source. The right to decide disputes had been delegated to trustworthy scholars by the imams, and there was evidence that Ja'far al-Sadiq had appointed scholars to do this himself.

At first there may have been a degree of reluctance to consider the problem of how judges could be appointed during the occultation of the Hidden Imam. Nevertheless, in time it was taught that a Twelver scholar who possessed the right attributes to be a judge could decide cases while the imam was absent.[33] These desirable attributes were depth of religious knowledge, piety and the respect of ordinary believers. In a somewhat similar way, Twelver scholars originally held that the portion of the *zakat*, the religious tax, that was to be paid to the ruler for administrative purposes and for the conduct of jihad (three eighths of the total) had lapsed during the occultation of the imam. However, as time passed this attitude changed, and it was held that these portions of the *zakat* should also be paid to the *fuqaha*, the religious scholars, alongside the portions of the tax payable in respect of other matters, such as the relief of poverty and the construction and maintenance of religious buildings. This change had been accepted by the sixteenth century, and occurred through a re-assessment of the texts of revelation and the teachings of earlier scholars.[34]

Another question that had to be considered was: what are the political consequences of all earthly governments being deemed unjust? The answer is that, until the Hidden Imam returns, there is no point in

trying to overthrow them. The religious scholars therefore followed the
traditional attitude of quietism. Yet they could also, if they deemed it
appropriate, co-operate with the secular power when they chose. This
may explain why the Buyid dynasty was content to control Baghdad
but never attempted to abolish the Abbasid Caliphate. Instead, they
manipulated the caliphs, whom, as we have seen, they could depose at
will. The policy the Buyids followed towards the caliphs was simple
expediency. Because the majority of those over whom the Buyids ruled
were Sunnis, the dynasty adopted a wise policy of live and let live in
religious matters.

VIII

As the Buyids declined from the late tenth century onwards, the
period sometimes called the Sunni revival began. The Caliph Qadir,
who ruled from 991 to 1031, was able to escape Buyid control to
an extent that permitted him to take a much more assertive role in
religious affairs than his immediate predecessors. Backed by popular
demonstrations, he was strong enough to refuse a Buyid choice for the
post of chief judge in Baghdad. It was under his successor, Qa'im, who
ruled from 1031–75, that the Buyid dynasty finally lost Baghdad. It
was to the Seljuqs: unruly Turkish tribes who had converted to Sunni
Islam and swept across Iran from Central Asia. Their leader, Tughril
Beg, sent envoys to Baghdad, where Qa'im conferred the legitimacy
on him that he had granted other Sunni rulers. In 1058, three years
after Tughril Beg had entered into Baghdad in person, the Caliph
appointed him 'the King of the East and West'. Tughril Beg was now
the Caliph Qa'im's protector. The Caliph was free of Buyid influence
and control at last.

The Seljuqs surged on, taking Greater Syria and, in a battle that
decisively altered the course of history, defeating the Byzantines at
Manzikert (or Malazgirt) in 1071. This opened up Anatolia to Turkish
settlement. However, their empire was short lived. After the death of the
third Seljuq sultan, Malik-Shah, in 1092, it began to disintegrate into
a number of smaller states which were at war with each other as much
as with their neighbours. Nevertheless, Sunni rule was restored in most

places over the whole of the eastern Islamic world. That world also now became more assertively Sunni. Seljuq rulers encouraged more rigorous study of the Sharia through the establishment of colleges set up by one or other of the four doctrinal law schools. These began to educate the bureaucratic elite of administrators, producing a class that was more outwardly observant in its religious practice than its predecessors, and was one of the pillars of society and the state. This did not mean the end of Twelver Shi'ism in the territories which were dominated by Seljuq rulers. It retained a presence in Baghdad and Kufa, as well in many parts of Iran. The shrine of the Eighth Imam, Ali al-Rida, at Mashhad near Tus remained an important pilgrimage centre. This was also the case, of course, with the shrines in Iraq.

The Twelvers were not seen as a political threat. The custom of having a *naqib*, or local leader of the descendants of the Prophet, continued, and he was a respected figure with whom the political authorities would deal. There were also many Twelvers appointed to government officers by Sunni Turkish rulers. These were often benefactors who endowed their community and sponsored the teaching of the Twelver version of Islam in response to the proliferation of Sunni scholars who graduated from the colleges established by Seljuq rulers.

The disintegration of the Seljuqs eventually gave the Abbasids some leeway to escape from the control of those who claimed to be their protectors. The Caliph Nasir, who reigned from 1180 to 1225, re-established political and military control over most of Iraq, but that control was only ever on a 'local' basis. The lands beyond had slipped away from political control by the caliph forever. The most the caliph could hope for was a continuation of the symbolic pledges of allegiance from local rulers, recognition of the caliph in the Friday prayers as the leader of the Muslim community, and handsome gifts. These may theoretically have been a form of tribute, but they were given at the local ruler's whim, or were the subject of negotiation. The caliph was in no position to extract anything from a reluctant ruler. Sunni Islam would soon find that it could exist perfectly well without him.

CHAPTER FIVE

Of Ismailis, Assassins, Druze, Zaydis, Gnostic Shi'is, Alawis and Sufis

I

By 874 – the year of the death of al-Hasan al-Askari, the Eleventh Imam of the Twelvers, and the beginning of the epoch of the Hidden Imam – there were many other Shi'is who belonged to different trends. Most of these maintained that the imamate had continued through the line of Ismail, the son whom Ja'far al-Sadiq had designated as his successor but who had predeceased him. They are known as the Ismailis, a name that denotes all those who believed the imamate continued through the descendants of Ismail. It is to these that we turn in this chapter before looking more briefly at other movements which are Shi'i, or at least Shi'i in origin. We will conclude by saying a few words about Sufism and its relationship to both Sunnism and Shi'ism.

The quietism of the Twelvers was probably greatly influenced by the decision of Ja'far al-Sadiq not to accept the office of caliph when it was offered to him – to say nothing of their general belief at that time that jihad, war declared in the name of Islam, could not be proclaimed during the imam's occultation. By contrast, Ismailism would be an intellectual and spiritual cradle for movements that, over the next couple of centuries, preached the use of violence to establish a new and just caliphate.

During the last decades of the ninth century, at approximately the time when the Twelvers were coming to the conclusion that the Twelfth Imam had gone into permanent occultation, a rival public preaching mission, or *da'wa*, began. This *da'wa* seems to have been started by a man known as Abdullah the Elder who lived in a small town called Askar Mukram on the river Karun in Khuzistan. He taught that Muhammad bin Ismail had been the last of the seven imams and would return in the End Times as the Mahdi to establish the true religion that had hitherto been known only to a few. This would mean that the rules of the Sharia would be lifted, and humanity would live once more in a blissful state like that in the Garden of Eden.

After preaching locally and then in Basra, constantly facing hostility, he ended up at Salamiyya, south-east of Hama in Syria, which became the centre for his missionary activity (and which remains an Ismaili centre to this day). This preaching spread the Ismaili word, not least among those Shi'is in Iran who were disillusioned after the death of the Eleventh Imam, al-Hasan al-Askari, and did not accept the existence of the Twelfth Imam. Abdullah the Elder was succeeded by his son and grandson, who continued his work. Effective missionaries were sent out to many corners of the Muslim world. They carried on trade in local markets where they could secretly tell their subversive message to the people they met. They also proselytised more openly among the nomadic tribes, where the level of religious knowledge was generally low. These tribes provided them with some of their greatest successes in recruiting new followers.

The missionaries taught that God had revealed his teaching in the Qur'an, which he had imparted to Muhammad, just as earlier revelations had been sent to the earlier prophets. The prophets, however, taught only the outward form of the religion God wanted to be established on earth: the rituals and sacred law that the believers must follow and obey. But these rituals and sacred law had an inner meaning, which was imparted not to the prophet but to his deputy, or *wasi*. Thus, in the case of Abraham, the *wasi* had been Isaac; the *wasi* of Moses had been Aaron; that of Jesus had been Simon Peter; and that of Muhammad had been Ali. Each *wasi* had communicated this inner teaching only to a small circle who kept it secret, and who were to be succeeded by a cycle of seven imams. The seventh imam after Ali was Muhammad bin Ismail. He had not died but had gone into occultation, where he remains until he reappears as the Mahdi and brings back the bliss of the Garden of Eden.

It is hardly surprising that the Ismailis became known as the *batinis*, 'those with a secret teaching' (literally, the 'interiorists'). Their *da'is*, or missionaries, would swear-in those they initiated, and stress that the name of the Mahdi was known to only a few. Ultimately, however, this far-flung preaching led Ismailism to split into different branches.

One branch originated in the Iraqi countryside of the Sawad near Kufa, among followers whom Abdullah the Elder had either left behind or who had been converted by *da'is* he sent from Salamiyya. In 875 or 878, a *da'i* won to the cause a man called Hamdan Qarmat, who gave his name to the powerful movement known as the Qaramitah, the Qarmatis (the form we will use), or even in an anglicised form as the Carmathians. Hamdan and his brother-in-law Abdan became local leaders of the movement, and spread the word among the nomadic and semi-nomadic people of the area who were soon causing havoc for the Abbasid authorities in Iraq and Syria. The word also spread among the tribes and in the oases of the southern coast of the Persian Gulf and its hinterland, where the movement was able to take control of a large area. This included the port of Qatif, which the Qarmatis took in 899.

Quite coincidentally, 899 turned out to be a very significant year for the Ismaili movement as a whole. Abdullah the Elder's grandson, Muhammad Abu'l-Shalaghlagh, died. His nephew Abdullah is disparagingly known to history as Ubaydullah or 'little Abdullah', as he was dubbed by the movement's opponents. Ubaydullah proclaimed himself to be a direct descendant of Muhammad bin Ismail, and despatched word to all Ismaili *da'is* to inform them that he was in fact the true Mahdi. This split the Ismaili movement. The Qarmatis refused to acknowledge him, and embarked on an attempt to spread their own movement instead.

The Qarmatis succeeded in raising support among the Bedouin of the Syrian desert; they besieged Damascus and devastated many of the cities to the north. They took the opportunity to sack Salamiyya, as well as Tiberias, before the Abbasid authorities were able to regain control. They were also active in the area south-east of Iraq, and sacked Basra in 923. The following year, as mentioned in Chapter Four, they attacked and pillaged the pilgrimage caravan to Mecca. Soon they were threatening Baghdad itself. They also committed a massive act of sacrilege in 930 when they removed the sacred black stone from the Ka'ba and took it off in triumph to their bases in eastern Arabia.

Soon thereafter, however, the Qarmatis started to feud among themselves. The movement appeared to have peaked, although it continued to control a large area along the Gulf coast, inland from Bahrain. It would flare into life again on several occasions later in the ninth century. Subsequently, during a period that lasted from the thirteenth century until at least the fifteenth, the Qarmatis of Greater Bahrain would convert to Twelver Shi'ism. One factor behind this may have been that Sunnis found Twelvers less threatening.[1]

II

The Qarmatis shook the Abbasids, but a far greater threat to them would come from the other main branch of the Ismaili movement, which sprang from the activities of Abdullah the Elder at Salamiyya. This was from the dynasty known as the Fatimids, which was founded by Ubaydullah when he declared himself Mahdi in 899. Forced to flee by the Qarmatis when they rejected his claim, he went to Ifriqiya (roughly modern Tunisia and eastern Algeria) where a *da'i*, Abu Abdullah al-Shi'i, had already spread the Ismaili message among the Kutama Berbers of the Atlas to the west. Just as the Caliph Mansour had disposed of Abu Muslim, so Ubaydullah disposed of Abu Abdullah once he had taken control of Ifriqiya and established his capital at Qayrawan in 909. He claimed authority as imam over all Muslims and their lands. He supplemented the power of his Berber tribesmen with slave soldiers who were Black Africans and Europeans, and built a strong navy. A new and very powerful rival to the Abbasids had been formed. The Fatimids claimed that they were the true caliphate, that of the descendants of Ali and Fatima. The Fatimid Caliph was the imam. He had a degree of authority equal to that of the Prophet, save for the fact that he did not receive new, Qur'anic revelation. For a while it seemed that they were going to sweep all before them.

In 969, a Fatimid army crossed the deserts of North Africa and seized Egypt. The taking of Egypt by the Fatimid general al-Jawhar, acting in the name of the Fatimid Caliph al-Mu'iz, was largely achieved by negotiation, although force was used when required. The arrival out of the desert of a huge army composed largely of fierce Berbers would no doubt have had a salutary effect on those inclined to resist. The old administration of government seems not to have been overthrown so much as absorbed, and notable figures such as the chief judge of Fustat (then Egypt's leading city) and the preacher at Egypt's oldest mosque – who was even a member of the Abbasid family – were permitted to continue in their posts.[2]

Jawhar established a new city which he called al-Qahira, or Cairo, less than an hour's walk from Fustat. Initially, the new Cairo would be a city for the Fatimid elite and army, where they could worship according to the Ismaili rites at their new mosque called Al-Azhar. An implication of the construction of this shining (and well-fortified) city was that the Fatimids would keep themselves apart from the Egyptian population, both Sunni Muslims and Copts (the Copts, the Egyptian Christians, were almost certainly still a significant majority). Four years after the submission of Egypt, the Caliph Mu'iz arrived from Ifriqiya, even bringing with him the bodies of his ancestors to be reburied in Egypt. He was forcefully making the point that Cairo, not one of the relatively remote cities of Ifriqiya, was now his capital and the centre of the true religion.

Economically, Egypt began an era of prosperity under the Fatimids, and the gold coins minted in the name of Mu'iz were valued everywhere for their high and reliable gold content. The trade route to India and the Far East moved southwards from the Persian Gulf, Iraq and Syria. Instead, cargoes were taken up the Red Sea to Egypt and the Mediterranean. It was around this time that Egypt displaced Iraq as the richest province in the central Islamic lands.

Although much attention was paid to training *da'is* and spreading the Ismaili message in lands which were not yet under Fatimid sway, it seems that little effort was made to convert the broad mass of people under their rule to the new creed. In fact, there is some evidence that the Fatimids were indifferent as to whether or not the ordinary people converted. This may have been a reason for their success. The most notable change was that prayers in the mosques were now said in the name of the Fatimid, not the Abbasid, Caliph. Shi'i, rather than Sunni, law was used in the courts (although it was sometimes enforced by judges who remained Sunni). The distinctive Shi'i call to prayer was introduced, and Shi'i commemorations such as the day of Ghadir Khumm and the anniversary of Hussein's martyrdom on the 10th of Muharram became public events. These changes may have caused resentment, and there were some disturbances, especially over the introduction of the Shi'i commemorations, but they did not shake Fatimid control. Such religious strife as took place in Fatimid Egypt was largely between Christians and Muslims, rather than within the Muslim family itself.

Now that they had absorbed Egypt, the Fatimids set out to extend their power into Greater Syria, where they soon found themselves in open warfare with both the Qarmatis and local Turkish warlords who were Sunni. Although they came to dominate the southern portions of Greater Syria, and were able to integrate some of the Turks into their own military system, Greater Syria with its many walled cities, forts, mountain ranges and deserts would prove a constant source of instability and theatre of war for them. On the other hand, in 975, Mu'iz was acknowledged as the protector of the Hajj. Prayers were said in his name in front of the pilgrims assembled in Mecca from all over the Muslim world. The Fatimids never established direct control in the Hejaz, but they paid subsidies to the local Bedouin to make sure they left the holy cities and the pilgrims in peace. They thus displaced the Abbasids from the role which they had once played as patrons of the Hajj, and which had been hugely important to their legitimacy. This must have been a profound humiliation for the Sunni Caliphate. The Fatimids also ensured that the Qarmatis left Mecca and the pilgrims alone. Even before they took Egypt, they had successfully negotiated with the Qarmatis to return the black stone to the Ka'ba. In 992, their caliphate was also acknowledged in Yemen. But the high watermark of their power was in 1058–59, when a soldier of fortune allied to them took Baghdad and prayers were said in the city's mosques in the name of the Fatimid, rather than the Abbasid, Caliph.

The entry of the Sunni Seljuqs into Baghdad put an end to the brief period when prayers in the name of the Fatimid Caliph had been said in the city of the Abbasids. The establishment of the Seljuq Empire placed a block on expansion by the Fatimids, and the Seljuqs drove them from most of Greater Syria. Gradually, the Fatimids declined until they were only a regional power based in Egypt. Their Ismaili Caliphate was finally extinguished by Saladin the Ayyubid in 1171, a few years after he had taken control of Egypt. This was when the Friday prayers in the Al-Azhar mosque in Cairo were said in the name of the Abbasid Caliph for the first time. Saladin ensured that there would never be another Fatimid imam. He had all sixty-three male members of the dynasty imprisoned for the rest of their lives, while all female members were kept captive for six months to confirm that they were not carrying a child that might have continued the line.

III

There was another sect that emerged from Fatimid Egypt. In 996, an eleven-year-old boy became caliph. His regnal name was Hakim. Four years later, when he was still only fifteen, he murdered the eunuch Barjuwan, who was his tutor and the person meant to supervise and, if necessary, restrain this young and inexperienced monarch. Hakim now took complete control himself. He would prove to be enigmatic and unpredictable throughout his rule. This ended when he disappeared, presumed murdered, in 1021.

It is sometimes suggested that he was mentally unstable, possibly a sufferer from a personality disorder or a psychopath, although, as the medieval historian and Islamic specialist Hugh Kennedy has pointed out, his madness 'was always guided by a kind of shrewdness'.[3] There were no major rebellions against him, and he managed to deal effectively with external threats, such as the attempt to invade Egypt by Bedouin from Cyrenaica led by al-Walid bin Hisham, who was of Umayyad ancestry. He also managed to keep in check the latent rivalry and tensions between the Berber and Turkish soldiers of the Fatimid Empire. Hakim was certainly one of those absolute rulers to whom it is dangerous to get too close. Many of those who were his immediate subordinates were executed, often apparently on a whim. He also persecuted Christians and Jews at times. One notorious act was his order to demolish the Church of the Holy Sepulchre in Jerusalem, an event that was a factor in sparking the wars we now call the Crusades. On the other hand, his decrees were often inconsistent and could be abruptly reversed – as when he banned Christians from showing crosses in public, then subsequently issued an abrupt order commanding them to wear crosses whenever they went out of doors.

It is not easy to detect a religious ideology behind his decrees. Some could be construed as enforcement of the Sharia, but others suggest the reverse, or are quite unintelligible in Sharia terms. It may

seem unsurprising for a caliph to ban alcohol, although the Sharia has
no problem with Christians and Jews drinking it. But why ban eating
watercress and fish without scales, or playing chess? Why did he issue
commands that all dogs should be killed, or that the markets should
open at night rather than during the day? As time went on, he became
increasingly retiring and ascetic, and is rumoured to have considered
himself divine. He took to wearing ragged clothes like some Sufis and
to disappearing in order to wander in the rocky hills that overlook the
Nile Valley to the east of Cairo. Some of his measures may have been
intended to placate the Sunni majority among Egypt's Muslims, such
as forbidding the cursing of Abu Bakr and Umar. On the other hand,
this could be construed as an example of the indifference he sometimes
showed towards religious practice as he grew older. He also neglected
the celebrations that marked the Hajj and other events in the Muslim
religious calendar, and is said to have been seen eating in public during
Ramadan.

His reign ended in 1021 when he failed to return from one of his
walks or rides in the Muqattam hills behind Cairo. He is generally
presumed to have been murdered on the orders of his sister, Sitt al-Mulk,
who became the real power behind the Fatimid throne in the years
following his disappearance. In any event, his body was never found.
This left it possible for followers to believe that he was still alive, or that
he had gone into occultation.

Three or four years before his disappearance a new and revolutionary
idea had appeared: Hakim was, indeed, God incarnate. Although there
is no firm evidence that Hakim himself believed this, he did not take
action to stop it being preached. Nevertheless, one of the propagators
of this idea, Muhammad bin Ismail ad-Darazi, was murdered by some
outraged Turkish soldiers. The movement that ad-Darazi had been
leading engaged in very active missionary work; but Hakim's successor,
Zahir, took firm action against it, and it was soon ruthlessly suppressed
by the Fatimids in Cairo and elsewhere in Egypt. Despite this, the
movement spread into Greater Syria where it took root in some areas,
especially on parts of Mount Lebanon, and has developed into what we
now know as the Druze faith. Druze communities today exist in parts
of Lebanon, the Hawran plateau and Golan Heights in southern Syria, a
few places elsewhere in Syria, and the Galilee in northern Israel.

The Druze teach that God had originally withdrawn from humanity after the fall of Adam, but had been reincarnated in the Fatimid caliphs up to and including Hakim. In response to humanity's ingratitude, the Divine Presence has now withdrawn once more. A new era of God's absence, or occultation, had begun. This was a new test (*imtihan*) for the faithful. The Druze divide themselves into two categories: the *'uqqal* (sing. *'aqil*) who are the religious scholars (literally: 'the intelligent'); and the *juhhal* (sing. *jahil*), the unlearned (literally: 'the ignorant'). Possibly reflecting the Fatimid practice that the secrets of the faith should be known only to an initiated elect, knowledge of the inner teachings of the Druze faith are restricted to the *'uqqal*, the religious scholars. To this day, not all the Druze scriptures have been published. These include many letters written by the early missionaries who spread the new faith.[4] Today, the Druze do not proselytise, admit converts or marry non-Druze. They have thus, like some other small sects, developed into a quasi-tribe.

IV

The Fatimid Caliphate, like that of the Abbasids, is remembered today for its vanished glories. After the end of the dynasty, Ismailism seems to have disappeared in Egypt, but Ismailism itself survived.

A feature of the Fatimid Caliphate was the fact that the succession on the death of a caliph was generally smooth – a striking contrast to succession under the Umayyads and Abbasids, which often led to prolonged periods of civil war. This was the case even when caliphs were still boys at the time they came to the throne. The eleven-year-old Hakim was not the only example of this. His successor, Zahir, was sixteen, and the latter's successor, Mustansir, was only seven. Nevertheless, strife over the succession to the office of caliph did eventually come to the Fatimid Caliphate when Mustansir died after a long reign of nearly sixty years in 1094.

Mustansir – as was his right – had designated his elder son, Nizar, as his successor; but the vizier and head of the army, al-Afdal bin Badr al-Jamali, instead appointed Musta'li, Nizar's younger brother, who happened to be al-Afdal's son-in-law. Nizar objected and tried to start a rebellion, but was arrested and executed, together with his sons. This led to a schism. Hassan-i Sabbah, a Fatimid *da'i* who had succeeded in seizing a number of castles in parts of the Elburz mountains in Iran, broke away. Hassan-i Sabbah had made his headquarters at Alamut, one of the most remote of these castles, and effectively established a small Ismaili fiefdom from which he carried out raids against the surrounding Seljuqs and the Baghdad Caliphate. In one of these raids, he had sent out an assassin dressed as a Sufi, who succeeded in approaching and killing the Seljuq vizier Nizam al-Mulk in 1092.

When he heard of the killing of Nizar, Hassan-i Sabbah refused to offer allegiance to Musta'li and made himself independent. He began his 'new preaching' (*al-da'wa al-jadida*) in which he may have taught initially that Nizar was still alive, but had gone into occultation. In time, however, another idea became predominant instead. One of Nizar's grandsons had become the imam and had escaped to Alamut where he lived in hiding. In other words, he was in a state of occultation although Hassan-i Sabbah was in personal communication with him and had been entrusted with the task of keeping him safe.

Hassan-i Sabbah's followers have become known to history as 'the Assassins'. Those who carried out the assassinations and other missions were called *fida'is*, an Arabic word that means literally 'those who offer their lives as a ransom'. This is the same word that in its Arabic plural form, *Fedayeen,* has entered English, and is used by various revolutionary movements today to denote their fighters. For a while, the power and influence of the Assassins grew. The fear that they inspired gave them a power that was out of all proportion to their small numbers. Their castles were sometimes established near major trade routes, from which they could exact tolls. They also demanded protection money from rulers in exchange for leaving them alone, secretly infiltrated the armies of the Seljuqs, and could also occasionally be persuaded to carry out assassinations for a fee. During the period 1126–29, following more than two decades of activity in Aleppo and the Orontes valley, they managed to establish themselves in the coastal mountains of Syria. By agreement with the Seljuq military leaders in Damascus, they occupied the castle of Marqab and threatened the Crusader states along the coast. They soon held other castles, and struck terror into the hearts of local Muslim and Crusader rulers alike. They twice nearly succeeded in killing Saladin, but it was probably Fatimid and Abbasid caliphs who were the most prized targets for them. In 1130, the Fatimid Caliph Amir was assassinated, as were two Abbasid caliphs: Mustarshid in 1135, and Rashid in 1138.

Hassan-i Sabbah died in 1124, before these successful assassinations of caliphs. He designated another *da'i*, Buzurg-Ummid, as his successor. The latter appointed his son Hasan to succeed him, effectively establishing a dynasty. Three years after his grandson Hasan II succeeded his father, he declared that the End Times had begun, since the Hidden Imam had abolished the Sharia. Up to this point, the Assassins had been scrupulous in observing the requirements of the Sharia, but now these had served their purpose. Unfortunately for Hasan, however, he did not carry all his community with him, and he was murdered. His son Muhammad succeeded to his place, and proclaimed that he and his father were, in reality, descendants of Nizar and that he was therefore the imam. When his own son, Jalal al-din Hasan III, succeeded him, he reintroduced the Sharia, and even established cordial relations with the Abbasid Caliph, allowing Sunni mosques to be constructed in his territories. It was an example of the normalisation of a charismatic, millennial sect, but it was not yet quite ready to become part of the mainstream. His own son Ala'al-din Muhammad III declared that the reintroduction of the Sharia had only been proclaimed in order to conceal the truth, and had been motivated by *taqiyya* (the practice permitted by the Shi'is of denying one's religion to escape persecution). He was to be the last ruler of the Iranian fiefdom of the Assassins. Alamut and some or their other castles negotiated their surrender to the Mongols, but Ala' al-din resisted. After he was taken prisoner, he had the distinction of being taken to the court of Kublai Khan, the overlord of the Mongols, and was subsequently executed.

The era of the Assassins was over, but their descendants still live around Masyaf and some of their other castles in the coastal mountains of Syria, as an Ismaili sect. Their practice of political assassinations ended, and they became tolerated, after a fashion, and were even recognised by the Ottoman Empire, which taxed them. Other followers of the line of Nizar remained in Iran. Their imam became known as the Agha Khan, but he and his followers fled to Afghanistan after an unsuccessful rebellion in 1842. Shortly afterwards, they went to India and made Bombay their centre. Today the peaceful Ismailism of the Agha Khan and his followers has spread around the world.

V

The division between Twelvers and Ismailis is not the only ancient split among mainstream Shi'is that survives to this day. An even earlier split occurred when Zayd, the son of Ali Zayn al-Abidin (the Fourth Imam) and half brother of Muhammad al-Baqir (the Fifth Imam), rose in rebellion in Kufa in 739 and was killed fighting against the Umayyad governor's forces in the streets of the city. We have already noted how Zayd's action contrasted with the quietism of the other imams after the events of Karbala. In time, his followers developed their own, distinctive legal tradition and also evolved their own theology of the imam. It is the latter that sets the Zaydis apart from other Shi'is and leads them to a very different world-view.

The theory of Zaydism is that any descendant of Ali is eligible to be the imam. The true imam will be the descendant of Ali who takes up his sword and establishes the imamate in battle. The Zaydis reject the notion of *taqiyya*, and believe that Muhammad al-Baqir, Ja'far al-Sadiq, and the other figures revered by the Twelvers as the imams, disqualified themselves by *qu'ud*, quietism or inactivity (literally, 'sitting'). Several consequences flow from this theory. There is no Hidden Imam, and therefore the whole edifice of Twelver dialectic about what the source of authority should be for Muslims during his absence falls to the ground. This is also the case with regard to the concept of the return of the imam as the Mahdi to usher in an era of justice during the End Times. The Zaydi imam is not infallible, cannot work miracles, and cannot be a child. In practice, therefore, Zaydism is much closer to Sunni Islam than any other Shi'i group.

There have been two successful Zaydi kingdoms. One was set up in Tabaristan, south of the Caspian Sea, during the late ninth century. This kingdom was the background to the emergence of the Buyid family of warrior princes, whose origins were probably Zaydi. The kingdom survived in various forms into the twelfth century. The last Zaydi communities in Tabaristan seem to have accepted the Twelver Shi'ism of the Safavid dynasty in the sixteenth century.

The other Zaydi kingdom was in Yemen and dated back to the end of the ninth century. Zaydism took deep root in the Yemeni mountains and the country was ruled by a Zaydi imam until 1962, when the last imam was overthrown in a military coup. Over its many centuries of existence, the Zaydi imamate of Yemen was contested by local Sunni forces, as well as by foreign dynasties and states, the last of which was the Ottoman Empire. Although the Ottomans repeatedly defeated Zaydi rulers, the Zaydi conception of the imamate meant that defeating, imprisoning or executing an imam could never be decisive; another imam would invariably appear in the mountains, unsheath his sword and summon his followers to battle against the invaders. It is by no means impossible that another Zaydi imam may yet proclaim himself in Yemen. Zaydis are a minority in Yemen: a little over a third of the population of the modern Yemeni republic is Zaydi, the remainder belonging to the Shafi'i doctrinal law school of Sunnism. Sectarianism has traditionally been absent from Yemen until now, the twenty-first century, when it has begun to spread.[5]

VI

There were other groups that were associated, sometimes unfairly, with Shi'ism and which can be traced back to the decades following the original Arab conquest of Iraq in the 630s. They were known collectively as the *ghulat* (singular: *ghali*), the 'exaggerators', or 'extremists', to give them the labels attached to them by their opponents. These groups were firmly rejected by the Shi'i mainstream for their unacceptable views, but the historian Moojan Momen (a specialist in Shi'ism and Baha'i studies) refers to them as 'Gnostic Shi'is' and this is the term we will use here.[6] They were often considered to have gone beyond the fringes of Islam. They were more of a tradition than a sect, although sects sprang from that tradition. They seem to have taken some of the metaphysical and cosmological ideas that were swirling around in the intellectual world of late Antiquity, and recast them in an Islamised form.

The tradition seems to begin with an obscure figure called Abdullah ibn Saba', who approached Ali in Kufa and worshipped him as God, much to the latter's horror and revulsion. This idea of *hulul*, by which God inhabits the body of a human figure who then makes utterances that actually come from God, would resurface from time to time during the Abbasid period and later. In particular, Gnostic Shi'is would often paint the imams as divine figures. Rather than being human, the imams were actually veils through which God appears to humanity. The Neo-platonic and possibly Manichaean background to such ideas is striking. The author of the ninth-century *Kitab al-Azilla*, 'The Book of Shadows', which allegedly contained the secret revelations of Ja'far al-Sadiq, wrote in the introduction that the soul is a divine spark imprisoned in the body. Later in the work, he proceeds to teach that Hussein did not die at Karbala. Instead, he went behind a veil and into occultation.[7]

Other ideas that reoccur in Gnostic Shi'ism are the transmigration of souls and antinomianism: the belief that the Sharia has a spiritual meaning, and that therefore there is no need to follow its precepts literally. We have already seen an example of a teaching that owed something to this in the proclamation by the Assassins that the Sharia had become redundant and should actually be proscribed. One common feature of Gnostic Shi'ism was that its truths were known only to a spiritual elect, and should not be imparted to ordinary believers who would be incapable of grasping them.

Two points should be made when we consider Gnostic Shi'ism. The first is that, because of the principle of *taqiyya*, it is difficult to know how widely such 'secret teachings' and Gnostic Shi'i ideas spread. The other is that the idea of a secret teaching was not confined to Gnostic Shi'is. There is no doubt that the Ismailis of the Fatimid Caliphate saw themselves as an initiated elect, and described themselves as the *awliya*, or 'friends', of God. To their enemies, such as the great Sunni polymath Abu Hamid al-Ghazali (d. 1111) who achieved a synthesis between Sunnism and Sufism, the Fatimid Caliph and his followers were the *batinis* or 'interiorists' who taught a pernicious, secret doctrine. Al-Ghazali may have been the arch opponent of the *batinis*; but he himself, from the pinnacle of his immense prestige as a mainstream Sunni religious scholar, taught some religious teachings were just for the elect, and too dangerous to impart to ordinary believers.[8]

We will come across Gnostic Shi'ism again, but there is a small Shi'i sect from a Gnostic background that is very much alive today. These are the Alawis, who used to be more commonly called the Nusayris. Alawism still preserves elements of an unbroken tradition of the Gnostic Shi'i trend. Alawi religious scholars still read, for instance, the Book of Shadows.[9] The sect can be traced back to the historical period when the split into Twelver and Ismaili branches occurred. Their beliefs stem from the teaching of Ibn Nusayr, who was (or claimed to be) a pupil of the Eleventh Imam, al-Hasan al-Askari, and based his doctrines on revelations which he said al-Hasan al-Askari imparted to him. These teachings were propagated by Abu Abdallah al-Khasibi, who lived in the Shi'i centre of Karkh in Buyid Baghdad, where he was a court poet and presumably taught his doctrine for a while. He subsequently became an itinerant preacher, passing through Mosul and ending up in Aleppo, where he died in 969.

At that time Aleppo was under the Hamdanid dynasty, who were Shi'i and to whose ruler, Sayf al-Dawla, al-Khasibi dedicated his 'Book of the Great Guidance' (*Kitab al-Hidaya al-Kubra*). His grandson Abu Said al-Tabarani moved to Lattakia in 1032, which was then temporarily part of the Byzantine Empire. He and his followers succeeded in converting many of the people in the coastal mountains of Syria, where Alawism survives and thrives to this day – as it does in some parts of the nearby Orontes valley. This was despite later attempts to convert them to Sunnism by Egyptian Mamluk sultans (rulers who were selected by a self-perpetuating caste of slave soldiers) such as Baybars, who finally drove the Crusaders from their last possessions in Greater Syria. Since the thirteenth century, they have also faced a fatwa by the famous Hanbali scholar Ibn Taymiyyah, who described them as more heretical than idolaters, and authorised jihad against them.[10] The Ottomans, however, recognised them as a separate group with their own legal practices. With typical Ottoman pragmatism, they also taxed them and conscripted them into the army.

Alawis practise *taqiyya* when expedient and do not disseminate their beliefs beyond circles of sheikhs who are the repositories of the sect's truths – even though among these sheikhs, too, there are gradations in knowledge. A word of caution is therefore necessary before mentioning their secret teaching. Yet it seems that they believe that there have been seven cycles of eras of humanity, in each of which God has made Himself manifest in human form and through two persons who emanate from Him. In the last such era, Ali represents God (the *ma'na*, or 'meaning'), Muhammad is the divine name (*ism*) or veil (*hijab*), and Salman al-Farisi (one of Muhammad's Companions) is the gate (*bab*) through which believers may reach the divine essence. Subsequently, God also revealed himself through al-Hasan al-Askari (the Eleventh Imam of the Twelvers), for whom Ibn Nusayr was the *bab*.[11]

VII

It will have been noted that most of the Shi'i sects described in this chapter share the idea of a secret, esoteric teaching – which was part and parcel of the interiorisation of the spiritual life – that is known only to an elect among the believers. There was one other trend in the early centuries of Islam where similar ideas appeared. This was in the pious movement we call Sufism. It is not a simple matter to characterise Sufism, but it must be stressed that it is not a sect. Although it is generally seen as part of Sunni Islam, it straddles both the Sunni and Shi'i traditions and could be a vehicle for Muslims to move away from one sect towards the other, or even to join the other sect. Sufism often transcended sectarian divides, and brought people from different traditions together. It is therefore unsurprising that Sufis have converted many non-Muslims to Islam across all the centuries of Islamic history and in most (if not all) parts of the Muslim world. They often allowed the new converts to retain old customs and elements of their former beliefs, which were recast in an Islamic guise. They have therefore tended to be very tolerant of diversity.

There is something mysterious about the origins of Sufism, which scholars have never completely explained, although it has unquestionably always been a movement among devout Muslims who deepened their religious experience through meditation on the Qur'an and following the example of the Prophet. The Arabic word *sufi* is generally accepted to come from *suf*, meaning wool, but *sufi* is perhaps a rather unusual-looking word in Arabic, and its etymology was a topic for discussion among Sufis at an early date. Sufis frequently wore wool, possibly in emulation of the Christian monks and ascetics of the Fertile Crescent with whom they discussed spiritual matters and for whom they frequently had a profound respect. Although the earliest figures actually called Sufis date from the eighth century, they trace their spiritual lineages back to the Prophet. The movement seems to have started as a reaction to the worldliness of the Umayyad polity. The words 'dervish' and 'fakir', which literally mean 'poor' in Persian and Arabic respectively, are synonyms for 'Sufi'.

Muhammad was seen by Sufis as having imparted esoteric wisdom to Ali, while other members of the Prophet's family were believed to have been endowed with mystical insights and to have pursued mystical practices – something that is reminiscent of Shiʿism.[12] The undeniable closeness between Muhammad and Ali is reflected in some Sufi ideas that could easily act as a door to Shiʿism, although not everyone who reflected on that closeness and was inspired by it went through that door. Veneration of Ali and the Prophet's family, and feelings of tenderness towards them, were widespread among all Muslims, and certainly not confined to Shiʿis.

Some key Sufi ideas have been traced back to Jaʿfar al-Sadiq, whose commentary on the Qurʾan teaches that there are four levels of understanding of the sacred text. These comprise a hierarchy: the level of the common people who understand only its literal meaning; the elite who can interpret it on a metaphorical level; the saints who are inspired with insights which come as flashes of grace; and the prophets who comprehend the reality. Such ideas would be developed in parallel by Shiʿis and Sufis, who would sometimes cross-fertilise.[13] Later, as Sufism was systematised by writers such as Abu Nasr al-Sarraj (d. 988), Abu Qasim al-Qushayri (d. 1072), and perhaps most of all by Abu Hamid al-Ghazali (d. 1111), it continued to spread and to penetrate more deeply right across Muslim society. One effect of this was the appearance of the Sufi 'brotherhoods' or 'orders' that emerged in the early twelfth century, although their origins were earlier and they claimed to trace their spiritual lineages back to the Prophet. Annemarie Schimmel, a prominent scholar of Sufism, suggested that the phenomenon of the Sufi brotherhoods may have been linked to the struggle between Sunni Islam and the *batinis*:

Gradually, the preaching of the Sufis began to attract wider groups of people. The basic rules of mystical education were elaborated during the eleventh century, and in a comparatively short period of time – beginning in the early twelfth century – mystical fraternities that included adepts from all strata of society were emerging. How the crystallization process itself worked is difficult to explain; it must have been a response to the inner need of the community that was not being met by the scholasticism of orthodox theologians; people craved a more intimate and personal relationship with God and with the Prophet. One cannot exclude the possibility that the orders came into existence as a movement to counter the strong Ismaili-Batini influence against which Ghazzali had fought so relentlessly. The esoteric interpretation of Islam, which threatened its very structure, was, thus, replaced by the interiorization of orthodox Muslim teaching.[14]

An example of how in later centuries Sufism could seem to come remarkably close to Shi'ism, while technically remaining Sunni, can be seen in the Bektashi order. Its founder, Hajji Bektash, was said to have been born in eastern Iran in 1247 and to have travelled to Anatolia. The order would become very influential among the crack Janissary troops of the Ottoman Empire, the most feared warriors in the service of the great Sunni sultan, but its teachings were full of Gnostic Shi'i ideas. Bektashi poetry celebrates Ali and the other Twelve Imams alongside the Prophet. God, Muhammad and Ali are also linked together in a way reminiscent of the Christian trinity, while Bektashis consider the Iranian ruler Shah Ismail (who made Iran a Twelver Shi'i country, and whom we will encounter in the next chapter) to be one of their greatest poets.[15]

CHAPTER SIX

How Iran Became Shi'i

I

The sack of Baghdad in 1258 by Hulegu the Mongol is one of those world-shattering events that are used to define the end of a period of history and the beginning of a new one. Yet dig a little deeper and a slightly different picture emerges. The event was certainly devastating for Sunni Muslims, but as the marker of the end of an era it was in many ways symbolic rather than causative.

As we have seen, the Abbasid Caliph had conferred legitimacy on many Sunni rulers. Yet even if his religious claim to be the leader of the Muslim community was absolute, it was contested. Apart from the opposition from the various Shi'i groups (and the Kharijis), there had already been rival Sunni caliphates that had existed simultaneously with the Abbasids in Baghdad. Both the Spanish Umayyads of Cordoba (929–1031) and the Almohads of North Africa (1130–1269) had established a caliphate within the geographical areas they aspired to control. Although they did not assert a putative jurisdiction over all Muslims in the manner of the Abbasids, their description of themselves as caliphs was a denial of the universality of the caliph in Baghdad.

On a practical level, the extinction of the Baghdad Caliphate made little if any difference for Sunni Muslims when it came to the formulation of the rules of the Sharia or the doctrines of Muslim religious belief. As we have seen, whatever authority the caliphs may have had to define these had long since ended. Yet the concept of the caliphate would live on among Sunnis, since it was still useful as a tool for legitimacy. The

Mamluk rulers in Cairo were sultans, that is to say rulers who swore to uphold the Sharia within their dominions and consequently claimed a God-given right to rule. They appointed a member of the Abbasid family to adorn their court as a puppet or shadow caliph, and he would be wheeled out for public relations purposes when appropriate. His authority was solemnly exploited to invest every new sultan, and he would sometimes accompany the sultan on campaigns. Occasionally, distant Sunni rulers would send gifts and request a letter of investiture from the caliph in Cairo, as Muhammad bin Tughluq, the sultan of Delhi, did in the first half of the fourteenth century. But, at the same time, other rulers such as the Tunisian Hafsid dynasty would claim the title of caliph for themselves. The Ottomans will be discussed in the next chapter, but the Ottoman sultan Murad I (r. 1360–89) would also assert that he was caliph. Despite this, the title was not used systematically by his successors until the late eighteenth century. Mehmed II, the conqueror of Constantinople (modern-day Istanbul) in 1453, seems never to have used it. For the Ottomans, who will be discussed in the following chapter, the status of sultan was always what really mattered. This was also the case with most other Sunni rulers.

A Sunni ruler took his legitimacy from the injunction in the Qur'an 'to command the good and forbid the wrong' – in other words, from upholding the Sharia in his dominions. This was the hallmark of a sultan, which was already the status to which most Sunni rulers aspired before 1258. The destruction of the Abbasid Caliphate thus made little difference except on the symbolic level, but on that symbolic level it was of massive importance. A century and a half before Hulegu's execution of the last Abbasid, the great theologian and mystic Abu Hamid al-Ghazali had written a blistering polemic against the Ismailism of the Fatimids. The work is known as the *Mustazhiri*, because it was dedicated to al-Mustazhir, the Abbasid Caliph of the day. Al-Ghazali contrasts him, as the true imam, with the false, *batini* imam in Cairo. Yet he opines that there must be an imam in every age. What if there were no imam of the age? Al-Ghazali answers, 'The conflict of wills and passions would lead to the neglect of the afterlife and the triumph of vice over virtue, and of the lowly over the learned with the consequent dissolution of religious and secular checks. So it is clear that the Imam is an indispensable necessity of men.'[1] Now Sunnis would find that

Ghazali had been proved wrong, and that their faith and way of life would survive the end of the caliphate.

Yet the feeling of loss caused by the sacrilegious execution of Musta'sim, the last Abbasid Caliph and his family, was amplified by the sheer horror that Muslims (and non-Muslims) experienced if they were unfortunate enough to live in the lands conquered by the Mongols. Apart from Baghdad and large areas of Iraq, the Mongols devastated Transoxania (roughly equivalent to present-day Uzbekistan), Khorasan and much of the rest of the eastern Islamic world. This included the probably unintended destruction of irrigated agricultural land both in Iraq and in sparsely watered regions of the Iranian plateau, where much agriculture depended on carefully maintained channels such as the underground systems known as *qanawat*. When peasants were slaughtered or fled in terror, there was nobody left with the skills needed to maintain irrigation works.

What may have been worst of all was the sheer indifference Mongols showed to Muslim sensibilities and to Islam in general, which Muslims would have found profoundly shocking. Muslims were well used to rulers who shortened their own lives by over-indulgence in alcohol and general hedonism. In this respect, the Mongols were no different from many Abbasids and Seljuqs, to say nothing of some Umayyads. What was different about the Mongols was the disregard they had for any and all religions apart from their own shamanistic beliefs and superstitions. Individual Mongols might convert to other religions. Thus, the general Kitbogha, who was sent by Hulegu to conquer Syria, was a Nestorian Christian, but as far as the Mongols were concerned his choice of religion was purely his own affair and nothing more. Similarly, when the Mongol ruler Teguder (r. 1282–84) converted to Islam, it did not imply that he would now re-establish Islam to the place it had enjoyed before the Mongol invasions.

None of this should be seen as a sign of an anachronistically modern tolerance by the Mongols; on the contrary, it was disdainful indifference or contempt. The indigenous beliefs of the Mongols were essentially pre-monotheistic. For Teguder's fellow Mongols, his conversion meant nothing except for an uneasy feeling in the back of their minds that he might now be reluctant to attack and plunder the territories of other Muslim rulers. In any event, he was soon deposed and executed in one of the Mongols' many dynastic disputes that probably had nothing to do with religion. When Hulegu himself had died in 1265, he was buried with treasure to take with him into the next world, and slaves were sacrificed to accompany him there. It would not be until 1295 that the Mongols adopted Islam. This was when Ghazan, a great-grandson of Hulegu who had already converted to Islam, took power. By this time, the Mongols were coming to realise that taxation was a more efficient way to raise revenue than letting their soldiers plunder and destroy the resources of Iraq, the Iranian plateau and the other the lands they ruled. Becoming Muslims was just one way of integrating themselves into the societies of these lands. Unsurprisingly, many Muslims doubted the sincerity of their conversion.

II

After the extinction of the Fatimid Caliphate in 1171, the last Ismaili militants were the sect known as the Assassins. Hulegu besieged them in their mountain fastnesses of western Iran and crushed their resistance in 1256, two years before he turned his attention to Baghdad. The Egyptian Mamluks would take the Assassins' strongholds in the coastal mountains of Syria in 1271–73. As we saw in Chapter Four, before the arrival of the Mongols, Sunnis had regained the dominance they had been in danger of losing to the Ismailis. Yet now that most of the eastern Islamic lands were ruled by non-Muslims they found themselves for a few decades on a level playing field with other religions and sects. They shared this playing field with Twelver Shi'is as well as with Christians, Jews, Zoroastrians, Buddhists and others. Buddhists – or particular forms of Buddhism – seem to have initially received more favour from Mongol rulers than the other religions, but this ended when Ghazan became the Khan (ruler) of the Mongols in 1295. He expelled Buddhists and reinstituted the protected status and disabilities under the Sharia for Christians and Jews.

Despite Ghazan being a Muslim, Islam took a while to become firmly established among the Mongol leadership. Oljeitu, who was Ghazan's brother and successor and ruled from 1304–16, had Christian and Buddhist phases before he became a Muslim, and may have faced calls to

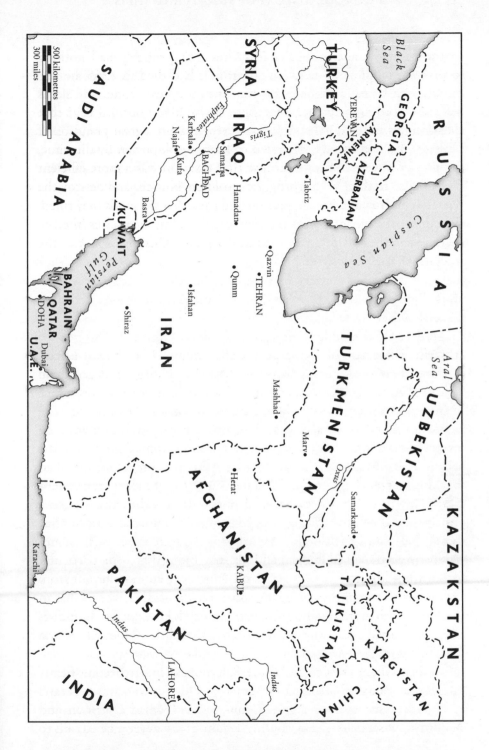

MAP OF IRAN AND NEIGHBOURING COUNTRIES SHOWING
IMPORTANT CITIES, AND WITH MODERN POLITICAL BOUNDARIES

restore the old shamanism of Genghis Khan. For a while at least, he seems to have been undecided between Sunnism and Shi'ism, but the scholar known as Allamah al-Hilli converted him to Twelver Shi'ism. Oljeitu had the names of the twelve imams put on his coins, and he planned a mausoleum in his capital at Sultaniya to which the remains of Ali and Hussein would be brought from Iraq. But this never happened. Instead, the grand mausoleum became his own. It seems that Oljeitu's preference for the Islam of the Twelvers brought a reaction from the Sunni majority. There were disturbances, especially in Isfahan where parts of the city were destroyed in riots.[2] This is probably the reason why, after Oljeitu's death, the Mongols reverted permanently to Sunnism. Sunnism was the sect of the majority of Muslims across the lands they ruled. After the mid-fourteenth-century break-up of the Mongol Empire centred on the Iranian plateau known as the Il-Khanate, most of the rulers who succeeded them were Sunnis.

Twelver Shi'ism underwent significant developments in this period, and was characterised by some notable thinkers. Twelvers tended to hope that the Mongols would be their liberators from both the Abbasids and the Assassins, and it has been suggested that the vizier of the last Abbasid caliph, who happened to be a Twelver, had a part in his downfall.[3] Nasir al-Din al-Tusi, the famous mathematician and medical practitioner who was also a leading Twelver religious scholar, had been imprisoned in Alamut by the Assassins before the arrival of the Mongols, and used his time there and the night skies of the high mountains to conduct astronomical observations. The Assassins sent him as their envoy to Hulegu, hoping he would negotiate with him on their behalf, but he felt no loyalty towards them. He became the chief vizier and confidant to Hulegu and his successor, Abaqa. Yet, although he did what he could to persuade the Mongols to favour the Twelvers, they suffered from the invasion, just as the Sunnis did. He was unable to save the shrines at Kazimayn or Karkh, the Twelver district of Baghdad, from destruction. On the other hand, in the lower Euphrates, the Twelvers of Hilla welcomed the Mongols, and even constructed a bridge across the river for them to use. As a result, their town and the shrines of Karbala and Najaf were spared.

Hilla developed into a pre-eminent place for Twelver learning during the Mongol period, becoming much more significant than either

Baghdad or the Iranian shrine city of Qumm, where Fatima, the sister of Ali al-Rida, the Eighth Imam, is buried. The man who is probably Hilla's most famous son was born in 1250/1, and saw the Mongols arrive when he was a boy. He came from a family of leading religious scholars and his father played a role in the surrender of the town. The boy became known as Allamah al-Hilli, 'the very erudite one of Hilla'. After studying with his father and uncle, he sat at the feet of the great Nasir al-Din al-Tusi. Allamah al-Hilli took himself to Oljeitu's court in Tabriz in 1305, and subsequently converted him to Twelver Shi'ism. He was able to play a role with Oljeitu similar to that which Nasir al-Din al-Tusi had played with Hulegu. So great was his learning that he earned himself a new and unprecedented title that reflected it: Ayatollah – 'The Sign of God'.

It was Allamah al-Hilli who brought the notion of *ijtihad* into Twelver Shi'ism. Hitherto, it had been a Sunni concept, and he did not try to hide his own intellectual debt to the Sunni jurist al-Shafi'i.[4] As we saw in Chapter Four, *ijtihad* meant the ability of a trusted scholar to use his knowledge of the Sharia to give a considered and independent judgement to reach a solution to an unanswered judicial question. A one-word and over-literal English translation for *ijtihad* might be 'striving', and the general idea is the expenditure of effort for a purpose. Allamah al-Hilli's own definition was 'the utmost exertion of the faculties to speculate on those questions of the law which are subject to conjecture'.[5] Neither the Prophet nor the Imams exercised *ijtihad*, because the inspiration they received from God gave them certainty. It followed that they had no use for conjecture or speculation – and *ijtihad* was actually forbidden for them, since it was preferable for them to wait for divine inspiration.

It was only when there was no prophet or imam available to consider a question that had no clear answer in the Qur'an and hadith that *ijtihad* came into play. But that meant that it was the province of scholars, who were fallible. Two eminent scholars might easily, in good faith, give different answers to the same speculative question. There was therefore a heavy burden on their shoulders, and they should revise their opinion if they were persuaded by the thoughts of other scholars, whom they had a duty to consult. Nevertheless, if they have looked into the question in good faith and to the best of their ability, they commit no sin if they are mistaken in the ruling they make. In the absence of the Imam, *kull mujtahid musib*: 'every mujtahid [i.e. a scholar who has the necessary degree of knowledge for ijtihad] is correct'.

The same applies to the unqualified laypeople who follow the teaching of a mujtahid. They, too, commit no sin when they follow his teaching, even if it is subsequently shown to have been in error on the point in question. Their consciences are clear. It is not right for laypeople to attempt *ijtihad* for themselves; they are neither required nor authorised to do so. They lack the necessary learning. Instead, every believer should seek out a mujtahid whom he can follow. He should choose one who is both learned and devout. If he has a choice of two mujtahids who fulfil both characteristics, he should choose the more learned.[6] Yet a mujtahid's opinions should be adhered to only while he is still alive. This followed naturally from the provisional nature of *ijtihad*, which, we might stress again, is only valid in the absence of the imam.

Important consequences flowed from Allamah al-Hilli's new doctrine. It meant that the process of discerning those areas of the Sharia that are a matter of conjecture must continue in every generation. In other words, Twelver teaching will always evolve and develop in those areas in which the teaching is not fixed or 'necessary', because the word of the Qur'an or hadith is clear. His new ideas also had a profound effect on the status of the scholarly religious class among the Twelvers. In practice, it gave them a status as lawgivers that, in theory, their counterparts among the Sunnis did not have. Although the Twelver mujtahids exercised no sacerdotal functions, for teaching purposes they had become a priesthood whom ordinary believers must strive to follow. In time, this would have an enormous impact on Twelver Islam.

III

The Mongols of Hulegu were followed by the last great invasion by nomadic tribes from the steppes of Central Asia. Timur, also known in English as Tamerlane or Tamburlaine, was of Mongol descent and spoke a Turkish language. Unlike Hulegu, he was a Muslim. This did not, however, mean that he was any less violent as a conqueror. He became famous for leaving pyramids of skulls outside cities that had been so foolish as to resist him, and his Muslim faith gave him convenient pretexts for some of his aggressive campaigns. He succeeded in becoming the ruler of Transoxania around 1366. For a period of more than thirty years, he then expanded his rule across Central Asia and as far west as Moscow. He went on to descend on Iran, northern India (where he sacked Delhi) and then the Middle East. Between 1399 and 1402, he stormed and pillaged Baghdad, Aleppo and Damascus. In a campaign in which he defeated the nascent Ottoman Empire and carried off its sultan in a cage, he even reached the Aegean coast before returning to his capital, Samarkand. He died in 1405 shortly after setting out to conquer China.

Timur has been contrasted with Ghengis Khan, the initiator of the wave of conquests that had brought Hulegu to Baghdad.[7] Ghengis Khan had been a state builder as well as a conqueror. He gave thought to such matters as the succession after his death and establishing a structure of government. Timur, by contrast, seems to have been concerned solely with his own position and power. The internal politics of his empire appear to have been geared solely towards ensuring that there could never be anyone able to challenge his position. Only limited power was ever granted to anyone else, and men he appointed were moved around so that they could not build up a local powerbase. When he died in 1405, his son Shahrukh established himself as sultan after a few years of dynastic civil war, but neither he nor his successors ever managed to gain control of the western regions of Timur's empire. Shahrukh moved from Samarkand to Herat in what is now Afghanistan, which remained the capital until the death of the last Timurid, Husayn Bayqara, in 1506.

The tribes that accompanied Hulegu and Timur into the lands of Islam in search of grazing and plunder were taking part in a process of emigration from Central Asia that had continued for centuries, going back to pre-Islamic times. The peoples who crossed the Oxus river all had much in common. They were nomads accustomed to life on the steppe. Virtually every man could ride his horse into battle, and was proficient at firing a bow from the saddle. They thus presented formidable adversaries for the professional but cumbersome armies of the more organised states that they encountered, particularly when they also acquired expertise at siege warfare. They were hungry, quite literally. They had been pushed westwards by a combination of famine and pressure from invaders driving them out of their ancestral pasturelands.

We do not know much about the Islam adopted by the wild, uncouth and illiterate Turkic tribes that flooded into the lands of Islam over many generations, including those that would become the Ak Koyunlu or 'White Sheep' confederation and would be very significant for the history of Iran. Important chapters in their story are lost to history, often beyond recovery. For instance, we do not even know whether and to what extent the tribes of the Ak Koyunlu were already in Iran and eastern Anatolia before the Mongol invasions, or whether (as scholars tend to think is more probable) they came there in the wake of Hulegu. When such tribes adopted Islam, they often did not know what it involved – and often did not care. They frequently subscribed to the teachings of the Hanafi doctrinal law school, but in many instances it took them generations before they began to follow its precepts properly. It seems that for them becoming Muslim was often adopting a badge of identity more than anything else. It was probably similar to the adoption of Christianity by many of the 'Barbarians' who crossed the Rhine or Danube to invade the Roman Empire, and saw their conversion as a step towards becoming accepted as part of the new and richer world they had entered.

The Turkish tribes were regularly introduced to Islam by wandering Sufi ascetics and even more shadowy figures. These figures frequently preached a version of Islam that was mixed with heterodox practices and beliefs. They would have had much in common with the shamans who were the holy men of the steppes. Both shamans and Sufis worked miracles. Some Sufis could be extremely lax in their interpretation of the Sharia. They were followers of a path to the Divine that many Muslims rejected as eccentric, dubious in terms of compliance with the Sharia, and sometimes downright blasphemous. Those Sufis who are sometimes referred to as the 'ecstatic mystics', such as Abu Yazid al-Bistami (d. 870s) and Husayn bin Mansur al-Hallaj (d. 922), made statements that appeared to suggest that they saw themselves as God, or at least were so consumed by the Divine Presence that they had no separate, personal consciousness. Such figures caused widespread horror, and were publicly rejected by many religious scholars. Hallaj was crucified for alleged heresy. But they were revered by later generations of Sufis who considered their only crime (if they had indeed committed any crime at all) was to make utterances that confused unenlightened, ordinary believers.

The key relationship in Sufism was between a teacher and his disciples. As has already been mentioned in the last chapter, this led eventually to the appearance of brotherhoods or orders. These were known as *tariqas* (literally: 'pathways'), which often had a considerable degree of formal organisation. The *tariqas* claimed a spiritual lineage that they traced back through the great teaching masters to the greatest of them all, Junayd of Baghdad, who had died in 910. Beyond him, they continued their spiritual pedigree through the first generations that had adopted the epithet of Sufi and, beyond them, to eminent Companions of the Prophet, and ultimately the Prophet himself.

Here, as in many other contexts, Ali is a key figure. His memory was venerated by many *tariqas* which claimed him, in some sense, as their first teacher after the Prophet. He was seen as the great exemplar to be followed. This was not just because of his many outstanding qualities but, above all else, because of his closeness to the Prophet. At the same time, he was revered by groups of urban young men who were often craftsmen carrying on a particular trade together, and who shared many bonds in common. They set up organisations that had something in common with the guilds of medieval Europe. Ali was seen as the exemplar of all the manly qualities to which their members should aspire.

None of this emphasis on Ali implies a link with Shi'ism. Reverence for Ali was natural –indeed, essential – for Sunnis, even though they did not see Ali as the First Imam. But looking to Ali as a great exemplar could open the door to the propagation of Shi'i teachings and ideas. Some *tariqas* also listed the Shi'i imams as figures in their spiritual pedigrees. This might, perhaps, be said to have made that door to Shi'ism even easier to open. At the same time, the belief among Sufis that there are higher forms of religious knowledge, known only to the adepts, could also be said to have parallels in Shi'ism.

It is probably wrong to see the divide between Sunnism and Shi'ism as clearly understood by the Turkmen tribes. One major Turkmen ruler, Jahan Shah (who died in 1438), produced coins with Shi'i formulae on one side and the names of Abu Bakr, Umar and Uthman on the other. Was this confusion, or was he just hedging his bets? Sufism is generally considered to have been a Sunni rather than a Shi'i phenomenon, but once again the distinction was not always clear-cut. The great Nasir al-Din al-Tusi could compose a treatise on the Sufi mystical path and dedicate it to his contemporary the Sunni vizier and historian Juvayni, while still being a major teacher of Twelver doctrine. This treatise retained the esteem of Twelvers after his death.[8]

The martial prowess of the Turkmen tribes made them the most formidable soldiers in Iran and the surrounding areas at that time. Their reverence for the figure of Ali, their indifference to formulations of religious doctrine, their attraction towards preachers who worked miracles and taught doctrines known only to a few, and the natural pull nomadic tribesmen can feel towards a charismatic leader – these were all factors that would make the tribes ripe for recruitment by a Gnostic Shi'i warrior who claimed that he was, in some sense, a God-King.

IV

The political power of the Safavids, the dynasty that was to make Iran a predominantly Shi'i country, really began during the rule of Uzun Hasan, who was the leader of the Ak Koyunlu, 'White Sheep', confederation. The Ak Koyunlu dominated eastern Anatolia and the areas further east after the Timurid Empire fell apart. Uzun Hasan took power after triumphing in a lengthy period of dynastic civil wars and defeating his main rival in 1457. He moved his capital to Tabriz a few years later. He was an empire builder, and went on to defeat Abu Said, the last of the Timurids, in 1469. He then gained control of Iraq and most of what is now Iran as far east as Fars and Kirman.

The Safavids, as a political force, can thus be traced back only to the second half of the 1400s. Their empire came to an end in 1722. It did not spread over such a vast expanse of territories as their Ottoman neighbours, nor did it last as long (the Ottoman Empire ended only after its defeat in the First World War). Another contrast with the Ottomans is that the Safavids did not become a maritime power, although they took control of the predominantly Shi'i island of Bahrain in 1602. Being centred on the arid Iranian plateau, the empire's agricultural base was relatively small, and it was heavily dependent financially on a single commodity: silk. But it is very important for our story. This is because the Safavids made Twelver Shi'ism their state religion. During their rule, Twelver Shi'ism became the predominant Muslim sect in Iran, and has remained so ever since. If this had not happened, Twelver Shi'ism might today be the majority sect only in relatively small areas such as the Jebel Amil region of south Lebanon, the shrine cities of Kufa and Najaf in Iraq, and Bahrain and its hinterland on the Arabian coast. The significance of Twelver Shi'ism in terms of the demographics of the Muslim world as a whole might not be much greater than that of Zaydism in Yemen, the Alawis in Syria, or the Ismaili sects and their offshoots such as the Druze. The story of how Iran became a predominantly Shi'i rather than a Sunni nation therefore requires some explanation.

The Safavids were originally Sunni. Their name comes from a Sufi brotherhood founded by a certain Sheikh Safi, who died in 1334. The brotherhood was probably influential in the Ak Koyonlu Empire at an earlier stage, but there is little that attracts the attention of historians to it until Junayd, the son of its fourth leader, was exiled and spent twelve years wandering in eastern Anatolia and northern Syria during the period 1447–59.[9] On these travels he picked up some obscure, unorthodox beliefs. He may well have learned them from Gnostic Shi'is. It is perfectly possible, for instance, that he encountered Alawi teachings while wandering through northern Syria.

He declared that he was a descendant of Ali, gathering a large number of followers from Turkmen tribes who passionately devoted themselves to him and saw him virtually as a God-King. They believed that Junayd, together with Ali himself, shared in the divine nature. Whatever the origin of the beliefs that Junayd had adopted, and which essentially led him to consider himself to be divine, on his return Uzun Hasan offered him his sister as a wife. A son, Haydar, was born of the union, but Junayd was killed in battle soon afterwards by a Muslim ruler whose territory he was seeking to cross so as to attack the Christians of Georgia on a campaign of jihad.

Haydar was brought up at the court of Uzun Hasan, who subsequently gave him a daughter in marriage, just as he had given his sister to the boy's father. These two marriages brought the Safavid brotherhood into the heart of Ak Koyunlu politics at a time when the confederation was turning in on itself and was greatly weakened by the almost inevitable round of civil wars that followed the death of Uzun Hasan in 1472. Haydar is said to have devised a red or crimson headgear for his followers, who now became known as the Kizilbash, or 'redheads'. The headgear had twelve gussets, each of which, it would be said, represented one of the twelve imams. Haydar's son Sultan Ali succeeded his father as head of the Safavid brotherhood, but was imprisoned and killed in 1494. Another son, Ibrahim, replaced him, but a militant faction followed his younger brother Ismail, who was then only seven. Ismail had to flee for his life from the Ak Koyunlu dominions.

The story of this boy is truly extraordinary. In 1499, when he was still only twelve years old, he appeared leading an army of Kizilbash tribesmen against the Ak Koyunlu. Two years later, in 1501, when he was about fourteen, he defeated the last effective Ak Koyunlu ruler, Alwand, at the Battle of Sharur, and took Tabriz. This is traditionally seen as the starting point of the Safavid Empire. Ismail immediately embarked on a dizzying campaign of conquest. He took Hamadan from another Ak Koyunlu prince, then turned west into the parts of eastern Anatolia around Diyarbakir and Mardin. He then marched into Baghdad in 1508, before extending his control all the way down to the Persian Gulf.

As we have seen, Ismail was a grandson of Uzun Hasan and was followed by men who gave him a semi-divine status. Their religion was essentially a Turkmen paganism, 'which Safavid propaganda merely provided with a thin Islamic varnish and "rendered Sufi and Shi'ite"', as one scholar has put it.[10] It may well be that at this stage Ismail envisaged establishing an empire for himself like that of the Ak Koyunlu, and he should certainly be seen as their successor. But he also conquered territories that the Ak Koyunlu had never taken. To the east, he was faced by another aggressive Turkish tribal confederation, the Uzbeks. Ismail marched into Khorasan, and defeated and killed the Uzbek leader, Muhammad Shaybani, near Marv. He established the River Oxus as his eastern boundary. Following a Mongol tradition, he had Muhammad Shaybani's skull mounted in gold as a drinking cup, which he sent as a present to the man who was his greatest and most powerful enemy: the Ottoman sultan.

This may not have been wise. His victory over the Uzbeks marked the high watermark of his conquests. Soon afterwards, a Safavid army was defeated at Ghujduwan by Uzbek forces that had crossed the Oxus. Although the Uzbeks retreated when Ismail approached in person, he was about to suffer a crushing defeat at the hands of the Ottomans. The Ottoman Sultan Yavuz Selim, best known in English as Selim the Grim, was worried by the spread of Kizilbash sentiment among tribes in Anatolia. When revolts broke out in 1511–12, they received encouragement from Ismail. The sultan had real grounds to fear that the tribes would abandon the Ottomans for Ismail, and marched east with a formidable army after massacring the Kizilbash in eastern Anatolia. Ismail at first adopted a scorched-earth policy and withdrew, but he accepted battle at Chaldiran in 1514, even though he was outnumbered. His army was composed of mounted archers, while the Ottomans were fielding artillery and musket-bearing Janissaries, as well as cavalry. Ismail suffered a devastating defeat in which many of his senior officers, as well as the highest Twelver religious dignitary in his empire, were killed. Selim the Grim even took Ismail's capital, Tabriz, but the Ottoman army was now too far from its bases for him to annex the city, and he decided to withdraw. Nevertheless, the defeat at Chaldiran seems to have ended Ismail's expansion for good. He lived for another ten years, but he would never lead an army into battle again.

Proof that Ismail posed to the Kizilbash as a semi-divine figure can be found in the poetry he composed under a pseudonym in his native language, Azeri Turkish. He considered himself to be the long-awaited Mahdi who will usher in the End Times, as well as a physical manifestation of Muhammad, Ali and the twelve imams. They, like him, are veils in which the divine light has clothed itself:

> I am identical to God...
> Come, look now at the divine truth, thou erring blind man:
> I am the Absolute Primal Moving Cause of whom men speak.[11]

Before Chaldiran, Ismail had never lost a battle. It would seem reasonable to suppose that the defeat might have dented this belief in his semi-divine status. Nevertheless, as has been pointed out by David Morgan, a historian of medieval Iran and the Mongols, his father and grandfather had also enjoyed a semi-divine status but had been defeated and killed in battle without this diminishing the Kizilbash movement's fervour. What Ismail's survival after Chaldiran does show is that the tribes were not the only basis of his regime's support, although by being their messianic leader Ismail skilfully harnessed their feelings of alienation from oppressive rulers. Yet he was also aware that, as a Chinese observer put it, 'the empire has been conquered on horseback, but it cannot be governed on horseback'.[12] He received support and assistance from Persian-speaking bureaucrats who had administered the area under previous regimes, including the Ak Koyunlu. In fact, during Ismail's rise the vizier at the Ak Koyunlu court had defected to him and encouraged him to attack his masters.[13] For the ten years that remained to him after Chaldiran (he died in 1524 at the age of only thirty-seven), he set about establishing effective administration over the territories he ruled. He also forged ahead with the project to turn his dominions into a Twelver empire.

Historians speculate over why he did this. The most likely reason is that it was a logical response to a crucial dilemma. On the one hand, he was the ruler of a large, predominantly Sunni empire. On the other, his powerbase consisted of fanatical Turkmen tribesmen who saw him as a God-King. We should remember that an adolescent boy who claims that, in some sense, he is God and who is followed by hosts of fiercely loyal tribesmen who are prepared to die for him in battle, does not look like a Muslim of either the Sunni or Shi'i persuasion. In fact, he does not look like a Muslim at all. The phenomenon of the young Ismail can only be understood against the backdrop of the epic story of the coming of the Turkmen tribes to the lands of Islam and their assimilation into that world, which we have sketched out above. Rule by a man who claimed some kind of divinity would have been anathema to the predominantly Sunni, Persian-speaking bureaucrats on whom he relied to collect taxes and administer the cities, as well as to the sedentary populations under their control.

At the same time, like any other ruler, he would have had to tend his powerbase. Attempts to impose or enforce the regulations of the Sharia had often been made by rulers with the aim to transform the basis of their rule. A taxation-based machinery of government was preferable to relying on the support of fickle tribes in search of opportunities for plunder. Ismail would have been very conscious that, when rulers attempted to impose the Sharia on tribes, this frequently led to revolts. Could it be that he saw adopting Twelver Shi'ism as a neat solution, a middle way between the Sunnism of the cities and agricultural areas, and the Gnostic ideas of the nomadic Turkmen? He would cease to behave as a God-King, but he could still claim a status superior to other rulers as a descendant of Ali and the imams. In fact, he still went beyond the tenets of Twelver Shi'ism. He saw himself as the political representative of the Hidden Imam, and forced his subjects to adopt this view. Nevertheless, the old ideas of the Kizilbash took a while to die. In 1555, Ismail's successor, Tahmasp, had to reject the attempt by some enthusiasts to proclaim him the Mahdi in succession to his father. The men who publicly advocated this were executed.

The imposition of Twelver Shi'ism was a top-down process. Ismail began by declaring it the compulsory form of Islam in his dominions as soon as he took Tabriz in 1501. For good measure, he also adopted the ancient Iranian title of Shahanshah, 'King of kings'. He ordered the ritual cursing of the first three caliphs, and this was followed up with persecutions of Sunnis – including burnings at the stake and other grisly executions when necessary – in areas over which his armies gained control. A genealogical table was produced that showed that Ismail was descended from the Seventh Imam, Musa al-Kazim. If Ismail was no longer portrayed as the Mahdi, he had become instead the representative of the Hidden Imam during his occultation – a role that claimed a universal jurisdiction over all Muslims. It may have been in response to this that the Ottoman Sultan began assertively to describe himself as the Caliph, as well as the Sultan, after the conquest of Egypt in 1517.[14]

No doubt many Muslim religious scholars in Ismail's empire would have been like the legendary Vicar of Bray: they bowed with the prevailing wind and happily changed their religious allegiance to Twelver Shi'ism so as to win preferment. Those who were willing to teach the new doctrine retained their posts; those who were not prepared to do so faced active persecution. But how could they learn the Twelver Shi'i interpretation of Islam and the Sharia? There were few scholars in Ismail's dominions with the knowledge to impart it to them. His answer was to invite learned scholars from the existing strongholds of Twelver Shi'ism: Jebel Amil in what is now Lebanon, Greater Bahrain, and the colleges at Hilla in Iraq. This was continued by his son and successor, Tahmasp, and would be the start of a long-lasting process of scholarly interchange between Twelvers in the Arabic- and Persian-speaking worlds that continues to this day. It must have taken some time for Shi'ism to percolate down through society, but the Shi'i-fication of the Safavid Empire seems to have been irrevocable, if incomplete, by the time the Safavids collapsed in 1722.

Only one Safavid, Ismail II, tried to revert to Sunnism in 1576–77, but he did not succeed.

The leading scholar Ismail persuaded to come to his empire was Sheikh Ali al-Muhaqqiq al-Karaki, who was from the Beqaa valley in what is now Lebanon. He had also studied at the school of Hilla in Iraq. He followed Allamah al-Hilli's teaching on *ijtihad*, and brought to the Safavid Empire the vision that the qualified religious scholars could perform many functions of the Hidden Imam during his absence. Twelvers had found the congregational prayers on Fridays problematic during the imam's absence, since only the imam was entitled to lead them. Now, al-Muhaqqiq al-Karaki taught that it was not just permissible for a qualified scholar to lead them, but a duty incumbent on him. The Twelver clergy were fast becoming a vital element in the Safavid state. They were to develop a hold over Safavid society.

V

An important lesson the Safavids learned from Chaldiran was the danger of offering battle to an invader. Although the Safavid Empire was much smaller than that of the Russian tsars, it presented some of the same challenges for an invader. Problems of logistics made it difficult to conquer if an invader was met with a scorched-earth policy and the defenders withdrew without offering battle. Although the Ottomans won back Iraq from Ismail's successor, Tahmasp, repeated Ottoman invasions of Azerbaijan often merely led to the occupation of Tabriz for the remainder of the campaigning season, since the Ottoman troops needed to return home for the winter. The Safavid capital was moved east to Qazvin, which was harder for the Ottomans to reach. There was a similar but less formidable threat from the Uzbeks to the east and north east of the Safavid Empire. Against these enemies, too, strategic withdrawal generally worked.

The greatest Safavid ruler after Ismail was Abbas I, who came to the throne in 1588 at only a slightly less tender age than Ismail himself (Abbas was sixteen). Shah Abbas soon showed his mettle by ordering the death of the Kizilbash leader Murshid Quli Khan, who was meant to be his mentor and a kind of regent: in other words, someone who was intended to control the young shah. By the time of his death in 1629 he had won back virtually all the territories that had been lost to the Ottomans and Uzbeks in the years since the death of Shah Ismail. He also transferred the capital to Isfahan, even further away from the Ottomans than Qazvin, and gained a greater degree of control over the Kizilbash leaders. Determined to break his almost complete dependency on them, Abbas set up a permanent army of slave soldiers of Caucasian origin – especially from Armenia and Georgia – as a counterweight to the Kizilbash tribesmen. They were paid from the revenues from crown lands, including whole provinces that had formerly been in Kizilbash hands. He also attempted to disperse some of the tribes by settling them in different parts of the empire. The Kizilbash remained important, but they were no longer the only source of fighting men for the empire.

The shrine of the Imam Ali al-Rida at Mashhad had been destroyed by the Uzbeks, but Abbas made a pilgrimage there on foot from Isfahan, a journey he completed in twenty-eight days. He afterwards restored the shrine to its full glory. He also built a madrasa (school) and a hostel at Qumm, which once again became a major place for pilgrimage as well as a popular burial place for the sayyids, or descendants of the Prophet. At the same time, the empire enjoyed a cultural flowering. Isfahan was adorned with beautiful new buildings. Illuminated manuscripts, painting and ceramics all flourished. In fact, his reign is often described as the high point of Persian painting. A philosophical movement also appeared. This was known as the school of Isfahan. It combined Neo-platonism, Sufi illuminationist thought and Twelver theology. Among its achievements was to ensure that the logical tools and philosophical ideas that had taken root in the Islamic world as a result of translations into Arabic from ancient Greek would continue to develop in the Twelver world. In the early 1600s, Shah Abbas extended his empire to the island of Bahrain and its coastal hinterland. These were already predominantly Shi'i areas. He then turned his attention westwards, and drove the Ottomans out of Iraq. This enabled him to visit the tomb of Hussein as a pilgrim and to restore the shrines of the other imams in Iraq. He also made his sectarian leanings clear. The Sunni shrines of Abu Hanifa, the great scholar of the Sharia and founder of the Hanafi doctrinal law school, and the Sunni mystic Abd al-Qadir al-Jilani were sacked, while much of the Sunni notable class of Baghdad was massacred or enslaved.

The era of Abbas was the highpoint of the Safavid Empire, but the empire would have virtually another century of existence. The governmental machine he set up served the empire well and kept it functioning for many years. He died in 1629. Without his forceful presence, a measure of decline was almost inevitable. In 1639, the Persians lost Iraq once again to the Ottomans. Nevertheless, the external threats to the empire were containable. Internal tensions brought about its end, possibly assisted by a period during which there were no major wars, which may have led to neglect of the armed forces.

VI

Muhammad Baqir al-Majlisi was the Sheikh al-Islam, the most notable religious scholar in the Safavid Empire, during the second half of the seventeenth century. He enforced a strict interpretation of the Shi'i form of the Sharia and produced a vast compendium of Shi'i traditions attributed to the imams for use by scholars. He was a hammer of Sunnis and Sufis, as well as an important figure in completing the imposition of Shi'ism as the national religion. He has been described as a kind of grand inquisitor who 'led an operation to cleanse the Shi'a in Iran of all trace of Sufism, philosophy and gnosis'.[15] His excess of zeal may have been a factor that led to tensions in the early eighteenth century in parts of the empire that remained Sunni and which are today in Afghanistan. A rebellion occurred among the Ghilzai Afghans in Kandahar. They marched west, defeating the Safavid army and besieging Sultan Husayn, the last Safavid shah, in Isfahan. When the city surrendered, their leader, Ghilzai Mahmud, was proclaimed shah but was unable to gain control of large areas of the country, while the Russians and Ottomans took advantage of the disintegration of central authority to snatch provinces from the empire. The Safavid Empire had come to an inglorious end.

Although the empire was destroyed by what was essentially an insurrection by an ethnic group who were Sunni, the territories that became Shi'i during the Safavid period largely remained so. After a period of chaos and an Ottoman invasion, order was restored again when a new strong leader appeared. This was Nadir Shah, who ruled at first through members of the Safavid dynasty, but proclaimed himself Shah in 1736. He was a great conqueror, although few of his conquests would be permanent. He marched east through Afghanistan and large areas of northern India, sacking Delhi and taking the Mughal peacock throne and Koh-i-noor diamond back with him as loot. To the north, he re-established Iranian control up to the River Oxus. He also drove the Ottomans out of parts of western Iran that they had occupied, and invaded Iraq and eastern Anatolia.

He was from the Afshar tribe, one of the tribes that had made up the Kizilbash confederation. This meant that his background was Twelver Shi'i, but he inclined to Sunnism and made the last serious attempt to reinstate Sunnism in Iran. Many of the soldiers in his army were Afghan Sunnis, and there may therefore have been a political aspect to this; but it has also sometimes been suggested that he had megalomaniac ambitions of establishing his rule over the entire Islamic world, and that this was the real reason he favoured Sunnism. Nevertheless, his army also contained many Shi'is, and he made his capital at Mashhad, the shrine city that contained the tomb of the Imam Ali al-Rida. As he had made the Oxus once again the boundary of the Persian Empire, and even made Bukhara which lay on the far side of it a vassal state, there may have been sound geographical reasons for this.

Nadir Shah attempted to close the gap between Shi'is and Sunnis. There would be tangible political benefits for him if he could achieve this. It would increase his prestige throughout the Muslim world. It would also put an end to a source of discord within his dominions, and would deprive the Sunni Ottomans of an important pretext for invading Iran: the grounds that they were fighting heresy.

The Ottoman fears about the spread of Gnostic Shi'i and subsequently Twelver ideas by the Kizilbash tribes in their eastern provinces, were deep-rooted. Moreover, the Safavids had practised *sabb*, the cursing of the first three caliphs. This was an affront to all Sunni Muslims, especially to Ottoman sultans who had themselves sometimes adopted the title of caliph, and it was something the Ottomans never forgave or forgot. They already considered the Safavids and their followers to be infidels at the time of the Battle of Chaldiran in 1514. Whenever they were at war with Iran, decrees and fatwas would be produced to remind the people (and the army) of this.

According to one decree issued by Ebussuud Efendi – the sixteenth-century Ottoman Sheikh al-Islam, who was the most senior religious dignitary in the empire – Twelvers were like the false prophet Musaylimah, sowing corruption and discord among Muslims. Ebussuud Efendi reminded his flock for good measure that 'killing this group is more important than killing other groups', and that no less an authority than Ahmad ibn Hanbal had declared the blood of anyone who cursed the first three caliphs to be lawful – that is, fit for of execution – even if he subsequently repented.[16] A similar example is contained in an opinion of Ibn Kemal Pasha-Zade, another sixteenth-century Sheikh al-Islam, who wrote that the Kizilbash are 'a *ta'ife* [i.e. sect] of the Shi'ah whose men must be killed, whose wealth and women are allowed to any Sunnis who wish to usurp them and against whom holy war is incumbent'.[17] Much more recently, while the last Safavids were reeling under the attacks from Sunnis in Afghanistan, the Ottomans invaded from the west in order 'to fight unbelief'. Their propaganda described Safavid soldiers as infidels who could legitimately be killed in battle, and whose property could be lawfully seized.[18]

Nadir Shah's idea was that Twelver Shi'ism would be considered as an additional *madhhab*, or doctrinal law school, alongside the four great doctrinal law schools of Sunnism. For Shi'is, this would have meant acceptance of the first three caliphs as legitimate, and an end to the practice of ritually cursing them. The suggestion was received coldly by the Shi'i scholars in his dominions. In fairness to them, Nadir Shah was not quite asking for mutual acceptance of each other by Sunnis and Twelvers, but was attempting something rather different: to find a place for Twelver Islam within the framework of Sunnism. His idea was also treated disdainfully in the Sunni world, and he eventually dropped his idea of the fifth, 'Ja'fari' *madhhab*. The name of the school itself would have appeared an insult to Twelvers. From their point of view, Ja'far al-Sadiq was the Sixth Imam – a status that was much more exalted than that of the founder of a doctrinal law school like Abu Hanifa or Ahmad ibn Hanbal.

He also made other moves towards Sunnism, or at least to a position of neutrality between Sunnism and Shi'ism. The Kizilbash headdress with twelve gussets symbolising the twelve imams was abolished and replaced with a new one with four points – which might be taken to indicate the first four caliphs. He also had Shi'i formulae removed from his coins. When he visited Iraq, he endowed both Sunni and Shi'i shrines. In an attempt to placate his Twelver subjects, he encouraged Shi'i practices – such as pilgrimage to the shrines of the imams – that were potentially compatible with Sunni Islam.

In 1743, after he had temporarily seized much of Iraq from the Ottomans, Nadir Shah held a kind of religious council at Najaf, the location of the shrine containing the tomb of Ali – and therefore a potential focal point for Sunni-Shi'i reconciliation. In reality it was a public-relations exercise aimed at preserving the unity of the Sunnis and Shi'is in his armies, where he was concerned at anti-Shi'i feeling among some of his Sunni troops. It was therefore only the legitimacy of Shi'ism that was in question.[19] Little if any serious theological disputation took place. Sheikh Abdullah al-Suwaidi, a Shafi'i jurist from Baghdad whom the Ottomans had cajoled into taking part, was unimpressed. When told by the Ottoman governor's deputy that he had been chosen to represent the Sunnis, he was shocked. His reaction included a succinct summary of the practical differences between the theological reasoning used by Sunnis and Shi'is, as seen from a firmly Sunni standpoint:

> You know that the Shi'a are people of deceit. How can they accept what I say when they are in their element and there are a great number of them, and this shah [Nadir Shah] is a tyrannical oppressor? How do I dare adduce proofs of the falseness of their *madhhab* and declare its opinion void? We can talk with them, and they will deny every hadith quoted by us, because they do not accept the soundness of the Six Books of hadith. For every Qur'anic verse that I rely on, they will make an esoteric interpretation of it, and they will say that when proof reaches the level of conjecture, it is futile to adduce any proofs at all. They will also say that the condition of proof is that the two sides must agree that in affairs involving the use of ijtihad, it is permissible to follow individual opinion.[20]

Al-Suwaidi was greatly lacking in trust towards the Twelver scholars, and assumed that they would distort his arguments when they repeated them to others. So suspicious was he that he even asked for a neutral religious scholar – a Christian or a Jew – to be appointed arbitrator:

We need an *'alim* [a scholar] who is Christian or Jewish or of some other faith, who is neither Sunni nor Shi'i. We will say to him, 'We are pleased with you. You will be arbiter between us, and God will hold you accountable on the Day of Resurrection. Listen to what we have to say until the truth becomes clear to you.' I reckoned that if [this arbiter] favoured the other side's position, I would argue with him and discuss the affair further, even if this led to me being put to death.[21]

Needless to say, this suggestion was rejected and al-Suwaidi did take part. The Twelver scholars who spoke claimed that they had abolished *sabb* (which Nadir Shah wrongly, but cleverly, asserted to have been an innovation of the Safavids). They also asserted that they had ended their tolerance of the practice of temporary marriage, which is allowed by the Twelver interpretation of the Sharia but is generally viewed by Sunnis with horror as a form of prostitution. Al-Suwaidi doubted their sincerity. He suspected it was just an exercise in *taqiyya*, deliberate dissimulation to placate the Ottomans and pull the wool over their eyes for a naked, political end.

As Nadir Shah aged, he became crueller and more capricious, and some doubt whether he retained his sanity. Discontent at excessive taxation and the increasing arbitrariness of his rule led to revolts. He was eventually murdered by Kizilbash tribesmen in 1747. With his towering personality gone, his army and realm soon fell apart. It would be a further half century before Iran was reconstituted in the 1790s under another dynasty which stemmed from another old Kizilbash tribe, the Qajars.

But two long-lasting consequences flowed from Nadir Shah's religious policy. The first was that his efforts at dialogue with the Sunni Ottomans (if it was, indeed, genuine dialogue) led to a new approach in the relations between the two mighty empires. The 1746 Treaty of Kurdan, which Nadir Shah and an Ottoman ambassador put in place shortly before Nadir Shah was murdered, set out a framework for relations between Ottoman Turkey and Iran that would endure. It established peace and also the frontiers between the two states that have survived more or less to this day. While it appeared to promise that Iran would convert to Sunni Islam, this has been described as entailing no more than 'what might be considered a superficial reorientation of practice'.[22] Iranians would refrain from *sabb*, but were formally granted the right to continue to make pilgrimages to the shrines of the tombs of the imams in Iraq where they could be expected to practise only their specifically Shi'i religious rites. This would lead, incidentally, to a long line of dissident Iranian religious scholars being able to take refuge in Najaf from the Iranian authorities. Very importantly, it also made obsolete the religious justifications that the Ottomans had used for war against Iran.

The other consequence was internal to Iran and concerned the relationship between the rulers and the religious leaders. Under the Safavids, it could be said that Mosque and State were united, and that the scholars who converted the population to Twelver Shi'ism were an arm of the State. Under Nadir Shah, and subsequently, this ceased to be the case. Some scholars left Iran in high dudgeon, many of them settling in India while others went to the shrines of Iraq. The resistance to Nadir Shah's attempt to convert Twelver Shi'ism into a fifth Sunni law school demonstrates how deeply entrenched Twelver Shi'ism had now become in Iran. But, following the end of the Safavids, religion was no longer 'almost a department of state'.[23] Whoever ruled the land could not take for granted the support of the religious leaders. These leaders were not under the control of the government, or even necessarily beholden to it. Moreover, for Twelver Shi'is, during the occultation of the Hidden Imam there was always a question mark over the legitimacy of any government. There was thus an inherent tension between the rulers and the religious leaders that would not go away. The scholars became those who collected and distributed religious alms and taxes that were the entitlement of the Hidden Imam. This enabled them, for instance, to fund institutions of learning such as madrasas without needing the involvement of the state.

But those religious leaders disagreed among themselves. They became divided into two main factions. One was known as the Akhbaris or 'traditionists'. In a methodology similar to their Sunni contemporaries, they saw the task of the scholar as being to discern the Sharia from study of the traditions of the Prophet and the twelve imams. The difference was that the source material for their scholarship was substantially different from that of Sunnis. As we have already seen, while both shared the Qur'an, Sunnis looked at the traditions of the Prophet, the first four caliphs and the Prophet's Companions and their successors. Shi'is rejected the sayings and practice of the first three caliphs and of those of the Prophet's Companions who had supported them. Instead, of those sources, they looked to the traditions attributed to the twelve imams.

The other trend or tendency was that of the Usulis. The Usulis followed the methodology originally developed by Allamah al-Hilli so that, where there were no clear teachings in the text of the Qur'an or hadith, learned scholars could use *ijtihad* to supply the believers with certainty in living the holy law and, where appropriate, apply it to new circumstances. This increased the authority of the scholars, thereby adding to their ability to influence social developments and, ultimately, political ones. The school had originally been brought to Iran during the days of Shah Ismail and his son Tahmasp. It had taken root and flourished. Over time, the position of the Usulis had been strengthened as the endowments supporting them grew, and they married into landowning and merchant families from which many of the next generations of scholars were drawn. This had the consequence that religious scholars could often be found who would take up the interests of these classes in disputes with the government.

The Akhbari tradition continued, but increasingly lost out to the Usulis. The main battlegrounds were the communities of scholars in the Iraqi shrine cities. The decisive figure was Agha Muhammad Baqir Wahid Bihbihani, a scholar from Isfahan who lived virtually his entire adult life in Karbala where he had originally gone to study. By the time of his death in 1793, he had driven the Akhbaris, whom he denounced as heretical innovators, from the shrine cities. He fatefully pronounced unbelief, *takfir*, against his opponents and was not above the use of violence, which was meted out by 'the masters of anger' (*mir-ghadab*). These were men armed with cudgels who patrolled the streets on his behalf. This domination of the Usulis spread to Iran and elsewhere, although the Akhbaris would continue to survive in Basra and Bahrain.

At the same time as the religious scholars had become a major force in the empire that was independent of government and beyond its control, Shi'i piety had spread among ordinary people. The Shi'i passion play became popular, the *ta'ziyya*, which told the story of the martyrdom of Hussein by the evil Caliph Yazid. Perhaps unsurprisingly, it was not liked by the religious scholars who tended to disapprove of folk piety that they could not control. But it was a sign that Twelver Shi'ism had become the religion of most of the ordinary people of Iran.

CHAPTER SEVEN

The Ottoman Empire, India
and the Muslim Reformation

I

The relentless pressure of nomadic invasions from Central Asia did not just provide the environment that led to the birth of the Safavid Empire. The influx also provided the genesis of the mighty Ottoman Empire. We now need to look at the Turkish Ottomans and (to a lesser extent) the Indian Mughals. At their height, these two Sunni empires, together with the Shi'i Safavids, contained the overwhelming majority of Muslims in the world, and ruled from Algeria to the mouths of the Ganges. These empires would dominate the Muslim world from the sixteenth century until well into the eighteenth century, and the Ottomans would survive into the twentieth century. There were very few predominantly Muslim lands which were never under the sovereignty or suzerainty of one or other of them. Of the lands conquered by the Arabs in the seventh and eighth centuries, only Morocco entirely escaped their control (the last parts of Andalusia in Spain had been finally reconquered by Spanish Christians in 1492). They also never penetrated the Malay peninsula and the archipelago that is today Indonesia, where Islam was being spread largely by traders and Sufis. The same applied to sub-Saharan Africa, where Islam had taken root in some regions, especially around the great bend in the River Niger.

Although at its height the Mughal Empire ruled over many more people, the Ottoman Empire is generally considered the greatest of the three. It covered the largest area, was both a land and a maritime power, and was by far the most enduring. It was also the strong defender of Sunnism. It would never have come into existence but for the fact that, in 1071, the Seljuq sultan Alp-Arslan came upon the army of the Byzantine Emperor Romanus Diogenes at Manzikert, or Malazgirt, to the north of Lake Van. Neither army was expecting to meet the other, but the encounter was a resounding Seljuq victory, and Romanus Diogenes was taken prisoner. Turkish tribes now swept westward and, for the first time, settled in Anatolia. They established a sultanate at Konya, whose rulers were known as the Seljuqs of Rum. In time, it disintegrated into a number of smaller principalities, which disputed Anatolia with each other, as well as with local Greek and Armenian warlords, the weakened Byzantines and, from 1097 onwards, the Crusaders.

The beginnings of the Ottomans are lost in legend. What we do know is that they came from one of the Turkish tribes that had swept over the eastern Islamic world in the days of the Seljuqs. They adopted Islam but, as with similar tribes, their Islam would have been mixed with many other elements: survivals of ancient shamanistic practices, unorthodox ideas learned from wandering Sufis, and Christian and other influences they would have picked up in Anatolia.

The half-legendary founder of the Ottoman dynasty was Osman Gazi (d. 1326) who established an entity that successfully expanded against its rivals until it controlled western and central Anatolia. It even crossed into Europe in 1352 after Osman's successor, Orkhan, was asked for military support by a contender to the Byzantine throne. That Byzantine invitation was foolish, and would lead to the Ottomans finally gobbling up the remnants of the Byzantine Empire itself a century later in 1453, when they used cannon to breach the land walls of Constantinople. By then, they already dominated the Balkans up to the river Danube and in some places beyond. They had also defeated numerous attempts to force them back by Balkan rulers such as the kings of Hungary and Serbia, as well as Crusaders and the forces of wealthy Italian merchant city states. They survived their crushing defeat at the hands of Timur, although it took them several decades to recover. But for that defeat, they might well have taken Constantinople half a century earlier than they did.

After the seizure of Constantinople, the Ottomans were a great power – in fact, one of the superpowers of the fifteenth and sixteenth

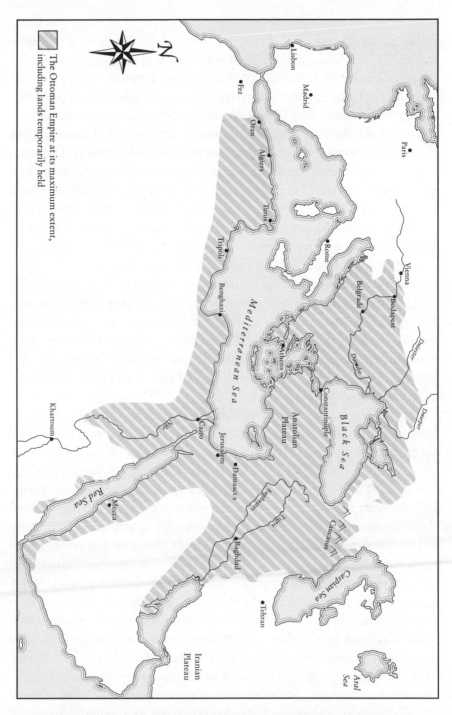

THE OTTOMAN EMPIRE AT ITS MAXIMUM EXTENT

centuries. They would spread their control over Greater Syria and Egypt in 1516–17, besiege Vienna in 1529 and 1683, and establish their rule along the coast of North Africa as far west as Algeria, becoming a major naval force in the Mediterranean. They would simultaneously turn the Black Sea into an Ottoman lake and control the Crimea, Moldova and an area of southern Ukraine and Russia, as well as most of Arabia and the Red Sea. Less successfully, they would try to resist the Portuguese and other European maritime powers as they penetrated the Indian Ocean. We have also seen how they never managed to extend their rule to the Iranian plateau. Although they were the terror of Europe during the century and a half between the two sieges of Vienna, by the end of the seventeenth century they were in retreat before Austria and Russia.

The Ottomans established order, which allowed agriculture, industry and commerce to flourish. Their sultan presided over an empire of many faiths in which Christians may have been at least as numerous as Muslims – or actually more numerous. The Ottomans recognised this reality. For this reason, in their heyday they received widespread support from many non-Muslims. Most of their Christian subjects were Orthodox, who generally preferred Ottoman rule to that of the Latin Christian powers of Western Europe. The elite troops of the army were the Janissaries, Christian boys taken in a levy called the *devshirme*, ordered to convert to Islam and brought up in special military schools. Separated from their family ties, they became well-trained professional soldiers with a strong *esprit de corps* – a combination that probably made them some of the best soldiers in the world. Despite their Christian birth, they sometimes achieved very high office, as did some other converts to Islam, many of them from leading families. At least two nephews of the last Byzantine emperor became Muslims, and one of them was made the governor of Rumelia, the generic name for the Ottoman provinces in Europe. The fact that this put him in charge of roughly half the Ottoman army shows the degree of trust in which the Ottomans held him.

It has been suggested that the important role given to such converts would have helped the Ottomans absorb the conquered areas. As the Ottomans required at least the passive acquiescence of the conquered Christians to their rule, it could also indicate that the conversion to Islam of such eminent individuals did not alienate them altogether from the Christian communities from which they came. Some Christians who did not convert fought voluntarily in the service of the Ottomans, although this became rarer as time passed. As the historian and political advisor Douglas Streusand has put it, 'Ottoman expansion clearly meant something other than the simple triumph of Muslim over Christian.'[1]

Following the conquest of Constantinople, the Ottomans saw themselves as the heirs to Ancient Rome as well as to the imperial sovereignty of the pre-Islamic Sasanian shahs of Persia and the Turkish khans of the steppes. Yet of greatest importance to them was their pre-eminence among Sunni Muslim rulers. When, after their conquest of Greater Syria and Egypt, they became the guardians of Mecca and Medina, they adopted old caliphal titles such as Khadim al-Haramain al-Sharifain, 'the Servant of the Two Holy Sanctuaries'. Indeed, on an emotional level their conquest of Syria and Egypt and control of the Holy Cities meant more to them than the taking of Constantinople, even though the European provinces of their empire were the richest. The Ottomans had become the leading Sunni Muslim power west of India. They were intensely jealous of this position. In 1578, when the Mughal Emperor Akbar made large donations to Mecca and Medina, the Ottoman Sultan Selim II responded by forbidding the receipt of any further donations from him.[2]

II

Sunni Islam was thus at the cornerstone of the Ottomans' sense of identity. The concept of 'the Peoples of the Book' provided the framework within which they viewed their numerous Jewish communities, as well as the Christians who made up something like half the population of their empire. Indeed, the Ottomans frequently encouraged inward Jewish migration and supported Hungarian Protestants against the Catholic Habsburgs. But what about their attitude to Shi'is? This was a more complex question, since for Sunni Muslims Shi'is do not fit into the framework for the 'Peoples of the Book'. They are still Muslims, but misguided heretics.

The Ottoman rulers were pragmatic men. When at war with the Safavids, the most extreme language would be used in religious opinions to justify attacking Shi'is. In the last chapter, we saw two examples of this in the opinions of Ebussuud Efendi and Ibn Kemal Pasha-Zade, who each filled the highest religious office in the empire as Sheikh al-Islam. The Shi'is who really scared the Ottomans were the Kizilbash tribes, which threatened their hold on eastern Anatolia. They were numerous. It looks like an exaggeration, but according to a Venetian source 80 per cent of the population of Anatolia was Shi'i.[3] The Kizilbash could easily provide a fifth column for the Safavid emperor if he ever decided to march westwards towards the Aegean, as Persian emperors had done before the coming of Islam. The Ottoman reaction could be drastic. In 1501, Sultan Bayezid forced 30,000 Kizilbash to migrate to the Peloponnese, while Selim the Grim ordered the massacre of 40,000 in eastern Anatolia as he marched east to Chaldiran. But it was their political support for the Safavids, rather than their doctrines, that caused such extreme measures.[4] The Ottomans also retaliated when they retook Iraq from the Safavids in 1638. Sunnis had been persecuted during the Iranian occupation, and the Sunni shrine of Abd al-Qadir al-Jilani had been damaged. The Ottomans extracted revenge, and killed all known persons of Persian descent.[5] This was a striking contrast with the earlier campaign of Suleyman the Magnificent, who had retaken Baghdad from the Safavids in 1533. He had restored the Sunni shrines of Abd al-Qadir al-Jilani and Abu Hanifa, but also visited the shrines of the Imams, thus gaining himself the respect of his Shi'i subjects.[6] Different rhetoric was deployed by the Ottomans when there was peace. At such times the Shi'i Safavids were greeted as brother Muslims.[7] The Ottomans had no scruples about alliances with Shi'is when convenient.[8]

Ottoman fears that Twelver Shi'is were sympathetic to the Safavid cause could be fatal for Twelvers in other parts of the Ottoman Empire. One instance saw the execution of Qur'an reciters, living in the shrine cities of Iraq, who took a secret stipend from Shah Tahmasp of Iran.[9] In another, a governor of Baalbek who came from the local Twelver Harfush clan was executed for suspected Safavid sympathies. But perhaps what is most interesting here is that, off and on, this Twelver clan provided Ottoman governors for the town from the sixteenth to the nineteenth century. It seems that the Ottomans did not care overmuch what the Twelvers, Alawis and Druze of Greater Syria believed, so long as taxes were paid and they posed no threat. Twelver Shi'is in what is now Lebanon were listed in the tax registers as Muslims, without a mention of their sect.[10] Very often, sect played little part. Nevertheless, there was an inherent insecurity for Shi'is in that their distinctiveness was not officially recognised. Merit could lead to Shi'i poets being present at the Ottoman court, but Shi'is did not have the opportunities open to their Sunni counterparts for advancement as religious scholars and bureaucrats. This meant that patronage received by Sunnis was often denied to them. Shi'is tended to be careful and reticent about their beliefs, an option that was open to them because of *taqiyya*. In the 1770s, Sayyid Mihdi Tabataba'i, a senior Usuli scholar from Karbala who was also a descendant of the Prophet, made the pilgrimage to Mecca. While there, he felt it necessary to evade questions about the doctrinal law school to which he belonged.[11]

It has been suggested that the Ottomans, both rulers and religious scholars, became more aware of their identity as Sunnis as a result of their confrontation with the Safavids. The Safavid practice of *sabb*, the cursing of Abu Bakr, Umar, Uthman, Aisha and most of the Prophet's Companions, which horrified Sunni Muslims, was a capital offence under the Ottomans.[12] 'Turk' and 'Persian' were sometimes used as synonyms for Sunni and Shi'i respectively, a conflation of sect and ethnicity that would continue into the modern era.

III

As the Arab conquerors rode east during the Umayyad period, their armies reached the river Indus and Sind in 711 during the reign of the Caliph Walid I. This was the same year in which a Muslim army first crossed the Straits of Gibraltar and entered Spain. From Sind, they conquered as far north as Multan in the southern Punjab. Some of the Arab soldiers settled in these areas, where Islam spread. Muslim rule penetrated further as a result of the conquests of the Turkish-speaking Ghaznavid dynasty in north India around the year 1000. Other Muslim armies came southwards through the Khyber Pass, and a sultanate was established in Delhi in 1206, but overthrown in 1398 by Babur, a descendant of Timur on his father's side and of Genghis Khan on his mother's. He was the grandfather of the emperor Akbar who is today considered to be the real founder of the Mughal Empire.[13]

The Mughal Empire had many more inhabitants than the Ottoman Empire and was considerably wealthier.[14] At its height, it covered almost all the Indian subcontinent. This was the achievement of Akbar, who came to the throne in 1556. By the time of his death in 1598, he had extended his dominions almost to the southern tip of India. He was followed by three energetic successors, Jahangir (r. 1598–1627), Shah Jahan (r. 1627–59) and Aurangzeb (r. 1659–1707), before decline set in during the eighteenth century as provincial governors increasingly asserted their autonomy and became practically independent. Nevertheless, the empire would survive, in attenuated form, until the mid-nineteenth century. In 1857, the last Mughal emperor was chosen as the symbolic alternative to British rule by the traditional rulers who took part in the great uprising known in Britain as the Indian Mutiny.

India was far too vast and populous to be permanently conquered and settled by Muslim invaders. There were many conversions to Islam, especially through the work of the Chishti order of Sufis, but over the subcontinent as a whole Muslims were a minority. Although the emperor Akbar was a Sunni Muslim, he devised a novel solution to this problem of ruling a vast empire in which the majority of the inhabitants were not Muslim. Instead of Islam being the cornerstone of his legitimacy, he claimed a special spiritual status of his own and propagated what was known as *sulh-i kull*, which meant 'peace with all' or universal toleration.[15] Loyalty to him flowed from this special spiritual status and the dynastic principle of his descent from Timur (who had conquered northern India but had not remained there) and his grandfather Babur, who had been a great conqueror in his own right. He certainly never abandoned Islam but, very unusually for a Muslim ruler, he followed Hindu court rituals that were designed to demonstrate that he enjoyed the same sovereignty as a Hindu king. He abolished the *jizya*, the poll tax on non-Muslim males; Muslims and Hindus alike could enter his service at the highest level, and he made no distinction between them. This also applied to Shi‘is, and there is no indication that either they or Hindus were less loyal to Akbar than Sunnis.[16] As a system, *sulh-i kull* seems for a while to have been very successful.

Albar's successors Jahangir and Shah Jahan backtracked from some aspects of *sulh-i kull*, but it was Aurungzeb, the last great Mughal emperor, who reversed the policy and made Islam, and the upholding of the Sharia, the basis of his legitimacy, as was the case with other Sunni rulers. When he won a dynastic civil war against his brother Dara Shikoh over who should succeed his father, Aurungzeb had his brother executed as an apostate. Yet even though Aurungzeb began to enforce the Sharia by such measures as reinstituting the *jizya* poll tax on non-Muslims and reimposing a Sharia ban on the construction of new places of worship by them, he retained the support of many Shi'is and Hindus. Nevertheless, he had altered the tone of Islam in the subcontinent and this would be permanent. What has been called the universalist strain of Akbar and the Chishtis was eclipsed.[17]

Sunnism would dominate the Islam of the Indian subcontinent, but Shi'ism was also present, although generally as a minority of a minority. Shi'is fleeing the Mongol invasions settled in the territory of the Bahmani sultanate in the Deccan, which was founded in 1347. Some of these refugees became soldiers in the sultanate's armies. It split into a number of different sultanates, which came under strong Safavid influence, and Shi'ism remained strong locally after the area was absorbed by the Mughals. There is still a sizeable Shi'i minority there today. Shi'ism became fashionable at the court of Emperor Akbar during his later years, and remained so under his successor Jahangir.[18] It was Jahangir who constructed the famous Taj Mahal as the mausoleum for his beloved Shi'i wife, Nur Jahan. Another stronghold of Indian Shi'ism is the area around Lucknow, the capital of the principality of Awadh (also often spelled Oudh), which became a separate Mughal province when a Shi'i who was a descendant of the Seventh Imam was appointed its governor in 1722. It subsequently became an independent kingdom. From the the late eighteenth century onwards there were links between Awadh and Najaf, which received much financial assistance from Awadh including the construction of a canal to give it a reliable water supply in the late 1700s. When direct rule by Britain was imposed in Awadh in the late 1850s, the Shi'is who had been the elite suddenly went to being merely a minority of the Muslim population, which was itself outnumbered by Hindus.

The Mughals looked to their Turkic ancestry as a major foundation for their legitimacy. By contrast, Mughal provincial governors from Shi'i families who became virtually independent rulers sought their own legitimacy by modelling themselves on the Shi'i Safavids. This happened not just in Awadh and the Deccan but also in Bengal and Sind. Their kingdoms became magnets for merchants and religious scholars from Iran. Shi'i devotional poetry was popular at the courts of Awadh and in the Deccan. In fact, in the eighteenth century Shi'i devotional poetry at the court in Lucknow played a role in the early development of Urdu as a written language.[19] Another significant Twelver Shi'i community in the Indian subcontinent is in Kashmir. This dates from the Chak dynasty in the sixteenth century, which converted to Shi'ism under the influence of a Sufi order that had many Shi'i elements. The Chak dynasty propagated Shi'ism vigorously, and much of the peasantry converted. A Shi'i community in Kashmir has since survived, despite persecution during a period of Afghan rule in the late eighteenth century and early nineteenth centuries.[20]

IV

By the eighteenth century, it was obvious to any thoughtful observer that Ottoman Turkey was falling behind the European powers. It would not be until the 1850s that Turkey would be dubbed 'the sick man of Europe', but Europe was now relentlessly moving ahead in terms of industry and technology. It was also the place where the exciting new ideas of the Enlightenment were emerging. For the time being, these had little if any impact on the Ottoman elite. The Ottomans studied the new European methods and sometimes adopted them, but they seem to have been painfully slow in benefiting from some of the innovations.

Printing is the obvious example. The Jews and some of the Christian peoples of the Ottoman Empire such as the Greeks and Armenians had long since established printing presses for books in their own languages, although, as Ottoman specialist Caroline Finkel has put it, this was 'not without problems'.[21] It was late as 1727 that the first Arabic script printing press was established in the empire. Even then, only a few books with short print runs were produced. It would not be until the nineteenth century that printing really took off in Turkish (which was written in the Arabic script) and Arabic. One factor that slowed down the spread of printing was the respect felt for the art and skill of the copyists, and a perhaps praiseworthy concern that printing could lead to the loss of their livelihoods. It probably also indicated a feeling of awe and reverence for the written word in a society where literacy was rare and therefore prized.

As the empire weakened, it began to lose vast territories in Europe to Austria and Russia, while elsewhere its control over some of its provinces decayed. Strong local personalities such as Mamluk soldiers, provincial governors, tribal leaders, tax gatherers and other notables often saw an opportunity to increase their power at the expense of the centre. The empire frequently found itself forced into a policy of negotiation and compromise with powerful local figures, since it lacked the strength to enforce its will without their support.

Many of the rebellions that took place during the eighteenth century left no lasting impact, except to weaken the empire further. But one locally based movement, which appeared in the central Arabian region of Nejd in the middle of the century, would have consequences for the history of Islam and especially for relations between Sunnis and Shi'is – consequences that are still very much with us today. This is the movement founded by Ibn 'Abd al-Wahhab, who lived during the period 1702–93 and whose life therefore almost spans the eighteenth century.

Ibn 'Abd al-Wahhab set out to purify and reform Islam from the remote, desert region where he was born and grew up. In some ways, he has something in common with certain Protestant reformers in the Europe of the Reformation. There are, for instance, eerie parallels with Protestants in the ways in which he sought to go back to the original scriptures of his religion (the Qur'an and hadith, in his case) rather than interpret them by sifting through the hallowed commentaries of long-dead scholars. He also concentrated on the lives of the Prophet and his Companions, and preached that believers should live according to the example of the first Muslims. This often meant ignoring and rejecting the scholarship and deep theological thought of the centuries in between.[22] He did not subscribe to the idea of a universal caliphate.

As a religious scholar, he seems to have been largely self-taught. He did not sit at the feet of any of the great scholars of his time or receive a certificate that confirmed the level of scholarship he had attained. This meant that, in the eyes of eminent Sunni scholars, he had no authority – and therefore no right – to teach. But he seems to have revelled in this. He taught that every man and woman should study the Qur'an for themselves. For him this meant that they would, virtually of necessity, come to the same conclusions from that study as he himself had done and therefore subscribe to his teachings. Those who acccepted his teaching were true Muslims; those who rejected it were apostates. Inevitably, opponents compared him and his followers to the Kharijis, who had declared that the Caliph Ali should be deposed because he had left the faith. Possibly in reaction to this charge, Ibn 'Abd al-Wahhab and his followers stressed their adherence to the Hanbali doctrinal law school, and their acceptance of the validity of the other three doctrinal law schools of Sunni Islam.

The mission he had taken on was to protect and purify Sunni Islam, especially against Sufism and Shi'ism.[23] He was as obsessed with fighting idolatry and destroying graven images as any Protestant during the Reformation. He also criticised religious scholars who gained property or money from their roles – as when they found ways to ease the consciences of Muslims who charged interest.[24] Although he saw himself as uniting Muslims, his actions divided communities against themselves, and those divisions persist to this day. Yet any similarities between him and figures such as John Knox or Calvin are purely coincidental; although Europe was now breathing down the neck of the Ottoman Empire, and European navies even dominated the seas surrounding Ibn 'Abd al-Wahhab's native Arabia, there was absolutely no European influence on his life or thought.

Ibn 'Abd al-Wahhab came from a family of Hanbali scholars at a time when Nejd was probably one of the few places in which this doctrinal law school was still influential.[25] He saw the state of the Nejdi tribes as 'ignorance', *jahiliyah*, explicitly using the Muslim term used to portray the pagan Arabs before Islam.[26] As a young man he certainly travelled to Mecca and Medina and also to Basra. He returned home by way of Hasa, the area on the east coast of Arabia that is now a province of Saudi Arabia and which was then thought of as part of Greater Bahrain. Twelver Shi'is formed the majority of its population. It is doubtful that he went further afield.[27] It is impossible to know for certain, but he may have been stirred into action in order to oppose the attempt by Iranian ruler Nadir Shah (r. 1736–1747) to bring Twelver Shi'ism into the fold of Sunnism.[28] Little is known for certain about his early studies, or even the precise years of his travels, but it is possible if not probable that his stay in Basra and travels through Hasa were in the 1730s at the time when Nadir Shah's power was at its peak.

While in Basra, Ibn 'Abd al-Wahhab agitated against Shi'is, Sufis and local practices he considered polytheistic. This was really the beginning of his career as a preacher. After his return to Nejd when he was probably in his mid-thirties, he never left the region again. He had been appalled by what he had observed which was, for him, the corruption of Islam by idolatry. What happened next was that, 'his perspective on the wider world froze in time just as his doctrines cohered into a corpus that he never revised substantially'.[29]

Tawhid, the affirmation of the Divine Unity, what we might call an absolute monotheism, is the point of departure for Islam and for all Muslims. It was therefore Ibn 'Abd al-Wahhab's point of departure as well. In the West, the movement he founded is known as Wahhabism, but he and his followers called themselves the Muwahhidun, those who affirm *tawhid*, the unity of God. In his writings, he elaborated on two forms of tawhid: *tawhid al-rububiyyah* and *tawhid al-uluhiyyah*. We might translate the first concept, very freely, as 'the affirmation of God's lordship' and the second as 'the affirmation of God's divinity'.

Affirmation of God's lordship is the monotheism that Islam shares with Christianity and Judaism. It is the acceptance that God is the creator of all. Yet, for Ibn 'Abd al-Wahhab it will not be enough to save believers from Hell. Although they accept that God is the creator, in his eyes they have not taken the next essential step and affirmed God's divinity. This involves the acceptance that all intercessionary prayer or supplication to saints and all other figures apart from God is idolatry and unbelief, and leads to eternal damnation.

He saw Shi'i commemorations of the deaths of the imams, all of whom were listed by Twelvers as martyrs, as idolatry. For him, the public expressions of grief at the fate of Hussein on the 10th of Muharram, which could involve breast beating, self-flagellation and other forms of self-harm, were forms of idol worship. They were an affront to all true Muslims that should be banned.

This applied also to those Sunni Muslims who prayed to saints or other figures. Veneration of saintly figures, including annual festivals at their tombs, was deeply engrained in Muslim culture everywhere. Now Ibn 'Abd al-Wahhab's 'affirmation of God's divinity' challenged the practice. The two main Muslim groups that offended were Shi'is and Sufis, and both made pilgrimages to tombs. In the case of Shi'is these were to the shrines of the Imams and other figures from the House of Ali, such as the shrine of Fatima, the sister of the Imam Ali al-Rida at Qumm. In the same way that he attacked Shi'i pilgrimages, he also attacked the Sufi practice of *ziyarat al-qubur*, literally 'visiting the graves'. Individuals might merely visit the tomb in order to be close to the dead saint and to ask for his intercession. This was bad enough but there were also festivals, the annual *moulids* or celebrations of the saint's life, which Sufi brotherhoods organised. These were joyful occasions for music, dancing and feasting which he abhored.

His view was that all Muslims who made intercessionary prayers should be declared unbelievers, a declaration called *takfir*. They had left Islam and were infidels. Their marriages to Muslim women should be dissolved, their property impounded, and their lives forfeited. He seems to have been most hostile to those groups, such as some Sufi brotherhoods, who made intercessionary prayers but at the same time observed the Sunni version of the Sharia scupulously. What he loathed above all was any attempt at compromise – to bring within the fold any strain of Islam that conflicted with his core beliefs.[30] It is also noteworthy that his greatest ire seems to have been reserved for religious scholars who disagreed with him.[31]

One objection that many other Muslims would make to his teaching – both then and now – was: by what authority could he pronounce *takfir*? It was the gravest of charges to bring against a fellow Muslim, and should only be alleged if there was clear proof against the individual concerned. His assertion that he could do so led to widespread condemnation, and even to counter pronouncements of *takfir* against him. He was denounced by many of his contemporary religious scholars. Yet he was adamant that he could declare not only individuals but entire groups or communities as guilty of *kufr* or 'unbelief'. The only requirement before pronouncing this dread sentence was that the apostates must first have had clear proofs taken from the Qur'an and presented to them, even if they failed to understand them.[32]

A test case seems to have arisen over a woman who publicly confessed to adultery. Although he tried to persuade her to retract her confession, when she refused he sentenced her to death by stoning, even though some other scholars declared that he did not have the authority to pronounce such a momentous sentence. Ibn 'Abd al-Wahhab won, both on that occasion and on many others. Religious devotion was not a private matter. The Muwahhidun also had to be seen to act publicly in the ways required by their faith; it was their duty to correct others who were neglecting their religious observance, or performing it badly. As he put it himself, 'a person's Islam is not sound even if he practises *tawhid* of God and deserts polytheism unless he is hostile to polytheists and declares to them his hostility and hatred'.[33]

He had an additional quarrel with Shi'is that went to the root of the differences between them and Sunnis. Echoing medieval scholars such as Ahmad ibn Hanbal and Ibn Taymiyyah, he found the Shi'i rejection of the first three caliphs and the many Companions of the Prophet who had supported them as absolutely unacceptable, since this rejection extended to the greater part of the hadith, which was for Sunnis the main source material after the Qur'an for discerning the Sharia. In his view, as in that of the earlier scholars, this demolished the foundations of true Islam. He also attacked Shi'is for disdaining Sunnis, practising *taqiyya* to hide their true beliefs, and indulging in forbidden practices like temporary, *mut'ah,* marriages. Worst of all, Shi'is had also subverted the teaching of the Qur'an. To hesitate over admitting they were unbelievers was itself an act of unbelief.[34] In fact, they were worse in their unbelief than Christians and Jews who at least frankly admitted that they were not Muslims. By contrast, the Shi'is claimed to be inside the tent of the Muslims, and risked undermining it from within.[35]

His aim was to recreate the Islam of the Prophet's Companions and the devout men and women of the next generation who had had intimate contact with those who had known the Prophet well. The Shi'i belief that most of the Companions had betrayed Ali meant that Shi'is considered them to be utterly unacceptable as witnesses to the true Sunna of the Prophet. Wahhabism and Shi'ism were therefore totally incompatible.

Ibn 'Abd al-Wahhab's doctrine was unswerving and rigid. But if compromise on matters of faith and the Sharia was impossible in his eyes, he sometimes showed a very pragmatic willingness to compromise when this was politically wise. He aimed to establish what the his modern biographer Michael Crawford has called 'the regime of godliness'. And he succeeded in marrying his status as the teacher of godliness with the political power of the small emirate of the al-Saud family at Dir'iyah in

Nejd. This led to the start of a partnership that endures to this day. The emirate expanded. As it did so, it implemented the regime of godliness but would also often make expedient compromises. This meant that it failed to enforce the regime of godliness entirely to the satisfaction of Ibn 'Abd al-Wahhab and the religious sheikhs of the Wahhabi movement after his death, when its leadership was taken over by members of his family.

Nevertheless, Ibn 'Abd al-Wahhab taught that Muslims must give unconditional obedience to a ruler, no matter how tyrannical he might be, provided he upheld *tawhid* and the Sharia, and rejected heretical innovations. It was only if the ruler failed to do this and did not govern in accordance with the Qur'an and Sharia that rebellion became legitimate – in fact, a duty. In such circumstances the justification for revolt was that the ruler had made himself an idol. By contrast, the ruler who upheld *tawhid* as envisaged by Ibn 'Abd al-Wahhab was entitled to the loyalty of the community, even if he acted oppressively. *Tawhid* and the regime of godliness thus united ruler and people. Any question of social justice was essentially irrelevant. It was not a concept that occurs in Ibn Abd al-Wahhab's teaching. The religious sheikhs would ensure religious conformity, and the warriors who fought for the ruler would enforce it.[36] In the late twentieth century, when Saudi Arabia acquired previously unimaginable wealth, it would use its resources to spread Wahhabism across the Muslim world.

The expansion of the Saudi emirate started with Ibn 'Abd al-Wahhab proclaiming jihad against those who opposed his teachings, and the taking of other small settlements in Nejd. This culminated in the seizure in 1773–74 of Riyadh, the capital of the emirate's main local adversary. While jihad was preached to extend the emirate, rebellions against its authority were treated as 'tantamount to apostasy'.[37] There were few, if any, Shi'is in Nejd, but as the emirate grew into what is now called the First Saudi State it took over many areas to the east with a substantial Shi'i population. In 1794, the Wahhabis began an educational campaign to eradicate Shi'ism from the areas of eastern Arabia that they had now conquered, even though up to three quarters of the population there were Twelvers. This was to be achieved through preaching, but the Wahhabi efforts met with little lasting success.

A few years later, in April 1802, Wahhabi warriors swept down on Karbala. They sacked and plundered the town and shrine, destroyed

Hussein's tomb, and massacred 2,000 people.[38] At the same time, they pressed on into the Hejaz, where the local protector of the holy cities was the Sharif Ghalib, a descendant of the Prophet through Ali and Hasan. Although he was a Sunni who acknowledged the jurisdiction of the Ottoman Sultan, the Wahhabis considered him to be a crypto-Shi'i. In 1806–07 they took control of both Mecca and Medina. They also closed the routes for Ottoman pilgrimage caravans. These snubs would temporarily be the undoing of the Wahhabis, as it forced the Ottomans to react. As the Ottomans lacked the military resources to regain the Holy Cities themselves, they turned to the governor of Egypt, Muhammad Ali Pasha. An Egyptian army under the capable command of his son, Ibrahim Pasha, now began a professional and very thorough campaign to regain control. It advanced into Nejd and reached Dir'iyah in September 1818, where the Saudis made their last stand. The Egyptians destroyed the town with an artillery bombardment. Ibrahim Pasha had the leading Wahhabi religious scholar, Sheikh Suleyman, executed after taunting him by forcing him to listen to music: something that the strict Wahhabi interpretation of the Sharia outlawed. It seemed at the time that the world had heard the last of the Saudis and of the movement established by Ibn 'Abd al-Wahhab, but that would not be so.

In the nineteenth century, the worlds of Islam and the West would come into contact in an unprecedented way. Thoughtful Muslim religious reformers like the Iranian Jamal al-Din al-Afghani and the Egyptian Muhammad Abduh, whom we will meet in the next chapter, would reflect on how Muslims could benefit from European thought while devoutly practising their faith and preserving their identity. As they learned about the Reformation that had set out to cleanse European Christianity, they pondered whether Islam needed its own Reformation in order to restore the religion to the purity that the Prophet had originally intended. Jamal al-Din al-Afghani even said that Islam needed its own Martin Luther figure. Later on, some Western observers would take up the idea, and even sometimes make comparisons between Islam in the modern world and Christianity in the Europe of the Reformation. One of the many things they overlooked was that in the eighteenth century Islam had already had a figure who could be said to have been its great Protestant Reformer. Progress of his ideas would be slow at first, but would then increase exponentially in the later twentieth century when it became financed by Saudi wealth. We would all do well to remember that the Thirty Years' War and the horrific religious persections that disfigured Christianity in Europe were part and parcel of the Reformation. Those who say Islam needs its own Reformation should be careful what they wish for.

PART TWO

CHAPTER EIGHT

The Long Nineteenth Century
and the Coming of Western Dominance

I

Part Two of this book deals with the Sunni-Shi'i divide over the past 200 years or so, and brings us up to the present day. The Muslim world has been a very different place during this period, no longer able to set its own terms of reference and decide its own agendas.

By the start of the nineteenth century even the great empires of Ottoman Turkey, post-Safavid Iran, and residually Mughal India could no longer deal with the major European powers on anything like equal terms. In the twentieth century, new states would come into being that were products of the colonial era. In earlier ages, boundaries had often been vague, represented by marchlands rather than neat lines on a map. They were rarely delimited on the ground unless they followed the course of a natural line such as a river (and this was, in any case, rare for boundaries in the Muslim world). The boundaries for the new states were often drawn by European powers, and reflected the interests of those powers rather than the aspirations of the people who lived in them. These people would generally have no choice but to become citizens of these new states, or to face exile.

As education became more secular, ideas such as nationalism, democracy and constitutionalism became the currency of debate in the new territorial units into which the Muslim world was now divided. This would often push questions of religion and sect into the background, but religion remained the bedrock of society virtually everywhere. Muslims – Sunnis and Shi'is alike – had to absorb the new ideas that spread from the West. A new dynamic occurred as a result of the impact of the West. In the modern era, the history of Sunnis and Shi'is cannot be treated in isolation from the broader questions of the thorny relations between Islam and the West and the impact of nationalism.

Religious and sectarian questions are not limited to the people of a particular country or state. Nevertheless, the carving up of the Muslim world into modern states defined by modern boundaries often leaves us with no choice but to deal with relations between Sunnis and Shi'is as they developed within particular territorial units. In this way, once we reach the twentieth century we focus in particular on Syria, Lebanon, Iraq and Saudi Arabia, while also looking at important developments elsewhere.

In the late eighteenth century, Muslim rulers of one stripe or another ruled over vast territories stretching from the Atlantic coast of Morocco, right through the Middle East, Central Asia and much if not most of the Indian subcontinent. Further east, Malaya and large parts of what we now call Indonesia were predominantly Muslim lands. Substantial areas of Africa south of the Sahara were also Muslim. By contrast, in 1914, only three completely independent Muslim states still survived: Ottoman Turkey, Iran and Afghanistan. And there were even question marks over how real the independence of Iran and Afghanistan was.

In the 1790s, most areas of the Muslim world were overwhelmingly, often entirely, Sunni. Twelver Shi'is predominated in Iran (which then included all of Azerbaijan), in Bahrain, and in parts of the Arabian mainland along the southern shores of the Persian Gulf. There were also some Twelvers in the Indian subcontinent, including several Twelver kingdoms, although most of their Muslim subjects were Sunni. In the Ottoman Empire, Jebel Amil in Lebanon, and the cities of Karbala, Najaf and Hilla in Iraq, were Twelver enclaves, and there were also pockets of Twelvers scattered around Central Asia. Zaydis predominated in large areas of the Yemeni mountains, while Alawis and Druze were locally dominant in some remote parts of Greater Syria.

The long nineteenth century was the period when the Muslim world fell under the hegemony of the West. The transformation that came to Muslim countries during this period and subsequently is essential background for understanding how Muslims would come to see themselves as they became part of the brave, new, Western-dominated world that emerged. It was not just Western technology, organisation, economic dominance and military might that changed their lives. It was also Western ideas. Foremost among these was nationalism. It was an idea that spread slowly but had begun to put down roots in many Muslim majority countries in the decades leading up to the First World War.

Nationalism is a sense of identity, a feeling of belonging to an 'imagined community' of people who share a passionate solidarity with each other even though they may have never met. It is a 'deep horizontal comradeship'; a 'fraternity' which can inspire men to die for their country by the million.[1] This solidarity comes from a consciousness of living in the same land, from sharing the same sense of history and a common culture, and speaking the same language. Religious identity, too, can play an important part in a sense of nationhood. The solidarity of nationalism binds people together against those who are perceived as outsiders, who thus come to be perceived as 'the other'. It is not for nothing that Ernest Renan (1823–1892), a French philosopher and historian of Semitic civilisations, once quipped that nationalists are people who are united in a false understanding of history and a hatred of their neighbours.

Local loyalties had always been extremely important throughout the Muslim World; but religious affiliation had generally been the prime marker of identity. In the second half of this book we shall see that, as nationalism spread, Islam would sometimes be seen as an important element of national identity. At the same time, nationalism had to compete for Muslim hearts and minds with another idea: pan-Islamic solidarity. There would be those who saw Muslims as an 'imagined community' that transcended all national and other geographical boundaries. To a considerable extent, this would reduce the significance of the Sunni-Shi'i divide.

Most Muslim states, including Ottoman Turkey and Iran, were forced to devote much of their energy to meeting the challenge posed by the onward march of the West. During earlier centuries there had been many wars between the Ottoman and Persian Empires. Antagonism between Sunnis and Shi'is, and the resultant sectarian propaganda, had played a role in them, as we have seen. Now, however, Ottoman and Iranian rulers had other preoccupations and did not have the time or energy to make war against each other. The settlement between Nadir Shah and the Ottomans, at which we looked in Chapter Seven, endured. This permanently ended a major irritant affecting Sunni-Shi'i relations.

II

In the nineteenth century, Ottoman sultans began to place stress on their status as 'caliph' in a way that was altogether new. Abdul Hamid II, who reigned from 1876 to 1909, may even have seen his title of caliph as more important than that of sultan.[2] In 1876 the Ottomans adopted a constitution: it began by proclaiming that 'His Majesty the Sultan is, in his capacity as supreme Caliph, the protector of the Muslim religion'.[3] As caliph, Abdul Hamid claimed a religious focus for the loyalty of his Muslim subjects – as well as for Muslims everywhere. It was a daring and clever idea – an attempt to assert jurisdiction over all Muslims across the world. In theory, this included Shi'is, whom the Ottomans saw as Muslims who had erred but were still Muslims. As a matter of principle, they did not recognise Shi'i sects as having the validity of a Sunni doctrinal law school, but were perfectly prepared to tax Shi'is and conscript them into their armies. What Abdul Hamid II had done was recast Islam as a kind of super-nationalism that could be used for political ends.

There were weak foundations to the Ottoman sultans' claim to be caliph in any sense that went beyond a title of honour. In the first place, as has already been shown at the beginning of Chapter Six, there had never been a successor to the Abbasid Caliphate with anything like a valid claim to attract the worldwide loyalty of Sunni Muslims. Since the ninth century, the role of defender and protector of Muslims was frequently exercised by a sultan, a ruler who exercised authority and claimed to be the protector of Muslims within his own dominions. The first sultans had appeared while the caliphate was still in existence, and drew their legitimacy from investiture by the caliph. By the time the caliphate was destroyed by the Mongols, the concept of sultanate was well established, and it was soon obvious that new sultanates could emerge even though there was no longer a caliph.

It was only as the Ottoman Empire was rolled back by the European powers that emphasis began to be laid on the sultan's role as caliph. In 1774 the Treaty of Küçük Kaynarca required the empire to cede territories to Russia, ending Ottoman domination of the Black Sea. It was specified that the Crimea – a territory then inhabited predominantly by Muslim Tatars – would become an independent Khanate. The treaty described the sultan as 'Caliph of all Muslims', leaving him a spiritual authority over the Crimean Tatars. It was also a face-saving quid pro quo for the Ottomans to match the designation of Russia as protector of Orthodox Christians in the Ottoman Empire. Its significance was stressed again in 1784 when Russia annexed the Crimea. But a quarter of a century after the Treaty of Küçük Kaynarca, when Napoleon invaded Egypt, Egyptians appealed to the Ottoman emperor to save them from the French invasion. Their approaches were made to him as sultan, not caliph.[4]

When Selim the Grim extinguished the Mamluk sultanate of Egypt in 1517 he brought the relics of the Prophet – his cloak, staff and seal – back to Istanbul. These had been kept at the Mamluk court in Cairo. He was accompanied on his way home by the last puppet Mamluk caliph, Mutawakkil III (r. 1508–1516 and again in 1517). Mutawakkil's presence in Istanbul does not seem to have been particularly significant, because he was subsequently allowed to return to Egypt. At some point, a story was devised that he had solemnly transferred the office of caliph to the Ottoman sultans. The Ottoman scholar Ahmed Cevdet Pasha, a conservative figure of great gravitas, wrote these words in 1861 at the time of the accession to the Ottoman throne of Sultan Abdulaziz, the first sultan to take the claim to be caliph seriously:[5]

> When Sultan Selim conquered Egypt and brought the Abbasid caliph to Istanbul, the Abbasid caliph girded Sultan Selim with the sword [of Umar] and thus transferred the Islamic Caliphate to the house of Osman.[6]

The fact that some but not all Ottoman sultans had intermittently claimed the title of caliph before 1517 is a glaring inconsistency with this account. Ahmed Cevdet Pasha was either unaware of this or chose to ignore it. Another problem for the Ottoman claim was that many scholars across the centuries had argued that a caliph must come from the Quraysh. As the Abbasid Caliphate receded ever further into history, less stress was placed on this requirement. It had become, after all, a purely academic discussion – and it was a point on which the Hanafi doctrinal law school, which was the official form of Islam in the Ottoman Empire, did not insist. The Ottomans were not from the Quraysh, nor even Arab. As the very first sparks of what would develop into Arab nationalism began to appear in the later decades of the nineteenth century, the question of the Ottoman Caliphate could be a sensitive topic among the Sultan's Arab subjects.

Abdul Hamid had a strategy to deal with this. Arab religious advisers were given important posts at court in a way that was new, and he created a kind of 'Islamic Vatican' at the Sultan's Yildiz Palace in Istanbul.[7] By the time he came to the throne, European concepts of nationalism were beginning to percolate into the elites of many Muslim countries. This already threatened to make a new sense of nationhood the focal point for identity, one that went beyond religious or sectarian boundaries. Islam as a political ideology – what was then called Pan-Islamism and is now generally called Islamism – recognised no racial or ethnic boundaries, but only those of faith. It could thus compete with the appeal of nationalism, and inculcate the sense of identity of belonging to an 'imagined community'. Efforts were also made to educate Ottoman Muslims in the teachings and practice of their religion. All this had the effect of promoting Islam as a focus of identity against nationalist sentiment.

III

After the Crimean War, which ended in 1856, the Ottomans were accepted as a member of the Concert of Europe (or 'Vienna Congress' – the system whereby Europe's conservative nations had maintained the balance of power since Napoleonic times). The thought that at least one Muslim power was recognised as an equal by the Western world was a great solace to Muslims everywhere; many were seeing their countries annexed or reduced to mere protectorates by colonial powers such as Britain and France. Ottoman envoys were sent to teach Muslims in the European colonial empires about the sultan-caliph and request that he should be remembered in the Friday prayers like the Abbasid caliphs of old. The universalist claims of the sultan-caliph to a right to suzerainty or even rule over all Muslims were deeply uncomfortable for the colonial powers. This was especially so as Ottoman Turkey was now doing what it could to modernise itself, even though 30 per cent of the budget had to service its debts to European bankers. Central control was spreading inexorably into even the outlying provinces of the empire, and was exemplified best, perhaps, by schemes to link it together by railways. Medina in the Hejaz was connected to Damascus and the rest of the empire in 1908 by a railway line crowd-funded by Muslims across the world. They contributed their money so as to facilitate the pilgrimage to Mecca, but the line also served to bring Ottoman administrators and troops to the Hejaz. The construction of the railway was a personal triumph for Abdul Hamid II, and a vindication of his policy of branding his empire as the Caliphate.

Yet the empire's problems were probably insuperable. Abdul Hamid II was autocratic, secretive and inclined to paranoia. Despite his best efforts, the empire's gradual dismemberment seemed set to continue. Things went from bad to worse. A coup was finally mounted in 1908 by nationalist officers known as the 'Young Turks', who took over the government. Although the Young Turks reconvened the Ottoman Parliament and saw themselves as liberals, their rule soon showed itself to be as autocratic as that of Abdul Hamid, who was deposed in 1909 after a failed counter-coup. His replacement as Sultan-Caliph, Mehmed V, was little more than a puppet. The Young Turks had much in common with violent revolutionaries elsewhere in the nineteenth and twentieth centuries. They did not hesitate to subvert the constitutional order that had been their rallying cry on their journey to power.

There were also two ironies about the revolutionaries. The first was that their numbers included members from other communities in the empire, as well as ethnic Turks: Albanian and other Balkan Muslims, Jews, and even some Armenians. Yet an aggressive Turkish nationalism would become their guiding star. They were essentially secularist, and some of their leading figures would dream of turning the empire into a pan-Turkish state. Yet the role of Islam – Sunni Islam – in Turkish identity would prove to be too great a factor for them to ignore. This brings us to the other irony. The Young Turk leadership would continue to revel in the status the sultan enjoyed as sultan-caliph (even though they had taken all power away from him). Pan-Islamist feeling and calls for jihad mounted by the sultan-caliph remained useful items in their political toolbox. It helped to ensure that large numbers of Arab and other non-Turkish Muslims remained loyal to the bitter end.

Although Sunni Islam had been able to survive and thrive perfectly well after the end of the Abbasid Caliphate in 1258, the caliphate had always been mourned. It had remained in the hearts of Sunni Muslims as a symbol of the unity and power of Islam. They also found it a source of pride, which was renewed as modern scholarship began to make its cultural achievements better known. Already by the mid-nineteenth century, Muslim scholars were beginning to notice the debt modern Europe owed to the philosophers and scientists of the Abbasid era. For many Muslims across the world, the reinvented Ottoman Caliphate became a potent symbol and focal point for identity.

IV

And what of Shi'i Iran, once the great rival of the Sunni Ottomans? From the 1790s through to the early 1920s, Iran was ruled by the Qajar dynasty, who stemmed from one of the old Kizilbash tribes. The Qajars were Twelvers who ruled a largely Twelver country, and made a point of ostentatiously demonstrating their piety. But their Turkic origins made it unrealistic for them to assert that they were descended from one of the imams as the Safavids had done, let alone claim to be a representative of the Hidden Imam.

They attempted to cultivate the religious scholars of the Usuli school, but with decidedly mixed results. The Usulis now predominated among Twelvers virtually everywhere except in Bahrain. The Usulis, it will be recalled, hold that analytical reasoning by learned and pious scholars should be used to establish the contents of the Sharia, which should not be determined purely on a literal reading of texts. These scholars were now completing the process of transforming themselves into a Usuli clerical class. They liked the institutional independence they had gained, and were not going to surrender it. They had also developed a hierarchy. At the bottom were the ordinary mullahs who gave judgments only on rules that were clear and unambiguous. Above them were the mujtahids, who had the knowledge of the principles on which the rules were based and were qualified to give independent rulings. At the very top, there were the scholars who had an absolute, all-embracing competence known as *ijtihad mutlaq*, literally 'absolute ijtihad'. During the first half of the nineteenth century there were probably only a dozen-or-so such scholars, but more than 175 such mujtahids have been identified as active during the reign of Naser al-Din Shah (r. 1848–96). Ordinary believers (and ordinary mullahs) now had to follow a mujtahid as a *Marja al-taqlid*, a 'source of emulation' onto whom the individual believer 'shifts his responsibility in matters of faith, subjecting himself to [the expert judgement of the source of emulation] and blindly following his decisions.'[8] Sometimes a senior cleric would be widely recognised as the major or even the sole source of emulation. If the latter was the case, the idea that he was the sole source of emulation had to arise spontaneously among Twelver Shi'is. In other words, it had to be discerned by the faithful. It was not something that could be imposed from above. On the death of a scholar who was the sole source of emulation, it would be unlikely that a single figure would already have the necessary pre-eminence to follow him. It was therefore probable that some time would elapse before another such figure emerged and, indeed, more than likely that this would not happen.

Outside Iran, the Usuli dominance of Twelver Shi'ism also continued. Twelvers in the shrine cities of Iraq and in India would also recognise a leading scholar as their source of emulation. New technologies added to the importance of the shrine cities, since the telegraph enabled mujtahids there to disseminate their opinions much more rapidly to Twelvers everywhere.

The new hierarchical structure led to eminent mujtahids feeling themselves able to declare *takfir* against an individual – that is, to declare that that person should no longer be considered a believing Muslim. This meant that the individual was an apostate, worthy of death. Leading clerics sometimes pronounced *takfir* against each other, but victims also included the Akhbaris, that is to say those Twelvers who did not accept the role that the Usulis gave to reason and *ijtihad*, and who preferred a rather more literalist approach to the reading of texts. They still survived in Basra and would remain dominant in Bahrain, despite the best efforts of the Usulis.

Other targets for *takfir* were Sufis, the Babi movement and the Baha'is. The Babi movement appeared on the 1,000th anniversary of the occultation of the Twelfth Imam in 1844, when Ali Muhammad, a young man from Shiraz who was a descendant of the Prophet, declared that the Hidden Imam would reappear at Karbala on 1 January 1845. He also declared himself to be the *bab*, or gateway to the Hidden Imam. He was hauled before a panel of religious scholars who forced him to recant, but he subsequently went on to declare that he was the Hidden Imam himself, and announced that the Sharia was no longer applicable because the End Times had begun. He was imprisoned, tried for heresy, flogged and eventually executed in 1850 after his followers began rising up in rebellion. Among the rebels was Mirza Husayn Ali Nuri Baha'ullah, who would become the founder of the Baha'i religion. Although the Baha'is are Iran's largest religious minority, they have frequently been subject to persecution as renegades who have abandoned Islam. This oppression has at times been very severe.[9]

The clergy thus attained great power in Iran. They used this to protect their position and hinder Qajar attempts at modernising reforms, which were aimed at strengthening the central government and might chip away at the clergy's influence. This was a period of increased foreign commercial penetration of Iran. Trade agreements with Russia and Britain granted many privileges to the merchants from the empires these two countries had established. This led to the clergy adopting a populist role as protectors of the Iranian merchants of the markets or bazaars (often called the 'bazaaris'), who tended to be devout. The clergy had close links with this class, into which they married, and from which many religious scholars were drawn.

In 1890, a monopoly over tobacco in Iran was granted to a British citizen. Clerical agitation was a key factor in a nationwide boycott of tobacco that continued until the concession was abolished. Not only did preachers thunder against the monopoly from the pulpit, but they also received strong support from leading clerics in the shrine cities of Iraq, who sent telegrams to the shah. One opinion was from Mirza Hasan Shirazi, a cleric in Samarra who was considered the highest source of emulation at the time. He denounced the consumption of tobacco while the boycott was in force as the equivalent of declaring war on the Hidden Imam. The government found itself forced to cancel the concession; only then would Shirazi send a telegram informing the populace that they could resume smoking.

The part the clergy played in fighting the tobacco monopoly has been described as a dress rehearsal for their role in the events that became known as Iran's Constitutional Revolution in the period 1905–11.[10] It began with protests among the bazaaris. They received clerical backing when the governor of Tehran had some merchants publicly whipped for allegedly profiteering from the price of sugar. The clergy thus played an important role in initiating the revolution. They also influenced the drafting of Iran's first constitution, which declared Twelver Shi'i Islam the state religion. The constitution also contained a provision that a committee of leading mujtahids would be established to vet legislation to ensure that it complied with Islam. However, this committee was never set up.

Although the clerics had given the constitutional project legitimacy at the very beginning, they soon lost out in terms of influence to intellectuals with a modern education, who also played a key role in the revolution. These intellectuals were at ease with the new language of constitutionalism, rights, and liberty used in the constitution, terminology that was unfamiliar to most clerics. Therefore the initiative in moving Iran forward would now pass to the intellectuals and their new ideas, and it would remain with them until the late 1970s. Some clergy soon noticed how the constitution limited the Sharia in many respects. They were also against secular measures such as the codification of laws, the creation of a new court system outside clerical control, and equality before the law, which abolished the old Sharia distinction between Muslims and non-Muslims.

The revolution did not last, but the institution of parliament survived. The constitution was 'well beyond the comprehension of most of the people it was intended to serve'.[11] Yet even though new, secular ideas now seemed to be the way forward for Iran, the clergy retained their importance among the bazaaris and in the countryside. This would remain the case in the decades that followed, even though it was often overlooked at the time.

V

Islam found itself on the defensive almost everywhere against the apostles of Western rationalism, as well as unprecedented attempts by Christian missionaries to win Muslim converts. These challenges applied equally to Sunni and Shi'i Muslims. The Western onslaught reduced the significance of the differences between the two sects when Muslims tried to defend their faith. Yet the long nineteenth century still saw some friction between Sunnis and Shi'is, as well as attempts to minimise their differences and to promote reconciliation. Many reforms carried out in the Ottoman Empire were aimed at producing a unified concept of citizenship on European lines; in theory these should have benefited all minorities, including Twelvers. Nevertheless, by and large, the Ottoman Twelvers 'occupied the more backward sectors of the empire's economy', as Juan Cole, the academic and commentator on Middle Eastern affairs, puts it.[12] The result was that the gap actually widened between urban Sunnis and the rural Twelvers in areas like the marshes of southern Iraq.[13]

The Ottoman authorities had cause to worry about the spread of Shi'ism in their empire, in much the same way as they fretted about the activities of Christian missionaries. Among illiterate populations, folk religion was intimately bound up with superstition, and heterodox ideas could easily acquire a dangerous resonance. The Ottomans had long had to cope with Gnostic Shi'i beliefs among the Alawis of Syria and the Alevis of Anatolia. Now another development took place: the spread of Twelver Shism among the tribes of southern Iraq, which led to most of the inhabitants of that area converting to Shi'ism.

Iraq was the location of four major Shi'i shrines: Najaf, Karbala, Kazimayn and Samarra. Najaf and Karbala were also homes of Shi'i scholarship, as was the town of Hilla. Iraq had therefore always been important to Twelver Shi'is. Given that Sunni and Shi'i Islam were the defining characteristics of the Ottoman and Safavid Empires respectively, and that Iraq lay at the edge of each of those empires, it is no surprise that historically it had been bitterly contested between them. After the conversion of Iran to Twelver Shi'ism, Iranian scholars and pilgrims came to live and study in these Iraqi cities.

When Sunni Afghans captured Isfahan in 1722, they expropriated much property belonging to Shi'i foundations. Many Shi'i clergy fled to Iraq, especially to Najaf and Karbala. The Iranians put down roots, which helped the Usuli school of Twelver Shi'ism to gain dominance in Iraq over its Akhbari rivals, while Persian was spoken alongside Arabic in Karbala, which had a majority Persian population for a while. The military and political weakness of the Ottoman Empire was reflected in its acceptance that Iran had a special status in Karbala and Najaf, which were at times virtually independent city states. But it was not only Iran that posed a problem for the Ottomans in Iraq. The weakness of their authority meant that, in the eighty-or-so years up to the 1830s, their rule was only indirect, and was subcontracted to Mamluks in Baghdad and Basra.

From the late eighteenth century, many tribes in southern Iraq – including new arrivals from Arabia – were converted to Twelver Shi'ism. Although this had already begun before the Wahhabi raids into Iraq which were mentioned in the last chapter,[14] there is no doubt that those raids encouraged this process. The Wahhabis saw Shi'is as idolators, and they besieged Najaf twice and stormed and pillaged Karbala in 1802. Lacking a local base of support against the Wahhabis (and also seeking local support with which to put pressure on the Ottomans), the Iranian religious scholars in Karbala set out to convert the tribes to Shi'ism. Karbala, Najaf and Hilla were important market towns for the tribes, which provided natural opportunities for preaching on market day. New irrigation works were also significant, including those financed by the chief minister of the Shi'i state of Awadh (Oudh) in India in order to secure the water supply for Najaf. Tribes began to settle on reclaimed land near Najaf and Karbala, exposing them to proselytisation from the sacred cities.

Later in the nineteenth century, as a result of Ottoman reforms and the push to integrate the Ottoman Empire into a globalised capitalist economy, other major irrigation schemes were carried out, with the intention of encouraging the tribes to settle. A new land law and system of land registration led to the splitting up of communal land into plots registered in the names of individual owners. This was all part of a nineteenth-century civilising mission – Ottoman style. The Ottomans hoped to reduce the power of the paramount tribal sheikhs. They succeeded in this to a considerable extent, and tribes themselves began to fragment. The nomads had always been ignorant of their religion and lax in observing it, and often preferred their own unwritten codes of law to the Sharia. The Ottomans intended to make them into better Sunni Muslims by persuading them to take up farming. Yet what they did was give the Shi'i preachers a golden opportunity to spread their message, since Sunni scholars who could counteract their activities were few in remote, southern Iraq. Despite this, Shi'ism seems to have stopped at the edge of the cultivated area. None of the tribes that remained desert nomads converted.

The Ottomans were aware of what was happening, and tried to think of ways to slow down or reverse the process of conversion. In 1894, Ali Galip Bey, the Ottoman ambassador in Tehran, wrote a report suggesting that the movements of Iranian religious scholars who entered Ottoman territory should be restricted, especially if they went to rural areas and moved among nomads, when they might spread sedition. He also advocated a ban on teaching religion by non-Ottomans and the expulsion of any Shi'is who proposed 'religious separation'. Another unsigned and undated report suggested that the government should set out to reconcile Sunnis and Shi'is, since 'now it is time for all Islamic peoples to perform their religious duty by uniting against the Christian powers'.[15] This was, after all, the policy of Sultan Abdul Hamid II himself who thus, whether consciously or not, recognised a certain legitimacy in Shi'ism.

One consequence was that the Ottoman authorities exempted students in Shi'i madrasas (religious schools) from conscription, leading to a fall in the number of recruits to the army from the district of Karbala. There was a positive Shi'i response to Abdul Hamid's policy. Sometimes, at least, Shi'i scholars silenced criticism of the Ottomans. They also considered appealing to Abdul Hamid as 'the strongest Muslim ruler' to ask the Shah of Iran to be less subservient to the Russians. One letter to him from the three most senior mujtahids in Karbala addressed him with the caliphal title of 'Commander of the Faithful', which Shi'is traditionally reserve for Ali, the first Imam and the figure they regard as the Prophet's appointed successor.[16]

The motivations behind the conversions to Shi'ism in Iraq are hard to unravel at this distance in time. However, Yitzhak Nakash (associate professor of Middle Eastern and Islamic studies at Brandeis University in Massachusetts) has probably done this to the greatest extent that is still possible. Factors he lists include: the hope that conversion would remove the fear of conscription into the Ottoman army; a bitter reaction against the transformation of some of their tribal sheikhs into Sunni landed aristocrats as the tribal system broke down; a convenient vehicle to express anti-government solidarity; and the opportunity to feel, as Nakash puts it, that they were better Muslims than their oppressors. It may also have seemed advantageous to convert to Shi'ism because of the influence of the shrine cities, which would have been local economic magnets.

The stories of the martyrdom of Ali and, even more so, of Hussein, the Prophet's grandson and, for Shi'is, the Third Imam, resonated deeply with the tribes. Tribal poetry remained vibrant even as the population became agriculturalists. The Shi'i martyrs began to be celebrated in heroic poetry in a way similar to the veneration of distant tribal ancestors. Shi'ism thus began to become ingrained at a popular level. When five leading scholars were sent to establish Sunni education in rural southern Iraq in 1905, they were unable to counteract the Shi'i preaching. Perhaps by then it was too late, although Istanbul lacked the funds to pay the scholars' salaries, and their endeavours may therefore have been half-hearted. The Shi'i clergy of the shrine cities were able to outspend them. Yet many tribes were still split between the two sects, and the process of conversion to Shi'ism continued well into the twentieth century. As with tribal Bedouin nomads throughout the history of Islam (and it is important to remember that the tribes of southern Iraq were Bedouin before they became settled), the extent to which they could really be considered to be Muslims in anything more than the most nominal sense was open to discussion. As Rashid Rida, the important Sunni scholar whom we shall meet in the next chapter, wrote in 1908:

> If those [Shi'i] emissaries preach [religion] among the [tribesmen], and teach them the Islamic duties, as well as what is permissible and what is prohibited, then, from the point of view of their religion, the current position of the tribesmen is better than their former status.[17]

Shi'is may have been seen as Muslims who had rejected the true Sunni faith, or had defected from it. But Rashid Rida still saw them as Muslims. One of his key motivations throughout his long career was to help

Muslim states and societies resist Western penetration. It is therefore unsurprising that he could sometimes be conciliatory towards Shi'is.

The Young Turk Revolution and the restoration of the Ottoman constitution in 1908 brought a considerable degree of freedom of the press. The years leading up to the First World War saw many Sunnis and Shi'is call for the unity of Islam against the West, and to argue that Islam was compatible with the modern world and could be reconciled with the new scientific discoveries. At the same time, Shi'i scholars in Iraq took full advantage of this to reach wider audiences, and to promote their own position. They also established a few modern schools for Shi'i youth alongside traditional madrasas teaching a religious curriculum. The new schools included the teaching of French and English in their curricula, and were intended to enable their pupils to acquire the modern, Western knowledge that was now so prized.

At times, the leading mujtahids were seen to be acting almost as though they were heads of state. Some of them felt free to support ideas such as the right or duty of the scholars to depose a sovereign ruler if this was necessary in order to defend Islam.[18] They also felt empowered to issue calls for a defensive jihad – something that the Ottomans permitted because it suited their own policies. Such a call was potentially controversial among Twelvers, because the declaration of jihad was a prerogative of the Hidden Imam. Yet, just as other functions of the Hidden Imam had been deemed to be delegated to religious scholars, so too in 1805 Sheikh Ja'far Kashif al-Ghita categorised the Wahhabis who had besieged Najaf as 'enemies of Islam' and proclaimed a jihad against them. This provided a precedent. In December 1910 a group of respected mujtahids called for the unity of Islam and a jihad to oust Russian troops from territories in northern Iran. It seems to have been welcomed by the Ottomans and by Rashid Rida in Cairo, who saw it as the first tangible sign that the Sunni and Shi'i religious scholars were prepared to act together to promote Muslim unity.

Other examples would follow. Shortly thereafter, Italy invaded the Ottoman territories we now think of as Libya, and the Iraqi Shi'is joined the Sunnis of the Ottoman empire in responding with calls to arms to defend Islam. This was also the case when, simultaneously, Britain and Russia colluded to occupy parts of Iran. But the greatest example was after the outbreak of the First World War. A British expeditionary force landed at the mouth of the Tigris and began to fight its way up river. The Shi'i mujtahids rallied the tribes of the south of Iraq to the Ottoman cause. The Shi'i tribes fought as auxiliaries alongside their Sunni comrades and the Ottoman army at the Battle of Shu'ayba in April 1915 in a forlorn attempt to throw the British back.

VI

By the second half of the nineteenth century, the penetration of Western ideas among the elite in Muslim majority countries was growing. The thought of Jamal al-Din al-Afghani (1838–1897), who addressed the question of how Muslims should react to the spread of Western political, economic and cultural hegemony, is of particular interest to us because of the way he also tried to move beyond sectarian differences between Sunnis and Shi'is. Therefore, before we leave the nineteenth century behind, it is worth pausing for a moment and attempting to encapsulate his influential teaching – and that of his most significant pupil.

He is one of the fathers of Islamic modernism and, it could be said, of Islamism.[19] The name 'al-Afghani' means 'the Afghan' in Arabic. Al-Afghani claimed to come from Afghanistan and to have been raised a Sunni, but in reality it seems he was born into a Twelver family of Sayyids (descendants of the Prophet) near Hamadan in Iran. He received a religious education in the Shi'i shrine cities of Iraq. He also visited India, where he began to learn about Western thought, of which he gained a good knowledge. While there, he developed a lifelong hatred of Western imperialism, especially that of Britain. Rousing the Muslim world from its torpor and corruption became his life's work.

His thought flowed from two passionately held convictions. The first was a sense that the West could destroy Islam if Muslims did not reform their religion; the other was an intense pride at the heritage of the civilisation that Muslims had created. Many younger intellectuals and religious reformers were his disciples. These included Muhammad Abduh (1814–1905), who would become the head of the Muslim religious establishment in Egypt at the end of the nineteenth century.

The perceived failures of Islam were the fault of Muslims themselves, he taught, especially corrupt and self-seeking rulers and scholarly elites.

Islam had suffered from stagnation and servile conformism, as well as from all kinds of deviance. This is what had left Muslims defenceless before the West. It was now time for Muslims to revive their faith and act upon it.

While he was certainly influential in the growth of nationalism in a number of separate Muslim countries, he taught that Muslims should have the same feeling of solidarity that binds a nation. He wanted Muslims to unite by developing social solidarity and helping each other, as well as the non-Muslim inhabitants of their countries. Unlike many other scholars, he taught that Muslims could revolt against an oppressive ruler.

Al-Afghani admired the Germans for having overcome the Catholic/Protestant split and forged a united nation, despite the immense strife and bloodshed of the Reformation. Muslims should emulate this example and overcome the Sunni-Shi'i divide. He called for Shi'i Iran and Sunni Afghanistan to unite. In the last decade or so of his life, he tried to develop a political formula to reconcile the Sunni Ottomans and Shi'i Iran.

Nevertheless, by claiming he was from Afghanistan rather than Iran, al-Afghani deliberately hid his Shi'i origins. For a period, he taught at the Al-Azhar mosque in Cairo, the foremost institution of learning in the Sunni world. To do so, he must have adopted the Sunni forms for saying the daily ritual prayers and abandoned the slightly different ones of Twelver Shi'is. On the other hand, his choice of texts for his class was unusual, and included books by Abbasid-era rationalist philosophers. At that time, scholars teaching at the Al-Azhar did not normally choose such books for their classes, but al-Afghani had studied them in the Iraqi shrine cities where they were an important element in the curriculum for aspiring Twelver mujtahids.

His pupil Muhammad Abduh noticed a contrast between his tutor's lectures and those of the other scholars. The latter taught by rote, and did not welcome critical discussion. Al-Afghani, by contrast, demanded that his class engage with the text and discuss it. This was the teaching methodology used in the Shi'i universities of the shrine cities.

On one level, the reason al-Afghani concealed his Shi'i origins was probably because he did not consider them important in the context of his desire to unite all Muslims against the colonial powers. But the fact that he found it necessary or at least advisable to conceal his Shi'i origins tells us that Sunni Muslims in Cairo and Istanbul would have been much less likely to heed the views of a Twelver. If he had been frank about these origins – let alone if he had presented himself as an Iranian Twelver rather than an Afghani Sunni – he would have made his task of uniting Muslims to resist the imperial spread of the West even harder to accomplish.

Yet Sunnism and Shi'ism are trends that can overlap, as well as sects. Muhammad Abduh, who would become his star pupil, would go on to become not only the head of Egypt's religious establishment but also the great modernist reformer in Sunni Islam. His work adapting the Sharia to the circumstances of the modern world had an immense impact on Sunni Islam that is with us still.

One of his more controversial opinions was that Islam can permit the paying of interest on a loan if this contributes to the public good. This meant reinterpreting the Qur'an, where *riba*, frequently translated into English as 'interest', is specifically forbidden. Muhammad Abduh seems to have done this by invoking the principle of *maslahah*, interpreting the Sharia in the way most beneficial to humanity, which is used by Sunni scholars. Yet is it altogether fanciful to see Abduh's approach to this question as being rather like that which a Twelver mujtahid might have taken? A mujtahid would have felt able to accord reason a much greater role in interpreting the literal meaning of the sacred text than most Sunni scholars would have done.[20] Whatever the case, there are clear signs of the influence of Twelver Shi'i thought in some of Muhammad Abduh's writings, and there is no doubt that these reflect al-Afghani's influence.[21] In the early editions of his major work *risalat al-tawhid*, 'the Theology of Unity', he subscribed to the old Mu'tazili view that the Qur'an was created by God, rather than being the uncreated speech of God.[22] This was extremely controversial – in fact, anathema – to most Sunnis. Yet it reflected the general Shi'i view. His editors dropped this from the later editions of the work, which were published after his death and which reached a much wider audience.

Muhammad Abduh gave Sunni Islam a mechanism that would help it to adapt itself to the modern world. He advocated a reversion to the teachings of the pious ancestors, *al-salaf al-salih*, and doing away with the accretions that Islam had acquired across the centuries. For him, these pious ancestors included the great thinkers of the Abbasid age to whom al-Afghani had introduced him, and whose logical thinking and aptitude for debate would enable him to put Islam in tune with the modern world at the same time as attacking popular superstitions. He saw this as far preferable to the previous practice, which was to follow rigidly the teaching of the doctrinal law school to which a particular Muslim belonged. Yet others who came after him would limit the concept of *al-salaf al-salih* to just the first three generations of Muslims, with an effect that was often the opposite of the one Abduh had intended. Rather than making Sunni Islam more open to rational debate, reducing the importance of the doctrinal law schools would pin the Islamic belief and practice of many Sunnis down to the strictest and narrowest possible construction of how those first generations had practised their faith. That is what the word 'Salafism' generally means today.

VII

In the long nineteenth century there was relatively little friction between Sunnis and Shi'is. Muslim societies were preoccupied with the new challenges they faced as a result of the nineteenth-century version of globalisation. Disdain for members of the other sect continued, as did discrimination, but the idea of unity among Muslims transcended sectarian divisions and was increasingly attractive. It provided a focal point for identity and was thus a counterweight to the new, Western idea of nationalism. At the same time, many Muslims embraced nationalism, and saw no contradiction between this and practising their religion. Even though the Ottomans looked askance at the spread of Twelver Shi'ism in Iraq, they were able to live with it. After all, Shi'is could be taxed and conscripted into the army just like Sunnis – and just like Christians and Jews. That was what mattered to the Ottomans most of all.

CHAPTER NINE

Between the Two World Wars

I

By the end of the First World War the Muslim world lay almost completely prostrate before the Western powers. In the Middle East, Britain and France gained new territories under League of Nations mandates. France's share was Syria and Lebanon, while Britain acquired Palestine (which included Jordan) and Iraq. Britain also became the dominant power in Iran.

The creation of these new and completely arbitrary divisions was greeted with dismay by most of the inhabitants of these lands. The new entities of Syria, Lebanon, Iraq and Palestine (out of which Israel would be created in 1948–49) were left with formidable problems in establishing a sense of nationhood. Religious differences were often significant. The peace settlement between Turkey and Greece included an exchange of populations in which Turks and Greeks were defined solely by their religious identity as Muslims or Orthodox Christians.

In British-mandated Palestine, Jews were seen by Britain as an ethnicity defined solely by religion. By contrast, the overwhelming majority of the population, the native Arabic speakers, were initially dismissed as the 'existing non-Jewish communities in Palestine'.[1] The Arabs of Palestine were predominantly Sunni Muslim (with a tiny Shiʻi element) and a large Christian minority. They would now rally behind the banner of Arab nationalism and the principle of national self-determination as they sought to defend themselves from colonisation by the European Jews. Sunni-Shiʻi divides existed in three of the mandated territories:

Syria, Lebanon and Iraq. Yet in none of these was it seen as sufficiently important to be a marker of ethnicity in drawing up the mandates.

At street level, Muslim solidarity and appeals to past glories often meant much more than calls by intellectuals for the establishment of a secular, pluralist Arab nation. When volunteers were raised to support the tiny Syrian army that forlornly tried to halt the French invasion in 1920, their cause was called *al-jihad al-watani*, 'the patriotic jihad'.

The same congruence of the new, nationalist sentiment with appeals to Islam's martial rhetoric reappeared only a few years later, when the Great Syrian Revolt of 1925 broke out. It would spread over much of the mandated territory before it was finally crushed in 1927 by reinforcements rushed to Syria by France. It followed earlier opposition to France among the Alawis of the Nusayri mountains and in the countryside of Aleppo. Perhaps because these areas had already been subdued, they were not greatly affected in 1925. But the great revolt spread from the Hawran to Damascus and its surrounding countryside, Hama and much of the southern half of Syria before France was able to reassert control.

Syria's great revolt cut across religious lines. It began among the Druze of the Hawran plateau over specific local grievances, especially questions of honour such as the mistreatment of Druze envoys by the French authorities. As the Druze drove the French out of much of the Hawran, they were joined by some local Muslims and Christians. Guerrilla fighting spread to the countryside around Damascus, the predominantly Sunni Muslim city of Hama, and then Damascus itself. The revolt also spread into parts of southern Lebanon, where there was concern at the possibility of a combined uprising among Druze and Twelver Shi'i peasants. There was a massacre of Maronite villagers at Kawkaba, committed by Druze.[2] The Maronites were a Christian sect that had thrown in its lot with the Crusaders many centuries before. They had had close ties with Catholic France for centuries. During the mandate, they were perceived – with considerable justification – as supporting the French.

The French policy was always to attempt to split off religious minorities from the Sunni majority. Sometimes they had an element of success but, except among the Maronites, this was always limited. Although the rebellion was crushed, France was forced to compromise with Arab nationalism in its aftermath and allowed a parliamentary republic to be set up under its control. When that republic became independent after the Second World War, the new independent Syria received enthusiastic support from its Shi'i minorities, Alawis, Druze and Ismailis, who together probably made up a little over 16 per cent of the population, It would really only be in the 1970s that sectarian politics would begin to have a major impact in Syria.

The French split Lebanon off from Syria and established it as a separate state. There was a strong desire for independence among the Maronites who predominated in large areas of Mount Lebanon. These were poor areas and not a viable independent state. Many of the areas surrounding the Maronite heartland were inhabited by Druze, Sunni Muslims, Twelver Shi'is and others. Nevertheless, the French were determined to create a Maronite-dominated state and expanded the Maronite heartland to include the other areas that form part of Lebanon today. No single sect had a majority. This was a potentially explosive mix, because the vast majority of Lebanese Sunnis and Shi'is, as well as a substantial number of Christians, would have preferred to be part of a united Greater Syria. A state was created with a fragile mixture of religious minorities and a constitution that entrenched sectarian differences; this meant that the Lebanese continued to focus on their religious sects as the prime focus of their identity. The Lebanese state was little more than the arena in which the different communities played out their power struggles, and scrambled for state patronage. It was therefore hard for a feeling of genuine Lebanese patriotism to emerge. It also meant that Lebanon was a weak state with weak institutions, although it was a democracy.

The Lebanese constitution allocated parliamentary seats to the different religious communities on what was called a 'confessional' basis, in rough proportion to their numbers. This was tweaked to favour the Christian groups, who had an overall majority of seats. In 1931–32 the only census ever conducted took place in Lebanon. Christians, when considered together, were only 52 per cent of the population; Sunnis were 22.5 per cent; and Twelvers a little under 20 per cent. Different posts in the government were also allocated to the different sects. Under the Lebanese national pact of 1943, which paved the way to independence from France, the president of the republic had to be a Maronite and the prime minister a Sunni, while the Twelver Shi'is were given the office of the speaker of parliament.

The way in which politics developed in Lebanon was very different from events in Syria, which could justifiably be described as the heartland of Arab nationalism. The Druze became enthusiastic Arab nationalists from an early date, as their role in the rebellion of 1925 demonstrates. In time, Syria's other Shi'i minorities, the Alawis and Ismailis, also took up the new, nationalist creed, with a similar degree of passion.

II

The name 'Iraq' is ancient. It was the Arab name for the area comprising the valleys of the Tigris and Euphrates, and extended into what is now Iran. In the aftermath of the First World War a new entity called Iraq was created as a British Mandate. It covered slightly different territory and was essentially composed of the old Ottoman provinces of Baghdad, Basra and Mosul. This is what we mean today when we refer to the country we know as Iraq. Its boundaries with the French Mandate of Syria were completely arbitrary: quite literally a line in the rocks and sand of the desert.

According to a British census in 1919, Shi'is constituted roughly 53 per cent of the population of Iraq. An Iraqi government survey conducted in 1932 put the figure at 56 per cent.[3] The majority of the remainder were Sunnis, but they were split between ethnic Arabs and Kurds (although there were some Kurdish Shi'is). The Sunni Arabs were slightly less than 20 per cent of the population, and the Kurds roughly the same. There were also Jewish, Christian and Yazidi Iraqis, as well as ethnic minorities such as Turkmen, who were divided between Sunnis and Shi'is, and Syriac-speaking Christians. However, these made up no more than a few percentage points of the total population. Iraq was thus an overwhelmingly Muslim country, but with a Sunni-Shi'i division among that Muslim majority, and an ethnic Arab-Kurdish split among the Sunnis.

What is interesting from our perspective is the extensive degree of cooperation between Sunnis and Shi'is in the years immediately after the First World War. Britain deliberated over how best to safeguard its interests in Iraq, while Sunnis and Shi'is struggled to escape from British control. This cooperation is encapsulated in an observation by Gertrude

Bell, the famous British political officer who was one of the officials involved in setting up the Iraq mandate. The Arab nationalists had, she wrote in a letter to her father on 1 June 1920, 'adopted a difficult line in itself to combat, the union between Shi'ah and Sunni, the unity of Islam.'[4]

This should have come as no surprise. The secret society al-'Ahd, which had been set up in 1913 by Arab nationalists in the Ottoman Empire, had Shi'i sympathisers in Iraq. When the 1916 revolt against the Ottoman Turks by Sharif Hussein of Mecca (Hussein bin Ali al-Hashimi) began, al-'Ahd put the Sharifian nationalists in touch with the leading Shi'i mujtahids in Iraq. The mujtahids saw themselves as more than the religious leaders of the Shi'i community. They aspired to play an important political role in the new Iraq, which they hoped they would come to dominate because of the greater numbers of Shi'is. Although the Sharifians would frustrate this desire, they were able to do so only because they persuaded a sufficiently broad section of Shi'i society to back the principle of an Arab kingdom under a son of the Sharif Hussein.

A petition signed by leading scholars in Karbala was organised by Mirza Muhammad Taqi Shirazi, the second most important Shi'i mujtahid in Iraq. It stated:

> We the people of Kerbala ... have decided to seek the protection of the Arab-Islamic banner and we have selected one of the sons of Sharif Husayn to be an Amir over us bound by an assembly elected by the people of Iraq [to] enact the rules approved by the clergymen of this nation and [to administer] its affairs.[5]

The Sharif Hussein was in the thirty-fourth generation of direct descendants from Hasan, the son of Ali and grandson of the Prophet. This would have appealed to Shi'is, but could not alter the fact that the Sharif and his family were Sunni. The petitioners aimed for a national assembly and political system that would constrain the king's actions and place him under the indirect control of the mujtahids.[6] Sunnis could hardly have supported this role for the Shi'i 'clergymen of this nation'. Nevertheless, the question of which religious scholars would exercise strong influence over the new order emerging in Iraq could be left for consideration at a later stage. The immediate priority was to ensure that Iraq remained under Muslim, not Western and Christian, rule.

Leading Sunnis and Shi'is thus joined together to call for the establishment of a Sharifian monarchy. Mirza Muhammad Taqi Shirazi – who became the pre-eminent Shi'i religious authority in Iraq after the death of Karim Yazdi in April 1919 – was able to influence Sunni as well as Shi'i opinion in this direction. At the same time, support for the Sharifian cause, and its non-religiously based but conservative Arab nationalism, spread among Shi'is. News reached Iraq that, at a conference in May 1920, Britain and France had agreed a carve-up of the predominantly Arabic-speaking former Ottoman provinces, thus finalising the mandate system. Mass protest meetings took place in Baghdad. The organisers chose to alternate between Sunni and Shi'i mosques so as to emphasise religious unity. That year, *ta'ziyas*, the Shi'i lamentations for the Imam Hussein, took place during Ramadan and on the feast of the Prophet's birthday. These were occasions on which Shi'is would not normally have considered such lamentations to be appropriate, and Sunnis might have felt alienated by them. The idea was to spread political awareness and encourage opposition to the British occupation. A nationalist fervour that transcended religious divides grew rapidly. As the nationalist poet Muhammad Habib al-'Ubaydi (a Sunni) put it:

> Do not talk of a Ja'fari or Hanafi
> do not talk of a Shafi'i or Zaydi
> For the Shari'a of Muhammad has united us
> and it rejects the Western mandate.[7]

A police report speculated whether such a phenomenon had ever occurred before in the history of Islam, and noted that the purpose of the ceremonies was to instil nationalist sentiment in the lower classes of society. These were the sections of the population which, as in Greater Syria, were new to such sentiment but for whom Islamic symbols resonated deeply. At the end of June 1920, a rebellion broke out among some of the tribes, especially along the Euphrates in parts of central and southern Iraq. It would take until October for the British forces to subdue it. The revolt drove home the realisation for Britain that controlling Iraq would be an expensive undertaking, unless local actors could be co-opted to share in the project. This was similar to the conclusion the French would reach in Syria after they quelled the 1925 uprising.

Prince Faisal (Faisal bin Hussein bin Ali al-Hashimi, 1883–1933) had been driven from Syria by the French and repudiated by many Syrians for his attempts at compromise with France; in August 1921 Britain placed him on the throne of the new kingdom of Iraq. At this stage, the boundaries between Iraq and Turkey had not been agreed. Turkey still claimed Mosul, and assembled an army behind the border that might invade to claim the province – or even the whole of Iraq. To support its position, Turkey opportunistically made appeals to pan-Islamic sentiment, and called on Iraqis for support. By this stage, reaction against Faisal was increasing, since many Iraqis came to see him as a British stooge. The result was that Turkey now received support from both Sunni and Shi'i religious scholars. On 12 April 1923, the Iraqi Shi'i mujtahids nailed a fatwa to the gates of the shrine of Kazimayn in Baghdad, forbidding Muslims to resist a Turkish invasion. Three months later, over 400 prominent Iraqis went further and called on the caliph in Istanbul to deliver Iraq from foreign rule. The signatories included Shi'is as well as Sunnis. The nailing of the fatwa took place only eleven months before the caliphate was formally abolished by the new Turkish republic of Kemal Ataturk (1881–1938), but it showed that the Shi'i religious establishment could contemplate Sunni, Turkish rule – or even welcome it. The appeal to the caliph also demonstrated how, despite the destruction of the Ottoman Empire, his office could still carry force as a symbol of Muslim unity –including, to an extent, for Shi'is as well as for Sunnis.

Yet the crisis soon passed. Prince Faisal was accepted as king without any great enthusiasm. His coronation took place on 23 August 1921, a date he chose because it was the anniversary of Ghadir Khumm in the Muslim calendar, an anniversary celebrated by Shi'is as the occasion when Muhammad endorsed Ali as his successor. This was a sign of how Faisal I wished to reach out to the majority Shi'i community.[8]His only firm supporters were the Sharifian officers, former Ottoman army officers who came predominantly from Mosul and Baghdad and had switched sides to join the Arab revolt against the Turks. Many of them were soon placed in prominent positions. Like the notables, the upper class families that had provided the Ottomans with senior bureaucrats and religious scholars, they were overwhelmingly Sunni. But Faisal's position as king enabled him to establish patronage networks of his own, especially through the distribution of state land. (The term 'patronage' will necessarily be used extensively in the remainer of this book, and in this context refers to the doling out of political appointments and privileges, as well as financial subsidies and land.) Baghdad became the centre, drawing in the most significant political actors, who formed a new power elite. Ideally, they lived in Baghdad; if they did not, they would move there. The exceptions were important tribal leaders among the Kurds of the north and Shi'i Arabs of the south, as well as those mujtahids who remained in Najaf and Karbala. In order to maintain their political influence, they appointed agents to represent them in Baghdad. The patronage that came from government became the glue that kept the new Iraq together.

Sunni Arabs received the lion's share of this patronage, but it was also directed at all other groups. There were few Shi'is with the necessary qualifications to take up administrative positions, and the revolt of 1920 made both the British and the Sunni elite suspicious of them.[9] But patronage could be used both to co-opt and to divide, while the new Iraqi parliament gave Shi'is a potential vehicle for the advancement of their interests.

In the summer of 1922, two political parties were established in which prominent Shi'i individuals figured. But the mujtahids opposed elections, fearing that they would lead to a Sunni-dominated state. They therefore issued fatwas calling on the Shi'i faithful to boycott them. King Faisal exiled a prominent Shi'i cleric, Ayatollah Mehdi al-Khalissi, in response. Others followed him to Iran. Yet this did not lead to nationwide expressions of support and demonstrations by Shi'is. Patronage had been successfully used to seduce the tribes of the Euphrates valley, reducing the strength of their link with the shrine cities. At the same time, the Shi'i politicians in Baghdad felt embarrassed by the actions of their clerics. The last thing they wanted was for other Iraqis to see the Shi'is as clients of Iran, which would lead to the permanent marginalisation of their community, even though it constituted a majority of the population. The result was a decline in the political influence of the Shi'i clergy over their flocks. Henceforth, the most influential political leaders in the Shi'i community would be laymen.

Yet Shi'i discontent simmered, while the Sunni elite continued to run Iraq just as it had done in the days of the Ottomans. An incident in 1927 showed the underlying risk of sectarian discord. A Syrian teacher working in a leading secondary school in Baghdad published a book on the Umayyad state in Greater Syria. It harked on about the glories of the Umayyad Caliphate – something that was, of course, offensive to Shi'is. The narrative of Arab history espoused by most Sunni pan-Arabists was deeply problematic for Shi'is. As a result, there were Shi'i protests against the recruitment of Syrian teachers by the government for Iraqi schools. Pan-Arabism also cut against the calls for Islamic unity made by Shi'i mujtahids.[10]

Despite this, ideas of a secular Arab identity that rose above religious differences gained currency. Simultaneously, class politics steadily gained in importance. In the early 1930s, the dangers of (predominantly Sunni) landowners holding a stranglehold over politics was shown when new laws increased the powers of landlords at the expense of their tenants. As tenants found themselves having to bear the financial cost of crop failures and consequently facing destitution, there was an increasing drift to the cities – above all to Baghdad – and the growth of an urban proletariat. Questions of class cut across sectarian lines. At a popular level, urban politics moved steadily in the direction of movements such as socialism.

In response, a new Patriotic Brotherhood Party was launched in 1931. This was a merger of two other parties. One of these had significant urban Shi'i representation, as well as connections with another predominantly Shi'i party enjoying a following in the shrine cities and among the Euphrates tribes. The Patriotic Brotherhood Party also cultivated trade unions. A power struggle took place. Strikes and demonstrations were used to bring pressure on the government, but they were successfully repressed, even though at one point some tribal disturbances broke out in the mid-Euphrates region.

The end of the mandate came in 1932, when, largely as a result of King Faisal's successful manoeuvring, Iraq became a full member of the League of Nations – though its independence was, for the time being, only partial. Faisal died in 1933, and was succeeded by his son Ghazi, who was then only twenty-one and would be killed in a car crash in 1939. Ghazi lacked his father's political acumen. During his reign the Sunni power elite would continue to dominate Iraq, despite simmering discontent among many Shi'is and the poor. His reign also saw the entry of the military into Iraqi politics. This was the first time this happened in a modern Arab state.

During the ten years from 1932, the army became an increasingly important national institution and grew from 12,000 to 43,000 men.[11] This was achieved through conscription, which was finally introduced in 1934. Its introduction was opposed by Shi'is and Kurds. It led to the resignation of two Shi'i cabinet ministers when funds intended for a dam project, which would have benefited farmers in a largely Shi'i area, were earmarked for the army instead. The army crushed rebellious groups in the provinces, beginning with the Syriac Christian community, which rose in revolt in 1933 after its hopes of autonomy were turned down. The threat it posed to the integrity of the Iraqi state was grossly exaggerated, but the officer who suppressed the rebellion, Colonel Bakr Sidqi, was treated as a national hero. He went on to put down revolts by some Shi'i tribes in the Euphrates valley in 1935.

The movements for reform in Iraq during the 1930s were motivated by resentment at how an elite, whose members were disproportionately Sunni, exercised huge influence through patronage and excluded others from power. Yet despite the power of this elite, by the mid-1930s Shi'i officials were coming to dominate the Ministry of Education. This enabled them to push for the spread of schools in rural areas, from the academic year 1933–34 onwards.[12] Those Shi'is who had the chance welcomed the opportunity for their children to acquire a modern, secular education. Education spread slowly but steadily across the rural communities of southern Iraq over the next twenty years. Yet although Shi'i representation at all levels of government steadily increased, the Shi'is were never able to acquire the dominance that reflected their numbers. Sunnis still dominated, especially in key ministries.[13]

Two nationalistic trends were appearing in Iraq. The first was pan-Arabism. This saw Iraq as the leader of the other Arab territories in the Fertile Crescent. The other was what became known as 'Iraq first' nationalism. Iraq was a predominantly Arab country, yet it was a unique society with major interests and concerns that did not affect other Arabs. Although Iraq's Shi'is were overwhelmingly Arabic speakers, the way in which they were often marginalised by the Sunni establishment, who were almost all pan-Arabists, made them receptive to the 'Iraq first' form of nationalism. However, it would be wrong to see the pan-Arab/'Iraq first' divide as identical to that between Sunnis and Shi'is. When a contingent of Iraqi volunteers was recruited to assist the Palestinian rebellion against the British Mandate in 1936, many of those who joined up were Shi'is.[14]

As the years leading up to the Second World War slipped away, high, nationalist ideals were preached even if they contained contradictions. The Iraqi state was strongly held together by coercion and patronage, two adhesives that can glue a state together but which are antithetical to democracy – and therefore ultimately antithetical to stability. The unity Sunnis and Shi'is showed in their opposition to the British Mandate did not lead to healing the divide once the new, fragile Iraq settled down to the politics of parliament and patronage. There was a disdain for Shi'is among the Sunni elite and a corresponding mistrust of pan-Arab nationalism among Shi'is. The split was still very much there.

III

In the 1920s and 1930s, Arabic speakers in the mandated territories were faced with a major question to which there was no simple answer. Should their national sentiment be bound up primarily with the wider Arab nation? Or should it be focused on the political units into which Britain and France had arbitrarily parcelled up the Arabic-speaking areas of the old Ottoman Empire? The wish among Syrians and Palestinians in the early 1920s to reunify Greater Syria, and the choice for Iraqis between an 'Iraq-first' ideal and pan-Arabism, posed complicated dilemmas to which there was no simple answer. Nevertheless, it is clear that nationalism was the ideology framing debate during this period. This was so even if religion could be a hallmark of identity. Pan-Muslim solidarity often crossed sectarian divides between Sunnis and Shi'is and was a sufficiently strong force for nationalists to manipulate. There were, however, some developments during this period that would lead in time to the resurgence of religious-based identity politics. One of these was the expansion of the Wahhabi emirate in central Arabia into the kingdom of Saudi Arabia, which was formally proclaimed in 1932.

After the destruction of the al-Saud family's emirate in 1818 by an Egyptian army, Wahhabism seemed initially to become more intent on surviving and preserving its identity than spreading its doctrine abroad.[15] Another Wahhabi emirate under the political leadership of the al-Saud family appeared in the nineteenth century, and is sometimes referred to as the Second Saudi State. This was based on Riyadh in the heart of Najd. When it tried to reconquer the province of Hasa in eastern Arabia, it came up against the Ottomans at a time when they were extending their reach in that area. When the Wahhabis took control of Shi'i areas, they demonstrated their hostility to the sect by destroying Shi'i places of worship. Nevertheless, this attempt at expansion was unsuccessful, and the Second Saudi State collapsed into civil war in the 1870s.

It was displaced by a tribal confederation led by their rivals, the Al-Rashid. But in 1902, the al-Sauds bounced back when the young prince Abdul Aziz ibn Abdul-Rahman ibn Saud (known simply as Ibn Saud), retook Riyadh and re-established his family's emirate. He took control of eastern Arabia from the Ottomans, and persuaded them to appoint him their governor. After the First World War he proclaimed himself the independent sultan of Nejd, adding the Al-Rashid's territories to his own in 1921, before conquering the Hejaz in 1924–25. When the Wahhabi soldiers took Medina, they went to the Baqi' cemetery and destroyed the tombs of the four Shi'i imams who were buried there: Hasan, Ali Zayn al-Abidin, Muhammad al-Baqir and Ja'far al-Sadiq. They saw them as places of idolatry.

The Kingdom of Saudi Arabia, to give it the title it officially adopted in 1932, had (and has) a diverse population. Its population centres were separated by immense distances of desert, and its creation can truly be said to have been the work of one man: Ibn Saud. Few observers thought that his kingdom would survive when this charismatic and astute man eventually died. It should be remembered that oil had not yet been discovered, and Ibn Saud's vast new country probably lacked even a single stretch of tarmac road.

The kingdom's inhabitants included Sunni Muslims from the Malaki, Hanafi and Shafi'i doctrinal law schools, as well as the Hanbalis of Nejd, who dominated, and from whom the new state's Wahhabi religious establishment was drawn. The Hijaz, now its western province, had a cosmopolitanism very different from the inward-looking tribal society of Nejd. This was the legacy of centuries of pilgrimage traffic to the holy cities of Mecca and Medina. Some of the villages along the mountainous spine that ran southwards from Mecca to Yemen had African inhabitants, some of whom still observed the customs and traditions of their old homelands. The women in some of these villages continued to be unselfconsciously bare breasted in public into the 1970s, when tarmac roads reached into the mountains for the first time. Apart from the eastern province where Twelver Shi'is were the majority, there was also a small Shi'i community in Medina and a substantial Ismaili community around Najran (a relic of Fatimid influence), just north of the Yemeni border.

The Wahhabi scholars saw the Shi'is as their main opponents. This would lead to an 'othering' of the Shi'i minority in the new state. The king and the royal family would modify this to a certain extent as part of the pragmatism that enabled them to hold the kingdom together, but this would never be in an even-handed way. When it came to it, the Wahhabis were far more important in the political order, even if the Shi'is may have been 10–15 per cent of the kingdom's population. As of 2015, no Shi'i has ever been made a minister in Saudi Arabia, and only one Shi'i has represented the kingdom abroad as an ambassador.[16] Although Ibn Saud made many dynastic marriages to help cement his influence across the country, he never married a Shi'i woman.[17]

The Ottoman authorities had cooperated with the Shi'i notables of eastern Arabia and enlisted them in their project to govern the area. They even appointed a local Shi'i, Ahmad bin Mahdi bin Nasrullah, as district governor of Qatif in 1875. His time in this post lasted only three years and he was the last local figure to hold a significant administrative appointment in this area;[18] even so, under Ottoman rule Shi'is were able to flourish and became wealthy. When Ibn Saud took control of the area in 1913–14, some emigrated to Bahrain and Iraq, another group advocated armed resistance, and others called for an accommodation with him. One Shi'i notable who called for resistance was publicly executed.[19]

Life was clearly not easy for the Shi'is of Hasa in the years immediately after their inclusion into what became Saudi Arabia; but matters would get worse. The Ikhwan were a religious brotherhood of Wahhabi fighters who had been the mainstay of Ibn Saud's fighting force. In 1927 they demanded that the Shi'is of Hofuf, the great inland oasis of eastern Arabia, be forced to convert to 'true Islam'. Their places of worship should be destroyed, and Wahhabi preachers should be sent to enlighten them. Ibn Saud acceded to the Ikhwan's request. Perhaps fortunately for the Shi'is, he fell out with the Ikhwan about a year later and had to crush them ruthlessly. Thereafter, the conversion of the Shi'is was not seen as a priority, but Wahhabi attempts continued. What had happened showed the degree to which the Shi'is were treated on sufferance. A local uprising against Saudi rule even occurred in 1930, and was defused by mediation.[20] Although the Shi'is were often left in relative peace, and many Shi'i notables continued to collaborate as they had with the Ottomans, the system the new kingdom established meant that they were inevitably excluded from its elite. No better formula could have been devised to arrange for them to maintain and develop a strong sectarian identity that marked them apart from other Saudis.

Wahhabism also began to expand outside Ibn Saud's domains. Word of Ibn 'Abd al-Wahhab's teachings diffused gradually across the Muslim world as a result of the encounters pilgrims to Mecca and Medina had with Wahhabi preachers. This had been especially the case during the brief period when the holy cities were occupied during the First Saudi State, but to a certain extent it continued afterwards. Now, with the Hejaz officially recognised as part of Ibn Saud's kingdom, the word began to spread once again.

Ibn Saud's seizure of Mecca and Medina came shortly after a moment of huge psychological shock for many Sunni Muslims: the abolition by Turkey of the Ottoman Caliphate in March 1924. In December that year, Ibn Saud took Mecca. Twelve months later, he entered the port of Jeddah. He soon received British recognition of his conquests as a fully independent ruler. There was no other Arab country (except Yemen) that could be said to be fully independent at that time. This was also the time of widespread dismay among Arab nationalists everywhere at the fact that Greater Syria and Iraq had been cheated of full independence and partitioned between Britain and France. Ominously, the new League of Nations had compromised its integrity by acquiescing in this carve-up. Abdullah and Faisal, the two sons of the Sharif Hussein, had been made the kings of Jordan and Iraq by Britain, thereby causing many nationalists to be disillusioned with the Sharifian cause.

IV

It is therefore not surprising that some nationalists in Arab countries formed a grudging respect for Ibn Saud, and even a broadly positive view of his achievements. This is despite his having no interest in Arab nationalism; furthermore, the Wahhabism of his new kingdom was widely disparaged. But in the late 1920s a major Sunni religious scholar endorsed Wahhabism for the first time. This was Rashid Rida, who was born in 1865 near Tripoli (then part of Ottoman Greater Syria) and became the pupil and biographer of the eminent Egyptian religious scholar Muhammad Abduh, the disciple of Jamal al-Din al-Afghani. Rashid Rida is seen as continuing the strand of Islamic modernism that began with al-Afghani, but he was much more conservative in his teaching than Muhammad Abduh. He has been described as advocating a return to a medieval, sectarian past,[21] although he also believed that the justice inherent in Islam would produce a better solution for religious minorities than secularism. His argument was that those who 'worshipped their own communities' but were not guided by a religious ethic could easily let their communal solidarity slide into a hatred of other communities. In his view, such a slide had occurred in the Middle East because of the decline in Islam. As an example, he cited the ethnic hatred that had followed the revolution of the secular Young Turks in 1908.[22]

As a young man Rashid Rida had become disillusioned with Sufism. He could also be scathing about Shi'ism, and wrote that it was 'full of fairy tales and illegitimate innovations'. Reviving an old charge, he also claimed that its doctrinal differences with Sunnism were the work of the first Jewish converts to Islam, who had inserted alien ideas into the new religion.[23] He was the originator of the term Salafi,[24] meaning a Muslim who restricts himself to looking at these first three generations of Muslims in order to establish the rules of the Sharia. Because of the importance of the Companions for Sunnis, and the fact that most of them were rejected by the Shi'is, this would have made it easy for Rashid Rida to move closer to the Wahhabi position on Shi'ism.

Nevertheless, as was seen in Chapter Eight, Rashid Rida almost welcomed Shi'i proselytisation among Iraqi tribesmen who did not know the tenets of their nominally Sunni religion. He called for unity among Muslims and saw an end to intra-Muslim sectarianism as essential. He suggested that Sunni and Shi'i should cooperate in the areas where they agreed and apologise to each other for their disagreements. And if a member of one sect made false and disparaging statements about the other, the scholars of his own sect should correct him. Yet he did not always practise what he preached. He had a habit of rushing to judgement to condemn Shi'i leaders if they said something that angered him.[25] His anger could also be turned against Christians and Jews. Enraged at the Zionist programme to transform predominantly Arab and Muslim Palestine into a Jewish state he descended into anti-Semitism. He brought the lies of *The Protocols of the Elders of Zion* (a forged document first published in Russia, alleging a Jewish conspiracy of world domination) into Arab and Muslim discourse, very probably for the first time.

Rashid Rida had once supported liberal constitutional ideas because they accorded with the Islamic principle of consultation and would lead to the upholding of the Sharia by consent. But he was shocked by the French invasion of Syria in the summer of 1920 and the hypocrisy of the League of Nations, which was meant to uphold self-determination for the Arab peoples in the former Ottoman provinces as 'a sacred trust of civilisation'.[26] Instead, it had placated the regional ambitions of Britain and France, as well as the Zionist lobby.[27] This led to a deepening of his hostility to the West, and would also have been a step on his path to anti-Semitism (as a younger man, he had actually written in defence of Dreyfus, whom he saw as a victim of Western racism).[28] It was also what led him, a few years later, to defend Ibn Saud and the Wahhabis. Their motivations were of the best, he argued, and their teaching was consistent with the Sharia since they followed the religion of the first Muslims. In fact, he asserted, Ibn Saud was maintaining and defending the essential principles of Islam better than anyone since the time of the first four caliphs. His endorsement included a savage attack on Shi'is, whom he accused of being Iranian agents.[29]

In his view the Wahhabis' concerns about saint worship were justified: they saw Muhammad as having the highest status of any man who had ever lived, but they were categorical that he was not a super-human being. They had also established a new Arab and Muslim kingdom that could help defend Islam from Western penetration. For Rashid Rida, Islamism and Arab nationalism were two sides of the same coin. Shi'ism might be a branch of Islam, but it was a very inferior branch.

V

This was a time when many people felt that the new world they were entering was cutting them adrift from their roots. There had already been Muslim revivalist movements. As was seen in Chapter Seven, Muhammad ibn 'Abd al-Wahhab lived and preached before the impact of the West reached Arabia. His message therefore cannot be seen as a reaction against Westernisation. But he was followed in the late nineteenth and early twentieth centuries by charismatic movements that tried to push back against the advances of the West and Westernisation. Examples are the movement led by the self-styled Mahdi in the Sudan and the Senussi Sufi Brotherhood that fought the Italians in Libya. Such campaigns were traditional in their style, and relied on propagating their messages among tribes in a primarily desert environment. But in the 1920s there was a completely new development: a Muslim revivalist movement in urban Egypt.

It was led by a young teacher called Hasan al-Banna, who founded the Muslim Brotherhood. A devout Muslim, he was devastated by the abolition of the Ottoman Caliphate. He saw this as a hammer blow to Islam, especially as Turkey itself had abolished the institution as a step towards making itself into a fully-fledged secular state. The abolition left many Muslims in Egypt feeling that they no longer had a protector on the world stage. In Cairo, the scholars of Al-Azhar mosque denounced the last Ottoman caliph as illegitimate, since he had accepted the separation of sultanate and caliphate when the Turkish republic was declared. They called on the Muslim community to find a replacement. Rulers including Sharif Hussein of Mecca and the king of Egypt indicated they would be prepared to put their names forward. The king of Afghanistan and the Zaydi Imam of Yemen (who, of course, was a Shi'i) were also suggested.

There was even an element of shock among Shi'is. In India, some Shi'i leaders supported the Khilafat movement, which in the years immediately after the First World War aimed to exert influence on Britain and Turkey to preserve the institution of the caliphate. Iraqi Shi'i scholars accompanied their Sunni colleagues to a conference convened in Jerusalem in 1931 to discuss the restoration of the institution. While the Shi'is did not consider the Sunni Caliphate legitimate, they shared the wider concern that its abolition was a threat to Muslim identity and to Islam itself.[30] But no practical steps were taken to restore the institution, and the matter soon seemed almost forgotten. Underneath the surface, however, a trauma had been inflicted on many Muslims. In time, this would manifest itself. Hasan al-Banna's call to activism was one of the first signs of that manifestation.

The Muslim Brotherhood's call was an emotional appeal for a return to Islam. Hasan al-Banna was a populist visionary and orator. He produced attractive slogans that encapsulated his audience's gut reactions to the problems of foreign domination. But these slogans were vague and ambiguous. 'Islam is the solution' and 'the Qur'an is our constitution'[31] were (and are) two well-known catchphrases of the Brotherhood. Those who saw them could decide for themselves what they meant – hence their appeal. Hasan al-Banna believed that all Egyptians should come together to fight colonial oppression under the banner of Islam. 'Humanity,' he wrote, 'is in dire need of the purifying waters of true Islam.'[32] He was scathing about Western capitalism, which he saw as the cause of the maladies affecting Europe in the 1930s. By contrast, Islam offered the values of thrift, respect for private property and a sense of fairness in commercial dealings.

He was also a formidable organiser. The Brotherhood began to spread as he reminded Egyptian Muslims of the tenets and practice of their faith. He encouraged them to take their religious practice more seriously. He and his companions began to build new mosques in places where there were few, and to establish social work and education programmes. As time passed, the Brotherhood became the largest mass movement in Egypt, especially as many 'liberal' politicians became discredited through corruption or the unpalatable compromises they found themselves forced to make in their negotiations with Britain. The Brotherhood also began to set up branches in other Arab countries.

Following the assassination of the police chief for Cairo, and then Prime Minister Nuqrashi Pasha, who had declared the Brotherhood a terrorist organisation and tried to close it down, Hasan al-Banna was himself assassinated in February 1949 by men who are presumed to have been sent by the Egyptian secret service. This made him a martyr for his followers. The era during which nationalism would be the dominant force in politics still had over a quarter of a century to run, but by the time of his death he had established political Islam as a permanent feature in Egyptian politics.

The arrival of the Muslim Brotherhood showed that Islamism was a serious alternative to nationalism in the sruggle for hearts and minds. Islamists, however, had a long way to go before they could hope to seize the initiative. As the Second World War loomed, few would have expected them to be able to do so. There were still sectarian tensions in Iraq. Nevertheless, there was little to indicate, outside Saudi Arabia, that one day there would be a widening of the gap between Sunnis and Shi'is.

CHAPTER TEN

Tides Ebb and Flow

I

Four decades separate the start of the Second World War from the Iranian Revolution of 1979. Much changed over that period, and the trends that triumphed were not always those that seemed to be gathering momentum at an earlier point. Albert Hourani, one of the foremost scholars of the history of the Middle East in the English-speaking world during the second half of the twentieth century, used to tell his students that Britain's domination of the Middle East had seemed so overwhelming to him in 1945 that he could not imagine it would end in his lifetime. Yet by the time of his death in 1993, not a single British imperial outpost remained in the region. The last British troops who had been stationed permanently in the Gulf left in 1971. The forces of Arab nationalism had, seemingly, triumphed.

Yet already by 1971 that nationalism was in decay, and there were the first signs that religion was making a triumphant comeback as the primary focus of identity. Two events that are inextricably connected with this are the Six Day War of 1967 and the 1973–74 oil price rise. In 1967, Israel defeated the armies of Egypt, Jordan and Syria comprehensively and occupied much extra territory. Gamal Abdel Nasser, the president of Egypt who was the Arab nation's great champion, was shown to be a colossus with clay feet. This led to slow-burning disillusionment with Arab nationalism. People turned in increasing numbers to religion for a solution to the dilemmas (and, frequently, the despair) that confronted them. The significance of the 1973–74 oil price rise was that it made oil producers such as Iran, Iraq and Saudi Arabia wealthy in a way that had previously been almost unimaginable. It also meant that Saudi Arabia was now able to spend lavishly on promoting its own brand of Wahhabi Islam with its hostility to Shi'ism.

II

Throughout the period 1939–79, Iraq's elite remained predominantly Sunni. It tended to look down on Shi'is and despise them, although many individual Shi'is became part of that elite, and the strongest currents in political life were secular throughout this period. Nevertheless, the elite feared the Shi'is because they made up most of the country's population – and most of its poor – and there was the risk of revolution from below.

One manifestation of Shi'i frustration was widespread support for the Iraqi Communist Party. In the six years from 1949–55, Shi'i representation in the upper echelons of the party rose from 21 to 47 per cent. The adoption of communism by many Shi'is did not necessarily indicate their acceptance of Marxist-Leninist ideology. It reflected their desire for a new, equality-based social order and their dislike of the links between Sunnism and pan-Arabism. Behind this lay the fear of the possible absorption of Iraq inside a massive pan-Arab state which would be led by Sunni cliques in the way that Iraq was.[1] The men who ran Iraq saw communists and populist Arab nationalists as the great dangers to stability, not the emergence of religion-based politics.

Before the end of the monarchy in 1958, some Shi'is were able to progress through parliamentary politics and become fully fledged members of the political elite. There had never been a Shi'i prime minister of Iraq before the Second World War. During the post-war monarchy, however, there were four Shi'i prime ministers. Some of them were able to establish patronage networks of their own, and to embody the aspirations of the new, young, educated Shi'i professionals who were increasing in numbers. Iraq's third Shi'i prime minister, Fadhil al-Jamali, was himself a strong Arab nationalist who appointed a cabinet of which half the members were Shi'i. This was a symbolic moment for many Shi'is but, like most Iraqi governments under the monarchy, the new administration was short-lived. It fell for two reasons. One was conservative opposition by the landed interest to reforms proposed by al-Jamali, an opposition that united Sunni and Shi'i landlords. His intended changes to the civil service also threatened the positions of the entrenched and predominantly Sunni groups that dominated it. His opponents hinted that he was showing favour to Shi'i co-religionists. They succeeded in forcing his resignation. He had encountered a wall of anti-Shi'i prejudice that remained solid throughout the period of the monarchy. That would also be the case under the revolutionary regimes that followed.

In 1958, the monarchy came to an end in a bloody coup in which the king, much of the royal family, and the prime minister were killed. It was also the end of parliamentary life in any real sense. Henceforth, Iraq would be under the control of groups of army officers with revolutionary agendas.

A great deal changed in Iraq over the years following the end of the monarchy. Socialist policies were increasingly implemented after President Nasser of Egypt adopted them. He had led the army officers who overthrew the Egyptian monarchy in 1952 and provided the model for other Arab revolutionary leaders during this period. State planning and public ownership of new industries were seen as the way forward, and a new emphasis was placed on education, healthcare and other social services.

But the greatest transformation, of course, was ideological: from a conservative monarchy to a revolutionary, populist regime which trumpeted Arab nationalism, paid a noisy lip service (but little more) to ideals of Arab unification, and tried to create a new, socialist Iraq. Yet none of Iraq's deep-seated problems of identity had been solved. The country's elite remained Sunni Arab, even if the faces at the top table had changed beyond recognition. The Kurdish areas in the north felt alienated, and increasingly experienced insurrections. Throughout this time, and indeed until the overthrow of Saddam Hussein by the US-led coalition in 2003, Shi'is remained poorly represented in the higher levels of administration and the officer corps.

The Iraqi branch of the nationalist and ultra-secularist Ba'ath party was founded by a Shi'i, Fuad al-Rikabi, in 1952. He did not manage to spread his Ba'athist message successfully among his co-religionists, and left the party in 1959. The reasons for this failure were probably the two problems for Shi'is with Arab nationalism that have already been mentioned: the association of pan-Arab nationalism in the minds of many Shi'is with Sunni hegemony, and the fact that they felt excluded by a Sunni Arab elite.

Brigadier Abd al-Karim Qasim, who headed the blood-soaked coup that overthrew the monarchy, was, in theory at least, probably a more appropriate person to rule Iraq then anyone before or since. His father was a Sunni Arab and his mother was a Faili, a member of the Kurdish Shi'i minority. He wanted to end the grotesque inequalities of Iraqi society, and made this his priority rather than starry-eyed visions of uniting Iraq with other Arab states. Whether or not he had a clear idea about how to go about transforming Iraqi society, he soon found himself trapped by Iraq's tradition of patronage and its murderous twin, coercion. Real parliamentary life was now over. Even if it had continued, patronage and coercion would have been the best – or perhaps the only – ways for him to secure his powerbase and to get things done.

Qasim's rule turned out to be the high watermark of the Iraqi Communist Party, and of Shi'i participation in it. The Communists provided him with an important counterweight to the pan-Arab nationalists. He became authoritarian, possibly despite himself, and a personality cult grew up around him. Although his popularity grew, he was overthrown in a coup by Arab nationalist officers on 9 February 1963. He and his associates were brought before a summary court and shot. His bullet-riddled corpse was then displayed on television. This may have been because the plotters genuinely feared his popularity and therefore wished to quash any rumours that he was still alive.

By the time of Qasim, the first signs of religious politics were beginning to appear in Iraq. To an extent, this was a reaction against the threat of communism, materialism and atheism. It was also, however, a response to the prevailing secularist assumptions that both the elite and the intelligentsia had held under the monarchy and after the coup of 1958. Among Sunnis, an Iraqi branch of the Muslim Brotherhood was formed. In 1957, a similar organisation called al-Da'wa, 'the Call', was set up by some Shi'is. It was led by a young religious scholar, Muhammad Baqir al-Sadr.

The impulse for an Islamic alternative thus occurred more or less simultaneously among a number of Sunnis and Shi'is. Initially, they were told to form a single Islamic party, so as to avoid the risk of sectarianism. Its leader was a Sunni, but it was sponsored by the Najaf-based Shi'i scholar Grand Ayatollah Muhsin al-Hakim. In 1960 it began to criticise legislation as contrary to the Sharia, and was harassed by the authorities. This harassment was part of a general crackdown that made open party politics difficult, and drove much political activity underground. Even though they were now often operating in secret, the Islamists were able to join nationalists in their fight against the communists. The communists turned out to be the big losers in the period after Qasim fell. They never recovered.

Apart from hostility to the old regime and anger at the state of the country, little united the officers who had overthrown Qasim. Factional bickering in the months following the coup led to another military strongman, Abd al-Salam Arif, taking power in Iraq in November that year. He followed a socialist path and issued a decree in July 1964 that nationalised banks, insurance firms and major industrial companies. Islamic organisations, both Sunni and Shi'i, were among those who objected. There was a revival of religion-based organisations in the Shi'i community, bolstered by leading mujtahids in the shrine cities denouncing the nationalisations as contrary to the Sharia. This may have had some effect, since Arif had always shown himself in public to be a devout Muslim, and he subsequently backtracked from this policy. However, it soon became apparent that the policy was disastrous for the economy – the probable reason for the political U-turn.

Abd al-Salam Arif was killed in a helicopter crash in April 1966 which seems to have been a genuine accident. His brother Abd al-Rahman, the acting army chief of staff, took over, but he lacked his brother's political abilities. He was overthrown in July 1968 in a coup mounted by the nationalist, socialist and secularist Ba'ath Party under Ahmed Hassan al-Bakr, who became Iraq's fourth president. Saddam Hussein, who was then thirty-one and secretary of the Iraqi Ba'ath party, was a relative of the new leader. He would now begin his rise to the very top and take full power in 1979.

The officers who were central to the new regime came disproportionately from the Sunni Arab areas of the north-west of Iraq.[2] They instinctively considered themselves superior to the Shi'i Arabs and non-Arab Kurds. It was thus first and foremost among fellow Sunnis in these areas of the north-west of the country that the regime would dispense its patronage, and from which it would recruit those to be given key positions. This was a disguised patron-client relationship, even if on the surface it appeared sectarian. The new rulers tightened their grip on power by purges in response to fictitious conspiracies and coup attempts. There was no ideological struggle. The Iraqi Ba'ath Party had become a vehicle with the sole purpose of supporting the rulers' power and control.

III

It was hardly surprising that the new regime's reliance on the support of a relatively narrow section of the population led to discontent. There were insurrections in Kurdistan. Troubles loomed with the Shi'i community when the Shah of Iran used his greater military muscle to pressurise Iraq into making concessions regarding the Shatt al-Arab waterway, where the boundary between the two states lay. Part of Hassan al-Bakr's response to the Shah's aggressive approach was an attempt to reach out to the leading Iraqi Shi'i religious scholars for support. He had a reputation as a devout (Sunni) Muslim; he was able to remind them of his hostility to communism and how the Ba'athists had been the major force that had defeated them. These points counted in his favour. On the other hand, the religious leaders could not overlook Ba'athist support for socialist policies which they believed conflicted with Islam. Probably most significant was the fact that Hassan al-Bakr's regime was built on a tight circle of Sunni Arab army officers who kept themselves in power by promoting their kinsmen and tribal connections. Socialist rhetoric increased, and was often mouthed by secularists who had risen to prominent positions because they came from Sunni tribal cliques; the disquiet of Shi'i religious scholars grew.

Matters came to a head in 1969 when Ayatollah Muhsin al-Hakim refused Hassan al-Bakr's request to condemn the Iranian government's position over the Shatt al-Arab. This began a process that turned into a nightmare for the narrowly based regime. It began with government measures expelling from the country many Iranian religious students in the shrine cities, and closing down a university in Najaf. The security services harassed Shi'is, citing 'the Iranian threat' as justification. This led to a reaction. Ayatollah Muhsin al-Hakim led a protest march from Najaf to Baghdad, and was greeted by thousands of Shi'i well-wishers when he arrived in the capital. The authorities stopped people visiting him, but protests only intensified. When a Sunni scholar, Sheikh Abd al-Aziz al Badri, gave a sermon at a Baghdad mosque in support of the ayatollah, he was seized and executed.

The regime was mindful of past cases of cooperation between Sunnis and Shi'is, perhaps especially those at the end of the First World War and time of the British occupation. Such inter-sectarian cooperation between religious scholars of both persuasions was probably what the regime feared above all else. In the big cities of Iraq, ordinary Sunnis and Shi'is co-operated together at grass-roots level and there was considerable intermarriage.[3] If their religious leaders could cooperate against the government this might have truly devastating consequences for the regime. The authorities therefore reacted with a clampdown on religion that was to some extent reminiscent of practice in the Soviet Union: Islamic instruction in schools was ended, and the state broadcasting networks stopped recitations of the Qur'an. Such moves were unprecedented in an Arab country. They triggered riots and demonstrations in the Shi'i south. As he fled into exile, Ayatollah Muhsin al-Hakim issued a fatwa banning membership of the Ba'ath party.

When the ayatollah died a year later, many Shi'is who had been his followers transferred their loyalty to another scholar, Muhammad Baqir al-Sadr, who had been one of the founders of al-Da'wa. He had been much more engaged in politics, and also had an appeal to many devout Muslims who were not Shi'i. He carried widespread respect, and this presented difficulties for the government. Its strategy was to undermine the social solidarity that he and other religious scholars might succeed in building across the Sunni-Shi'i divide, on the basis of common Muslim values. The way it could do this was through patronage, that old stand-by of every Iraqi government since independence.

The Ba'athist regime was shortly to have greater resources at its disposal than any previous government. Subsidies, welfare payments and other benefits were now introduced. They were expanded massively when Iraq received its windfall from the oil price rises following the 1973 Arab-Israeli War. Between October 1973 and December 1975,

Iraqi oil revenues increased by 800 per cent. Even though 40 per cent of the budget was earmarked for defence, vast sums were available to foster patronage networks.[4] Unsurprisingly, some of this was directed at Shi'is, many of whom responded by allowing themselves to be co-opted.

Yet Shi'i discontent continued to simmer. This was inevitable given the close-knit, in some ways almost tribal, nature of the regime. In 1977 at the time of Ashura, the commemorations of Hussein's martyrdom, the security services were caught off guard when a traditional march from Najaf to Karbala turned into a massive protest against the regime and degenerated into riots. When the army was called in, some soldiers deserted. The response was harsh. Two thousand arrests were made, and a special tribunal was set up to deal with them. Many of those involved were imprisoned, but eight religious scholars were executed.

But toughness was not the only response of the regime. There was the carrot, as well as the stick. By this time, Saddam Hussein was the real ruler of Iraq, although Hassan al-Bakr was still head of state. Saddam Hussein began to use Islamic rhetoric in a way that was new for a senior Ba'athist. He extended his patronage to religious scholars as part of a wider strategy by which he would be the sole dispenser of patronage across all sections of Iraqi society.[5] He also appointed some Shi'is to the Revolutionary Command Council, the supreme organ of government. This had never happened before.

But Saddam Hussein also had to cast his eyes to the east, where events were building up over which he could have no control. There was now increasing unrest in Iran, and it had a religious flavour. Some of this was linked to scholarly activity in the shrine cities of Iraq. An exiled Iranian ayatollah called Ruhollah Khomeini had been quietly lecturing in Najaf for some time, expounding his ideas on Islamic government. The Shah asked Iraq to expel him. Relations between Iraq and Iran were not good, but eventually, in November 1978, the Iraqi government did so, and the ayatollah took up a new residence in France. In Iraq, there was much Shi'i discontent, but it was not a force that seemed able to threaten the Ba'athist state.[6]

IV

At the start of this period, Syria was probably the Arab country where secularism was most deeply entrenched. The last French troops withdrew in 1946. The new, fully independent Syria was a parliamentary republic in which the members of parliament elected the president. Although the notables who dominated the Syrian parliament were chiefly Sunni Muslims with socially conservative, Muslim attitudes, religious politics were not a major factor. It would be several decades before this would change and sectarianism would become significant.

Although the Sunni Muslim Brotherhood set up branches in the major cities, it was chiefly engaged in campaigning against the Westernisation of society, not in trying to find a route to power. In politics, it showed itself to be flexible. The most powerful political force of the era aimed to remove all religious and sectarian divisions from politics. During the Second World War, Michel Aflaq, a proudly Arab, Orthodox Christian in Damascus, was formulating an Arab nationalist ideology based on aspirations for freedom, unity, and socialism. He fought passionately against religious involvement in politics, but also saw Islam as the supreme achievement of the Arabs. For him Islam was something that all Arabs, Muslim or non-Muslim, Sunni or Shi'i, believer or atheist, should recognise as the crowning glory of the civilisation their people had created. The Ba'ath ('renaissance') party which he co-founded had the slogan *ummah arabiyyah wahidah dhat risalah khalidah*, 'one Arab nation with an eternal message'. The Ba'athists had considerable success recruiting among Syria's Shi'i minorities, the Alawis, the Druze and the Ismailis.

Although the party contested elections, Ba'athist army officers soon began to conspire to take control of the government. They finally eliminated their rivals in a coup in 1966. After a chaotic period, Hafez al-Assad, a Ba'athist general who was an Alawi, took control. He proved to have hands of steel, and he kept the country in his grip until his death in 2000. He was the dictator who reduced the Ba'ath party to an instrument to maintain him in power. Alawis had been a despised and very poor peasant minority at the bottom of Syrian society. However, Hafez al-Assad selected many Alawis for key positions, and as the foot soldiers of the security and intelligence networks which expanded vastly under his rule. The military also expanded. In 1973, the army had five divisions. Two were commanded by Alawis. By 1992, it had nine divisions, and seven were commanded by Alawis.[7]

The resentment of those who had lost property in the Ba'athist revolution – a group that included many Sunni merchants – was joined by the anger of those who missed out on opportunities because of the regime's corruption and cronyism. Then there was a third category: those who had suffered at the hands of the security state. Parliament was now just a rubber stamp, while the security services had been exempted from judicial oversight since 1963. There was no legal opening for political opposition, or even for any public criticism. Yet after the end of real parliamentary life in Syria, there was still one possible source of opposition that was harder to control: rallying behind the banner of Islam. The mosque was a natural meeting place for men, especially after the noon prayers on Fridays. It became much easier for religious elements to organise demonstrations or shopkeepers' strikes than it was for secular forces.

Hafez al-Assad always took care to portray himself as a devout Muslim. There is no reason to be cynical about this in itself, but he definitely saw religion as an item to be deployed for political purposes when appropriate. He was also well aware of the dangers of sectarian politics. Conscious that some doubted whether Alawis were true Muslims, he obtained a fatwa from Musa al-Sadr, the eminent Twelver Shi'i religious scholar in Lebanon, that Alawis should be considered Muslims of the Shi'i persuasion. During Ramadan and at Muslim festivals, the public would see their president praying in some of the country's most famous mosques, flanked by eminent Sunni religious scholars. His son Bashar, who was chosen to take over the presidency when his father died in 2000, married a Sunni Muslim, as did the children of many other Alawi Ba'athists.

Yet the Alawism of so many figures at the top of the regime, and the easily identifiable accents of secret policemen from parts of the country where there were many Alawis, made sectarianism a potent weapon for the government's opponents. In the second half of the 1970s, militants started to take action against the regime of Hafez al-Assad. In 1976, assassinations of prominent Alawi figures began, coupled with bomb attacks on government targets. Many people felt excluded from the

Ba'athist revolution and hated the path on which it was taking Syria. They saw it as intended to take them away from their roots and, perhaps most of all, from their Islam. The regime responded by encouraging Sunni scholars and preachers who were prepared to work with it, some of whom publicly stressed the dangers that sectarianism would bring. Some pro-regime scholars would pay with their lives for supporting it.[8] It also succeeded in co-opting many Sunnis. Yet the absence of any other way for expressing opposition to the regime made Sunni Islamist politics a kind of default option for many people. Trouble was being stored up for the future.

V

Oil was discovered in the Eastern Province of Saudi Arabia in 1938. Its wealth from this new resource would transform the country – and to some extent the world – in many different ways. It also made Saudi Arabia a crucial American strategic interest, since it was ARAMCO, a consortium of American oil companies, that would be responsible for production.

As the 1950s progressed, the secular Arab nationalism of Egypt's President Nasser had a strong appeal to the workers in the oil fields. Many of them were native Saudi Shi'is, who were the inhabitants of the area where the oil was exploited. Nasser's policies also attracted many other Saudis, notably in the kingdom's most sophisticated province, the Hejaz. Political awareness grew. A Saudi branch of the Ba'ath party was formed in 1961 which, like other nationalist organisations, was cross-sectarian. It attracted recruits among intellectuals and in Shi'i areas, but dissolved into factions following a split in the Syrian Ba'ath in 1963.[9] After the Six Day War in 1967, the Ba'athists and other organisations successfully staged demonstrations. Attempts to plot a coup (which cannot have involved many Shi'is, as there were very few, if any, in the army) led to arrests in 1969-70. This dealt a serious blow to the Saudi Ba'ath and other opposition networks.

After the oil price rises of 1973–74, Saudi Arabia became the epitome of a 'rentier state', one that lives on the revenues from its resources. Left-wing political prisoners were released from jail or allowed to return home from abroad, and were showered with patronage. In other words, most of the former activists allowed themselves to be bought off. Once they had compromised themselves in this way, they were able to take up a new life as bureaucrats, businessmen, or even journalists. Some of the Shi'is among them also returned to the old politics of the Shi'i notable families, seeking to represent their community (or part of it) in their dealings with the organs of the Saudi state. But there remained memories of the times when some young people had dreamed dreams of subversion, although these had turned bitter. Secular opposition had failed. Nor could anyone forget the harshness and disdain with which the security forces treated the Shi'is. An irony resulted. Members of Shi'i notable families who might once have made a career out of religious scholarship now chose other paths instead. The same pattern could be seen in the classes that had provided the religious scholars in some other Arab countries, notably Syria.[10] Among Saudi Shi'is, the old, respected elite of religious scholars ceased to enjoy the status in the Shi'i community that it had once enjoyed. This left a gap that others might one day be able to fill.

The impulse behind the spread of religious politics in Arab and some other Muslim countries from the late 1960s onwards was the revival of Islam and its defence against Western ideologies like socialism and Marxism. Socialism and Marxism had become popular among the intellectual elite across the Muslim world, just as they were in many Western countries at the time. Their hostility to imperialism and thirst for social justice made them especially attractive to young people. There were figures who succeeded in introducing many of their ideas to an educated and youthful public in a way that allowed them to be blended with Islam. One such figure was the devout but anti-clerical Iranian Ali Shariati (1933–1977).

He is regarded as one of the greatest Iranian intellectuals of the twentieth century and, in many ways, was the thinker behind the 1979 Islamic Revolution in Iran. He was a hugely popular figure and it is more than possible that, had he not died in exile in 1977, the Iranian Revolution would have gone down a very different track. A sociologist by training, he set out to reconcile Islam with Western thought including the principles of democracy and the variant of Marxism that was so fashionable at that time.

He was fascinated by Abu Dharr al-Ghifari, one of the Prophet's earliest companions whom he contrasts with the caliphs Uthman and

Mu'awiya, both of whom Abu Dharr upbraided in public for their pomp, fine living and extravagance. Abu Dharr even rose in revolt against Uthman. Ali Shariati wrote a biography of Abu Dharr, portraying him as someone who spoke truth to power and campaigned passionately for social justice. He presents Abu Dharr as a model for Muslims in the modern world. Under the Caliph Uthman's rule, 'the humiliated working masses and the helpless were suppressed under the heels of usurers, slave merchants, the wealthy, and aristocrats'. It was easy for a reader to see these references to Uthman's rule as coded references to that of Shah Muhammad Reza Pahlavi who then ruled Iran. The unabashed Marxist influence is also apparent. 'This capital, wealth, gold and silver which you have hoarded,' Ali Shariati's Abu Dharr tells Uthman, 'must be equally divided among all Muslims. In Islam's economic and ethical system, everyone must share in the others' benefits, and in all blessings of life.'[11]

One of the criticisms from the Iranian religious scholars who were upset by Ali Shariati's radical message was that he had departed from Shi'i doctrine by teaching that Abu Bakr had indeed been the first successor to the Prophet Muhammad, and had been validly elected to that position. Although Ali Shariati was actually very much a Shi'i (note how he cites the Caliph Uthman as an archetype of injustice), there is no anti-Sunni polemical strain in his writing. His focus on Abu Dharr is interesting in this context. Abu Dharr is one of the few Companions of the Prophet who are accepted by both Sunnis and Shi'is. On the Sunni side, he is seen among Sufis, including major mainstream figures such as al-Ghazali, as a figure of great piety who renounced the world and was the exemplar of the spiritual ideals of *faqr*, poverty and of *tawakkul*, trust in God. For Shi'is, his courage in confronting Uthman and Mu'awiya made him a hero.

Although Ali Shariati was not necessarily focusing on Abu Dharr as a figure to unify Sunnis and Shi'is, he intended his teaching that Islam should be the answer to the problems of the modern world to be shared equally by Sunnis as well as Shi'is. For him as for many other leading voices, the dichotomy was not between Sunnis and Shi'is but between Islam on the one side and capitalism and imperialism on the other. Sunni-Shi'i sectarianism was not an issue; the struggle was between Islam and the 'West' and its local stooges. This was also the view of many conservative voices, who would have abhorred the Marxist influences on Ali Shariati's work.

Nevertheless, when looking back on this period we can see with hindsight that the building blocks for Sunni-Shi'i discord were slowly but surely being put in place. The role Wahhabism played as Saudi Arabia's official ideology ensured that official attitudes to Shi'ism in that country would be at best disdainful. This would ensure that the Twelvers of the Eastern Province would be corralled off from any real participation in the public life of the kingdom, and be forced to retreat into their own identity. Even worse, now that Saudi Arabia had vast sums to spend on disseminating its brand of Islam across the world, this disdain for Shi'is and Shi'ism would be one of its principal exports (after hydrocarbons, of course).

At the same time, in both Iraq and Syria the government was in the hands of a clique largely drawn from a religious minority. While in theory each government was Ba'athist and therefore thoroughly secular, in reality the dictators who ruled these countries were forced to rely on patronage for much of their support. Although they succeeded in recruiting the support of many individuals from all sects, while many other people backed them because they feared civil strife if the regime fell, members of the president's minority sect received a grossly disproportionate share of state patronage. What could be a better place to seek the foot-soldiers for your brutal security services than among the members of your own minority religious grouping? And what could be more calculated in the long run to sow the seeds of sectarian hatred?

CHAPTER ELEVEN

The Iranian Revolution and The Iran-Iraq War

I

This chapter concerns just two events: the Islamic Revolution in Iran in 1979 and the Iran-Iraq War that broke out in September 1980. That war continued until 1988 and ended just over a year before the death of Ayatollah Khomeini in 1989. As he was the figure who led the revolution and whose ideas shaped the new Islamic Republic of Iran, his death seems a fitting point at which to close this chapter.

The Shah who ruled Iran before the revolution was a controversial figure. He was a friend of the West, but it was well known that his regime was extremely repressive and that torture was widely used by his secret police, the much-feared SAVAK. When his days in power began to seem numbered, most people in the West who followed the events in Iran hoped that the country would be able to join the ranks of the democracies. It already seemed to be well on the path to becoming an industrialised nation, so such an expectation did not seem unreasonable. Instead, observers were forced to watch in bafflement and sometimes horror as Iran took a seemingly bizarre and regressive path. As commentators in the Western media grappled for ways to explain this, the words Sunni and Shi'i began to creep out of the rarefied academic discourse of Islamic studies faculties in universities, and into the media for the first time.

There is no doubt that the Iranian Revolution changed the world. We need to understand the forces that drove it, because in a short space of time Shi'i Iran became characterised by many other regimes as a threat to stability, both within and between nations. The events, and their outcome, also provided a motivation for Shi'ism itself to be condemned. What happened in Iran in 1979 would open up the sectarian split in Islam as a fault-line. Yet there is a paradox here: the revolution had no sectarian agenda and aimed to unite all Muslims against the onslaught of the West.

II

The history of Iran in the century or so before the Iranian Revolution of 1979 can be summarised only very briefly here. Throughout the nineteenth century the ruling Qajar dynasty were unable to provide anything more than weak government, while Britain and Russia engaged in imperial power politics that eventually led to the country being divided into spheres of influence. In the 1920s a tough professional soldier called Reza Khan seized power, proclaiming himself Reza Shah in 1925 and taking Pahlavi as the name of his dynasty. He would rule Iran with a rod of iron until he was ousted by Britain and Soviet Russia in 1941. His son Muhammad Reza Shah then ruled, until he was overthrown in the revolution in 1979. Both shahs treated parliament and the constitution as a mere process of administration.

The Pahlavis changed Iran from a country of peasants and tribal nomads into an urban, industrial society. But a repressive security state stifled any form of opposition, and the country was corrupt to the core. 1976 saw the Iranian economy overheat, while the following year oil revenues began to fall. Inflation, commodity shortages and rising unemployment all arrived together.

Many Iranians were angry at what they saw as the Pahlavi shahs' subservience to America and Britain. This fed into the existing distrust of Britain that went back to the nineteenth century. Reza Shah was perceived by many as someone who had sold Iran to Britain. For a long time, the British government received more money from Iranian oil than did the Iranian government. His son, Muhammad Reza Shah, kept very close to America and Britain, remaining their firm ally in the Cold War. In return, he was showered with state-of-the-art military equipment sold on very favourable terms.

The cultural side of the Pahlavi modernisation programme rode roughshod over traditional values. This was especially the case with regard to the values of Shi'i Islam that the peasants brought with them as they flocked to the cities. The Pahlavis disparaged the clergy as relics of the old Iran they were trying to drag into the modern world, but unfortunately for them the clergy were part of the warp and weft of traditional society.

At times it almost seemed as though Muhammad Reza Shah deliberately passed measures that he knew the clergy would dislike, so as to taunt them by displaying his power. He issued decrees instructing Iranians how they should dress. Turbans were replaced with various sorts of headgear, including a brimmed hat for men that meant that they could not touch the ground with their heads while prostrating themselves in prayer. Only the clergy were exempt, but this gave him the chance to decide who the members of the clergy would be. He encouraged women to reveal their faces and hair, forbade head coverings for female teachers, and ordered officials to be accompanied by their wives at state receptions. Chairs were to be installed in mosques to end the immemorial custom of worshippers sitting on the floor, while street commemorations of Muharram and the feast of Zahra, when the period of mourning for Hussein comes to an end, were banned.

The clergy became increasingly aghast at some social reforms under the Pahlavis, especially those concerning the position of women. These chipped away at the traditional interpretation of the Sharia, and granted women the vote. In the late 1970s, political activism increased. Religious scholars who were hostile to the Shah began to establish a network of sympathetic mosques and other religious establishments.

Demands grew for the authorities to allow the return from exile of a religious scholar called Ruhollah Khomeini. Few people outside Iran and the world of Twelver Shi'ism had heard of him. When the Shah and his empress were on an official visit to Washington in November 1977, both the empress and the American ambassador to Iran, who was meant to know the country well, saw demonstrating students carrying posters with a picture of Khomeini. Both were surprised that the students had chosen the face of such an obscurantist figure to symbolise their opposition to the Shah.

At the end of 1977, the British ambassador to Tehran reported home that the political and economic difficulties Shah Muhammad Reza

Pahlavi of Iran faced were 'no threat to basic stability'. Yet the following twelve months saw a wave grow until it swamped the ship of state. Once several demonstrators had been shot, protests spread across the country against the 'Government of Yazid' (a reference to the second Umayyad caliph, blamed for the death of the Shi'is' Third Imam, Hussein). Leading religious scholars issued calls for restraint, fearing that the protests would lead to action against religious institutions. Yet from the safety of his base near Paris, Khomeini called for the demonstrations to continue. Those protesting increased in numbers, and dissent spread across a wider segment of society.

Demonstrations in Tehran on 4 September took place to mark the feast at the end of Ramadan. Up to half a million people walked through the city carrying pictures of Khomeini. Three days later another march openly called for an Islamic republic. That night the Shah appointed a hard-line general as military governor of Tehran, and the following day troops fired into the crowds, killing around eighty people and injuring many more.[1] Many of those who marched had little idea of Khomeini's own thought, which was controversial even among other religious scholars. The old man was a figurehead, a person of towering integrity but someone who had no political experience and no idea at all about how to run a major country like Iran as it blazed its way into the modern world. But the protestors knew what they wanted to end: the Shah's regime, together with its repression, corruption, kowtowing to foreign interests, and contempt for the traditional values still held by most ordinary Iranians.

The situation continued to deteriorate. Khomeini steadfastly insisted that the Shah had to go, as a precondition for any settlement of the crisis. This made any compromise impossible. By December, strikes had led to paralysis of the economy and shortages of many commodities, including fuel. On 11 December, the anniversary of Hussein's martyrdom, over one million people attended demonstrations in Tehran. The crowd listened to speeches from all corners of the opposition, who had combined to produce a manifesto. Its demands included: a call for Khomeini to be made the leader of the country; an end to the monarchy; the establishment of an Islamic government; social justice for the poor; the revival of agriculture; and the protection of minorities.[2]

What support there was for the old regime either melted away or wisely kept a low profile. The Shah left the country on 16 January, officially for a holiday and rest and recuperation. Khomeini arrived on 1 February to a tumultuous reception.

III

Who was this seventy-seven-year-old man with a long white beard, who wore black robes and a turban, held meetings while sitting on a carpet on the floor, and whose name had been enough to unify the protesters who had brought down the Shah? He was a descendant of the Prophet through the Seventh Imam, Musa al-Kazim. His forebears had for generations been important local religious scholars in Khomein, a town in central Iran between Isfahan and Hamadan. He was born in 1902 and lost his father when he was one, and his mother when he was sixteen. These bereavements may have left him with a certain independence as well as an ambition to succeed.[3] He received the traditional education for an aspiring religious scholar, especially in the Sharia and judicial reasoning, and he was attracted to classical Persian poetry and Sufi mysticism. These were somewhat unusual interests for a religious scholar. Like Jamal al-Din al-Afghhani, whose ideas he studied, he was interested in the philosophical writings of the seventeenth-century Iranian philosopher Mulla Sadra, and the School of Isfahan, associated with a cultural renaissance in the Safavid era. He also wrote a commentary on the *Fusus al-Hikam* by the early thirteenth-century Sufi mystic and poet Ibn Arabi.[4]

These were texts that more conservative religious scholars disdained as frivolous flirtations with heresy, and it is quite wrong to see Khomeini as a brittle, religious fundamentalist. As well as being a revolutionary, he was an intellectual – but an intellectual rooted in a tradition that owed nothing to modern Western thought (although it stretched back to Plato and Aristotle). He was a rather unusual religious scholar who was more outward-looking than many: he had a greater intellectual curiosity than most, a confidence in the strength of his own intellect, and was prepared to stand out from the crowd when he thought it was right to do so. Unlike many others, he also thought that politics were important.

In the 1950s and 1960s, Khomeini taught in Qumm, and in 1961 he became an ayatollah (a title given to high-ranking Shi'i clerics with expert knowledge of theology and jurisprudence). He began to make political statements, showing an ability to voice popular grievances while steering clear of issues that might prove divisive for those inclined to listen to his message. Thus, although he was privately against constitutionalism, he spoke positively about it in his public pronouncements.[5] In this way, he managed to reach out to nationalists and others who might have been suspicious of a religious scholar. Yet, at the same time, he did not trust secular forces; they were mere allies of convenience. His own thought moved in the direction of rule by religious scholars, by the mujtahids. In 1964 he was sent into exile and lived most of the time in Najaf. He continued to make pronouncements on internal matters in Iran, but also began to develop his theory of Islamic government.

The starting points of his theory were the doctrinal tenets of the Usuli school of Twelver Shi'ism. The dilemma Twelvers have faced since the occultation of the Twelfth Imam was the following: the Sharia is the only true law, but in the absence of the Imam how is it to be discerned, interpreted and enforced? As was noted in Chapter Six, for the Usulis questions of interpretation are for each era's mujtahids, those deemed sufficiently expert, pious and enlightened to evaluate law. Khomeini went a crucial stage further, although others had hinted at this idea before: only the mujtahids could confer legitimacy on secular rulers. In other words, it was for the mujtahids to choose them. Like earlier Islamic reformers, he saw Islam as under attack from the materialism of the West, especially from the educated classes in Muslim countries who saw the world through the false prism of Western ideas. For him, there was a binary distinction between imperialism and Islam. 'Islam', he wrote, 'is the religion of militant individuals who are committed to truth and justice. It is the religion of those who desire freedom and independence.' But the religious scholars were also to blame. They had withdrawn from the political sphere in order to concentrate on discussion of minute points of ritual and observance. Monarchy, he taught, was contrary to Islam, while the principles that had been adapted from Western thought for the 1906 constitution were not Islamic; they were 'alien and borrowed'.[6]

This was strong stuff; but Khomeini did not give detailed proposals for what Islamic government should consist of. His statement 'Islamic government may be defined as the rule of divine law over men' does not take us far in political terms. It is even reminiscent of the Muslim Brotherhood's simplistic 'The Qur'an is our constitution' and 'Islam is the solution'. All Khomeini suggests in order to give effect to this is that a simple planning body should be set up so that programmes for a government's ministries should be produced 'in the light of the ordinances of Islam'. This meant that no legislative assembly would be needed.[7] The mujtahids should be entrusted with government because they had knowledge of law and justice.

Before 1978–79, few Iranians outside scholarly religious circles would have read Khomeini's ideas, which have become known as *velayat-e faqih*, 'the government (literally, "trusteeship") of the mujtahid'. But his consistent calls for the Shah's overthrow and his populist appeal to the Islam of the Iranian masses were combined with his own charisma and canny political skills. After his return to Tehran, and the ecstatic welcome he received, there would be a testing time. Even if he could persuade Iranians to implement his ideas, those ideas had not been fleshed out. And it is less than altogether clear what he himself intended to achieve with the vast moral power that he now held in his hands.

IV

At the end of March 1979 there was a referendum: did Iranians want an Islamic Republic or a monarchy? Of those who voted, 98.2 per cent chose the Islamic republic, although many leading figures and political groups were unhappy that this binary choice obscured the question of what an Islamic republic would mean. The drafting of the Islamic Republic's new constitution continued over the rest of the year. In its final form it gave the *faqih* (the Islamic jurist, in this case Ayatollah Khomenei) tremendous power. He must approve candidates for president before they are allowed to run for office; and it is he who appoints the heads of the armed services, as well as the heads of national TV and radio. His role is leadership. As the introduction to the constitution puts it, his leadership 'will prevent any deviation by the various organs of government from their essential Islamic duties.'[8] Underneath the *faqih* there are the normal organs of a modern republic: the president, the legislature and the judiciary, but they must all act in accordance with the principles of Islam, of which he is the ultimate interpreter. A Council of Guardians can reject legislation if it considers it to be incompatible with Islam.[9]

The constitution also makes it clear that the Islamic Republic has a mission: 'to ensure the continuation of the revolution at home and abroad'. It is to strive with other Islamic and popular movements 'to prepare the way for the formation of a single world community of Muslims' and 'to assure the continuation of the struggle for the liberation of all deprived and oppressed peoples in the world'.[10] The ambition that the Islamic Republic will unite all Muslims is spelled out in Article 10:

> In accordance with the [Qur'anic] verse *This your nation is a single nation, and I am your Lord, so worship Me,'* all Muslims form a single nation, and the government of the Islamic Republic of Iran has the duty of formulating its general policies with a view to the merging and union of all Muslim peoples, and it must constantly strive to bring about the political, economic, and cultural unity of the Islamic world.[11]

Although the Islam of the Islamic Republic is Twelver Shi'ism, the constitution also explicitly recognises other Muslim schools, including the doctrinal law schools of Sunni Islam. These are listed by name and have official status. They 'are free to act in accordance with their own jurisprudence in performing their religious devotions'. In areas where members of one of these law schools predominate, local regulations are to be in accordance with that school's precepts, so long as this does not affect others adversely. Zoroastrians, Jews and Christians are fully recognised as religious minorities, but all non-Muslims are to be treated in an ethical fashion and in accordance with Islamic justice and equity and their human rights.[12] Yet there is no mention of Iran's largest religious minority, the Baha'is, who originated in the Iranian Shi'ism of the nineteenth century. They had often faced persecution in Iran. This would intensify under the Islamic Republic.

The constitution demonstrates how Khomeini and his followers saw the Iranian Revolution as a struggle under the banner of Islam against the oppression that flowed ineluctably from Western imperialism. This was intermeshed with the struggle against cultural imperialism and Westernisation. Because Iran was a predominantly Twelver country, it was natural enough for Twelver Shiʻism to be the form of Islam inscribed on Khomeini's banner. But it is important to stress that the aims of the revolution were universalist; it was in no way a sectarian struggle that pitted Shiʻi against Sunni, or counted Sunni Muslims as part of the forces of oppression it was combating. As the revolution wanted to export itself (just as the French and Russian revolutions had done in their early stages), this meant that its ideas should be spread everywhere – among Sunnis as well as Shiʻis.

Yet it would have been strange if this enthusiastic impulse had not been accompanied by a hope that the scales would fall from Sunni eyes and they would come to see the true light of Shiʻi Islam. Shiʻi proselytisation (both among non-Muslims and other Muslims) would be encouraged as part of the revolution. Although this was distinct from spreading the Islamic revolution's radical message, the two would inevitably become linked in the minds of many Sunnis. This was especially the case for those Sunnis who were hostile to the aims of the revolution – and they probably included all Sunni rulers across the Muslim world. On the other hand, liberation movements everywhere might now hope for support from the Iranian Revolution. This could easily lead to revolutionary solidarity among Sunnis and Shiʻis. It would now be very easy for rulers of other countries to see Iran as public enemy number one, for Shiʻi populations to be suspected of clandestine support for the Iranian Revolution, and for Shiʻism itself to be feared. There would also be a counterblast. Some Sunni rulers would urge Sunnis to rally together in a way that excluded, and sometimes demonised, Shiʻis. They would find religious justification for this in the Wahhabism of Saudi Arabia.

V

In September 1980, Iran was suddenly attacked by the Iraq of Saddam Hussein. The attack was opportunistic, and the reasons for it must be sought in developments in Iraq, as well as in Iran.

As was seen in Chapter Ten, the dominant cliques that made up the Iraqi Baʻath were composed of Sunni Arabs who feared the Shiʻis because of their numbers. Although the Ba'athists were certainly not friends of the Shah, they viewed the progress of the revolution in Iran with disquiet, and were unnerved when his regime collapsed. Iraqi Shi'i religious movements like the al-Da'wa Party had been driven underground, but they were emboldened by the Iranian Revolution. The response was a firm crackdown, which led to opposition. When the Iraqi regime placed the al-Da'wa Ayatollah Muhammad Baqir al-Sadr under house arrest in June 1979, it sparked widespread protests in Najaf, Karbala and Kufa, as well as the huge Baghdad housing district then known as Medinat al-Thawra, which was virtually a Shi'i ghetto. In Medinat al-Thawra, the force of the protests was such that the regime's surveillance apparatus temporarily broke down. Control was brutally re-established, but Muhammad Baqir al-Sadr's speeches attacking the regime continued to circulate on cassettes which were listened to by both Shi'is and Sunnis.[13] The possibility that events in Iran might trigger an uprising among Shi'is was bad enough for the regime. That it might also receive Sunni backing was even more worrying.

The crisis had a major consequence. In July, the Iraqi vice president and prominent Ba'athist Saddam Hussein took complete control of the country. This was followed by an Iraqi Ba'ath party conference. While the new president presided on the podium, a member of the Revolutionary Command Council – Iraq's supreme organ of government – publicly announced that he had taken part in a Syrian-led conspiracy to overthrow the new president. He also gave the names of some other members of the conspiracy. While these men were frogmarched out of the hall, Saddam Hussein smoked a large cigar and read out a list of others who were implicated (and who were also promptly removed). He broke out in tears several times as he wept at their treachery. Most of those taken from the hall would be tried and executed shortly afterwards. A wider purge led to a total of perhaps 500 executions.[14] Everyone already knew Saddam Hussein's ruthless side, which he so devastatingly displayed in this way in his first days in power. He combined it with charm and his extensive powers of patronage. He would ensure that every person of any importance in Iraq was either dependent on him or, at the very least, terrified of crossing him. This fear would often have applied to the bearers of bad news, who must often have shielded him from unpleasant realities. He would push Iraq into the abyss.

A little over a year later, in September 1980, Saddam Hussein invaded Iran. The Iran-Iraq War was a conflict in which the Western media took relatively little interest, except when it threatened to disrupt oil supplies. Despite this, it was the bloodiest of all the wars that have taken place in the Middle East region between the Second World War and today. One reason for the absence of Western interest was the lack of sympathy in America and Europe for either side. Henry Kissinger is reputed to have said that it was a pity both sides could not lose. Yet the conflict may have killed a million or more people.

The question is often debated: why did the war start? In 1980, Saddam Hussein's Ba'athist state was very powerful indeed. It was certainly concerned about Shi'i unrest, and that concern was a factor in Saddam Hussein taking complete control in July 1979. By then the al-Da'wa Party (in whose formation Muhammad Baqir al-Sadir had been instrumental) and other specifically Shi'i organisations were endorsing the use of violence against the government. The Society of Religious Scholars (Jama'at al-'ulama') added its voice to them in October, and the government responded to this with a retroactive decree in March 1980 making membership of al-Da'wa a capital offence. When an unsuccessful assassination attempt on Saddam Hussein's foreign minister was made in March 1980, the brutal response included the execution of Ayatollah Muhammad Baqir al-Sadr and his sister, Bint al-Huda, who was a noted religious scholar in her own right. The Ayatollah was probably paying with his life for a message he managed to send his followers from jail. In this, he had addressed the Iraqi people as a whole and called for unity between Sunni and Shi'i Arabs and Kurds. The message passionately attacked Saddam Hussein for trying to split Sunnis and Shi'is in order to divide and rule:

> The idol-Satan [Saddam Husayn] and his henchmen are trying to persuade our pure Sunni sons that the issue is that of Shi'i and Sunni... I want to tell you, O [Shi'i] sons of Ali and al-Husayn, and [Sunni] sons of Abu Bakr and Umar, that the battle is not between the Shi'is and a Sunni rule! The Sunni rule represented by the Rightly guided Caliphs... and based on Islam and justice, Ali used his sword to protect it! ... The present rule is not Sunni rule, even though the hegemonic clique belongs... to the Sunna, because a Sunni rule is not

that which is controlled by a man born to Sunni parents. Rather, it is the rule of Abu Bakr and Umar that is challenged by the tyrants in Iraq today.[15]

This plea for Shi'is and Sunnis to combine against a manifestly unjust government had resonances of the Sunni-Shi'i unity at the end of the First World War. It was just about the most worrying call that the Ba'athist regime could face. The execution of Muhammad Baqir al-Sadr was the first time a Ba'athist ruler had executed an ayatollah. Ayatollah al-Kho'i, Iraq's most senior mujtahid, was also placed under house arrest. Many Shi'is who could be designated as Iranian because of their ancestry were deported to Iran. With Shi'i scholarly networks and other bonds within the Shi'i community disrupted, the power of government patronage was now used to a greater extent than ever before to split Shi'i solidarity and tie much of the community to the regime.[16]

Was attacking Iran, which would lead to all the uncertainties of war, the obvious next step for Saddam Hussein to take in order to cope with Shi'i discontent?[17] This has to be doubtful. The precise reasons why Iraq invaded were probably only ever known to him and those close to him. They are to be found in his vaingloriousness and arrogance, and the sycophancy with which his entourage treated him, since to challenge his views was to court death. An important event in his decision-making process may have been Egypt's peace treaty with Israel in May 1979. This had caused Egypt to be thrown out of the League of Arab states. With Egypt temporarily removed from the equations of Arab politics, Iraq was now the Arab world's largest military power, as well as a major oil producer.

Saddam Hussein believed it was now time for Iraq to flex its muscles and show leadership. What could be better than a war that would demonstrate Iran's weakness and Iraq's strength, and force Iran to negotiate a humiliating peace? It would compel all the rulers of the Gulf and his arch-rival, Hafez al-Assad of Syria, to acknowledge him as the leader of the Arab world. It might also add the oil-rich area of the Arabic-speaking Iranian province of Khuzistan to Iraq and be fitting revenge for the Shah's previous humiliations of Iraq.

Iraq's decision to invade Iran thus may have had little to do with religion. The motive behind it, insofar as it can be disentangled from

Saddam Hussein's narcissism, was Arab and Iraqi nationalism. The war soon proved to be a disaster, a massive self-inflicted wound. Saddam Hussein had underestimated how his attack would put Iranian backs to the wall. On the Iranian side in particular, there was much religious rhetoric. There were calls to liberate Najaf and Karbala, as well as to advance to Jerusalem by way of Baghdad. The first of these would have appealed only to Shi'is but, it will be observed, the second was aimed at all Muslims. The Iraqi side, meanwhile, invoked the great battles in the Arab conquest of Iran by the soldiers of the first caliphs. Possibly through dire military necessity, an increasing number of able Shi'i officers were promoted to positions of responsibility in the Iraqi army. Much effort was also given to propaganda that Saddam Hussein's regime aimed at Iraq's Shi'is, including a fanciful claim that he was descended from the Imam Ali.[18]

In April-May 1982, Iraq made a strategic withdrawal, effectively suing for peace. But Khomeini was persuaded by military leaders that the war was winnable and therefore endorsed their wish to carry the fight into Iraqi territory in order to drive Saddam Hussein from power. By 1988 it was obvious that the Iranian forces were losing, and were being steadily driven back. Khomeini reluctantly accepted the need for a ceasefire, and in mid-August the guns fell silent.

No aggressive war had been waged by Iran since the days of Nadir Shah (r. 1736–1747). Yet now, by deciding in 1982 not to end the war when Iraq called for a ceasefire, and by actually invading Iraq, it was perceived as an aggressor. It had also failed to abide by the norms by which sovereign states are meant to behave. It was not just the wider international community that noted this. On the southern shores of the Gulf, Saudi Arabia, Kuwait and the UAE had Shi'i minorities, while Bahrain had a Shi'i majority. These states had been nervous about the nationalistic swaggering of the Shah. Now revolutionary Iran posed a much greater threat. Part of this stemmed from its use of religious rhetoric aimed at winning Shi'is to its cause and sparking revolution among all Muslims. It had also used the war as an opportunity to spread its revolutionary ideology among Shi'i soldiers from the Iraqi army who became prisoners, as well as Shi'i exiles from Iraq. In 1982, some of them formed the Supreme Council for the Islamic Revolution in Iraq (SCIRI) which subscribed to Khomeini's idea of the *velayat-e faqih* (government of the mujtahid). SCIRI formed its own military formation, the Badr Brigade, which fought against the Iraqi army on the Kurdish front. On one level, this was a portent of things to come. It also led to a rift among Iraqi Shi'is in exile or prisoner of war camps in Iran, since the main Iraqi Shi'i movement, the al-Da'wa Party, did not accept Khomeini's ideology.

VI

Iran had failed to force an Iraqi surrender, to overthrow the tyrant Saddam Hussein and to achieve a convincing victory for the revolution beyond its own borders. There are indications that this left Khomeini in a spiritual crisis, becoming confused and downhearted. He appears to have come to see himself as God's chosen instrument to achieve the divine purpose on earth. He must have asked why God had not granted Iran the victory it deserved. Surely, that victory would have consolidated and spread the Islamic revolution? And was not that revolution the divine will?

Ruhollah Khomeini died on 3 June 1989, less than a year after the end of the Iran-Iraq War. This last period of his life saw two events that are greatly to his discredit and deserve to be mentioned because of the light that they shed on him. Each also illustrates different aspects of the Iranian Revolution.

The first concerned Salman Rushdie, the British novelist from an Indian Muslim background. In September 1988 he published his satirical novel *The Satanic Verses*, which uses the techniques of magical realism. The book is about the problems immigrants experience when trying to settle in Britain, and the frosty attitude of the host culture. But the plot includes a dream sequence revolving around a story preserved by the Abbasid historian Muhammad bin Jarir al-Tabari. This concerns some verses that the Devil temporarily tricked the Prophet Muhammad into including in the Qur'an. Had these verses remained part of the holy text, they would have allowed idol worship. Airing this episode in a novel was bound to be controversial for Muslims, since some can find the story that al-Tabari recorded a stumbling block to their faith. Yet, quite apart from this, other features of the book are deeply offensive to many Muslims, and it is not hard to see why. There were demonstrations against the novel in Muslim communities in Britain, and these soon spread to Pakistan, Bangladesh and Kashmir, the countries from which those communities originated. Some of these demonstrations turned violent.

Six months later, in February 1989, Khomeini issued an order sentencing the author as well as 'those publishers who are aware of [the book's] contents' to death. The order continued: 'I call on all zealous Muslims to execute them quickly, wherever they find them, so that no one will dare insult the Islamic sanctities. Whoever is killed on this path will be regarded as a martyr, God willing.'

Nothing could have been more calculated to ensure that Iran would remain an international pariah. Violent attacks were made on Salman Rushdie's Norwegian, Japanese and Italian translators over the next few years. The Norwegian was killed, and the other two injured, while Rushdie himself went into hiding. Khomeini's stance demonstrated two things: the first was that the revolution's radicalism still survived ten years after the fall of the Shah. So long as the supreme *faqih* continued to support that radicalism, no Iranian government would be able to turn aside from it. The other point, which is often overlooked today, is that Khomeini's death sentence on Rushdie was a call to all Muslims of whatever sect. The overwhelming majority of those who had demonstrated against *The Satanic Verses* before he issued his order were Sunni Muslims. Khomeini hoped they would now fall in behind his lead.

Khomeini frequently attacked the Saudi monarchy; as his thought developed he came to see monarchy as un-Islamic. However, he always stressed his belief in the unity of Muslims, something that we have seen was set out by implication, if not more strongly, in the Iranian Constitution of 1979. He took steps to reduce discord between Shi'is and Sunnis and make it easier for Sunnis to see Twelvers as their brothers in faith. Thus, he opposed *sabb*, the ritual cursing of the three caliphs who had preceded Ali. Consequently this ritual that goaded Sunnis did not become a feature of the Islamic Republic. He also had the shrine of Abu Lulu closed down. The cult of Abu Lulu had grown among some Iranian Shi'is. He was the Persian Christian who had been taken to Medina as a slave during the very first Arab conquests, and had assassinated the Caliph Umar.

The period immediately after the Iran-Iraq War would lead to another serious blot on Khomeini's reputation. The most deadly opponent of his Islamic Revolution had been the Mujahideen-e khalq, a group that had blended Marxism and Islam and had been prominent proponents of armed struggle against the Shah. In a travesty of justice by any standards – including, it should be emphasised, the standards of the Sharia – Khomeini had them condemned for apostasy and hanged by slow strangulation. An estimated 4,000–5,000 people died.

Khomeini died less than four months after issuing his death sentence on Rushdie. He had made his brand of Twelver Shi'ism and its *velayat-e faqih* triumphant within Iran, but that triumph had come at a price. Dr Michael Axworthy, who headed the Iran Section of the UK's Foreign and Commonwealth Office from 1998 to 2000, asserts that, by the time of Khomeini's death, 'the principles of religion had become wholly subordinated to the requirements of power'.[19] Opposition to *velayat-e faqih* would continue among many Shi'is worldwide. In Iran itself there would be much resentment at the strictures on daily life that it had led to, as well as dismay at the way in which principle was so often overridden by expediency. The regime's use of torture, for instance, was in reality even worse than under the Shah. Expediency, placating populism, and putting means before ends, were all characteristic of Khomeini and his followers, and they led to disillusionment. That sometimes extended to disillusionment with Islam itself.

CHAPTER TWELVE

From the Iranian Revolution to the 2003 Invasion of Iraq

I

After the Iranian Revolution, the Middle East and the entire Muslim world could never be the same again. Monarchs, military rulers and other autocrats felt genuine fear as they contemplated what had happened. Their security services, like those of the Shah, had focused chiefly on left-wing activists such as communists, socialists and (in Arab countries) Ba'athists. Not only were these subversive forces still around, but a new threat had appeared: a movement of newly urbanised Muslim masses stirred up by an ideology that had Islam as its root. It took the autocrats some time to recognise that this new force was the greatest threat they faced. Left-wing activists were also slow to understand that reality.

In Saudi Arabia in 1979, left-wing organisations had joined Shi'i Islamists in the Eastern Province in widespread protests. Communists and Ba'athists published their own versions of events, in which they refused to acknowledge that the Shi'i activists had been the leaders of the popular discontent. As late as 1986, a spokesman for the Saudi Communists in exile in Lebanon condemned as 'backward' the Organisation for the Islamic Revolution in the Arabian Peninsula (OIRAP), one of the most important political groups behind the protests. But he was the one who was being left behind by history. OIRAP retorted that the events had coincided with the commemorations of the martyrdom of Imam Hussein, not a communist anniversary. The real 'vanguard', they added, were the Islamists, and it was they who had persuaded people to take to the streets.[1] They were right.

In the Middle East, rulers found it prudent to stress their own credentials as good Muslims. This was a trend that had begun before the Iranian Revolution; now it accelerated in response to a genuine religious revival. There were increasingly public manifestations of piety. More men could be seen with the callous on the forehead known as the *zabib*, or raisin, which is caused by the same patch of skin repeatedly touching the ground in regular prostrations for prayer. At the same time there was a dramatic increase in the numbers of women covering all their hair and wearing identifiably 'Islamic' dress. Behind the new stress on Islam as a badge of identity lay an uneasy resentment: the West, despite all the progress it had offered, despite all its achievements, had proved to be a false messiah. This was coupled with anger at many Western policies that had been imposed in the region since the spread of Western hegemony.

II

Autocrats in the Arab world (and elsewhere) did not have absolute power and were not equally repressive. In each country it was necessary for the ruler to keep the loyalty of a powerbase, and it was in his interest for that powerbase to be as broad as possible. This meant that prudent rulers needed to negotiate and compromise with the wishes and aspirations of ordinary people. In the monarchies, most kings and emirs could rely on a sense of legitimacy among a large section (frequently, but not always, the majority) of the population. Yet it was doubtful, for instance, that the Sunni royal families could claim such legitimacy in the eyes of most of their Shi'i subjects, save to the very appreciable extent that they were able to provide a stable regime from which Shi'is, as well as Sunni, could benefit.

The relationship between rulers in the Arabian peninsula and their tribal followers was contractual. Rulers had to make it worthwhile for their subjects to remain loyal. Revenue came from customs duties, not from taxation of tribal followers. In return for their loyalty, the followers would expect largesse from their ruler according to unwritten customs that dated from before the advent of Islam. When oil revenues

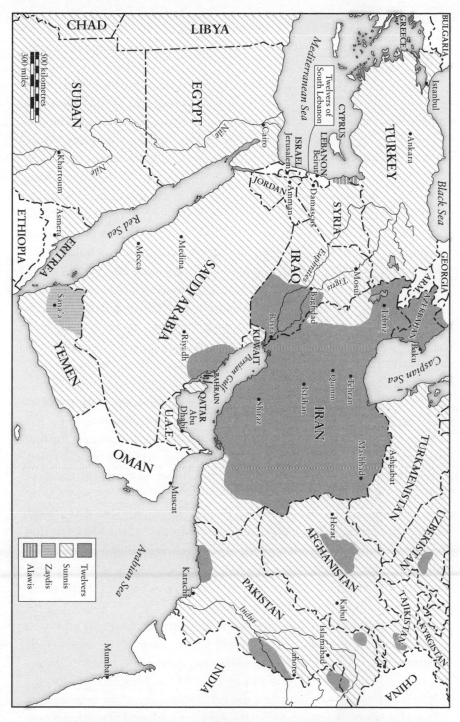

THE CENTRAL ISLAMIC LANDS SHOWING AREAS
WITH MAJORITY SUNNI AND SHI'I POPULATIONS

appeared, the expectation of increased largesse accompanied them, and the ruler's generosity would now be expected to include the provision of schools, clinics, roads and government jobs. The followers – who were now rebranded as 'citizens' or 'nationals' – would not be given any say in governing their country. Democratic institutions were not on the agenda. But the ruler's subjects could still go and talk directly to the ruler, or at least to his local governor, and petition in the old, customary way.

A wise ruler would listen, but the decisions were for him to take. It was not a question of no taxation without representation. It is sometimes suggested that in fact it was the opposite: no representation without taxation. In other words, the fact that citizens did not pay income tax meant that the government had no necessity to grant them democratic institutions. Traditional rulers of Arabian tribal societies had to listen to their followers and sound out their opinions if they did not want to risk their authority ebbing away. However, the vast financial resources that were now often at their disposal – especially after the oil boom of the mid-1970s – meant that they could frequently imprison or exile opposition leaders and buy off the constituencies to which the opposition appealed. There was always an apparatus of repression quietly present in the background. When needed, it would be used ruthlessly.

To an extent, these patterns also occurred in the military dictatorships, although they frequently lacked the same wealth and they were, by and large, not tribal societies – or at least much less so than was the case in Arabia. Yet military rulers and other dictators often depended on patronage in similar ways in order to stay in power. They had used socialist and nationalist ideologies as their original justification for kicking out the previous incumbent of the presidential palace, and were expected to expand education, healthcare, roads, mains electricity and piped water across the entire country – as well as to provide government jobs. They also needed a powerbase, and in some cases – notably Syria and Iraq –that basis for authority was to a considerable extent provided on sectarian lines. A central element of these powerbases consisted of members of a religious minority, meaning Alawis in the case of Syria, Sunnis in that of Iraq. This was almost an open invitation for poisonous religious politics to enter each country. As was seen in the last chapter, before 1979 militant groups in Syria were already trying to use solidarity among Sunnis to resist a regime dominated by members of the Alawi minority from which the president came. In Iraq, similar use of patronage by a president from the Sunni minority almost invited the Shi'i majority to turn to sectarian politics.

Several factors meant that governments in the non-oil states could no longer provide the services ordinary people had come to expect, These included rising populations, fluctuating oil prices, inefficiency, corruption, failed socialist policies (such as the promise of a civil service job to every graduate) and harsh neo-liberal ones (such as ending that promise of the government job and cutting subsidies on basic commodities). Activists associated with a liberal opposition political movement were unable to step into the breach, since they did not have the necessary base or funds, and the government was determined to keep it that way. On the other hand, those religious organisations prepared to work with the government were presented with a vacuum that they could fill. They distributed food to the poor and offered medical care, while at the same time providing classes for people to learn about the teachings and practice of their faith. All this helped them to anchor Islam more deeply as the bedrock of identity for millions of people. Sunni and Shi'i organisations carried out such work in their own communities, as did Christian groups in theirs. Although this helped cement the religious identities of those who benefited, there was no necessary reason for this, of itself, to lead to sectarian strife.

III

Such was the backdrop during the 1980s and 1990s against which two radical forces would seek to expand. The first was the revolutionary Islamist ideology coming out of Iran. The other was a radical, revolutionary impulse that gained traction among some Sunnis. It blended Wahhabism with movements such as the conservative Deobandis in the Indian sub-continent and the ideology of Sayyid Qutb.

Sayyid Qutb was a Sunni Islamist theorist born in Egypt in 1906. He was convicted of plotting against the Egyptian state and executed in 1966. But by then he had published books that would lead to his being perceived as the intellectual godfather of radical Islam and the terrorism that is today seen as its hallmark. He came from a devout family and had memorised the Qur'an as a boy, but he also received a modern education and was respected as a gifted secular intellectual when he was a young man. He was well into his forties before he joined the Muslim Brotherhood in 1953. A religious arch-conservative as well as a theoretician of Islamist revolution, he advocated reinstating the inferior status for Christians and Jews that was enshrined in the Sharia but had been abolished in the nineteenth century, and rolling back the gradual improvements which secular reforms had made to the position of women. 'Only in the Islamic way of life,' he wrote in *Milestones*, his last book, 'do all men become free from the servitude of some men to others and devote themselves to God alone.'[2]

In the end, he rejected Western ideologies like nationalism, socialism and communism outright in favour of a sense of Islam as the sole feeling of identity that should unite all Muslims. He knew that those who would set out to establish this vision were few, but they were a vanguard that would spread its word from individual to individual until a new, righteous generation was created that would bring Egypt (and other Muslim countries) back to the Islam of the *salaf*, the pious forebears who had known and loved the Prophet and the following two generations. Although the primary task of the members of the vanguard was preaching and showing how to live Islam by example, Sayyid Qutb taught that they should also use violence when necessary, so as to stop those whose actions hindered the preaching of Islam. This teaching would have ominous consequences.

Both of the new, radical movements mentioned above had as their main objective the rolling back of Western political and cultural domination of the Islamic lands. Although in theory they might have appeared to be allies, the clash between them would lead to sectarian discord.

But it did not start that way. The Iranian Revolution caused an initial groundswell of pride in Islam among many Muslims the world over. This was not restricted to Shi'is. Some enthusiastic Sunnis even saw *velayet-e faqih* ('government by the [Shi'i] mujtahid') as a new version of the caliphate. In Egypt the Muslim Brotherhood at first applauded the Iranians for overthrowing the secular identity that they had been forced to adopt by the Shah, whose rule they saw as characterised by lax religious observance and general misery. Some Malaysian Islamists saw the Islamic republic as a symbolic triumph of the Islamic ideal and Islamic identity.[3] In these countries – as in many other parts of the Muslim world where there were no Shi'is or there was a minimal Shi'i presence – a few Sunnis might decide to convert to Shi'ism after being inspired by Khomeini's anti-imperialist rhetoric. Generally speaking, however, such conversions had little lasting impact and very often the converts were re-absorbed by Sunni Islam. In Senegal a group of young intellectuals sparked enthusiasm for Islamism after visiting Iran in the early 1980s. They founded a newspaper in which they called for unity between Sunnis and Shi'is, while attacking Saudi Arabia and Egypt, as well the local Muslim religious establishment. But they were unable to establish alternative networks to those provided by traditional Senegalese Sufi brotherhoods. Over time, many of them became members of the religious establishment they had once condemned, while their newspaper (*Wal Fajri*, 'The Dawn' in the Senegalese language Wolof) evolved into a mainstream liberal publication.[4]

Saudi Arabia suddenly found itself faced by a challenge from the Shi'is of the kingdom's Eastern Province. Ever since the Saudis had gained control of the area, before the First World War, the public processions commemorating the martyrdom of Hussein at Karbala had been generally banned. In 1958 there had been sectarian clashes in Qatif, when Sunnis made fun of the Shi'i rituals. Since then, commemorations had generally taken place only behind closed doors, in private colleges or confined spaces, or in towns and villages that were exclusively Shi'i.[5] But in 1979, no doubt emboldened by the Iranian Revolution, and following calls from religious scholars, Shi'is tried to hold their commemorative processions publicly in the streets. This was an open act of defiance, especially as the commemorations held in Iran a year earlier had been an important milestone in the collapse of the Shah's regime. Twenty-thousand members of the National Guard, all recruited from Sunni tribes, had to be sent to disperse the crowds of mourners.[6]

Protests culminated in demonstrations across the province on 27 November, in which as many as 70,000 may have taken part. The following day there was violence, and demonstrators in the old town of Qatif carried pictures of Ayatollah Khomeini and chanted slogans from the Iranian Revolution. One of these was '*La sunniyya la Shi'iyya...*

thawra thawra islamiyya.' This catchy slogan (it is a rhyming couplet in Arabic) means in English, 'No Sunni, no Shiʿi... [we want] a revolution, an Islamic revolution!' Subsequently, Qatif had to be sealed off as protesters looted the offices of the Saudi British Bank and the Saudi Arabian national airline. Ominously, too, the protesters reconvened to march on 12 January, the fortieth day – the *arbaʿeen* – of the killing of the first demonstrator, as well as on 1 February 1980, the first anniversary of the return of Khomeini to Iran.[7]

But what was possibly most threatening for the Saudi regime was an attempt by some Shiʿis to link their own protests to the seizure of the mosque complex of the Kaʿba in Mecca by a Sunni militant called Juhayman bin Muhammad bin Sayf al-Otaybi (see below). The demonstrations in Qatif had begun only five days after the seizure of the mosque, while some other demonstrations started on the day of the seizure. The possibility of joint action by both Sunni and Shiʿi dissidents, combining along Islamic lines against the corruption and oppression of the regime, was as much a nightmare for the Saudi authorities as it was in Iraq.[8] Once again, we see how the Iranian Revolution was sparking a new assertiveness among Shiʿis outside Iran while also providing an inspiration to Sunni revolutionaries.

IV

Palestine was an interesting case. The Shah had been a close friend of Israel, seeing it as a valuable strategic ally as he tried to establish Iranian hegemony in the Gulf. Khomeini, by contrast, had been known as an outspoken supporter of Palestinian rights well before the Islamic revolution. As Shiʿis were a tiny minority among Palestinian Muslims, it was inevitable that Palestinian Islamist movements would be Sunni. Yet for some Palestinian Sunni Islamists the Iranian Revolution was an inspiration. Fathi Shiqaqi was the leader of Palestinian Islamic Jihad, a movement set up in 1980 with a programme of immediate armed struggle against Israel. In those early days, Islamist movements among Palestinians were sometimes encouraged by Israel, which saw them as a useful antidote to Arab nationalism. Shiqaqi contrasted the boldness and willingness to innovate shown by Khomeini, with the tepid and indecisive attitude of Sunni Islamists, who were all too frequently preoccupied with the minutiae of religious observance.

For Shiqaqi, Khomeini was 'the man of the century'. He had turned Islam into a faith for those prepared to fight and sacrifice their lives for justice. He had also correctly identified the Palestinian call for justice as the point around which the struggle between Islam and the West revolved, whereas so many of the Sunni Islamists were more concerned with domestic political struggles in their own countries. The result was that, for Shiqaqi, Tehran had acquired the right to political leadership of the Muslim world in a way that transcended geographic, ethnic and sectarian boundaries. Shiqaqi saw Khomeini as a disciple of Jamal al-Din al-Afghani, and argued that he had ensured that there would be no purely sectarian identity in the Iranian Revolution. On the contrary, the Iranian Revolution had been formulated on the basis of the Qur'an. Sunnis, as well as Shi'is, could line up behind it.[9] After Hamas (a Sunni organisation) emerged from the Palestinian branch of the Muslim Brotherhood in 1987, it, too, would receive generous support from Iran. This would continue across the decades.

In Egypt, where the number of Shi'is was extremely small, the Iranian Revolution actually hindered Sunni-Shi'i relations, for reasons that are not hard to fathom. In 1947 some Sunni-Shi'i dialogue began, when the Association for the Rapprochement of the Islamic Doctrinal Law Schools was established by an Iranian scholar, Muhammad Taqi al-Qummi. With government encouragement during the Nasser era, attempts were made to reach out to Iranian Shi'is. Possibly as a result of this, in 1959 the rector of the Al-Azhar Mosque in Cairo, Sheikh Mahmud Shaltut, issued a fatwa that Twelver Shi'is should be seen as a fifth doctrinal law school alongside the Malikis, Hanafis, Shafi'is and Hanbalis of Sunni Islam. This, of course, echoed earlier attempts at ecumenism such as those at the time of the powerful Iranian ruler Nadir Shah. Shaltut stated that in his view conversion from Twelver Shi'ism to one of the four traditional Sunni doctrinal law schools or vice-versa was permissible. Subsequently, however, after Egypt broke off diplomatic relations with Iran in 1960, anti-Shi'i religious polemic reappeared. This intensified after the Iranian Revolution, when the Egyptian government saw the new Iran and the export of its revolution as a major threat.

From the 1980s onwards, a few Egyptians have publicly announced their conversion to Shi'ism. This has caused outrage and led to passionate calls for an end to all Shi'i missionary activities and the banning of Shi'i publications. The desire for *taqrib*, or 'rapprochement', and the restoration of the unity of Islam has been countered by the fear of *fitna*, civil strife and subversion. It is not hard to see political subtexts behind official attitudes to Shi'ism in Egypt, including behind those expressed by the Al-Azhar Mosque. On the one hand there is genuine fear of subversion spreading from Iran. This is coupled with a kind of guilt that, since the time of President Sadat's peace treaty with Israel in 1979, Egypt has been complicit in fostering policies of Western governments in the region. Those policies are widely perceived as benefiting the interests of those governments, and not those of the people of the region, with the consequence that Egypt has failed in its duty to stand up for the oppressed. On the other hand, the steady Wahhabisation of Egyptian Islam at a popular level, which has followed on from the rise of Saudi Arabia as the wealthiest oil-producing state, has made rapprochement between Sunnis and Shi'is harder in Egypt, as it has elsewhere. In this respect, a revealing suggestion was put forward in 2007 by Sheikh Muhammad Sayyid Tantawi, a former rector of the Al-Azhar Mosque: that reverence for those of the Prophet's Companions who are rejected by Shi'is should be considered an essential part of a Muslim's faith.[10] It will have made rapprochement with Shi'is much harder, but would have been well received in Saudi Arabia, which is a major donor of aid to Egypt.

In Syria, the Iranian Revolution had paradoxical consequences. In June 1979, a disaffected Sunni Ba'athist let militants into the artillery academy in Aleppo, where they shot and killed at least thirty-two officer cadets who were chiefly Alawis. The artillery school massacre was a major escalation in the low-intensity guerrilla war already waged against the Syrian regime by Islamist militants inspired by the ideas of Sayyid Qutb. These militants were the Fighting Vanguard, an offshoot of the Muslim Brotherhood founded by followers of Marwan Hadid, a Muslim Brother from Hama. Hadid, unusually for a Syrian Muslim Brother, had been advocating the violent overthrow of the Ba'athists for a decade, before he died in regime custody in 1976. After the artillery school massacre, violence grew worse. In June 1980 an assassination attempt on President

Hafez al-Assad nearly succeeded, and a mass execution of Islamist detainees in the notorious prison of Palmyra took place in retaliation. There were also attempts on the lives of other prominent Alawis and some leading Sunni religious scholars who supported Assad's regime. Some of these were successful.

The culmination of the unrest was the uprising in Hama in February 1982 when the Fighting Vanguard and local members of the Muslim Brotherhood seized control and slaughtered dozens of local Ba'athist officials. Their hope was to spark similar uprisings across Syria, but these did not occur. The regime's response was brutal and comprehensive. Thousands of ordinary men, women and children died in the indiscriminate shelling by the regime's tanks before it retook control. The lowest estimate for those who died in the regime's recapture of Hama is 5,000, while figures of 10,000–20,000 (or even higher – up to 40,000) are frequently cited.

The Hama uprising and the violent campaign that preceded it was an attack on the kind of secularist regime against which Sayyid Qutb had advocated violence. At the same time, many of the members of the Fighting Vanguard who fought it had also been inspired by the Iranian Revolution. Specifically Sunni and Shi'i revolutionary currents had thus come together against the secularist Ba'ath of Hafez al-Assad. There was also another paradox. While the centre of Hama was being consumed by fire, the Iran-Iraq War was in progress and the Iranians were now on the offensive. The Syrian regime was revolutionary Iran's major Arab ally throughout that conflict. Only a couple of months after the uprising had been crushed, Syria would help Iran by closing the pipeline for Iraqi oil exports that crossed its territory.

V

In terms of exporting the Iranian Revolution, the greatest success was in Lebanon. It is not an exaggeration to say that this small state, once part of Ottoman Greater Syria but now wedged uncomfortably between Syria and Israel, would be permanently changed as a result.

At the time of the creation of Israel in 1947–49, Lebanon paid lip service to the general Arab view that the partition of Palestine was morally wrong and unjust; but the Lebanese army played only a nominal role in the fighting. The creation of Israel as a Jewish state necessitated the expulsion of a large number of Palestinian Arabs. Many were pushed over the border into Lebanon where they were forced to become long-term refugees. They were predominantly Sunni Muslim, with a fair number of Christians. Some managed to make their way in Lebanon but, for the most part, they were forced by the Lebanese government to remain in refugee camps and prevented from integrating into Lebanese society.

During the Six Day War in 1967, Israel seized the West Bank as well as the Egyptian Sinai peninsula and Syrian Golan Heights. This led to increasingly well-organised armed retaliation from Palestinian groups. Many of these had established a presence among the displaced Palestinians of Lebanon. For a while, the southern tip of the country became known as 'Fatahland', after the Palestinian guerrilla movement Fatah, which used the area to launch attacks on Israel. By the early 1970s these attacks were becoming more numerous and more professional. Israel retaliated on many occasions, often deliberately striking at non-military targets (as did Fatah in its attacks on Israel). One of its aims was to alienate the Palestinian guerrillas from the host population. In southern Lebanon this population was, for the most part, Twelver Shi'i.

The Shi'is were the poorest of Lebanon's many confessional groups ('confessionalism' is the political system in Lebanon whereby government posts are distributed between the country's sects according to a set formula). Predominantly rural, they lived in the south (the old Jebel Amil) and the Biqa valley, although many were also drifting to the cities, especially the southern suburbs of Beirut. They tended to have the highest birth rates among Lebanese and to be the least educated. They were at the bottom of the Lebanese social ladder (just as the Alawis had once been in Syria, and the Twelver Shi'is still were in Iraq). Although many Shi'i fighters joined the Palestinians, the community had also come to resent the Palestinian militias, which lorded it over them. When they also suffered from Israeli shelling and bombing as retaliation for Palestinian attacks on Israel, that anti-Palestinian resentment deepened.

In 1982 Israel invaded Lebanon. It had two sets of objectives. The first was to destroy the Palestinian militias and drive the Palestinian leadership out of the country. The Israelis hoped that this would deal a mortal blow to Palestinian nationalism. The second was to intervene in the civil war which by then had already raged intermittently in Lebanon for some seven years, a conflict between broadly Christian groups on one side, and on the other, leftist groups that were predominantly made up of Muslims. From 1979 onwards, Iran began to spread its revolutionary message among Lebanon's Shi'is, who were increasing in numbers and as a proportion of the Lebanese population. Today the Shi'is are generally assumed to be Lebanon's largest sect. Shi'i politics were originally dominated by village leaders, but from the 1950s onwards left-wing secular parties had a strong appeal. Although Ba'athist secularism attracted increasing numbers of Lebanese Shi'is,[11] many others had the same reservations about secular Arab nationalism that occurred among their Iraqi co-religionists: fear that it would lead to domination by the Sunnis, who were a large majority across the Arab world as a whole.[12]

Sectarian politics spread to the Lebanese Shi'is from 1969 onwards, when a Shi'i Supreme Islamic Council was established. It was chaired by Musa al-Sadr, a religious scholar who was born in Iran of Lebanese ancestry and was a cousin of the Iraqi Ayatollah Muhammad Baqir al-Sadr. He worked with other left-leaning groups against Maronite Christian domination, and founded the Amal movement (*amal* means 'hope' in Arabic), which had its own militia. He disappeared in 1978 while on a flight to Libya, and is thought to have been murdered on the orders of the Libyan dictator Muammar Gaddafi. When the Lebanese civil war and the concomitant Israeli invasions began, Amal grew steadily in importance, both as a militia and a political party. However, as its power increased it suffered the fate of some other left-wing political parties in Arab countries, such as the Ba'ath parties of Syria and Iraq and the Palestinian movement Fatah: it became a part of the patronage-dispensing political establishment.

Iranian Revolutionary fervour was already spreading among some Lebanese Shi'is, but the process was accelerated by the Israeli invasion of 1982. As the former Israeli Prime Minister Ehud Barak put it with admirable frankness in a *Newsweek* interview in 2006, 'When we entered Lebanon ... there was no Hezbollah. We were accepted with perfumed rice and flowers by the Shia in the south. It was our presence there that created Hezbollah.'[13] Only six days after the start of Israel's invasion in June 1982, a contingent of Iranian Revolutionary Guards and regular troops – some of them battle-hardened from urban fighting in the war with Iraq – flew into Lebanon. Some would remain and train a core of fighters for what would become Hezbollah.[14]

The movement gained momentum during Muharram in 1983 when several trucks full of Israeli soldiers blundered into an Ashura procession, apparently as the result of a map-reading error. There could have been no more apt targets to represent the tyrant Yazid, since Israel was understandably often cast in this role during Ashura events throughout the years of occupation. When the soldiers were stoned, they responded with bullets. Several people were killed. The incident is seen as something of a formative moment in the development of Lebanese resistance to the Israeli occupation and Hezbollah.[15]

There is a radical side to Hezbollah which the movement has never repudiated. This is set out in an open letter written in 1985 to 'The Downtrodden of Lebanon and the World'. It sees Islam as the only answer to the world's problems and is addressed to 'the Arab and Islamic peoples'. The letter is a black-and-white, simplistic document placing all blame for whatever is wrong on imperialism, colonialism and Westernisation. Where fractiousness has existed among Muslims, it has thus been a product of imperialism. Islam is the banner under which to fight back, especially against America, Israel and France. The Islam in question is that of Ayatollah Khomeini:

> Each of us is a combat soldier when the call of *jihad* demands it and each of us undertakes his task in the battle in accordance with his lawful assignment within the framework of action under the leadership of the guardian jurisprudent [i.e. Khomeini].

The reference to Khomeini is a sign that Hezbollah had subscribed to his theory of *velayat-e faqih*. Yet, despite this, the open letter calls, at least implicitly, on Sunni religious scholars, as well as those of their Shi'i counterparts who do not support Hezbollah, to educate the Muslim masses to practise their faith and fight oppression. It is therefore not a purely sectarian document.[16]

By the time of the open letter, Hezbollah had already proved itself to be highly effective on the battlefield and in achieving its political goals. It had played an important part in securing the withdrawal of American,

French and other international forces that had come to Lebanon in 1983, even if the suicide bombings that had played a large part in achieving this had shocked the world. It had also been instrumental in frustrating Israel's attempt to impose a victor's peace treaty on Lebanon, and in persuading Israel to withdraw from its costly occupation of much of Lebanon. (Israel would eventually draw back unilaterally to the international border in May 2000.)

In 1992, Hezbollah contested parliamentary elections for the first time. It meant an obvious step away from the brittleness and intransigence of the 'open letter' in favour of pragmatism and compromise. Ever since, Hezbollah has been represented in the Lebanese parliament. Its electoral programmes do not stress religious issues but focus on economic exploitation and underdevelopment as well as security. During this period, Lebanese of all faiths came to see Hezbollah as vital for their security. As well as militantly Shi'i, the movement can justifiably be described as Arab nationalist. This was brought home in the run-up to the US-led invasion of Iraq in March 2003. A week before the invasion began, the leader of Hezbollah, Hassan Nasrallah, warned the Americans what would await them if they went ahead:

> We tell the United States, don't expect that the people of this region will welcome you with roses and jasmine. The people of this region will welcome you with rifles, blood and martyrdom operations. We are not afraid of the American invaders and will keep saying 'death to America'.[17]

The Americans had given numerous reasons for their proposed invasion of Iraq, and these were often tailored for different audiences. When addressing people concerned by issues such as justice and human rights, they often argued they were going to Iraq to liberate the Shi'i majority and the Kurds from the tyranny of Saddam Hussein. They found no shortage of eloquent Iraqi Shi'is to put forward this case. What this statement by Hassan Nasralluh shows is that Hezbollah might be a Shi'i movement that had been inspired and aided by the Iranian revolution, but it was capable of putting solidarity between Muslims of all denominations, as well as between all Arabs, before solidarity with other Twelver Shi'is.

VI

The Iranian Revolution provided an inspiration for revolutionary Sunni Islamists as well as for Shi'is. But Iran's resources to be spent on revolutionary propaganda abroad were small compared to those that Saudi Arabia was now devoting to spreading its Wahhabi message. Consequently that message reached Muslim communities everywhere. Its thrust was inherently anti-revolutionary as well as ultra-conservative, since Wahhabism teaches that a ruler who enforces the Wahhabi brand of Islam in his domains must always be loyally supported by his subjects. It followed from this that, in the Saudi view, all Muslims everywhere should be expected to look up to Saudi Arabia as a beacon of Islam and good Sharia practice.

Yet by now there was interaction between the Wahhabism of Saudi Arabia and the revolutionary impulses that flowed from ideologues such as Sayyid Qutb. This development tested Wahhabism as a conservative ideology. Precisely how a strain of Saudi Wahhabism began to blend with revolutionary ideas has only been partially disentangled by scholars, although the broad outline seems clear.[18] Muslim Brothers were offered asylum by Saudi Arabia after they were forced to flee from Egypt after Nasser's crackdown on the Brotherhood in the 1950s. They were often given teaching positions, especially at the Islamic University of Medina after it opened in 1961 with the objective of exporting the Wahhabi variety of Islam. It was natural at that time – when educational levels in Saudi Arabia were still very low – for young Saudis to look up to these Egyptian teachers with great respect. Some of these teachers definitely had considerable influence on their pupils. One of them was Muhammad Qutb, who published *Milestones*, the work of his brother, Sayyid Qutb, while teaching in Saudi Arabia. It appears that Muhammad Qutb taught a young man called Osama bin Laden.

As has already been mentioned, in November 1979 Juhayman al-Otaybi led a militant group that stormed and occupied the Ka'ba and the Grand Mosque in Mecca. Most of his followers were former students of the Islamic University of Medina. His ideology can be seen as Wahhabism blended with the ideology of Sayyid Qutb as developed by Muhammad Abd al-Salam al-Faraj – whose teachings inspired the assassination of President Anwar Sadat of Egypt in 1981. Mixed in with these was a strain of millenarianism that has been described as 'altogether foreign to Wahhabism'.[19]

Juhayman al-Otaybi interpreted the Sharia in a way that demonstrated to his own satisfaction that the Wahhabi religious establishment had abandoned it. Thus, he was outraged at being asked to supply a passport photo in order to enrol at an Islamic university, since the most literal interpretation of Islam prohibits the reproduction of images. He also objected to images of the king on banknotes, to 'shameful' pictures of women on television, and to women entering the workplace in a way that involved contact with men. Such ideas were shared by many hard-line Wahhabis. But al-Otaybi went further. He did something that had no precedent since the days of Ibn Saud: he publicly attacked what he saw as the corruption and personal immorality of the royal family.[20]

In his view, the monarchy had only ever ruled according to its own whim. Thus, Ibn Saud had refused to support the Sultan-Caliph's call for jihad against Britain and its allies in the First World War. Instead, he had opportunistically used the conflict to undermine the Hashemite Sharif of Mecca, who was a fellow Muslim. Subsequently, he had used the Wahhabi fighters known as the Ikhwan to spread the faith, but, having secured his position, allied himself with the Christians (the United States and Britain). Juhayman did not merely reject the Saudi monarchy; he also rejected the Wahhabi religious establishment that had collaborated with it and was therefore equally discredited in his eyes. Wahhabism teaches that only a legitimate ruler may proclaim jihad. But Juhayman felt able to take that duty upon himself.[21]

VII

Many of the positions taken by Juhayman took will seem familiar in those subsequently adopted by Osama bin Laden, the founder of the group known as al-Qa'ida. This came into existence as a result of the Afghan jihad against the Soviet invasion of Afghanistan. The USSR had entered Afghanistan in December 1979 to prop up a communist government that had taken power in a recent coup and did not have widespread support. Ten to 15 per cent of the population of Afghanistan are Shi'is, and the remainder Sunni Muslims. The Shi'is come chiefly from the Hazara minority, which speaks its own dialect.

The communists and their Russian allies quickly alienated much of the population with the consequence that the country was soon in flames. The insurrection was tribally based or led by local warlords, who were often bitter rivals. Islam became the obvious rallying cry to unite Afghans against the communists. The USA and the Gulf monarchies, especially Saudi Arabia, therefore provided weapons and finance to the rebels to fight under an Islamic banner. They were also helped by the Pakistani intelligence services. It was at this time that the Taliban (literally, 'the students of religion') emerged. After the Soviet withdrawal in 1989, this movement gradually spread its control over most of Afghanistan. It took Kabul, the capital, in 1996, and most of the country over the following couple of years.

It is often asserted that the Taliban are Wahhabi in their inspiration and practice, but that is not quite correct. The Taliban belong to the Deobandi movement. This emerged in late nineteenth-century India as a reaction to British domination and the fear that living under non-Muslim rule would cause Indian Islam to atrophy. Unlike the Wahhabis, who follow the Hanbali doctrinal law school of Sunni jurisprudence, the Deobandis are members of the Hanafi school. Nevertheless, they share with the Wahhabis an obsession with the tiniest details of correct religious observance and a literalist interpretation of the strictest provisions of the Sharia. The Deobandis were therefore exactly the kind of movement that it was logical for the Saudis to encourage and target with extensive funding. As a result, the Deobandis expanded and absorbed Wahhabi ideas which are now widespread among Deobandis generally, and especially so among the Taliban. This led the Taliban – and many Deobandis outside Afghanistan – to consider Shi'is to be apostates who merit death.

In areas that came under Taliban control there were massacres of Shi'is, most notably in the northern city of Mazar-e Sharif in 1998. In 2001, the Taliban went on to destroy the giant Buddhas carved into the rock at Bamyan, the stronghold of the Hazaras, the predominantly Shi'i people who make up Afghanistan's third-largest ethnic group. One factor behind the destruction may have been the fact that the statues played a role in Hazara folk religion.[22] The Taliban declared jihad against the Hazaras. Iran was able to do relatively little to help them and other Afghani Shi'is during the Soviet occupation. But after the Soviet withdrawal in February 1989 it supported the group known as the Northern Alliance, which the Hazaras joined. The Northern Alliance would take Kabul from the Taliban in late 2001 after American and other NATO nations also intervened to support it, following the terrorist attacks of 9/11.

One feature of the struggle against the Soviet occupation was the large number of Sunni Muslims from other countries who went to Afghanistan. They went to fight a jihad to liberate the country's people from infidel control. They were predominantly Arab, and Saudis were especially numerous among them. As we have seen, by the early 1980s Islamism was fast replacing Arab nationalism as the most dynamic political force in Arab countries. The secular ideas of resistance and revolution were easy to incorporate into the struggle against the Soviets in Afghanistan. In Islamic terms, fighting to repel the infidel Soviet invaders in Muslim Afghanistan was technically a defensive jihad, which its advocates could argue was binding on the Muslim community as a whole. The problem was: who was authorised under the Sharia to proclaim jihad? In the absence of a legitimate caliph, this task would have fallen on the rulers of predominantly Muslim states. But that would have entailed declaring war on the Soviet Union, and no Muslim majority state was about to do that. The solution was for the volunteers who had gone to fight the Soviets to take the Sharia into their own hands and wage their own jihad. This is very reminiscent of Juhayman al-Otaybi.

By 1982, the Saudi and Pakistani intelligence services were co-operating, arranging for jihadi volunteers to assemble in and near the Pakistani city of Peshawar. The CIA also helped with arms and funding. Over the next ten years it is estimated that 35,000 young volunteers passed through Peshawar, of whom 12,000 to 25,000 were Saudis.[23] A key facility in Peshawar was the so-called Services Centre run by Abdullah Yusuf Azzam, a Palestinian who had sublimated his struggle to regain his own homeland into the jihadi cause. He now saw that cause as part of a much wider call to regain all the lands Islam had lost across the centuries, which he listed as: 'Palestine, Bokhara, Lebanon, Chad, Eritrea, Somalia, the Philippines, Burma, Southern Yemen, Tashkent and Andalucia.'[24]

In the late 1970s, he had been on the faculty of the King Abdulaziz

University in Jeddah, where he had taught Osama bin Laden, and seems to have been an important influence on him. In 1984, Osama bin Laden became involved in Abdullah Azzam's activities in the jihad and supplied funds and assistance for the establishment of training camps. Two years later, he journeyed to Peshawar himself and in 1987 saw action against Soviet forces inside Afghanistan. After the Soviet withdrawal, he returned to Saudi Arabia where he became an anti-American activist calling for, for instance, a boycott of American goods.[25]

To some Sunni dissidents in Saudi Arabia, the decision to use non-Muslim forces was problematic on religious grounds. The defence of the holy cities of Mecca and Medina should fall to Muslims, not to soldiers who were Christians, Jews and atheists. The stationing of these forces on Saudi soil was argued to be a violation of the Sharia. Moreover, their real role was seen as being to occupy Arabia and control the Muslim world. For Osama bin Laden, this seems to have been the point at which he began the career which would see him become the mastermind for the attacks by hijacked airliners on the World Trade Center and the Pentagon of 11 September 2001, and force him to become a fugitive after the consequent invasion of Afghanistan by an American-led coalition. It would end in his death at the hands of American special forces in his hideaway in Pakistan on 2 May 2011. The Kuwait crisis thus proved to be something of a watershed for the growth of violent, international jihadi Islamism among Sunni radicals.

On 2 August 1990 Iraq invaded the neighbouring state of Kuwait, which it occupied for a seven-month period. Defying a deadline imposed by the United Nations, Saddam Hussein refused to withdraw. Kuwait was eventually liberated in February 1991 by an American-led coalition. From then on, Saddam Hussein's strategy was survival. He held back his elite republican guard, which was recruited among the Sunni tribes close to the area from which he came. Because of a no-fly zone imposed by the UN and enforced by America and its allies, a rebellion among the Kurds of northern Iraq was successful in creating an autonomous Kurdish region. In the south of Iraq, however, the Republican Guard crushed rebellions among the Shi'is with relative ease. These were only locally based, and many areas remained quiet as they waited to see which way the wind would blow. Others did not wish to lose the benefits of Saddam Hussein's politics of patronage.

Nervous that Saddam Hussein was trying to acquire the atom bomb, and well aware that his forces had used chemical weapons extensively in the war with Iran, the UN under American leadership imposed a draconian sanctions regime on Iraq. This would last until it was proved that the regime had abandoned its weapons programmes. These sanctions made any real rebuilding of the shattered country impossible. Their effect was made far worse by Saddam Hussein's continued use of patronage to sustain the groups on which he relied, and which basically left the rest of the population to fend for itself. Many children died of malnutrition. In the meantime, he retained complete control of Iraq except in the Kurdish areas in the north. Although it seems he divested himself of weapons of mass destruction, he was careful not to declare this unambiguously, since he considered that the belief he might have them acted as a deterrent against an invasion. It was this ambiguity, however, that would lead to his overthrow by another, less broadly based, US-led coalition in 2003.

The period between the liberation of Kuwait and the overthrow of Saddam Hussein in 2003 saw the onward march of Sunni Islamism. Side-by-side with the blood-drenched actions of militants in countries such as Egypt and Algeria, to say nothing of attacks on Western targets, there were also Islamists who renounced violence and strove for a cultural revolution to make Muslim countries and societies more 'Islamic'. Much of this was successful, and was carried out by organisations like the Muslim Brotherhood, as well as by Salafis. Salafis, it will be recalled, were Sunnis who tried to return to the purity of the practice of the Prophet and his Companions, and avoiding the accretions which had become seen as part of Islam across the centuries. They attempted to live a scrupulously devout life and played a major role in the 're-Islamisation' of many Muslim countries. Initially they did not engage in politics or armed struggle; but that would change over time.

VIII

In Pakistan relations between the Sunni majority (approximately 85 per cent of the population) and the Shi'i minority (approximately 15 per cent)[26] deteriorated sharply during the twenty years or so after 1979. Pakistan was founded in 1947 in response to the demand by many Muslim politicians and leaders of British India for a separate, predominantly Muslim state. It was conceived as a secular state inhabited by Muslims, not an Islamic state. Many refugees from the mob violence that raged across India at partition fled there. They were Sunnis and Shi'is alike, although the impulse that had led to the partition had come chiefly from Sunnis. Some Muslims, especially many Shi'is, had opposed partition and would have preferred to remain in an undivided India. Many were able to do so.

The idea of Pakistan was, at first, inclusive of Shi'is and Sunnis, as the make-up of its institutions of state indicated. Muhammad Ali Jinnah – the founder of Pakistan who is revered among its people to this day – was from an Ismaili Shi'i background. He adopted Twelver Shi'ism, although he was lax in his religious observance. It took a while for the Sunni-Shi'i divide to become significant in Pakistani politics,[27] but that is what happened in the last two decades of the twentieth century. One factor that deepened the divide and made it toxic was the weakness of the Pakistani state. This led to governments trying to manipulate sectarianism for their own purposes. There had already been sectarianism in Pakistan aimed at the Ahmadiyya community (a Muslim movement that originated in the late nineteenth century). The position of the Ahmadis in Pakistan became impossible after 1974, when the Prime Minister Zulfikar Ali Bhutto (who was a Twelver Shi'i) caved into pressure from hard-line Sunni groups and a law was passed forbidding them from describing themselves as Muslims. After 1979, Iran and Saudi Arabia behaved as though Pakistan's Sunnis and Shi'is were their proxies. The descent into Sunni-Shi'i sectarianism seems to have been sparked by the Iranian Revolution and the ideological struggle between Iran and Saudi Arabia that ensued.

In 1979 Pakistan was ruled by General Zia ul-Haq, who had come to power in a military coup two years earlier. He was engaged in an Islamisation campaign that sought to end his country's secularism by putting Islam and the Sharia at the heart of the constitution and the institutions of the state. It was very much a Sunni form of Islam that he had in mind. His programme was intended to make Sunni rules of inheritance compulsory for all Muslims, and also to enable the government to collect the *zakat*, or charitable tax, which Shi'is already paid to their clergy. This would have meant that devout Shi'is would, in effect, have to pay the tax twice. Shi'is campaigned to be exempted from the legislation, while Iran supported them by placing external pressure on Pakistan.

This combination was successful in making the government back down, but it had the effect that henceforth Shi'is would be regarded as a separate religious minority. This meant that Shi'i activism would be seen as a threat to Pakistan's unity and the authority of the state. There had been a history of anti-Shi'i polemic and agitation in British India, and colonial officials had often been concerned whether Ashura commemorations would pass off peacefully. Kipling had recorded disturbances during Ashura in Lahore in the 1880s.[28] In theory, the Islamisation campaign in Pakistan during the 1980s was meant to be about transforming and uniting Pakistan by applying universal, Islamic values. Yet the understandable refusal of Shi'is to accept aspects of the programme as applicable to all Muslims meant that it became specifically Sunni. It led to division, not unity. Sunni Islamists refused to accept Shi'is as a distinct but legitimate sect, with the result that Shi'is became perceived as 'disloyal' to Pakistan. In reponse, Shi'is joined Pakistan's pro-democracy movement and looked to it for support. But this enabled the military regime to use anti-Shi'i feeling among Sunnis as a weapon in its fight against the restoration of democracy.[29]

Zia ul-Haq's regime now openly promoted Sunnism as the distinctive identity of Pakistan. The president encouraged the construction of Sunni madrasas and opened the public sector to their graduates. Many madrasas were deliberately set up with assistance from the Pakistani military in areas with strong Shi'i populations or close to the Iranian border. Saudi Arabia provided funding for them as part of its policy of seeking to harden the Sunni identity of countries surrounding Iran. Links between the military and Islamist groups such as the Taliban fighting the Russians in Afghanistan increased over time, and Wahhabi-style anti-Shi'i feeling steadily consolidated itself. In 1988, the government permitted Sunni groups to attack Shi'is in Gilgit, the one district in the tribal areas in the north-west of the country that had a Shi'i majority. One hundred and fifty Shi'is were killed. The government's reaction was to construct a large Sunni mosque there.

The dangers of the strategy soon became apparent as the sectarian strife and disorder that had now become part of Pakistan's life proved hard for the state to control. It was genuinely difficult for the state to oppose actions that were claimed to be carried out in the name of Islam. Some madrasas were involved in the campaign against the Soviets in Afghanistan, and provided training and volunteers for the struggle. This made it even harder for the state to untie itself from the juggernaut it had set rolling. Vitriolic rhetoric against Shi'is steadily increased, and was connected with rivalry among militants as they competed for Saudi funding. Even when the Pakistani government tried to curb religious militancy at home, it was still encouraging it in Afghanistan as a weapon against the Soviets.

General Zia ul-Haq was killed in August 1988 by a bomb planted on his plane. The rise of sectarianism in Pakistan that took place during his rule has not been reversed to this day, despite the reversion of the country to democracy. Attacks continue on Shi'is and Sufis and any other group deemed by Wahhabi-inspired movements to be engaging in idolatry. A militantly anti-Shi'i organisation called Lashkar-e-Jhangvi is blamed by the government for the attack in August 2016 on the police academy in Quetta in which at least sixty people were killed. In February 2017, nearly ninety people were killed in a bomb blast at a Sufi shrine in rural Sindh. Such attacks are sadly part of a pattern that now extends well beyond Pakistan.

IX

The period from the Islamic Revolution in Iran to the US-led invasion of Iraq in 2003 saw the reaffirmation of Muslim identity in a way, and to an extent, that few would have predicted at the start of the 1970s. This reaffirmation of identity did not of itself imply sectarian conflict among Muslims, but there were forces working in that direction. These can be seen clearly in the ominous developments in Pakistan, where the growth of sectarianism was a consequence of Saudi Arabian and Iranian interference on the one hand, and manipulation by the Pakistani government on the other. In the final chapter of this book there will unfortunately be all too many similar examples.

Another harbinger of what was to come was the discrimination against Shi'is in Saudi Arabia. The existence of the sectarian divide in that country turned out to be the perfect way to defuse calls for real reform, which might have led to a united front among Sunnis and Shi'is. The pursuit of sectarianism would become almost a deliberate strategy, while the weakness of so many states and the reliance on quasi-tribal patronage as the basis of power would make unity across sectarian divides much harder to achieve. Few foresaw the Iranian Revolution in, say, 1977. In the same way, few in early 2001 would have predicted that two years later the USA would invade Iraq to topple Saddam Hussein. And few of the policy makers in Washington and London who were engaged in the planning of that invasion seem to have foreseen that it would unwittingly open the gate to a sectarian Hell.

CHAPTER THIRTEEN

Wedges into Fault-Lines

I

When George W. Bush took the momentous decision to invade Iraq in 2003, his forces had little difficulty reaching Baghdad. But the Americans and their allies had convinced themselves that they would be greeted as liberators. They hardly acknowledged that they were occupying a country that they had defeated in war, however hated its government may have been, and that they had responsibilities to safeguard its people under the laws of war. The result was a rapid breakdown of law and order. This was compounded as the Americans and their allies set out to dismantle the corrupt and brutal old dispensation, but failed to put anything effective in its place. Like many of the Americans brought in to work under him, Paul Bremer, the man chosen by Washington to govern Iraq for the immediate future, had no background knowledge of the Middle East. Even more crucially, he had no understanding of Arab or Muslim society. The Americans had their own ideas about how to rebuild Iraq. It was these ideas that would now be implemented, as well as the dictates of policies that were often crafted to gain approval from ideologists back in America (e.g. on opening up Iraq to free markets and rolling back 'big government'). There was a complete failure to establish any records of Iraqi civilian casualties. The Iraqi state, which had been under extreme stress before the invasion, quite simply collapsed. At the same time, what has been called the 'shadow state', the networks of patronage and clientelism that had sustained Saddam Hussein's rule, shattered into smithereens. People fell back on their own communities and networks.

They would look to these, first, for their security and wellbeing. Only secondarily would they give thought to Iraq itself.

The American intention had been to create an Iraqi democracy. Yet, once they set out to achieve this noble aim, they soon encountered unwelcome realities. As it has been put by Charles Tripp, professor of politics with reference to the Middle East at SOAS:[1]

> Public ministries became partisan fiefdoms, farmed out to powerful factions, made more powerful by their ability to command militias that were used to terrorise political enemies and whole neighbourhoods or communities seen as hostile to their sponsors. The elected National Assembly, although the formal seat of authority, was not where power resided. This lay in the hands of men made powerful by the support they could muster in local ethnic and sectarian communities, by the weapons at their disposal, by the share of the national resources which they had managed to appropriate or by the patronage of the United States. In short, a range of mutually suspicious leaders were being encouraged to emerge as the new oligarchy of Iraq.[2]

In these circumstances sectarian identities were bound to come to the fore.

Muqtada al-Sadr, a firebrand Shi'i militia leader who was the son of Ayatollah Muhammad Sadiq al-Sadr, was able to benefit from the prestige of his deceased father's name. This included the goodwill attached to the network his father had set up to help the Shi'i poor, and over which the son now presided. Ayatollah Muhammad Sadiq al-Sadr had been a highly respected figure. After apparently following a policy of quietism (that is, religious withdrawal from politics), he had become a public critic of the Saddam Hussein regime. He had followers among Sunnis as well as Shi'is. Not only did he conduct joint prayer meetings, but he also encouraged Shi'is to pray behind Sunni imams. He was reported to have had ambitions to become the leader of all Iraqi Muslims, although he never wavered in his strong Shi'i positions on such matters as the history of the early caliphate. Despite this, his attempt to appeal across the sectarian divide had made him potentially a very dangerous figure for the regime of Saddam Hussein.[3] He was executed in 1999.

The overwhelmingly Shi'i working-class district in Baghdad once known as Madinat al-Thawra ('City of the Revolution') had been rebranded as Madinat Saddam ('Saddam City') in an act of sycophancy towards the dictator. But after the American invasion it soon became known as Madinat Sadr ('Sadr City'). Muqtada al-Sadr's militia, which called itself the Mahdi Army, used violence against anyone who opposed Muqtada al-Sadr in Sadr City and large parts of the Shi'i south. During the period immediately after the start of the American occupation, he initiated contact with Sunni insurgents. This might conceivably have led to cooperation between Sunni and Shi'i militant groups against the occupiers, but it did not.

Muqtada al-Sadr also faced opposition from Ayatollah Ali al-Sistani, the most senior source of emulation in Iraq for Shi'is. It will be recalled that Sistani had rejected Khomeini's *velayat-e faqih* (government of the mujtahid). He believed that religious leaders should hold back from day-to-day politics. This put him at odds not only with Muqtada al-Sadr, but also with the Supreme Council for the Islamic Revolution in Iraq (SCIRI) and many in the al-Da'wa Party. These two Shi'i organisations had returned in force to Iraq as soon as Saddam Hussein fell. They had grown and been strengthened during their period in Iranian exile and also had their own fighting men. There was potential not only for strife between Sunnis and Shi'is, but also within the Shi'i community itself.

Acts of resistance to the occupiers increased. As early as July 2003, the Americans were forced to admit that they were facing 'a classical guerrilla-type campaign'.[4] The following month bombs killed the newly arrived UN representative Sérgio Vieira de Mello in Baghdad and Ayatollah Baqir al-Hakim, the leader of SCIRI who had just returned to Najaf from Iran. Attacks on those working for the new authorities or queuing up at recruitment centres became commonplace – especially in Shi'i areas, where they were designed to intimidate Shi'is who might volunteer for the police or government jobs. The resistance gradually became a full-blown insurgency, but it had no central leadership. It intended to make life for the occupiers so uncomfortable that they would leave. It included Ba'athists who had lost out as a result of the dismantling of Saddam Hussein's patronage networks, as well as assorted nationalist and Islamist elements. Some of them wanted a return to the way things had been before the invasion, while others were motivated by instinctive revolt at the thought of America running their country.

The Shi'i militias did not take part in this insurgency and generally stood on the sidelines, but using violence for their own purposes. They deeply resented the Americans and the disorder they had brought, but they were certainly not about to join forces with those who wished to see Saddam Hussein's henchmen returned to power. In these circumstances, unity between Sunnis and Shi'is against a foreign occupier became very difficult. Saddam Hussein's manner of rule had ensured that this would be the case. For their part, much of the hostility among Sunni Muslims towards the new emerging dispensation targeted the Shi'i community. They saw it as collaborating with the Americans to displace the Sunnis from their dominant position in Iraq.

At the same time, the breakdown in law and order following the invasion led to theft, robbery, kidnapping, drug smuggling and general criminality on a massive scale. One of the last acts of Saddam Hussein's government had been to open the prisons and release the criminals from jail. This was followed at the time of the invasion by the disappearance of the police from view – often because they feared for their lives if they were seen in uniform. People were left with no support and protection, save what they could get from their extended family and those they could trust on a personal level. This was yet another stage in the Iraqi state's retreat from the services it had once provided. That withdrawal had begun with the sanctions imposed during the Kuwait crisis, when Saddam Hussein could no longer provide the bulk of the population with their needs. Instead, he had cunningly encouraged the re-emergence of the tribal system, which previously had been in decay.

Despite the best efforts of Ayatollah Sistani and many other religious leaders (both Shi'i and Sunni), the cycle of violence spiralled out of control. The situation made it possible for the type of Islamism that viewed Shi'is as idolaters, worthy of death, to become increasingly prominent among Sunnis. Simultaneously on the Shi'i side, SCIRI and its military wing, the Badr Brigade, were able to enmesh themselves at the heart of the government. Militias like the Badr Brigade and the Mahdi Army carried out attacks against Sunnis. According to a report by the International Crisis Group (a Brussels-based organisation researching ways to avert and resolve conflict): 'what they lacked in popularity they made up in resources, military organisation and patronage'.[5] After elections in January 2005, some of the Badr Brigade operatives moved into the Ministry of the Interior. The borderline between them and the Ministry's troops became blurred at a time when death squads were targeting Sunnis in Baghdad.

Increasingly, Sunnis and Shi'is living in neighbourhoods dominated by the other sect left to live among members of their own in a different district. Bombs targeted mosques and markets in Shi'i areas, and were paralleled by equally horrifying attacks on Sunnis. In this way, Baghdad gradually ceased to be a mixed city and become a predominantly Shi'i one, with some Sunni enclaves.

In the wider Muslim world, the occupation of Iraq by the Americans and their allies was widely perceived (with considerable justification) as a move intended to lead to American and Israeli hegemony in the Arab Middle East. This inevitably sparked calls for a jihad to expel the invaders. Sunni fighters from other countries began to make the journey there. Iraq's borders were now largely unguarded. Syria was nervous at neoconservative sabre-rattling in Washington that called for Syria to be invaded as soon as Iraq had been sorted out. The result was that Syria quietly let many Sunni fighters across its border. Many linked up with Iraqi Sunni Islamists and others fighting the American occupation. As time passed, large numbers of Sunni Ba'athists and other nationalists would join the jihadi Islamists and adopt their ideologies.

Some of the newly arrived foreign fighters became followers of the Jordanian jihadi Abu Musab al-Zarqawi, who horrified the world with his apparently psychopathic behaviour. He seems to have been one of the first to take pleasure in decapitating prisoners with a knife and depicting the grisly scene on a video. He is best known in the West for beheading the kidnapped British civil engineer Ken Bigley and other Western hostages. It is probably he, more than any other single individual, who lit the spark that ignited what can only be described as a sectarian civil war between Sunnis and Shi'is in Iraq.

II

Abu Musab al-Zarqawi was born in the Jordanian town of Zarqa in 1966. Zarqa had become home to destitute Palestinian refugees, many of them expelled in 1948–49 by the armies of the new state of Israel. They came to constitute perhaps 80 per cent of the town's population. It was a town where bitterness against Israel, the West and the Jordanian monarchy (which was perceived as collaborating with Israel) was widespread. It soon became a stronghold of support for radical Palestinian nationalist organisations. As militant Islam grew, much of this support transferred itself to political Islamism. Abdullah Azzam, Osama bin Laden's Palestinian spiritual mentor, had made his home in Zarqa for a period. The town would send a significant number of jihadi 'foreign fighters' to Afghanistan and subsequent jihadi conflicts, including Iraq after 2003.

Like a number of other jihadis, al-Zarqawi rediscovered Islam after a life of crime that allegedly included sexual assault. He did not have a secondary education. He travelled to Afghanistan where he saw action. On his return to Jordan he was imprisoned for possessing firearms and false documents. It appears that he was tortured while in prison. He said that he 'loved jihad' but did not have 'the patience to learn, teach or preach.'[6] After a further period in Afghanistan in which he ran a training camp, he seems to have been active in the border regions between Iraqi and Iranian Kurdistan, and also to have organised terrorist attacks in Jordan and possibly in Europe. These may have included the Madrid train bombings of 2004. The 2003 invasion of Iraq gave him new opportunities for jihad.

What distinguishes al-Zarqawi and his group is his extreme anti-Shi'i line. His group became the franchise known as 'al-Qa'ida in Iraq' and he pledged allegiance to Bin Laden in October 2004 after eight months of contacts with the al-Qa'ida leader. Some of his group's attacks were aimed at queues at government recruitment centres in Shi'i areas such as Hilla, but they were also responsible for the killing of religious scholars like Ayatollah Baqir al-Hakim, who was murdered in a mosque in Najaf along with eighty-three other worshippers on 29 August 2003. Other targets were Ashura commemorations in 2004 and 2005. In a letter in which he swore allegiance to Osama bin Laden, Abu Anas al-Shami, one of the leading religious scholars in al-Zarqawi's group, explained the anti-Shi'i strategy:

> The only solution is for us to strike the heretics [i.e. the Shi'is], whether they are men of religion, soldiers or others, until they submit to the Sunnis. You might object that it is too soon, and unfair to throw the nation into a battle for which it is unprepared; that this will cause losses and spill blood; but this is precisely what we want.[7]

Abu Musab al-Zarqawi himself wrote another letter to Osama bin Laden and his deputy Ayman al-Zawahiri to give them a report of the situation in Iraq as he saw it.[8] In this he asserts that America had entered Iraq in order to create a Greater Israel. America had done a deal with the Shi'is, 'the dregs of humanity', so that they will stand by 'the Crusaders' against the Mujahideen (the jihadis fighting in Iraq). Extreme language is used to describe the Shi'is: they are 'a lurking snake, a crafty and malicious scorpion, a spying enemy and a mortal venom'. They 'wear the garb of a friend', but 'the true face of their creed is war against the people of sunna and the community'. In this view, Shi'is have betrayed Islam throughout history: the Safavids stabbed the Ottomans in the back, and prevented them taking Vienna and spreading Islam in Western Europe. The Shi'is are also accused of helping the Mongols and the Franks (i.e. the Crusaders) to attack Islam. A direct charge of unbelief and treachery, as well as a list of ways in which the Shi'is reject the beliefs of Sunnis, is included in the letter:

> History's message, confirmed by the current situation, demonstrates most clearly that Shiism is a religion that has nothing in common with Islam except in the way that Jews have something in common with Christians as people of the book. From patent polytheism, tomb worship, and circumambulating shrines to calling the companions of the Prophet infidels and insulting the mothers of the believers [i.e. the Prophet's wives] and the best of the Muslim nation, they arrive at distorting the Quran as a logical means of defaming those who know it, in addition to claiming that the imams are infallible, that believing in them is a tenet of faith, that revelation came down to them, and other forms of unbelief and heresy that fill their favourite books and

reference works – which they continue to churn out incessantly.

The dreamers who think that a Shiite can forget this historical legacy and the old hatred of the *nawasib* [a pejorative term used by Shi'is for Sunnis, meaning 'swindlers'], as they say, are deluded... These are a people who gathered in their unbelief and marked their heresy with political cunning and a feverish effort to seize on the crisis of governance and overturn the balance of power in the state: with the assistance of their allies, the Americans, they are trying to redraw this state and determine its size by means of their political banners and organisations.

The letter concludes with an outline of the strategy he proposes to implement in Iraq. The key to this is igniting religious war between Shi'is and Sunnis:

In our opinion, [the Shi'is] are the key to change, because attacking their religious, political and military aspects will reveal their rage against the Sunnis. They will bare their fangs and show the secret rage simmering in their hearts. If we manage to drag them into a religious war, we will be able to awaken the slumbering Sunnis, who will sense the imminent danger and the cruel death that these Sabaeans [a Gnostic sect in Mesopotamia that is mentioned in the Qur'an] have in store for them.[9]

Such attitudes led to disquiet and opposition from other Sunni militants. Some regarded him as little more than a desperado. He was eventually rebuked in June 2005 by Ayman al-Zawahiri, Osama bin Laden's eventual successor. Al-Zawahiri's criticism may, however, have been more concerned with tactics – the risk that al-Zarqawi's campaign would alienate other Muslims – than principles.[10] Al-Zarqawi met his end on 7 June 2006 from a bomb dropped by an American F-16C fighter plane while he was attending a meeting of jihadi leaders in a safehouse. But by then, a sectarian civil war was well under way. That month, the World Health Organisation and the Iraqi Ministry of Health estimated that 151,000 people had been killed since the invasion.[11]

On 22 February 2006, a massive act of deliberate sacrilege had taken place. The golden-domed shrine of the Tenth and Eleventh Twelver

Imams in Samarra was blown up. Not only did it house the tombs of the imams Ali al-Hadi and al-Hasan al-Askari, but it was the spot where the Twelfth Imam, Muhammad al-Mahdi, had begun his occultation. It was a pilgrimage destination for Twelvers in their millions, and was also a place venerated by Sunnis – who, while not accepting the Twelver claims concerning the imams, respected the holiness of the two devout descendants of the Prophet who were buried there. It was also located in a predominantly Sunni town. Within hours, some 1,300 Sunnis (or people assumed to be Sunnis) had been slaughtered by the Mahdi Army. Up to this point, some Iraqis had seen Muqtada al-Sadr as primarily a nationalist leader with whom Sunnis could cooperate against the Americans. Any such nebulous dream of a united Sunni-Shiʻi front against the occupiers was now well and truly over.[12]

This barbarous act and its cruel aftermath finally ended any dream of a secular Iraq for the foreseeable future. It ensured that the new dispensation that had arisen after the invasion, and which saw power being channelled through the sectarian and ethnic communities, would now continue. A 'unity government' was formed under Nouri al-Maliki, a member of the al-Daʻwa Party, but there would be no national unity; instead, there would be yet more rule through patronage networks. The difference was that the Shiʻis now had control, and they believed that their hour had come. Nouri al-Maliki's government instituted a new sectarianism that favoured Shiʻis and reflected this new reality of power. Although the minister of defence was a Sunni, the Ministry of the Interior remained with SCIRI, and an ally from his own party, al-Daʻwa, controlled the ministry of national security. But real power did not reside in Iraq's new parliament. It remained with the various Shiʻi militias and the Kurdish militia known as the Peshmerga. Death squads often operated with apparent impunity, not just assassinating political opponents but carrying out sectarian killings that often had no motive except revenge and intimidation.

In 2007–08, a military 'surge' saw an additional 35,000 American troops come to Iraq to reinforce the 130,000-or-so foreign troops in the US-led coalition. This was combined with serious attempts to prise Sunni Arabs away from the insurgency – and to drive a wedge into the split that had developed between most Sunni Arabs and the ultra hard-line 'Islamic State in Iraq', which was the rebranded 'al-Qaʻida in Iraq' of

Abu Musa al-Zarqawi. These initiatives met with considerable success, not least because the vicious anti-Shiʿism of al-Zarqawi's followers did not resonate with many Sunnis, who saw how destructive it was. Nor did they support the extremely restrictive version of the Sharia that the jihadis enforced. One grievance that went deep was the attempt by Islamic State in Iraq to take over local business activities in Anbar Province, including lucrative smuggling across the Syrian border.

The result was what became known as the Sahwa, or 'Awakening' movement. Tribes in the Sunni north west of Iraq began cooperating with the government and the Americans, and were provided with arms to turn against the jihadis, as well as promises that they would eventually be incorporated into the Iraqi security services. Local councils were also set up. Over 80,000 men, many of them former insurgents, joined groups that were part of the Sahwa. By the summer of 2007, the insurgency had faded (although it had not ended) and major insurgent strongholds, such as Ramadi and Fallujah, were in the possession of the Sahwa militias.

In November 2008 the Sahwa were put under Iraqi government control. This is the point at which matters began to deteriorate. Prime Minister Nouri al-Maliki tried to split the movement so as to neutralise it. Only a few Sahwa fighters were incorporated into the security services, while attempts were made to disarm many others by withdrawing their weapons permits and subsidies. The Shiʿi (and Kurdish) political groupings that dominated Maliki's government did not want to have to compete with a movement that would revitalise tribal Sunni influence. Moreover, some of those most outspoken in their opposition to the Sahwa were the predominantly urban Sunni bloc in parliament, the Iraq Accord Front. This feared that whatever the Sahwa gained would be at their expense. There was also another old Iraqi dynamic at work: Baghdad versus the countryside. Many of the leaders of the Sahwa and their followers bitterly resented central government control. Once the government had shown that it was not on their side, it became inevitable that many of them would begin to drift back to supporting the insurgency of Islamic State in Iraq.[13] This was also in response to the increase in corruption, pervasive throughout the institutions of the Iraqi state. There was no real will to tackle it, since the political parties in parliament making up the government were dependent on it.

At the end of 2010 a series of demonstrations calling for freedom and dignity swept through many of the autocracies of the Middle East and North Africa, beginning an event that became known as the Arab Spring. In early 2011, a few breezes from this wind of hoped-for change blew into Iraq. Youth activists designated 25 February as a national day of rage against the corruption in Iraq's democratic politics. There were calls for demonstrations across the country, demanding that the government be cleaned up. Although demonstrations did take place in sixteen cities, the security services had taken pre-emptive action beforehand by intimidating and beating up potential ringleaders. According to the International Crisis Group, on the day of protests up to twenty demonstrators were killed by the security services, and many more were wounded.[14]

But as far as many Sunnis in the north-west of the country were concerned, matters were getting close to the point of no return. In March the Arab Spring also reached Syria, where the government resisted calls to reform, and then demands for its resignation. Syria descended into a prolonged civil war, which also became a proxy conflict. By 2012, the Syrian government's hold on the east of the country was slipping, and in April 2013 it lost the important city of Raqqa in the Euphrates valley. This was the month in which Abu Bakr al-Baghdadi, who had become the leader of Islamic State in Iraq in 2010, changed the movement's name to 'The Islamic State of Iraq and Sham [i.e. Greater Syria]'[15] – also known as ISIS or Daesh (its Arabic acronym), which is the name we will use. Raqqa became its de facto capital. It could now use much of eastern Syria to give itself strategic depth. In 2013 there was an escalation in Daesh attacks in Iraq, including many attacks aimed at releasing captives held in jail. Many of these, such as the raid on the notorious Abu Ghraib prison, were successful.

In the summer of 2014, in a blaze of well-coordinated attacks, Daesh finally burst onto the international news channels and shocked the world. In the space of three months, it swept across much of northern and western Iraq and took Mosul, Iraq's second- or third-largest city. Abu Bakr al-Baghdadi, dressed in Abbasid black, proclaimed himself caliph and claimed jurisdiction over all Muslims worldwide. The world seemed bemused as the Iraqi army turned and fled. Yet, as has been pointed out by the journalist Patrick Cockburn, who has first-hand knowledge of Iraq and Syria at this time, what had happened should scarcely have come as a surprise. However daunting al-Baghdadi and Daesh appeared, the

Sunni Arabs of north-west Iraq were 'even more frightened' of the Iraqi army and the Shi'i and Kurdish militias which often fought alongside it.[16] They saw the Shi'i soldiers virtually as a foreign occupying force.

Sometimes the officers commanding army units would abandon their troops and flee by helicopter. Much of the army was not fit for combat. It had become a vehicle for the dispensing of patronage. Corruption, as ever, played its part. People would pay a bribe to join the army, seeing it as an investment because of the salary they would receive.[17] Another example was the decision taken by the Americans that supplies of food to the army should be outsourced. Perhaps in the context of public procurement in a Western state this might have saved money and increased efficiency, but in Iraq after 2003 it could only ever have become an opportunity for kickbacks.[18] Most professional soldiers in the officer corps had been sent home by the Americans because they were Ba'athist and Sunni, and were not taken on again when the army was later rebuilt. When Tikrit fell to Daesh, defeated soldiers were divided into Sunnis and Shi'is. Many of the Shi'is were machine-gunned, and a video of the atrocity was posted on YouTube. Unsurprisingly, the populations of some towns and areas taken by Daesh were likely to fear the return of the forces of the Shi'i-dominated government in Baghdad as much as they feared Daesh itself.

III

After the 2003 invasion, the fault-line in Iraqi society between Sunnis and Shi'is was always going to be exploited by those seeking to destabilise the country. Iraq was reconstituted as a democracy – but in a form that encouraged politics to be conducted by parties and organisations that appealed to distinct sects and ethnic groups. The way to win votes was to attract support from your own community, and to try to bring them a greater share of the cake that constituted the Iraqi state. By definition, this meant that there would be less of that cake available for the competing groups. This helped to push many Sunnis and Shi'is towards a quasi-tribal allegiance with members of their own sect, excluding those who did not belong to it. This was not so very different from the way in which the Iraqi state had always been run; the difference was that now, for the first time, politicians from the Shiʻi majority controlled the government and would be the dispensers of patronage. The sad consequence was that the extreme version of Wahhabi disdain and hatred for Shiʻis propagated by Abu Musa al-Zarqawi could be grafted all too easily onto the sense of dispossession felt by many Sunnis after the American invasion.

The tsunami of sectarian strife that was unleashed in Iraq is with us still. It was made much worse by the underlying struggle for hegemony between Iran and Saudi Arabia, which had been an important part of the regional background before the invasion. A feature of the period after 2003 was the steady increase of nervousness about Shiʻism among conservative, Sunni-led regimes. The catchphrase 'the Shiʻi Crescent' was coined by a Jordanian intelligence officer in late 2004 and popularised by King Abdullah II of Jordan in an interview with the *Washington Post*. The crescent was allegedly composed of Iran, Iraq, Syria (implying that it was ruled by the Alawi minority from which the president and many of his henchmen came) and Hezbollah in Lebanon. The accusation was that a sectarian brand of politics was now radiating out from Tehran across the region.[19] The phrase (and the idea behind it) caught on, not just in the Arab world but also in the Western media.

The last two chapters have shown that Tehran was actually promoting Iran's revolutionary brand of Islamism, rather than sectarian strife. It should also be emphasised that the Alawis of Syria follow a very different creed from that of Iran's Twelver Shiʻism, and that Iran's alliance with secular Syria was in any case pragmatic, not religious. Be all that as it may, the Shiʻi Crescent was a deeply threatening concept that could only ratchet up feelings of insecurity among Sunnis as they watched the disaster unfold in Iraq. Fear of the spread of Shiʻi power linked to Iran was also observable among Sunni rulers at the time of the Israeli invasion of Lebanon in 2006. Hezbollah overreached itself in an incident on the Israeli border when it kidnapped two Israeli soldiers. In retaliation, Israel bombed Lebanon, deliberately devastating its infrastructure and, over the course of the conflict, killing many civilians. Hezbollah responded with untargeted rocket attacks on Israel, which also killed civilians.

The credibility of King Abdullah of Saudi Arabia and other major Sunni Arab leaders was strained when they failed to push for an immediate ceasefire. When Israel sent in ground troops, it seemed to many people in Arab countries that King Abdullah and other Sunni rulers, such as Hosni Mubarak of Egypt and Abdullah II of Jordan, were quietly hoping that Israel would draw the teeth of this Iranian-backed, revolutionary, Shi'i movement. As the fighting continued, the deafening silence of these rulers became increasingly embarrassing for their (overwhelmingly Sunni) subjects. They were eventually forced to change their tune and call for a ceasefire and Israeli withdrawal. President Bashar al-Assad of Syria taunted them as 'half-men'.[20] That would not have gone down well in Riyadh, Cairo or Amman. The incident showed that feelings of Arab solidarity still existed among ordinary people, and transcended the Sunni-Shi'i divide.

Nevertheless, it was all too easy for Sunnis across the Muslim world to see their co-sectarians as oppressed by regimes dominated by Shi'is, and for this to transform itself into sectarian anger while Saudi Arabian sheikhs denounced Twelvers and Alawis as infidels whose blood was lawful. Next door to Iraq lay Syria. Syria was a majority Sunni country where Islamist politics were outlawed (it was a criminal offence to be a member of the Muslim Brotherhood). It was also a surviving bastion of secular, Arab nationalism. In the Syrian context, it was easy for Sunni Islamists to blend their struggle against secularism with anti-Alawi sectarianism. There was reprinting and recirculation of ancient opinions by scholars such as Ibn Taymiyyah (1263–1328) that anathematised Alawis as a fifth column working to help Mongols and Crusaders destroy Islam; more recent ones by Haj Amin al-Husseini and Musa al-Sadr, stating that Alawis were indeed Muslims, were disregarded. Ibn Taymiyyah's more general attacks on Shi'is were also resurrected. They had once been influential on Muhammad ibn 'Abd al-Wahhab and more recently on Abu Musab al-Zarqawi. Now they would reach a much wider audience. The concept of the Shi'i Crescent also raised the spectre of insurrections among other Shi'i populations in Arab countries, Pakistan and Afghanistan. This was especially so with regard to the Shi'i minority in Saudi Arabia and the Shi'i majority in tiny Bahrain.

Even in countries like Egypt, where there were very few Shi'is, strong anti-Shi'i polemic appeared and was a sign of the 'othering' of Shi'is. In 2006 President Mubarak accused all Shi'is everywhere of being loyal to Iran in a way that negated their allegiance to their native country. Sheikh Tantawi, the rector of Cairo's al-Azhar Mosque at the time, called for reverence for the Prophet's Companions to be considered an essential pillar of the Muslim faith, which implied that Shi'is were not true Muslims. The numbers of Egyptian Shi'is is unknown, but conversions to Shi'ism did occur. It has been suggested that some Egyptian Sufi brotherhoods may have provided a door into Shi'ism, an allegation that was treated sufficiently seriously for it to require a vehement denial by the supreme sheikh of the Sufi brotherhoods in 2007.[21] This reflected a fear of Shi'ism as a denial of the country's perceived Sunni Muslim identity. In 2013, when Egypt was under the rule of the democratically elected Muhammad Morsi, four converts to Shi'ism were burned to death by an angry mob while the police stood by and claimed that they did not have the numbers to intervene.

IV

Before we conclude, we will look briefly at how Sunni-Shi'i relations have played out in three other countries since 2003: Syria, Saudi Arabia and Yemen. As we saw in Chapter Twelve, there was a certain similarity between the way many Alawis were privileged in Syria through patronage, and the role played by certain Sunni groups in Iraq before 2003. Just as ordinary Shi'is were likely to feel excluded from politics in Iraq under Saddam Hussein, so could ordinary Sunnis in Syria under the Assads. Yet in neither case was support for the regime conditioned by sect. As with the many Shi'is who were co-opted under Saddam Hussein's regime – and under earlier Iraqi governments – so, too, in Syria there were large numbers of Sunnis who supported the Assads.

In Syria, the extensive protests that rippled across the country in March 2011 calling for reform led to an aborted revolution, which gradually evolved into an insurgency. This was to a considerable extent taken over by jihadi groups, which often proved to be generally the best-organised and most effective fighters on the opposition side. In Syria, as in Iraq, Daesh were able to use a poisonous sectarian narrative against the religious sect most closely identified with the country's government. Other militant organisations did the same.

A book that charts the descent of Syria's revolution into a proxy conflict dominated by Sunni militants is Samar Yazbek's *The Crossing: My Journey to the Shattered Heart of Syria*. Yazbek is an Alawi supporter of the opposition who now lives in exile in Paris. Before Syria exploded, she was a writer and a presenter on Syrian television. In 2012 and 2013 she made three crossings into northern Syria from the Turkish border, visiting areas where government authority had collapsed. These are inhabited overwhelmingly by Sunni Muslims. Her story is heartrending. Several things stand out.

The first is the military inability of the Assad regime, without massive external help, to regain the large areas that had escaped its control – even at what seems in retrospect a relatively early stage in the Syrian conflict. Yazbek went to districts south of Aleppo close to the motorway linking Syria's great northern city with Damascus. Sections of this strategic artery were now in rebel territory. This forced the regime to re-route all transport with Aleppo along minor roads through the desert to the east. If the regime had had sufficient troops to retake the motorway we can be certain that it would have done so. Its loss was a major blow to its prestige and created significant logistical problems for the Syrian army. Yazbek was an eyewitness to the alternative strategy it employed. It bombed towns and villages indiscriminately, using the crude and infamous barrel bombs rolled out of the open doors of helicopters, as well as ordnance dropped from military aircraft. This was nothing less than terrorism from the skies. It was directed towards forcing the inhabitants of these areas to flee, or at least at cowering them into submission.

The second strong theme to emerge from this book is the strength and indefatigability that the author observes in the ordinary people of these largely rural areas. They are proud of their revolution. On her first visit, in August 2012, she watched as they tried to build what they hope will be the civil society of the new Syria. But then comes her third, tragic, observation. By the time she returns a year later, a process of hard-line and coercive Islamisation is well underway. Part of this is the spread of a vicious sectarian narrative that demonises Alawis and other non-Sunnis. To a large extent, this process of hard Islamisation is imposed by the numerous foreign fighters, Sunni Muslims who have come from other countries to battle for the establishment of a state in Syria based on a strict and narrow interpretation of the Sharia that stems, ultimately, from Wahhabism. Yet there are also plenty of Syrians taking part in this project. It has become inextricably linked to the fight to overthrow the regime.

V

The imposition of anti-Alawi and anti-Shiʻi Islamism in rural northern Syria brings us naturally to Saudi Arabia, the home of Wahhabism, which is the primary source of the anti-Shiʻi discourse that has spread so widely since 2003. At the same time, Saudi Arabia has a substantial Shiʻi minority in its eastern province. As was seen in earlier chapters, that community has often faced exclusion and has regularly been the object of hate-preaching. This is despite intermittent attempts by the Saudi monarchy to win its support; at times its treatment has been less harsh than at others.

There have also been attempts at reform in Saudi Arabia, especially during the reign of King Abdullah, who ruled for ten years from 2005. Before then, there had been a major reconciliation with a Shiʻi reform movement in 1993, which had led to many Shiʻi activists returning home from exile, and a sharp reduction of Iranian influence among Saudi Shiʻis. Nevertheless, while there may have been some small improvement in the position of Shiʻis in Saudi Arabia, the underlying issues were not addressed and dissatisfaction grew.[22] Although since 2004 Ashura processions have been allowed in predominantly Shiʻi towns and villages including Qatif, they have remained forbidden in mixed areas where they might cause communal tensions.[23] At the same time, what can only be called anti-Shiʻi hate-preaching has never ceased; its quantity has merely waxed and waned.

In 2003, an 'Islamo-Liberal' alliance of Sunnis and Shiʻis in Saudi Arabia presented a petition for reforms which included an end to sectarian and regional discrimination as well as a national parliament and anti-corruption measures. Demands for Twelver Shiʻism to be recognised as a separate doctrinal law school followed. But a terrorist campaign inside the country by al-Qaʻida from May 2003 onwards knocked discussions of such issues off-track. The sad truth is that for much of the Wahhabi establishment (and parts of the ruling family) anti-Shiʻi discourse remains to this day a powerful way to gain legitimacy against the claims of Sunni revolutionary groups like al-Qaʻida.[24] Anti-Shiʻi rhetoric has also been an instrument of Saudi foreign policy,[25] which is tied in with the kingdom's struggle with Iran for hegemony over the Muslim world. Even after King Abdullah came to the throne, this still applied, though he fostered dialogue with his country's Shiʻis. Thus, expressions of sympathy for Hezbollah among Saudi Shi'is (and some Sunnis) during the Lebanese crisis in the summer of 2006 led to further anti-Shi'i preaching in Saudi Arabia.[26]

In February 2009, there were clashes between Sunni and Shi'i pilgrims (the latter largely from the eastern province) at the al-Baqi' cemetery in Medina where the first Shi'i imams and other members of the Prophet's family are buried. Riots and demonstrations spread to the eastern province. Sheikh Nimr al-Nimr, a passionate Shi'i preacher, disobeyed instructions from the security services to use his sermons to subdue the protests. Instead, he preached that the Eastern Province should have the right to secede from Saudi Arabia. Sectarian tensions simmered over the following two-year period, then blew up again in February 2011, at the time when the demonstrations of the Arab Spring reached nearby Shi'i majority Bahrain.

The protests in Saudi Arabia were as much calls for equality and democratic participation as for the remedying of specifically Shi'i grievances, although the lack of equality underlay the latter. King Abdullah responded to the protests with promises of massive additional government expenditure to provide jobs, but some of that expenditure was for religious institutions and the Ministry of the Interior, in neither of which are Shi'is usually employed. Although the protests were dampened down by this policy, there were demonstrations by several hundred people in Qatif on 9 and 10 March calling for the release of prisoners. One of the slogans was 'Not Sunni, not Shi'i, Islamic Unity'.[27] But when on 14 March Saudi Arabia sent troops to Bahrain to stiffen the resolve of the government against protesters calling for democracy, for a while the protests grew again. It was this risk of its citizens combining across sectarian divides that frightened the government above all else. The protests were quelled by a mixture of repression and pleas for calm from religious leaders. Yet that autumn and over the winter they flared up again, and a number of people were killed.

Since then, the tensions between Sunnis and Shi'is in Saudi Arabia have not gone away. They were made worse by the execution of Sheikh Nimr al-Nimr on 2 January 2016. He had been on death row since his conviction in 2014 on charges of 'disobeying the ruler', 'inciting sectarian strife' and 'encouraging, leading and participating in demonstrations'.[28]

It was surely pure hypocrisy to have him executed for inciting sectarian strife, when anti-Shi'i hate-preaching is so widely tolerated in Saudi Arabia. The angry reactions from Iran, the Iraqi Prime Minister Nouri al-Maliki and from across the Shi'i world illustrate how this execution ratcheted Sunni-Shi'i tensions up another notch.

Saudi Arabia's repression of its Shi'is is also linked to its use of its armed forces in two nearby countries, Bahrain and Yemen, where its actions have aided a process of 'sectarianisation'. In Bahrain, the Arab Spring protests brought people from across the sectarian divide together, but fear and mistrust between Sunnis and Shi'is rendered fragile any attempts to build a united front calling for reform. Shi'is make up 60– 70 per cent of the Bahraini population. Toby Matthiesen, an author and researcher specialising in Middle Eastern politics, was an eyewitness to the demonstrations of February-March 2011 that called for a degree of democracy. His conclusion was that, at least in the first days of the protests, they were not sectarian. Rather than 'the people want the fall of the regime', which had been the call in Tunisia and Cairo, the shout in Bahrain was 'the people want the reform of the regime'. Yet the government, with Saudi backing, exploited fears of the Iranian bogeyman to pre-empt the emergence of a mature opposition movement that spanned the divide: something to which Iran also contributed through the use of unhelpful rhetoric.

Another example of sectarianism being fed by Saudi foreign policy has been Yemen, where the kingdom has supported the Yemeni government against the Houthi rebellion from 2009 onwards. The Houthis are from the Zaydi minority that constitutes a little over a third of Yemen's population. The Zaydis, it will be recalled, are distinct from Twelver Shi'ism. Their school of the Sharia is much closer to the Sunni doctrinal law schools, and sectarian differences have historically played little or no part in Yemen. Until 1962, North Yemen was ruled by a Zaydi Imam. When he was overthrown in a coup, civil war ensued between, on one side, royalists who were loyal to the Imam's son, and, on the other, republicans; but religious sect was entirely absent as a factor in the conflict. In the 1960s, the Saudi Arabians actively supported the cause of the Zaydi Imam. At that time, they did not care that he was a Shi'i. They saw him as something of a traditional Arab and Muslim ruler who was fighting the same good fight that they espoused against the Arab nationalism and socialism of President Nasser of Egypt. At that time, sectarianism was absent from Yemeni politics.

Yet today in Yemen, tragically, a new sectarian divide is being opened up. Salafi proselytisation aimed at the Zaydi minority has been encouraged by Saudi Arabia, and sectarianism has reared its ugly head. The Houthi movement was a Zaydi reaction led by a family of Zaydi religious scholars who feared the marginalising of their community. Fighting between the government and Houthi rebels began in 2004. As elsewhere, the 2011 Arab Spring protests in Yemen were non-sectarian in nature, but negotiations for a new constitution broke down over the question of federalism, which the Houthis saw as rigged against them. Since the first half of 2014, the country has been destroyed in a complex civil war in which the former president, Ali Abdullah Saleh, and his supporters are allied with the Houthis. It has suited Saudi Arabia, and its Gulf allies that have intervened in the conflict, to consider Yemen another battlefield between Sunnis and Shi'is, while the Houthis have received some support from Iran and Hezbollah. In Yemen there is now a danger of a wholly new sectarianisation redefining allegiances.

VI

In early 2002 the French scholar Gilles Kepel, a respected authority on Islamism, published a book called *Jihad: The Trail of Political Islam*. It was the translation of a work he had published in his native language in 2000, and its thesis was that Islamism had peaked and was in decline. The book had been updated to take account of 9/11, but for Kepel that event only added grist to his mill. He saw it as a clear act of desperation: a sign that Islamists knew they had lost the argument.

Many people will dismiss this view as simply an expert getting it completely wrong. But Kepel's thesis is not nearly as mad and out-of-touch as they might assume. Since 2003, there have been mass movements in a number of Middle Eastern states in which millions of people have gone on to the streets to demonstrate with immense courage for democracy, freedom of speech, freedom of assembly, human rights, the rule of law, and the creation of a corruption-free economy that provides jobs. These demands are problematic for Islamists, since their main source of inspiration is from the West, not Islam. By their nature, they are also un-sectarian.

The first of these expressions of people power was in Lebanon in February to March 2005, and was dubbed the Cedar Revolution. Large numbers of people from different sectarian backgrounds across the Christian-Muslim and Sunni-Shi'i divides demonstrated angrily but peacefully together in the aftermath of the assassination of Lebanon's prime minister, Rafiq Hariri. Syria was widely believed to be behind the assassination, so the demands included an end to Syrian interference in Lebanon, the withdrawal of Syrian troops from the country, and fresh elections. The largest of these demonstrations was on 14 March, in which hundreds of thousands, possibly one million, took part – perhaps one in every five-or-so inhabitants of the country. This phenomenon led to massive international pressure on Syria to withdraw, and Syria removed its forces within weeks. Even though a large rival demonstration was organised by Hezbollah in reply (and Hezbollah has been accused of involvement in Rafiq Hariri's murder), it did not call for the withdrawal to be reversed. Instead, it gave the Syrians an enthusiastic send-off and thanked them for their role in helping to protect Lebanon against Israel.

These mass protests left a legacy. Ten years later, in 2015, a campaign called 'You Stink' once again brought Lebanese people of all sects together to demonstrate against the government's incompetence and corruption, which had led to the breakdown of rubbish collection in Beirut. Lebanon's sectarian political system is too deeply entrenched for it to be uprooted easily, but increasing numbers of Lebanese are coming to the conclusion that one day this has to be done. Possibly connected with this are two factors that have tarnished Hezbollah's revolutionary credentials. The first is its intervention in the Syrian conflict on the side of Bashar al-Assad's regime, where Hezbollah's militias have actually been serving as counter-revolutionary troops. The other concerns its role in Lebanon itself, and shows how movements that are based on a sect/tribe can be ill-suited to serving the true interests of their followers. As it is now a major force in Lebanese politics, with seats in parliament and ministers in the government, Hezbollah has become compromised in exactly the same way as the other sect-based political parties in Lebanon. Like them, it has opposed measures such as increases in workers' salaries and insurance. It has done this because it is reluctant to see collaboration among trade unionists that transcends sectarian divides and is a potential threat to its hold over its Shi'i followers. It also wants to preserve its relations with the other sect-based parties with which it needs to do deals, and to safeguard its own, considerable business interests.

In Iran in 2009, there was a surprise presidential election result in Iran. The leading reformist candidate, Mir Hossein Musavi, who was widely expected to win, was beaten by the incumbent, the hard-line Mahmoud Ahmadinejad. There were a number of surprising things about the way the result was declared and the distribution of votes across the country. These suggested a very high probability of electoral fraud (this has not been proved – but the evidence to settle the question categorically is not publicly available). Peaceful but angry demonstrations followed, and on several occasions demonstrators were shot. Pro-regime thugs were also active, and even attacked Mir Hossein Musavi when he was walking in a funeral procession. These events became known as the Green revolution. The name caught on because many of the protesters wore green bandanas, wristbands and clothing. Green is the colour associated with Ali and with Islam. The demonstrators took to the rooftops in some districts at night to shout 'Allahu akbar' as a protest, a tactic that had been used in the Islamic Revolution that toppled the Shah. Although the regime eventually managed to bring an end to the demonstrations, it had received a nasty shock. In the short term, the events strengthened the hard-line elements; but next time there was a presidential election in Iran, in 2013, there were no suggestions of serious attempts at tampering with the result. The moderate candidate, Hassan Rouhani, was elected, and he increased his share of the vote when re-elected in 2017.

But the greatest wave of mass protests in favour of democracy, the rule of law, freedom of speech and a corruption-free economy was the aforementioned Arab Spring, which began in Tunisia in December 2010. In early 2011, it reverberated across many other Arab countries, most notably Egypt, Libya, Syria, Bahrain and Yemen. Its ripples travelled further, including to Saudi Arabia, Morocco, Jordan, Iraq and Oman. It led to the transformation of Tunisia into a democratic state, but in some of the other countries the experience was much less positive. In Egypt, the dictator Hosni Mubarak was brought down; but the aftermath of his fall was mishandled, and today Egypt is once again under military rule. In Libya, the overthrow of Muammar Gaddafi almost led to the disintegration of the country, and it has not yet reassembled itself. Syria and Yemen dissolved into civil wars in which outside powers have treated warring factions, including the Syrian and Yemeni governments, as proxies. In Bahrain, protests calling for democracy and reform unnerved the monarchy and led to a crackdown backed up by troops sent in support by Saudi Arabia. Saudi Arabia also increased the suppression of its own Shi'i population.

Initially, none of these expressions of people power had anything to do with Islamism or sectarianism between Sunnis and Shi'is (or between Muslims and Christians or other minorities). When taken together, they make a powerful statement about the direction in which the peoples of the Middle East wish to travel. Islam, of course, plays a role: it is the bedrock of the region's culture and identity for the vast majority of its people. It is therefore unsurprising that Iranians protesting against a stolen election result should chant 'Allahu akbar' from the safe anonymity of rooftops at night. In 2009 this Islamic slogan was used to taunt what might now be called the Iranian revolutionary establishment. One can detect similarities between this and the use of Islamic rhetoric on many earlier occasions. In Tunisia in 2011, the Nahda Party won the largest number of seats in the country's first democratic election (but not enough to gain a majority). This was a moderate Islamist movement with a socialist outlook. However, it lost seats in Tunisia's second democratic election and accepted the result. It now rejects the epithet 'Islamist' and considers itself to be a 'Muslim democratic' party. It thus seeks to take inspiration from the tenets of Islam in its democratic politics in the same way that, say, Germany's Christian Democrats aim to take inspiration from Christian social teaching.

Yet in the aftermath of the Arab Spring, Islamist forces were often best placed to exploit the ensuing vacuum as military regimes fell or found themselves with their backs to the wall. As so often before, the dictators and the monarchies had made sure that leaders of liberal opposition groups were in exile, had been co-opted, or were too weak to build up a powerbase that could challenge them. The success of Islamist parties and other groups followed on naturally from the symbiotic relationship between rulers and Islamists that had grown over the previous twenty or thirty years. This had allowed those Islamist groups that were willing to play the game according to the rules set by the regime to be the best-organised political forces in the country. At the same time, whenever they could, oppressive rulers would claim that opposition to their rule was sectarian, and use sectarianism to divide and rule.

VII

There have always been tensions between Sunnis and Shi'is, but there has never been sectarian strife between them to compare with the wars of religion and persecutions of the Reformation in Christian Europe in the sixteenth and seventeenth centuries. Sectarian strife did play a role at times in rivalries like that between the Ottomans and Safavids. But by the beginning of the nineteenth century, that had faded away. Ever since, Turkey and Iran have had peaceful relations. Any problems that exist between them today certainly do not have their roots in the fact that Turkey is predominantly Sunni, while Iran is predominantly Twelver Shi'i.

The toxic sectarianism that has broken out since 2003 has been the unlovely flowering of seeds that were planted much earlier. Some of the most important, such as the hostility of Wahhabism to Shi'ism, date from before the spread of Western political and cultural domination of the Muslim world. But if we look at the ways in which Sunni-Shi'i sectarian politics have appeared in the Middle East, they cannot be examined without considering them against the backdrop of the reaction to the West and the spread of nationalism from the nineteenth century onwards. Before the appearance of nationalism and its rival, pan-Islamism, people in the Middle East and other Muslim countries – like pre-modern peoples everywhere – were much less self-aware with regard to their various feelings of identity. That does not mean that their senses of identity were any less powerful. Indeed, belonging to a faith community was one of the strongest manifestations of that, and there has always been a feeling of clannishness among members of religions and sects. An English-speaking audience ought to be able to understand this by considering how religion in Ireland took on a quasi-tribal aspect at some point in the past, and how this led to intense sectarian strife in Northern Ireland over many decades. In a similar way, the danger of 'othering' the members of another religion or sect was always present among the quasi-tribes of the Muslim world.

This brings us to the flawed state formation in the Middle East. In some countries, important factors worked against the people developing a cohesive sense of national identity. The glaring example that is frequently pointed out is the imposition of state boundaries that ignored significant facts of human geography. The British and French Mandates over Greater Syria and Iraq are an obvious case in point. Another that is perhaps stressed less often is the culture of patronage, which has been almost a leitmotif in the later chapters of this book. Patronage has deep roots in Arab society, and can pose a serious obstacle to the development of genuinely democratic politics. As noted above, Iraq and Syria are prime examples of this. In each case, patronage was an important factor both in frustrating democracy and in leading the two countries down the road to civil conflict, in which sectarianism would play a prominent role. The intense pressure that was put on the Iraqi state from 1980 onwards and on the Syrian state since 2011 has not helped either. As states begin to fail, people are forced back on their family, on their tribe (if they have one), and on whatever other trusted support networks they can find. Their religious community is usually one of these. When a religious community hears hate speech directed against it and perceives itself as under attack from members of a rival sect or religion, it is not surprising if this leads to sectarianism. Sectarianism between Sunnis and Shi'is has proved to be most destructive when it has been grafted on to existing grievances. Indeed, in the absence of such grievances, serious sectarian discord has been rare.

Then there has been the manipulation of religion by powerful states as a way of promoting their hegemony, and by states that have created or exacerbated sectarianism among their citizens for short-term political ends. Saudi Arabia and Iran have been guilty of exploiting religion as a tool of foreign policy. As we have seen, from 1979 onwards, conservative Saudi Arabia and revolutionary Iran have been in ideological conflict for the leadership of all Muslims across the globe. This struggle has been exacerbated by Saudi Arabia's wish to assume the mantle of leadership of the Sunni world, and Iran's corresponding role as the self-appointed leader of Shi'is everywhere. These relations were not helped by the consequences of the 2003 invasion of Iraq. When a second major country with a coast on the Gulf came under Shi'i rule, this could only make the Saudis and other Sunni rulers in the Gulf nervous.

It is not only powers seeking hegemony, like Saudi Arabia and Iran, that can exploit sectarian divides. When a state that has a sectarian divide but no firm democratic tradition is weak, its own government can manipulate the divide. Yet sect-based movements in a divided society ultimately lead their followers into a cul-de-sac. Co-operation across the sectarian divide has always been possible. There is nothing inevitable about conflict between Sunnis and Shi'is.

The Family of the Prophet

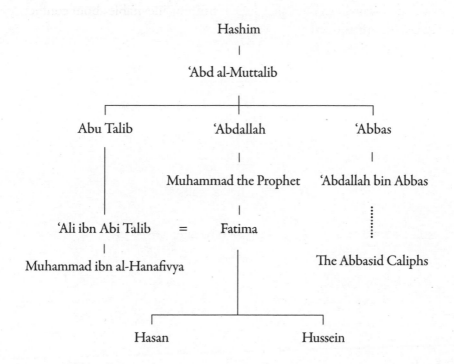

Hashim

|

'Abd al-Muttalib

Abu Talib   'Abdallah   'Abbas

Muhammad the Prophet   'Abdallah bin Abbas

'Ali ibn Abi Talib = Fatima

Muhammad ibn al-Hanafivya   The Abbasid Caliphs

Hasan   Hussein

The Twelve Imams

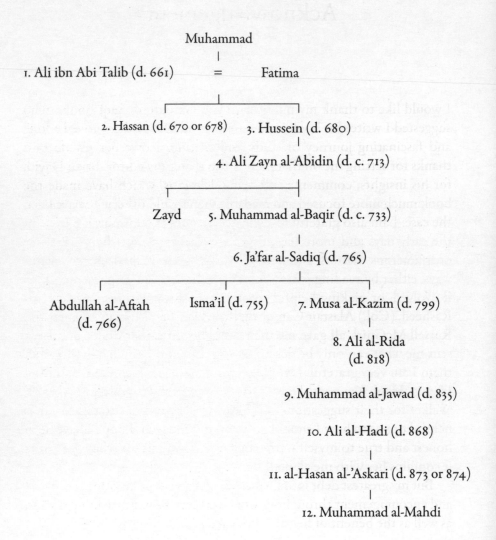

Muhammad
|
1. Ali ibn Abi Talib (d. 661) = Fatima

2. Hassan (d. 670 or 678) 3. Hussein (d. 680)

4. Ali Zayn al-Abidin (d. c. 713)

Zayd 5. Muhammad al-Baqir (d. c. 733)

6. Ja'far al-Sadiq (d. 765)

Abdullah al-Aftah Isma'il (d. 755) 7. Musa al-Kazim (d. 799)
(d. 766)

8. Ali al-Rida
(d. 818)

9. Muhammad al-Jawad (d. 835)

10. Ali al-Hadi (d. 868)

11. al-Hasan al-'Askari (d. 873 or 874)

12. Muhammad al-Mahdi

Acknowledgements

I would like to thank my publisher, Lynn Gaspard of Saqi Books, who suggested I write this book in the summer of 2015. It has proved a long and fascinating journey of study and writing. I owe her my deepest thanks for setting me on that path. I also thank my editor, Brian David, for his insights, comments and many deletions, which have made the book much more focused and readable than would otherwise have been the case. I am also grateful to Lynn's colleagues at Saqi, Sarah Cleave in the early days and more recently Elizabeth Briggs, for their assistance on numerous matters. Many other people have helped me in various ways, either by reading parts or all of the draft, discussing my project as it evolved, or making helpful comments and suggestions. Madawi Al-Rasheed, (Col.) Alastair Campbell, Rose Hadshar, Moojan Momen and Russell McGuirk all gave me their thoughts on earlier drafts, and Rose sent me what can only be described as a root-and-branch edit. To all of them I am very grateful. I would also like to thank Juan Cole, Edmund Herzig, Hugh Kennedy, Daisy Livingston, Derek Plumbly and 'Hooky' Walker for their suggestions and ideas on particular matters, as well as helpful tips as to how I should go about my research. I hope I have been honest and true to myself in the final text. The fault for whatever errors it contains lies with me alone.

But my greatest debt is to Diana. She has given me emotional support and encouragement throughout what has often been a gruelling process, as well as the benefit of her own knowledge and insights.

Notes

Preface

1. V. Nasr, *The Shia Revival*, p. 47.
2. 'The terms Sunni and Shi'a exist today in reciprocal relationship and any attempt to understand one is simultaneously a journey into the other.' See Pierce, *Twelve Infallible Men*, p. 149. See also the final section of Chapter Three below.
3. https://www.nytimes.com/2015/04/01/opinion/thomas-friedman-tell-me-how-this-ends-well.html?_r=0
4. See Hashemi and Postel, p. 2 and note 3 for further details.

Chapter One

1. This was how it was meant to be. Nevertheless, although Islam would succeed in ending conflicts between Muslim tribes during the remainder of the Prophet's life and the years immediately after his death, Islam did not succeed in eradicating these pre-Islamic customs. Blood feuds and activities such as cattle rustling among Arabian tribes have persisted into modern times.
2. Montgomery Watt, *Muhammad at Mecca*, p. 10, citing Ibn Sa'd.
3. Ibid., p. 27.
4. Madelung, p. 57, referring to Qur'an 8: 72–74 and 9: 100, 117.
5. Montgomery Watt, op. cit., p. 288.
6. Article 'Umar' in *The Shorter Encyclopedia of Islam*, ed. H.A.R. Gibb and J.H. Kramers, E.J. Brill, Leiden, 1974
7. Abbott, p. 8.
8. Madelung, p. 33.
9. Montgomery Watt, *Muhammad at Mecca*, p. 288.
10. Lings, p. 244.
11. Madelung, p. 67.
12. Madelung, pp. 18–27. Madelung shows that the accuracy of the

attributions of their accounts to Aisha and Abdullah bin Abbas is, so far as these things ever can be established, extremely plausible. My summary of these events is based on Madelung's work.

13. Madelung, pp. 62–63.
14. Ibid., p. 24.
15. Ibid., p. 23.
16. Ibid., pp. 45–46.
17. Ibid., pp. 40 ff.
18. Ibid., p. 58.
19. Ibid., p. 61.

Chapter 2

1. Madelung, p. 79.
2. Ibid., p. 80.
3. Ibid., pp. 81–82.
4. Ibid., p. 96.
5. Ibid., p. 113
6. Ibid., p. 108.
7. Ibid., pp. 121–23.
8. Ibid., p. 127.
9. Ibid., p. 127.
10. Ibid., pp. 112–13.
11. Ibid., p. 211.
12. Ibid., p. 145.
13. Ibid., p. 150.
14. Ibid., pp. 150–52.
15. Ibid., p. 149.
16. Ibid., p. 155.
17. Ibid., p. 161.
18. Ibid., p. 169.
19. Ibid., p. 179.
20. Ibid., p. 174.
21. Ibid., p. 175.
22. Ibid., p. 201. See also p.205.
23. Ibid., p. 205.
24. Ibid., p. 231.
25. Ibid., p. 203.
26. Ibid., p. 216.
27. Ibid., p. 231.

28. Ibid., p. 235.
29. Ibid., p. 238.
30. Ibid., p. 238.
31. Ibid., p. 244.
32. Ibid., p. 245.
33. Ibid., p. 246.
34. Ibid., p. 247.
35. Ibid., p. 252.
36. Ibid., pp. 255–56.
37. Ibid., p. 276.
38. Ibid., p. 279.
39. Ibid., p. 304.
40. Ibid., p. 308.
41. Ibid., pp. 311–12.
42. Ibid., p. 319.
43. Ibid., p. 323.

Chapter Three

1. V. Vaglieri, article on Hussein in *Encyclopaedia of Islam*, 2nd ed.
2. Jacob Lassner, 'Responses to unwanted authority in early Islam', in Bengio and Litvak, p.33.
3. El-Hibri, p. 271.
4. Kennedy, *The Prophet and the Age of the Caliphates*, p. 134.
5. Daftary, 'Varieties of Islam', in *New Cambridge History of Islam*, vol. 4, p. 112.
6. Pierce, p. 13.
7. Ibid., p. 13.
8. Ibid., p. 45.

Chapter Four

1. This paragraph is distilled from the first chapter of Norman Calder's PhD thesis, pp. 1–23.
2. Madelung, pp. 80–81.
3. Crone and Hinds, pp. 5–6, 13–15.
4. Rodwell's translation. There are other candidates for 'the rope of God' apart from the caliph. One is the Qur'an itself.
5. The Arabian poet al-Farazdaq (641–732), quoted in Crone and Hinds,

p. 33.

6.   Crone and Hinds, p. 41.
7.   For the emergence of the Sharia and Islamic Law, see Hallaq, pp. 142–83.
8.   Hallaq, pp. 157–58.
9.   Crone andHinds, pp. 86–87.
10. Crone andHinds, pp. 88–90.
11. The expression is that of Wael Hallaq: Hallaq, p. 162.
12. Hallaq, pp. 164–65
13. Ibid., p. 166.
14. Crone and Hinds, p. 93.
15. El-Hibri, in *The New Cambridge History of Islam*, vol. 1, pp. 291–92.
16. Melchert, p. 10.
17. Calder, p. 25–26.
18. Ibid, p. 301.
19. Calder, see pp. 29–48 passim.
20. Madelung, p. 216.
21. Ibid., p. 298.
22. Definition in Hans Wehr's Dictionary, 1966 English Edition.
23. Quoted in Halm, p. 37.
24. Quoted by Hurvitz in 'Early Hanbalism and the Shi'a', in Bengio and Litvak, p. 46.
25. Hurvitz, p. 47.
26. Pierce, p. 31.
27. Halm, p. 48.
28. Ibid., pp. 49–51.
29. Ibid., p. 53.
30. See Halm, pp. 53–54, which is also my source for this quote.
31. Halm, p. 55.
32. Calder, pp. 70–71.
33. Ibid., p. 78.
34. Ibid., pp. 110–13.

Chapter Five
1.   Cole, *Sacred Space and Holy War*, pp. 31–37; Momen, pp. 90–91.
2.   Kennedy, p. 316.
3.   Ibid., p. 334.
4.   Halm, p. 180.
5.   The material in this section is based on Halm, pp. 202–05.
6.   Momen, *Shi'i Islam: A Beginner's Guide*, pp. 4–5.

7. Halm, p. 155.
8. See, for instance, Ghazali's discussion of the fourth and highest level of tawhid in the first chapter of Book XXXV of the *Ihya' 'ulum al-din*, translated by this writer as 'The Book of Divine Unity and Trust in God', The American University in Cairo, unpublished MA Thesis 1976, pp. 1–48, especially at e.g. 11, 13.
9. See Halm, p. 157 and Daftary, 'Varieties of Islam' in *New Cambridge History of Islam*, vol. IV, pp. 136–37.
10. Daftary, p. 138.
11. Ibid., p. 138.
12. Schimmel, p. 27.
13. Ibid., pp. 41–42.
14. Ibid., p. 231.
15. Ibid., p. 238.

Chapter Six

1. R. McCarthy, *Deliverance from Error, An Annotated Translation of al-Munqidh min al Dalal and Other Relevant Works of Al-Ghazali*, 1980, p. 235.
2. Halm, pp. 62–63, Momen, pp. 208–11. Fuad Khuri states there are six, not seven 'cycles'. See Khuri, 'The Alawis of Syria', in *Syria: Society, Culture and Polity*, pp. 49–61.
3. Halm, p. 61.
4. Calder, p. 233.
5. Halm, p. 65.
6. Calder, p. 240.
7. The comparison is made and explored by David Morgan in *Medieval Persia, 1040–1797*.
8. Halm, p. 69.
9. Junayd is presented as the head of the Safavi order in the version of history promulgated by the Safavids. However, it seems that the real head of the order at that time was his uncle Ja'far, who forced him into exile. See Morgan, op. cit., p. 107.
10. Halm, p. 77 referring to Melikoff, 'Le probleme Qizilbas', *Turcica* 6, 1975, pp. 51 ff.
11. Halm, p. 78 quoting Khunji, *Tarikh-i 'alam-ara-yi Amini*, translated by Minorsky, No. 204.
12. Quoted in Morgan, p.117.

13. Morgan, p. 117.
14. Halm, p. 81.
15. Ibid., p. 93.
16. Tucker, p. 19.
17. Cole, *Sacred Space and Holy War*, p. 18.
18. Tucker, p. 24.
19. Litvak, *Encounters between Sunni and Shi'i 'Ulama' in Ottoman, Iraq,* in Bengio and Litvak, pp. 71–72.
20. Quoted in Tucker, p. 82.
21. Quoted in Tucker, pp. 82–83.
22. Tucker, p. 98.
23. Morgan, p. 155.

Chapter Seven

1. Streusand, p. 68.
2. Ibid., p. 68.
3. Scherberger, 'The Confrontation between Sunni and Shi'i Empires', in Bengio and Litvak, p. 53.
4. Cole, *Sacred Space and Holy War*, pp. 17–18.
5. Cole, op. cit., p. 19.
6. Scherberger, pp. 58–59.
7. Ibid., p. 60.
8. Ibid., p. 65.
9. Cole, *Sacred Space and Holy War*, pp.18.
10. Cole, op. cit., p. 19.
11. Ibid., p.21.
12. Scherberger, p. 55.
13. Streusand, p. 201.
14. Dale, p. 77.
15. Streusand, p. 209.
16. Ibid., p. 243.
17. Ibid., p. 279.
18. Schimmel, p. 367.
19. Cole, p. 8.
20. Momen, *Shi'i Islam*, pp. 79–80; Halm, p. 134.
21. Finkel, p. 366.
22. He did, however, apply a version of Hanbali *fiqh* himself. See Crawford, p. 54.
23. Crawford, pp. 51–53.

24. Ibid., p. 105.
25. M. Crawford, p. 20.
26. Crawford, p. 21.
27. Ibid., p. 22. It is sometimes claimed he also went to Iran, but Crawford dismisses this possibility.
28. Ibid., p. 25.
29. Ibid.,p. 27.
30. Ibid., p. 31.
31. Ibid., pp. 37–38.
32. Ibid., p. 63.
33. Ibid., p. 59.
34. Ibid., p. 87.
35. Guido Steinberg, 'The Wahhabiyya and Shi'ism', in Bengio and Litvak, pp. 166–67.
36. Crawford, p. 97.
37. Ibid., p. 42.
38. Halm, p. 98.

Chapter Eight

1. B. Anderson, *Imagined Communities: Reflections on the Origin and Spread of Nationalism*, Verso, 1983/2006, pp. 5–7.
2. Finkel, p. 492.
3. Hourani, *Arabic Thought in the Liberal Age*, 1798–1939, p. 106.
4. J. Cole, *Napoleon's Egypt*, p. 151.
5. Hourani, op. cit., p. 106.
6. Quoted in Finkel, p. 493.
7. The expression is Caroline Finkel's. See Finkel, p. 495.
8. Halm, p. 99.
9. The information contained in these paragraphs is taken from Halm, pp. 98–104.
10. Halm, p. 108.
11. Ansari, *Iran: A Very Short Introduction*, p. 94.
12. Cole, *Sacred Space and Holy War*, p. 30.
13. Cole, op. cit., p. 27.
14. Litvak, 'Encounters between Sunni and Shi'i "Ulama"' in Bengio and Litvak, p. 81.
15. Derengil, 'Legitimacy Structures in the Ottoman State: the Reign of Abdulhamid II', *International Journal of Middle East Studies*, 23, 1991,

pp. 347–48.

16. Litvak, 'Encounters between Sunni and Shi'i "Ulama", in Bengio and Litvak, p. 82.

17. Nakash, *The Shi'is of Iraq*, p. 44.

18. See Nakash, p. 55, where there is reference to the publication of a speech by Jamal al-Din al-Afghani in which he called for the overthrow of Nasir al-Din Shah for endangering Islam.

19. The thought and career of this once seemingly contradictory figure have been unravelled by Albert Hourani in *Arab Thought in the Liberal Age 1789–1939*, pp. 103–29; and Nikki Keddie in her book *An Islamic Response to Imperialism*.

20. For this, see Tripp, *Islam and the Moral Economy*, pp. 129 ff. Unfortunately Muhammad Abduh's reasoning on this issue has not survived.

21. Sedgwick, pp. 11–12, p. 68.

22. Hourani, *Arabic Thought in the Liberal Age*, p. 143; Sedgwick, p. 64.

Chapter Nine

1. This is how they are described in the famous letter from the British foreign secretary, Arthur Balfour, to Lord Rothschild of 2 November 1917 in which Britain promised to use its best endeavours to facilitate the achievement of 'a national home for the Jewish people' in Palestine. It became known as the Balfour Declaration and was incorporated into the British Mandate over Palestine. It is hard to reconcile this with the 'sacred trust of civilisation' which Britain took upon itself to ensure the 'well-being and development' of the Palestinian people under Article 22 of the Covenant of the League of Nations.

2. Khoury, p. 181.

3. Nakash, p. 13.

4. Allawi, p. 357.

5. Quoted in Nakash, p. 64.

6. Nakash, p. 64.

7. Quoted in Nakash, p. 70.

8. Allawi, *Faisal I of Iraq*, p. 379.

9. Tripp, p. 45.

10. Nakash, p. 114.

11. Tripp, p. 76.

12. Nakash, p. 125.

13. Nakash, p. 127.

14. Parsons, p. 119.

15. Crawford, p. 118.

16. T. Matthiesen, *The Other Saudis*, p. 10.

17. Matthiesen, op. cit., p. 52.

18. Matthiesen, op. cit., p. 33.

19. Matthiesen, op. cit., p. 49.

20. Matthiesen, op. cit., p. 51.

21. Achcar, pp. 110–11.

22. Hourani, *Arabic Thought in The Liberal Age, 1789–1939*, p. 244.

23. Hourani, op. cit., p. 231.

24. Nasr, *The Shia Revival*, p. 103.

25. Hourani, p. 231.

26. Covenant of the League of Nations, Article 22.

27. Thompson, p. 157.

28. Achcar, p. 110. Dreyfus was a French army officer who was Jewish. In 1894 he was wrongly convicted of high treason on trumped-up charges motivated by anti-Semitism. The affair split France down the middle at the end of the nineteenth and beginning of the twentieth centuries. Dreyfus was eventually exonerated.

29. Achcar, pp. 111.

30. Nasr, *The Shia Revival*, p. 106.

31. This slogan, of course, is reminiscent of what the future Caliph Umar said to the Prophet when the latter lay on his deathbed.

32. Thompson, p. 163.

Chapter Ten

1. Nakash, p. 133–34, referring to Batatu, *The Old Social Classes and the Revolutionary Movements of Iraq*, Saqi, 2004.

2. Tripp, p. 186.

3. A. Baram, 'Religious Extremism and Ecumenical Tendencies in modern Iraqi Shi'ism', in Bengio and Litvak, p. 105.

4. Tripp, p. 200.

5. Ibid., p. 209.

6. Nakash, p. 137.

7. H. Batatu, *Syria's Peasantry, the Descendants of its Lesser Rural Notables and their Politics*, Princeton, NJ, 1999, p. 227.

8. Pierret, *Religion and State in Syria*, p. 65.

9. Matthiesen, pp. 82–83.

10. On this, see Thomas Pierret, *Religion and State in Syria*.

11. Quoted from a published translation modified by Elizabeth Thompson, *Justice Interrupted*, Harvard, NJ, 2013, p. 286.

Chapter Eleven

1.   Axworthy, *Revolutionary Iran*, p. 112.
2.   Ibid., op. cit., pp. 121–22.
3.   Ibid., p. 134.
4.   Ibid., p. 134.
5.   Ibid., pp. 135-36.
6.   Quoted in Axworthy, p. 138.
7.   Axworthy, pp. 138–39.
8.   Algar, p. 21.
9.   Article 94.
10. Algar, p. 19.
11. Algar, p. 31.
12. Articles 12–14.
13. Tripp, *A History of Iraq*, p. 213.
14. Tripp, op. cit., p. 214.
15. A. Baram, 'Religious Extremism and Ecumenical Tendencies', in Bengio and Litvak, p. 111.
16. For this, see Tripp, *A History of Iraq*, pp. 224–5.
17. Contrast Axworthy, *Revolutionary Iran*, p. 188 with Karsh, *The Iran-Iraq War, 1980–1988*, pp. 12–14.
18. Tripp, op. cit., p. 238.
19. Axworthy, op. cit., p. 307.

Chapter Twelve

1.   Matthiesen, *The Other* Saudis, p. 109.
2.   Quoted in Thompson, p. 283.
3.   Martin, pp. 189–91.
4.   Kepel, *Jihad*, pp. 131–32.
5.   Matthiesen, op. cit., p. 102.
6.   Al-Rasheed, p. 142.
7.   Matthiesen, op. cit., pp. 106–07.
8.   Ibid., op. cit., p. 103.
9.   M. Hatina, 'Debating the "Awakening Shi'a": Sunni Perceptions of the Iranian Revolution', in Bengio and Litvak, pp. 205–07.
10. R. Brunner, 'Egypt and Shi'ism at the Beginning of the Twenty-First Century', in Bengio and Litvak, pp. 231–32.

11. Norton, p. 19.
12. Ibid., p. 16.
13. *Newsweek*, 18 July 2006, quoted in Norton, p. 33.
14. Axworthy, *Revolutionary Iran*, p. 222.
15. Norton, p. 66.
16. The information about the open letter, including the translated extracts from it, is taken from Norton, pp. 35–41.
17. al-Intiqad, 14 March 2003, quoted in Norton, p. 119.
18. Commins, p. 172.
19. Ibid., p. 164.
20. Al-Rasheed, p. 139.
21. Commins, pp. 163–71.
22. Kepel, *Jihad*, pp. 233–34.
23. Commins, p. 174.
24. Ibid., p. 175.
25. Ibid., p. 187.
26. The CIA Factbook gives Shi'is as 10–15 per cent; Vali Nasr suggest they are more numerous – 15–25 per cent. See 'Sectarianism in Pakistan, 1979–1988, in *Sectarianization*, ed. Hashemi and Postel, p. 78. The percentages I quote ignore the fact that there are 3–4 per cent who are not Muslim.
27. V. Nasr, 'International Politics, Domestic Imperatives and Identity Mobilisation: Sectarianism in Pakistan, 1979–1998', in *Sectarianization*, ed. Hashemi and Postel, 2016, p. 80.
28. Nasr, p. 45.
29. Ibid., pp. 84–86.

Chapter Thirteen

1. Formerly the School of Oriental and African Studies.
2. Tripp, *A History of Iraq*, pp. 277–78.
3. A. Baram, 'Religious Extremism and Ecumenical Tendencies', in Bengio and Litvak, p. 112.
4. Tripp, op. cit., p. 285.
5. International Crisis Group Report, 'The Next Iraqi War? Sectarianism and Civil Conflict', 27 February 2006, p. 17.
6. Kepel and Milelli, p. 243.
7. Ibid., p. 249.
8. The authenticity of this letter is not established beyond doubt, but Kepel and Milelli include it the anthology he edited, *Al-Qaeda in its own Words*.

See pp. 248–50.

9.   Kepel and Milelli, pp. 253–54.

10. Kepel and Milelli, p. 246, Emily Hunt, 'Zarqawi's "Total War" on Shiites Exposes a Divide Among Sunni Jihadists', *Policywatch* 1049, The Washington Institute, 15 November 2005.

11. A. Baram, 'Religious Extremism and Ecumenical Tendencies', p. 116, note 21.

12. For the information contained in this paragraph, see Allawi, *The Occupation of Iraq*, pp. 443–45.

13. See M. Benraad, 'Iraq's Tribal Sahwa: its Rise and Fall', Middle East Policy Council, Spring 2011, vol. XVIII, No.1.

14. International Crisis Group, 'Failing Oversight: Iraq's Unchecked Government, 26 September 2011, p.2.

15. Sham is the Arabic name for Greater Syria. It is sometimes translated into English as 'the Levant'.

16. Cockburn, p. xvii.

17. Ibid., p. 77.

18. Ibid., p. 64.

19. I. Black, 'Fear of a Shia Full Moon', *The Guardian*, 26 January 2007.

20. al-Rasheed, p. 256.

21. See R. Brunner, 'Interesting Times: Egypt and Shi'ism at the Beginning of the Twenty-First Century', in Bengio and Litvak, pp. 223–35.

22. Matthiesen, *The Other Saudis*, p. 165.

23. Ibid., op. cit., p. 179.

24. For some examples in 2008, see Al-Rasheed, p. 266.

25. Mathiesen, op. cit., p. 184.

26. Ibid., op. cit., p. 186.

27. Ibid., op. cit., p. 203.

28. Amnesty International, 15 October 2014, https://www.amnesty.org/en/latest/news/2014/10/saudi-arabia-appalling-death-sentence-against-shi-cleric-must-be-quashed/

Bibliography

N. Abbott, *Aishah: the Beloved of Muhammad*, Chicago University Press, 1942.

G. Abdo, *The New Sectarianism: The Arab Uprisings and the Rebirth of the Shi'a-Sunni Divide*, Oxford University Press, 2017.

E. Abrahamian, *A History of Modern Iran*, Cambridge University Press, 2008.

G. Achcar, *The Arabs and the Holocaust: The Arab-Israeli War of Narratives*, Saqi Books, 2010.

F. Ajami, *The Dream Palace of the Arabs*, Vintage Books, 1998.

J. al-Askari, *A Soldier's Story: From Ottoman Rule to Independent Iraq*, Arabian Publishing, 2003.

S. al-Harez, tr. anon, *The Others*, Saqi Books, 2009.

M. Al-Rasheed, *A History of Saudi Arabia*, 2nd edition, Cambridge University Press, 2010.

M. Al-Rasheed, 'Sectarianism as Counter-Revolution: Saudi Responses to the Arab Spring', in (q.v.) Hashemi and Postel, eds, *Sectarianization*, pp. 143–58.

H. Algar, tr., *Constitution of the Islamic Republic of Iran*, Mizan Press, 1980.

A. Allawi, *The Occupation of Iraq: Winning the War, Losing the Peace*, Yale University Press, 2007.

A. Allawi, *The Crisis of Islamic Civilization*, Yale University Press, 2009.

A. Allawi, *Faisal I of Iraq*, Yale University Press, 2014.

C. Allen, *God's Terrorists: The Wahhabi Cult and the Hidden Roots of Modern Jihad*, Da Capo, 2006.

M. Allen, *Arabs*, Continuum, 2006.

B. Anderson, *Imagined Communities: Reflections on the Origins and Spread of Nationalism*, Verso, 1983/2006.

A. Ansari, *Modern Iran since 1921: The Pahlavis and After*, Longman

(Pearson Education Series), 2003.

A. Ansari, *Iran: A Very Short Introduction*, Oxford University Press, 2014.

R. Aslan, *No God but God: The Origins, Evolution and Future of Islam*, Arrow Books, 2006.

M. Axworthy, *Iran: Empire of the Mind*, Penguin Books, 2007.

M. Axworthy, *Revolutionary Iran: A History of the Islamic Republic*, Penguin Books, 2013/4.

F. Balanche, *La région alaouite et le pouvoir syrien*, Editions Karthala, 2006.

A. Baram, 'Religious Extremism and Ecumenical Tendencies in Modern Iraqi Shi'ism', in (q.v.) Bengio and Litvak, eds, *The Sunna and Shi'a in History*, pp. 105–24.

H. Batatu, *Syria's Peasants: The Descendants of its Lesser Rural Notables and their Politics*, Princeton University Press, 1999.

O. Bengio and M. Litvak, eds, *The Sunna and Shi'a in History: Division and Ecumenism in the Middle East*, Palgrave Macmillan, 2011.

A. Bennison, *The Great Caliphs*, I. B. Tauris, 2009.

M. Benraad, 'Iraq's Tribal 'Sahwa': Its Rise and Fall', *Middle East Policy Council*, spring 2011, vol. XVIII, No. 1.

I. Black, 'Fear of a Shi'a Full Moon', *The Guardian*, 26 January 2007.

N. Brehony, *Yemen Divided*, I. B. Tauris, 2011.

R. Brunner, 'Interesting Times: Egypt and Shi'ism at the Turn of the Twenty-First Century', in (q.v.) Bengio and Litvak, eds, *The Sunna and Shi'a in History*, pp. 223–42.

R. Burns, *Aleppo: A History*, Routledge, 2016.

N. Calder, 'The Structure of Authority in Imami Shi'i Jurisprudence', unpublished PhD Thesis, SOAS, 1980.

N. Calder, *Studies in Early Muslim Jurisprudence*, Clarendon Press, 1993.

W. Cantwell Smith, 'The Concept of Sharia', in *Arabic and Islamic Studies in Honor of Hamilton A. R. Gibb*, E. J. Brill, 1965.

Z. Chehab, *Inside Hamas*, I. B. Tauris, 2007.

P. Cockburn, *The Rise of Islamic State: ISIS and the Sunni Revolution*, Verso, 2014/5.

J. Cole, *Napoleon's Egypt: Invading the Middle East*, Palgrave Macmillan, 2007.

J. Cole, *Engaging the Muslim World*, Palgrave Macmillan, 2009.

J. Cole, *Sacred Space and Holy War: The Politics, Culture and History of Shi'ite Islam*, I. B. Tauris, 2002.

J. Cole and M. Momen, 'Mafia, Mob and Shi'ism: The Rebellion of Ottoman Karbala, 1823–1843', *Past and Present*, No. 112, August 1986, pp. 112–43.

D. Commins, *The Mission and the Kingdom: Wahhabi Power behind the Saudi Throne*, I. B. Tauris, 2009/2016.

M. Crawford, *Ibn 'Abd al-Wahhab*, One World, 2015.

P. Crone and M. Hinds, *God's Caliph: Religious Authority in the First Century of Islam*, Cambridge University Press, 1986.

A. Crooke, *Resistance: The Essence of the Islamist Revolution*, Pluto Press, 2009.

F. Daftary, 'Varieties of Islam', in *The New Cambridge History of Islam*, vol. IV, Cambridge University Press, 2010.

J. Daher, *Hezbollah: The Political Economy of Lebanon's Party of God*, Pluto, 2016.

S. Dale, *The Muslim Empires of the Ottomans, Safavids and Mughals*, Cambridge University Press, 2010.

N. DeLong-Bas, *Wahhabi Islam: From Revival and Reform to Global Jihad*, Oxford University Press, 2004.

S. Derengil, 'Legitimacy Structure in the Ottoman State: The Reign of Abdul Hamid II', *International Journal of Middle East Studies*, vol. 23 No. 3, 1991, pp. 345–59.

T. El-Hibri, 'The Empire in Iraq, 763–861', *New Cambridge History of Islam*, vol. I, pp. 269–304

C. Finkel: *Osman's Dream: The Story of the Ottoman Empire, 1300–1923*, John Murray, 2005.

R. Fisk, *Pity the Nation: Lebanon at War*, 3rd edition, Oxford, 1990–2001.

R. Fisk, *The Great War for Civilisation: The Conquest of the Middle East*, Fourth Estate, 2005.

D. Gardner, *Last Chance: The Middle East in the Balance*, I. B. Tauris, 2009.

F. Gardner, *Blood and Sand*, Bantam, 2006.

J. Gelvin, *Divided Loyalties: Nationalism and Mass Politics in Syria at the Close of Empire*, University of California Press, 1998.

F. Gerges, *The Far Enemy: Why Jihad went Global*, Cambridge University Press, 2005.

A. Ghazali, *Deliverance from Error: Five Key Texts Including his Spiritual Autobiography, al-Munqidh min al-Dallal*, tr. McCarthy, Twayne, 1980.

J. Gordon, *Invisible War: The United States and the Iraq Sanctions*, Harvard University Press, 2010.

D. Gutas, *Greek Thought, Arabic Culture: The Graeco-Arabic Translation Movement in Baghdad and Early 'Abbasid Society*, Routledge 1995.

W. Hallaq, 'Islamic Law', in *The New Cambridge History of Islam*, vol. IV, pp. 142–83.

H. Halm, *Shi‘ism*, Edinburgh University Press, 2004.

N. Hashemi and D. Postel, eds, *Sectarianization: Mapping the New Politics of the Middle East*, Hurst, 2017.

M. Hatina, 'Debating the "Awakening Shi‘a": Sunni Perceptions of the Iranian Revolution', in (q.v.) Bengio and Litvak, eds, *The Sunna and Shi‘a in History*, pp. 203–22.

L. Hazleton, *After the Prophet: The Epic Story of the Sunni-Shi‘a Split*, Doubleday, 2009.

M. Hodgson, 'Dja‘far al-Sadiq' in 2nd edition, *Encyclopaedia of Islam*, Brill, 1954–2005.

M. Hodgson, *The Venture of Islam*, University of Chicago Press, 1974.

A. Hourani, *Arabic Thought in the Liberal Age, 1798–1939*, Oxford Paperbacks, 1962/1970.

A. Hourani, *A History of the Arab Peoples*, Belknap, Harvard University Press, 1991.

R. Hoyland, *In God's Path*, Oxford University Press, 2015.

J. Hurewitz, *Diplomacy in the Near and Middle East: A Documentary Record, vol. 2, 1914–1956*, D. Van Nostrand Co., 1956.

N. Hurvitz, 'Early Hanbalism and the Shi‘a', in (q.v.) Bengio and Litvak, eds, *The Sunna and Shi‘a in History*, pp. 37–50

International Crisis Group Report: *The Next Iraqi War? Sectarianism and Civil Conflict*, 2006.

International Crisis Group Report: *Failing Oversight: Iraq's Unchecked Government*, 2011.

C. Kanaan, *Lebanon 1860–1960*, Saqi Books, 2005.

E. Karsh, *The Iran-Iraq War, 1980–1988*, Osprey, 2002.

N. Keddie, *An Islamic Response to Imperialism: Political and Religious Writings by Sayyid Jamal al-Din 'Al-Afghani',* Berkeley, University of California Press, 1968.

N. Keddie, *Qajar Iran and the Rise of Reza Khan, 1796–1925,* Mazda Publishers, 1999.

H. Kennedy, *The Prophet and the Age of the Caliphates: The Islamic Near East from the Sixth to the Eleventh Century,* Pearson Longman, 1986/2004.

H. Kennedy, *The Caliphate,* Pelican (A Pelican Introduction), 2016.

G. Kepel, *Jihad: The Trail of Political Islam,* tr. A. Roberts, I. B. Tauris, 2002.

G. Kepel and J. Milleli, eds., *Al-Qaeda in its own Words,* tr. P. Ghazaleh, Belknap, Harvard University Press, 2008.

P. Khoury, *Syria and the French Mandate,* Princeton University Press, 1987.

F. Khuri, 'The Alawis of Syria: Religious Ideology and Organization', in *Syria: Society, Culture and Polity,* ed. R. Antoun and D. Quataert, State University of New York Press, 1991.

P. Kinross, *Atatürk: The Rebirth of a Nation,* Phoenix, 1964/2001.

G. Kraemer, *Hasan al-Banna,* One World, 2010.

R. Lacey, *Inside the Kingdom: Kings, Clerics, Modernists, Terrorists and the Struggle for Saudi Arabia,* Hutchinson, 2009.

N. bin Laden, O. bin Laden and J. Sasson, *Growing Up Bin Laden,* St Martin's Press, 2009.

A. Lambton, *State and Government in Medieval Islam,* Oxford University Press, 1981.

H. Laoust, 'Ibn Taymiyya' in 2nd edition, *Encyclopaedia of Islam,* Brill, 1954–2005.

H. Laoust, 'Les agitations religieuses à Baghdad aux IVe et Ve siècles de l'Hégire', in Richards, *Islamic Civilisation,* pp. 169–86.

H. Laoust, *Comment définir le sunnisme et le chiisme,* Geuthner, 1985.

J. Lassner, 'Responses to Unwanted Authority in Islam', in (q.v.) Bengio and Litvak, eds, *The Sunna and Shi'a in History,* pp. 17–36.

R. Lefèvre, *The Ashes of Hama: The Muslim Brotherhood in Syria,* Hurst, 2013.

B. Lewis, *The Middle East: 2000 Years of History from the Rise of Christianity to the Present Day,* Weidenfeld & Nicholson, 1995.

M. Lings, *Muhammad: His Life based on the Earliest Sources*, Islamic Texts Society, 1983/1991.

M. Litvak, 'Encounters between Shi'i and Sunni "Ulama" in Ottoman Iraq', in (q.v.) Bengio and Litvak, eds, *The Sunna and Shi'a in History*, pp. 69–86.

D. Livingston, 'Life in the Egyptian Valley under Ikhshidid and Fatimid Rule: Insights from the Documentary Sources', *Journal of the Economic and Social History of the Orient* (forthcoming).

J. McHugo, 'The Book of Divine Unity and Trust in God, being a translation of Book XXXV of al-Ghazali's Ihya' 'ulum al-din', unpublished MA thesis, the American University in Cairo, 1976.

W. Madelung, *The Succession to Muhammad*, Cambridge University Press, 1997.

S. Maher, *Salafi-Jihadism: The History of an Idea*, Hurst, 2016.

G. Makdisi, 'The Sunni Revival', in Richards, *Islamic Civilisation*, pp. 155–68.

V. Martin, *Creating an Islamic State: Khomeini and the Making of a New Iran*, I. B. Tauris, 2000/2003.

T. Matthiesen, *The Other Saudis: Shiism, Dissent and Sectarianism*, Cambridge University Press, 2015.

T. Matthiesen, *Sectarian Gulf: Bahrain, Saudi Arabia and the Arab Spring that Wasn't*, Stanford Briefs, 2013.

C. Melchert, *Ahmad ibn Hanbal*, Oneworld (Makers of the Modern World), 2006.

B. Metcalf, *Deoband: Islamic Revival in British India, 1860–1900*, Princeton University Press, 1982.

M. Momen, *An Introduction to Shi'ite Islam: The History and Doctrines of Twelver Shi'ism*, Yale University Press, 1985.

M. Momen, *Shi'i Islam*, Oneworld (Beginner's Guides), 2016.

W. Montgomery Watt, *Muhammad at Mecca*, Clarendon Press, 1953.

W. Montgomery Watt, *Muhammad at Medina*, Clarendon Press, 1956.

D. Morgan, *Medieval Persia, 1040–1797*, 2nd edition, Routledge, 2016.

Y. Nakash, *The Shi'is of Iraq*, Princeton University Press, 1994.

V. Nasr, *Meccanomics: The March of the New Muslim Middle Classes*, Oneworld, 2010.

V. Nasr, *The Shia Revival*, W. W. Norton & Co, 2006.

V. Nasr, 'International Politics, Domestic Imperatives and Sectarian

Mobilization: Sectarianism in Pakistan', *1979–1998*, in (q.v.) Hashemi and Postel, eds, *Sectarianization*.

N. Noe, ed., *Voice of Hezbollah: The Statements of Sayyed Hassan Nasrallah*, Verso, 2007.

A. Norton, *Hezbollah: A Short History*, Princeton University Press, 2007.

R. Owen, *The Rise and Fall of Arab Presidents for Life*, Harvard University Press, 2012.

L. Parsons, *The Commander: Fawzi Al-Qawuqji and the Fight for Arab Independence, 1914–1948*, Saqi Books, 2017.

M. Pierce, *Twelve Infallible Men: The Imams and the Making of Shi'ism*, Harvard University Press, 2016.

T. Pierret, *Religion and State in Syria: The Sunni Ulama from Coup to Revolution*, Cambridge University Press, 2013.

D. Pipes, *Greater Syria: The History of an Ambition*, Oxford University Press, 1990.

M. Provence, *The Great Syrian Revolt and the Rise of Arab Nationalism*, Austin, 2005.

S. Qutb, *Milestones*, tr. anon, Islamic Book Service, 2001/2008–09.

S. Qutb, *The Sayyid Qutb Reader: Selected Writings on Politics, Religion and Society*, ed. A. Bergeson, Routledge, 2008.

D. Richards, ed. *Islamic Civilisation: 950–1150*, Cassirer, 1973.

E. Rogan, *The Arabs: A History*, Allen Lane, 2009.

E. Rogan, *The Fall of the Ottomans*, Allen Lane, 2015.

I. Rutledge, *Enemy on the Euphrates: The British Occupation of Iraq and the Great Arab Revolt, 1914–1921*, Saqi Books, 2014.

M. Scherberger, 'The Confrontation between Sunni and Shi'i Empires: Ottoman-Safavid Relations between the Fourteenth and Seventeenth Centuries', in (q.v.) Bengio and Litvak, eds, *The Sunna and Shi'a in History*, pp. 51–68.

A. Schimmel, *Mystical Dimensions of Islam*, University of North Carolina Press, 1975.

P. Seale, *The Struggle for Syria: A Study of Post-War Arab Politics*, I. B. Tauris, 1965/86.

P. Seale, *Asad, The Struggle for the Middle East*, I. B. Tauris, 1988.

M. Sedgwick, *Muhammad Abduh: A Biography*, American University of Cairo, 2009.

E. Sivan, *Radical Islam: Medieval Theology and Modern Politics*, Yale University Press, 1985/90.

G. Steinberg, 'The Wahhabiyya and Shiism from 1774/5 to 2008', in (q.v.) Bengio and Litvak, eds, *The Sunna and Shi'a in History*, pp. 163–82.

D. Streusand, *Islamic Gunpowder Empires: Ottomans, Safavids and Mughals*, Westview Press, 2011.

E. Thompson, *Justice Interrupted: The Struggle for Constitutional Reform in the Middle East*, Harvard University Press, 2013.

C. Tripp, *Islam and the Moral Economy*, Cambridge University Press, 2006.

C. Tripp, *A History of Iraq*, 3rd edition, Cambridge University Press, 2007.

C. Tripp, *The Power and the People: Paths of Resistance in the Middle East*, Cambridge University Press, 2013.

E. Tucker, *Nadir Shah's Quest for Legitimacy in Post-Safavid Iran*, University Press of Florida, 2006.

L. Vaglieri, 'Ghadir Khumm' in 2nd edition, *Encyclopaedia of Islam*, Brill, 1965.

L. Vaglieri, 'Husayn b. 'Ali' in 2nd edition, *Encyclopaedia of* Islam, Brill, 1965.

N. van Dam, *The Struggle for Power in Syria: Politics and Society under Asad and the Ba'th Party*, I. B. Tauris, 1979/2011.

P. Walker, *Fatimid History and Ismaili Doctrine*, Routledge, 2008.

S. Yazbek, *The Crossing: My Journey to the Shattered Heart of Syria*, tr. Ahmedzai and Gowanlock, Rider, 2015.

B. Zollner, *The Muslim Brotherhood, Hasan al-Hudaybi and Ideology*, Routledge, 2009.

Sources and Further Reading

In writing this book I have consulted the best available scholarly works I could locate. They are all included in the bibliography, together with a number of works by journalists who have been eyewitnesses to events, as well as a few memoirs, novels and biographies.

I feel it is right to mention the principal scholarly sources on which I have relied, and to express my deepest gratitude to their authors, since without them this book could not have been written. I would also like to draw them specifically to the attention of readers who wish to look further into the topics covered by this book.

For the early history up to the beginning of the Umayyad Caliphate I have relied on Wilferd Madelung's magisterial *The Succession to Muhammad*. For the history up to the Abbasid era, my main sources have been Hugh Kennedy's *The Prophet and the Age of the Caliphates* and Amira Bennison's *The Great Caliphs*, as well as the contributions cited in the *New Cambridge History of Islam* by Farhad Daftary, Tayeb El-Hibri and Wael Hallaq. For the history of Iran, I have relied in particular on David Morgan's *Medieval Persia* and Michael Axworthy's *Iran: Empire of the Mind*. For the Ottoman Empire, I have relied in a similar way on Caroline Finkel's *Osman's Dream*. For the history of Iraq in modern times, I have used Charles Tripp's *A History of Iraq* and Yitzhak Nakash's *The Shi'is of Iraq*. For Saudi Arabia I have used Madawi Al-Rasheed's *A History of Saudi Arabia*, Toby Matthiesen's *The Other Saudis* and David Commins's *The Mission and the Kingdom*. For the history of Shi'ism, my main sources have been Heinz Halm's extraordinarily detailed *Shi'ism*, Moojan Momen's more accessible *Shi'i Islam: A Beginner's Guide*, Juan Cole's *Sacred Space and Holy War* and Vali Nasr's *The Shia Revival*. Other specialist books I have found very helpful are Hugh Kennedy's *The Caliphate*, Matthew Pierce's *Twelve Infallible Men* and Michael Crawford's biography of *Ibn 'Abd al-Wahhab*. A very useful collection of essays on Sunni-Shi'i relations on which I have also relied extensively is Bengio and Litvak's *The Sunna and Shi'a in History*. Finally, the collection of essays entitled *Sectarianization*, edited by Nader Hashemi and Danny Postel, provided me with much food for thought when writing the final chapter.

Index